The Chinese Astronomical Bureau, 1620–1850

This book offers a new insight into one of the most interesting and long-lived institutions known to historians of science, the Chinese imperial Astronomical Bureau, which for two millennia observed, recorded, interpreted, and predicted the movements of the celestial bodies.

Utilizing archival material, such as the résumés written for imperial audiences and personnel administration records, the book traces the rise and fall of more than 30 hereditary families serving at the Astronomical Bureau from the late Ming period to the end of the Qing dynasty. The book also presents an in-depth view into the organization and function of the Bureau and succinctly charts the impacts of historical developments during the Ming and Qing periods, including the Regency of Prince Dorgon, the influence of the Jesuits, the relationship between the Kangxi and Yongzheng emperors and the He family and the failure of the bureau to predict correctly the solar eclipse of 1730.

Presenting a social history of the Qing Astronomical Bureau from the perspective of hereditary astronomer families, this book will be of interest to scholars and students of Chinese Imperial history, the history of science and Asian history.

Ping-Ying Chang is Adjunct Assistant Professor of mathematics at the National Taiwan Normal University, Taiwan, where she teaches courses on the history of mathematics and mathematical thinking in fictions and films.

Needham Research Institute Series
Series Editor: Christopher Cullen

Joseph Needham's 'Science and Civilisation' series began publication in the 1950s. At first it was seen as a piece of brilliant but isolated pioneering. However, at the beginning of the twenty-first century, it became clear that Needham's work had succeeded in creating a vibrant new intellectual field in the West. The books in this series cover topics that broadly relate to the practice of science, technology and medicine in East Asia, including China, Japan, Korea and Vietnam. The emphasis is on traditional forms of knowledge and practice, but without excluding modern studies that connect their topics with their historical and cultural context.

Celestial Lancets
A history and rationale of acupuncture and moxa
Lu Gwei-Djen and Joseph Needham
With a new introduction by Vivienne Lo

A Chinese Physician
Wang Ji and the Stone Mountain medical case histories
Joanna Grant

Chinese Mathematical Astrology
Reaching out to the stars
Ho Peng Yoke

Medieval Chinese Medicine
The Dunhuang medical manuscripts
Edited by Vivienne Lo and Christopher Cullen

Chinese Medicine in Early Communist China, 1945–1963
Medicine of revolution
Kim Taylor

Explorations in Daoism
Medicine and alchemy in literature
Ho Peng Yoke

Tibetan Medicine in the Contemporary World
Global politics of medical knowledge and practice
Edited by Laurent Pordié

The Evolution of Chinese Medicine
Northern Song dynasty, 960–1127
Asaf Goldschmidt

Speaking of Epidemics in Chinese Medicine
Disease and the geographic imagination in Late Imperial China
Marta E. Hanson

Reviving Ancient Chinese Mathematics
Mathematics, history and politics in the work of Wu Wen-Tsun
Jiri Hudecek

Rice, Agriculture and The Food Supply in Premodern Japan
The Place of Rice
Charlotte von Verschuer
Translated and edited by Wendy Cobcroft

The Politics of Chinese Medicine under Mongol Rule
Reiko Shinno

Asian Medical Industries
Contemporary Perspectives on Traditional Pharmaceuticals
Edited by Stephan Kloos and Calum Blaikie

The Chinese Astronomical Bureau, 1620–1850
Lineages, Bureaucracy and Technical Expertise
Ping-Ying Chang

For more information about this series visit: https://www.routledge.com/Needham-Research-Institute-Series/book-series/SE0483

The Chinese Astronomical Bureau, 1620–1850

Lineages, Bureaucracy and Technical Expertise

Ping-Ying Chang

LONDON AND NEW YORK

First published 2023
by Routledge
4 Park Square, Milton Park, Abingdon, Oxon OX14 4RN

and by Routledge
605 Third Avenue, New York, NY 10158

Routledge is an imprint of the Taylor & Francis Group, an informa business

© 2023 Ping-Ying Chang

The right of Ping-Ying Chang to be identified as author of this work has been asserted in accordance with sections 77 and 78 of the Copyright, Designs and Patents Act 1988.

All rights reserved. No part of this book may be reprinted or reproduced or utilised in any form or by any electronic, mechanical, or other means, now known or hereafter invented, including photocopying and recording, or in any information storage or retrieval system, without permission in writing from the publishers.

Trademark notice: Product or corporate names may be trademarks or registered trademarks, and are used only for identification and explanation without intent to infringe.

British Library Cataloguing-in-Publication Data
A catalogue record for this book is available from the British Library

Library of Congress Cataloging-in-Publication Data
Names: Chang, Ping-Ying, author.
Title: The Chinese Astronomical Bureau, 1620–1850 : lineages, bureaucracy and technical expertise / Ping-Ying Chang.
Description: Abingdon, Oxon ; New York : Routledge, 2023. | Series: Needham research institute series | Includes bibliographical references and index.
Identifiers: LCCN 2022017187 (print) | LCCN 2022017188 (ebook) | ISBN 9780367439675 (hardback) | ISBN 9781032354903 (paperback) | ISBN 9781003008255 (ebook)
Subjects: LCSH: Qin tian jian (China)—History. | Astronomy, Chinese—History.
Classification: LCC QB33.C5 C43 2026 (print) | LCC QB33.C5 (ebook) | DDC 520.951—dc23/eng/20220711
LC record available at https://lccn.loc.gov/2022017187
LC ebook record available at https://lccn.loc.gov/2022017188

ISBN: 978-0-367-43967-5 (hbk)
ISBN: 978-1-032-35490-3 (pbk)
ISBN: 978-1-003-00825-5 (ebk)

DOI: 10.4324/9781003008255

Typeset in Times New Roman
by Apex CoVantage, LLC

To the Memory of My Parents,
Tsang-Lang Chang and Emmy Chou Chang

Contents

List of Tables xi
List of Figures xii
Acknowledgments xiii
Reign Titles of the Qing Emperors (1644–1911) xiv

1 Introduction 1

2 The Organization of the Qing Astronomical Bureau 16

3 From the Old Method to the New Method 35

4 Kangxi Calendar Dispute 68

5 Emperors and the He Brothers 99

6 The Solar Eclipse of 1730 126

7 Knowledge Reproduction 144

8 Maintaining a Familial Career 161

9 The Decline of Missionary Influence and the Nineteenth-Century Reforms of the Astronomical Bureau 182

10 Conclusion 200

Appendix A Reconstructed Family Tree of the Baos 204

Appendix B The Ge Family 205

Appendix C The He Family 208

Appendix D The Zhou Family 211

Appendix E The Huang Family 212

Appendix F The Si Family 213

Appendix G Register of Metropolitan Officials According to the Shunzhi Imperial Screen 215

Appendix H Units Used in the Qing Era 219

Index 221

Tables

2.1	Personnel quotas for Student Astronomers	23
2.2	Civil service ranks of Qing Astronomical Bureau officials, mid-Kangxi reign	27
3.1	Personnel quotas and civil service ranks for late Ming Astronomical Bureau officials	37
3.2	Numbers of Astronomical Bureau officials reported by Schall in 1645	38
3.3	Schall's disciples in Ming Calendar Department and Astronomical Bureau, 1644	51
3.4	Organization of Qing Astronomical Bureau proposed by Schall in 1645	51
3.5	Numbers of Astronomical Bureau officials, 1658	53
3.6	Endorsers of Schall's *Response to Concerns over the Notes on Civil Calendar*	54
4.1	Officials purged from the Astronomical Bureau during the Kangxi Calendar Dispute	70
4.2	Personnel quotas of Astronomical Bureau, 1690	75
4.3	Personnel quotas of Astronomical Bureau, 1732	76
4.4	Personnel quotas of Astronomical Bureau, 1764	76
4.5	Personnel quotas of Astronomical Bureau, 1818	77
4.6	Personnel quotas of Astronomical Bureau, 1899	77
8.1	He officials appeared in the Timely Modeling calendars	165
9.1	Triennial examinations, Qianlong and Jiaqing reigns	187
9.2	Triennial examinations, Daoguang and Tongzhi reigns	191
9.3	He officials who failed the 1828 examination	193

Figures

2.1	Map of Qing Beijing, 1644–1900	17
2.2	Organization structure of Qing Astronomical Bureau, after 1745	28
3.1	Reconstructed family tree of the Ges	41
3.2	Ming Great Concordance calendar, the fifteenth year of the Yongle reign (1417)	48
4.1	Career ladder for a Manchu official at the Astronomical Bureau	80
4.2	Career ladder for a Mongol official at the Astronomical Bureau	81
4.3	Career ladder for a military Han official at the Astronomical Bureau	82
4.4	Career ladder for a Han official at the Astronomical Bureau	83
4.5	Early generations of the He family	86
4.6	Schall's and He Luoshu's predictions of the 1665 solar eclipse in *I Have No Alternative*	87
4.7	Yang Guangxian's observation of the solar eclipse of January 16, 1665, in *I Have No Alternative*	88
5.1	Personnel serving in mathematics in *The First Collection of the Imperial Birthday Ceremony*	103
6.1	A solar eclipse prediction produced by the Astronomical Bureau, 1849	129
8.1	Qing Timely Modeling calendar, the eighteenth year of the Qianlong reign (1753)	162
8.2	Numbers of He officials in the Timely Modeling calendars	164
8.3	Age distribution of high Astronomical Bureau officials when receiving transfer orders	171

Acknowledgments

I am most grateful to Professor Joseph W. Dauben for teaching me the joy of historical research. Without his patience, my journey to earning a PhD would not come to a happy conclusion; without his encouragement, I would not have started the new journey to turning my doctorate dissertation into this book. I also wish to express my sincerest appreciation to Professor Christopher Cullen and Professor Catherine Jami for having kindly read the manuscript of this book and made many insightful suggestions. Particular thanks are due to Professor Wang-Sheng Horng for his timely and humorous advice that has rescued me from excessive anxiety during the long process of revising the book.

Ping-Ying Chang
Taipei, Taiwan

Reign Titles of the Qing Emperors (1644–1911)

Shunzhi	順治	1644–1661
Kangxi	康熙	1662–1722
Yongzheng	雍正	1723–1735
Qianlong	乾隆	1736–1795
Jiaqing	嘉慶	1796–1820
Daoguang	道光	1821–1850
Xianfeng	咸豐	1851–1861
Tongzhi	同治	1862–1874
Guangxu	光緒	1875–1908
Xuantong	宣統	1909–1911

1 Introduction

1.1 The Research Question

In the ninth month of the twelfth year of the Qing Yongzheng 雍正 reign (September 1734), Bao Qinhui 鮑欽輝, the Supervisor of the Winter Office (*Dongguanzheng* 冬官正) of the Astronomical Bureau (*Qintianjian* 欽天監), attended an imperial audience along with a group of officials from other institutions who were seeking to finalize their recent job promotions. An audience such as this represented the only occasion for lower-ranking civil servants like Bao to communicate directly with the emperor.[1] At the time, Bao was about 45 years old and had worked at the Astronomical Bureau all of his adult life.[2] Three years earlier he had been promoted to one of the highest positions in the Calendar Section (*Li ke* 曆科) and had been in charge of calculating the official calendar for the dynasty.[3] As a result of his long and excellent service record, Bao was granted a new position as Department Secretary at the Ministry of Works (*Gongbu zhushi* 工部主事)[4]. However, while the other officials at this imperial audience hoped to be approved for new jobs, Bao's object was to convince the emperor to let him remain in his old post. Uncertain about how much time he would be allowed to talk to the emperor, Bao Qinhui elaborated his concerns in the résumé that the emperor would be browsing through during the audience. Bao began by recounting his lineage:

> Although my intrinsic quality is mediocre and foolish, I have had the fortune to meet such a prosperous era that the profession of computation and observation has been showered with favor and grace. My grandfather, Bao Yinghua, 鮑英華, was an Erudite (*Boshi* 博士) of the Astronomical Bureau. My grandfather's elder brother, Yingqi 英齊, was a Senior Vice-Director (*Zuo jianfu* 左監副). My father, Kewei 可畏, was a Student Astronomer (*Tianwensheng* 天文生), and his younger brother, Kecheng 可成, was the Supervisor of the Spring Office (*Chunguanzheng* 春官正). From grandfather to grandson, every generation [of my family] has learned the method of calendar making (*li fa* 曆法) and received grace from the imperial state.[5]

DOI: 10.4324/9781003008255-1

After reminding the emperor that his family members had proudly served the dynasty for generations with their specialty in mathematical astronomy, Bao Qinhui recounted his own contributions. He listed three mathematical projects in which he had participated: the Office of Compiling Mathematical Treatises (*Xiu suanshu chu* 修算書處) in the previous reign, the modification of the calendar-making system in the 1730s, and the new mathematics education program in the Eight Banners Official Schools (*Baqi guanxue* 八旗官學) that had commenced earlier in the current year. Bao concluded his résumé by informing the emperor, "I worry about my stupidity. Except for the knowledge of calendar making, there really is not anything that I can contribute."[6] Bao's petition successfully convinced the Yongzheng emperor, and he remained in his position as the Supervisor of the Winter Office of the Astronomical Bureau until he died two decades later.[7]

The stories of Bao Qinhui, his family, and many other astronomer families, together with Bao's résumé and tens of thousands of Qing state documents that lie silently in archives, have attracted little attention from historians. Indeed, at first glance, Bao Qinhui's résumé is hardly exciting or inspiring. Mathematical astronomy as a hereditary profession has long been a historical phenomenon in China, but the Bao family was almost unheard of. Unlike other Qing astronomers, such as He Guozong 何國宗 (1687–1766), Mei Juecheng 梅瑴成 (1681–1764), and Minggantu 明安圖 (c. 1692–c. 1763), neither Bao Qinhui nor any of his family members had previously been considered distinguished enough to be included in the series of *Biographies of Mathematicians and Astronomers* (*Chouren zhuan* 疇人傳) that Ruan Yuan 阮元 (1764–1849) and other late-Qing mathematicians and historians compiled.[8] The Qing official history includes very few descriptions of the two Yongzheng-period mathematical activities in which Bao Qinhui was involved—the modification of the calendar-making system and the new mathematics education program. Similarly, historians are typically more interested in an earlier and larger-scale project, namely, the compilation of the *Origins of Mathematical Harmonics and Astronomy* (*Lüli yuanyuan* 律曆淵源), which Bao Qinhui also participated in but was not included in the state-approved list of major contributors.[9] Few historians perceive the Yongzheng period mathematical activities to be relevant or important in the development of Chinese mathematics.[10]

Nonetheless, historical research is about revisiting the stories that have been told and investigating the parts of the stories that have not been told. In particular, the purposes of research are to find out what storytellers have purposely hidden from the readers, reassess the significance of the stories, and reconstruct the stories if necessary. For instance, Bao Qinhui was indeed from one of the oldest hereditary astronomer families that had served the Qing court since its establishment in Beijing, and he appeared thankful for the rewards that Yongzheng and preceding emperors had bestowed on his family.[11] However, knowing that the formidable Yongzheng emperor had banned the dissemination of Christian teachings, Bao Qinhui did not mention in his résumé that he was from a Christian family. Bao Qinhui's granduncle, Bao Yingqi, had once been banished to the northeast borderland in the early Kangxi 康熙 reign (1662–1722) for being a member of the Jesuit faction.[12] In August 1702, Bao Yingqi and Bao Kecheng led their family and more than 40 Chinese Christians to send a collective testimony to the Pope regarding the Rites Controversy (*Liyi zhi zheng* 禮儀之爭), and they all signed the testimony with their official titles at the Astronomical Bureau.[13] The Bao family's career development in fact relied more on the Jesuits than on the Qing rulers' imperial grace. It is not a coincidence that the number of archival records related to the Bao family decreases as the Jesuits' status in the Qing court declined, and no record bearing the surname Bao dated after the end of the Jiaqing 嘉慶 reign (1796–1820) has been found (see Appendix A for a reconstructed family tree of the Baos).[14]

According to mid-Qing scholar and mathematician Tan Tai 談泰 (a. 1786), the character "*chou*" 疇, could best be interpreted as passing on a familial profession generation after generation (*Jiaye shishi xiangchuan zhiwei chou* 家業世世相傳 之為疇).[15] While this interpretation would not limit the meaning of "*chou ren*" 疇 人 to astronomers or the career of calendar-making, Tan points out that astronomical officials' learning particularly esteemed generational inheritance and that the tasks of predicting celestial phenomena were often given to hereditary officials.[16] Zu Chongzhi 祖沖之 (429–500) and Zu Gengzhi 祖暅之, for example, were a famous father–son pair of Chinese mathematicians and astronomers.[17] Zu Chongzhi's calculation found that π must lie between 3.1415926 and 3.1415927. This approximation not only was the best of his time but also would not be surpassed until the end of the sixteenth century by François Viète (1540–1603).[18] Zu's treatise *The Method of Threading Together* (*Zhui Shu* 綴術), now lost, was listed in the curriculum of the College of Mathematics (*Suanxue* 算學) in the Tang dynasty (618–907) as the most advanced textbook; studying it would take four years.[19] Zu Gengzhi was also an accomplished mathematician. Although we do not know exactly how much Gengzhi contributed to his father's achievements mentioned earlier, it is through Gengzhi's continuous efforts that Zu Chongzhi's Daming calendrical system (*Daming li* 大明曆) was finally adopted by the Southern Liang (Nan Liang 南梁) dynasty (502–557) as the official method of calendar making in 510.[20] In the Qing period, Minggantu 明安圖, who is known to historians of Chinese mathematics for his calculations of infinite series, and his son Mingxin 明新 were a father–son pair of Mongolian imperial astronomers.[21] Minggantu's most important contribution was working on the theory of the power series expansions of sine and versed sine. Minggantu's work was completed and published posthumously in the *Quick Methods for the Circle's Division and Precise Ratio* (*Geyuan milü jiefa* 割圜密率捷法), by Mingxin with assistance from his disciples Chen Jixin 陳際新 and Zhang Gong 張肱.[22]

It is noteworthy that although both Bao Qinhui and Minggantu worked at the Astronomical Bureau until their deaths, there are more differences than similarities in their career experiences. The Bao family learned the method of calendar making from Jesuit missionaries, but Minggantu claimed his mathematical lineage from the Kangxi emperor and became a major compiler of the *Origins of Mathematical Harmonics and Astronomy*.[23] When the treatise was completed, he was rewarded with the position of Supervisor of the Five Offices (*Wuguanzheng* 五官正). Minggantu devoted his later years to researching the analytic formulas that his Jesuit colleague Pierre Jartoux (1669–1720) had refused to explain.[24] Although Mingxin inherited the profession of astronomer, Minggantu's intellectual achievements seemed to be built on more by his disciples than by his own descendants.

The comparison between Bao Qinhui and Minggantu suggests that famous pairs of father-son mathematicians, such as Minggantu and Mingxin, are not necessarily the most representative cases of the hereditary astronomer families. It calls for more complete and in-depth research into the astronomer families that had worked for the Astronomical Bureau generation after generation. Only after such research is completed can we understand the systematic design that discouraged Minggantu and other non-Han imperial astronomers from passing knowledge and skills to their descendants and the family interests that Bao Qinhui had in mind when he considered whether or not he should accept the new position offered to him.

This book aims to construct a social history of the Qing Astronomical Bureau from the perspective of hereditary astronomer families. When the research for this book began, the initial goal was to understand the life and career of an imperial astronomer in the Qing period. It soon found that these astronomers should not be considered merely as individual officials at the Astronomical Bureau because familial relation was a crucial factor to their career. Most astronomers learned the mathematical knowledge and skills needed for a career at the Bureau as part of their early family education. In the workplace, their colleagues were often relatives from their extended families. It was not unusual for them to attend periodical examinations administered by their own senior relatives. As such, the research gradually turned its attention to the relationship between an individual official's career progression and an astronomer family's collective interests. Re-examining historical incidents has deepened the understanding of how astronomer families dealt with external challenges and navigated through political crises. In particular, it becomes clear that the historical significances of the two Yongzheng-reign mathematical activities that Bao Qinhui was involved in need to be reassessed. Although later Qing official documents downplayed the importance of these activities, this book hopes to demonstrate that such vagueness, in fact, is a byproduct of the continually changing and never-ending power struggle between the Qing monarch, European missionaries, and different hereditary astronomer families.

1.2 The Sources

Because of the nature of the research question, many archival materials that are already familiar to researchers of Qing history are less helpful to this study than one might expect. The focus of this study, the astronomer families associated with the Qing Astronomical Bureau, has two distinct characteristics: their members were low-ranking officials of the central government and their profession depended on mathematical knowledge. Because their ranking in the civil service hierarchy was low, the Astronomical Bureau officials did not have the right to communicate with the supreme ruler directly.[25] Therefore, popular archival materials such as the vermilion rescripted palace memorials (*zhupi zouzhe* 硃批奏摺)—the secret written communications between the emperor and a small group of trusted officials—contain very few records related to the astronomer families. Although some superintendents and Directors of the Astronomical Bureau were granted the privilege of submitting palace memorials, they mostly memorialized the monarch for affairs related to the jobs they held concurrently in other institutions that had nothing to do with the Astronomical Bureau. Similarly, the *Veritable Records* (*Shilu* 實錄) and the *Imperial Diary* (*Qiju zhu* 起居注) focused on the emperors, who—with the exception of the Yongzheng emperor—seldom paid attention to the routine operations and personnel administration of the Astronomical Bureau. These sets of archival sources are useful for gaining access to information on the monarch and his high ministers, whose policy decisions affected the Astronomical Bureau, but rarely do they provide insight into the lives of the astronomer families. The biographies contained in the *Draft History of the Qing* (*Qingshi gao* 清史稿), *History of the Qing Empire* (*Qing guoshi* 清國史), and the *Biographies of Mathematicians and Astronomers* have not fared much better.[26] They include about 20 persons who were associated with the College of Mathematics or the Astronomical Bureau. However, how these individuals studied and worked at the two institutions is rarely mentioned.

Traces of the astronomer families have to be found in other types of sources. The *Collected Statutes of the Great Qing* (*Da Qing huidian* 大清會典), which was updated and amended several times throughout the lifespan of the dynasty, contains laws that governed the organization and administration of every government institution of the Qing dynasty. These laws proved essential for understanding how the Astronomical Bureau operated and what the career path of an astronomer at the Astronomical Bureau typically looked like. However, as a set of laws, the *Collected Statutes* include almost no record of individual officials; only in the precedents that were added to the later versions of the *Collected Statutes* can some descriptions be found to include personal information about the officials involved.[27] Indeed, even locating the names of those who served at the Astronomical Bureau is not always easy.

Fortunately, previous researchers, such Qu Chunhai 屈春海 and Shi Yumin 史玉民, have laid inspiring groundwork for this study. Qu's "A Chronological Table of Officials Serving in the Qing Dynasty's Imperial Board of Astronomy and Section of the Almanac" (*Qingdai Qintianjian ji Shixianke zhiguan nianbiao* 清代欽天監暨時憲科職官年表) collected the rosters attached to the Qing official calendars.[28] A typical roster on the calendar consists of the titles and names of the Astronomical Bureau directorate and the higher-level Calendar Section officials. Qu's table suggests that the published calendars could be used to trace the personnel change among the higher-level Calendar Section officials, although the names of lower-level officials and trainees—Erudites and Student Astronomers—must be found elsewhere. Shi's "A Chronological Table for Officials Serving in the Division of Astronomy of the Qing Dynasty Qintianjian" (*Qing Qintianjian Tianwenke zhiguan nianbiao* 清欽天監天文科職官年表) provides similar information for the officials of the Section of Heavenly Signs (*Tianwen ke* 天文科).²⁹ Compared to Qu, who conventionally compiled his table from a single type of source, namely, the official calendars, Shi had to search the routine memorials (*ti ben* 題本) preserved in the First Historical Archive in Beijing to abstract the names of the Astronomical Bureau officials.³⁰ Shi's table has the advantage that it sometimes includes officials of the Erudite level. However, the number of officials that Shi located fluctuated during different periods, and he did not explicitly explain which types of routine memorials he used.³¹ Nonetheless, Qu Chunhai's and Shi Yumin's tables have been handy references for this research, and their works suggest that routine memorials and regular state documents could contain records related to the lower-level staff members of the Astronomical Bureau.

Among the 300,000 Qing state documents housed in the Archive of the Grand Secretariat at the Institute of History and Philology (IHP) of the Academia Sinica in Taiwan, approximately 1,400 are related to the Astronomical Bureau and the College of Mathematics.³² The majority of these documents are reports on routine duties and personnel affairs administered according to the regulations prescribed by the *Collected Statutes*. Their contents include the nominations of officials when vacancies arose, requests for imperial approvals to hold periodical and entrance examinations for the Astronomical Bureau and the College of Mathematics, reports on examination outcomes, the submission of sample calendars and predictions of solar and lunar eclipses to the emperor, and so on. When the Bureau submitted a progress or final report on the assigned task, it often attached the rosters of the officials responsible for that activity. If the report was related to personnel administration, then brief information about the officials in question—such as their ages, hometowns, academic degrees, and job performance reviews—often had to be included. Such reports provide personal information about Astronomical Bureau staff, from the highest-level Directors down to the lowest-level trainees. Moreover, information found in the process can be used to correct some of the errors in Qu's table that resulted from incorrect typesetting, and it can also help to clarify some administrative regulations that the *Collected Statutes* did not explain.

The *Complete Collection of the Qing Officials' Résumés* (*Qingdai guanyuan lüli dang'an quanbian* 清代官員履歷檔案全編) is another set of documents that have been indispensable to this research.³³ This published archive consists of records related to the imperial audiences, including lists of the officials who attended the imperial audiences, individual officials' service records kept by the government, and the résumés prepared by individual officials. Among these records, the résumés were the most useful to this research. Before the Qianlong 乾隆 reign (1736–1795) commenced, the format of the résumés was less restricted, and officials were permitted to introduce themselves more freely or to make suggestions related to their jobs. That is why some Astronomical Bureau officials like Bao Qinhui could describe their families' connection with the Bureau and state their preferences pertaining to their career transitions on their résumés. However, by the mid-Qianlong reign, lengthy résumés were no longer permitted, and the contents of these résumés became much less informative. Nevertheless, audience résumés are one of the rare types of documents to include records about the ages, places of origin, and degrees of lower-ranking officials.

Other sets of archives are useful for some special topics in this research. The IHP, together with the Qing Dynasty Palace Memorials and Grand Council Archived Memorials, housed in the National Palace Museum (NPM) in Taipei, contains relatively few records related to the Astronomical Bureau in the Yongzheng period. As such, the *Sources Related to the Personnel Administration in the Qing Dynasty* (*Qingdai lizhi shiliao* 清代吏治史料) becomes a great complement to them.[34] Note that the title of the latter set of archives is misleading, for it includes only records from the Yongzheng reign, not from the entire dynasty. The *Sources Related to China in the Veritable Records of the Chosŏn Dynasty* (*Chaoxian Lichao shilu zhong de Zhongguo shiliao* 朝鮮李朝實錄中的中國史料) complements Qing official records in a different way.[35] The *Veritable Records* of the Korean Chosŏn Kingdom included numerous descriptions related to the Qing court that Qing state historians would rather omit or alter than allow to embarrass their dynasty. This research makes use of evidence in the Chosŏn *Veritable Records* that exposes the deterioration of the Qing official calendar in the Yongzheng period.

Finally, it is noteworthy that the digitization of archival records played a critical role in this research. Due to the astronomers' low status within the giant bureaucratic system, finding records related to them was sometimes like searching for a needle in a haystack. Even when armed with the knowledge of which types of sources were more likely to contain useful material, locating useful details, which were often buried in tens or even hundreds of thousands of records, was challenging. To build a pool of members of the Qing Astronomical Bureau that was large enough to show the familial relations between them, a working environment that the researcher could effectively examine, abstract, and process the contents of archival records was important. The IHP and NPM archives can be accessed online, and the majority of the other sources used are published photocopies of archives. The author scanned or photographed all potentially useful records found in these archives to turn them into digitalized image files. After this extra step of digitization, collected records could be reviewed on computer screens as often as necessary. The rest of the process of data abstraction, filing, and analysis could also be accomplished much faster with computers than with traditional pen-and-paper methods. The time and effort spent on digitization undoubtedly repay itself for research involving large amounts of archival records.

1.3 The Plan of This Book

The process of scrutinizing the archival papers related to the Astronomical Bureau from the late Ming 明 dynasty (1368–1644) to the end of the Qing dynasty has found over five hundred Bureau members who were from about 30 astronomer families. To convey the stories of the astronomer families that served the Qing Astronomical Bureau effectively, the He 何 family was used as a representative case. The He family began serving the Astronomical Bureau in Ming times.

8 Introduction

Before the last He departed the Bureau in the Daoguang 道光 reign (1821–1850), the family had worked at the Astronomical Bureau for two hundred years, and more than 50 members of the He family had left their traces in Qing state records. Among them was He Guozong 何國宗, one of the most famous astronomers of the early Qing period. The richness of the records related to the He family and the roles it played in important junctures of the history of the Astronomical Bureau made it a perfect case study in this research.

To facilitate an understanding of the contents of this book, the next chapter will give an overview of the Qing Astronomical Bureau by describing its organization and functions on an institutional level, including the job requirements for each employee in the Bureau. This chapter aims to remove the difficulties that readers might have when reading this book or examining Qing state papers related to the Astronomical Bureau, rather than burdening them with too much detail.

Chapter 3 begins by describing the historical context of the Ming period that gradually transformed the profession of serving at the Astronomical Bureau from a mandatory career into an inheritable family interest. It then investigates the political concerns of China's new Manchu rulers that led Regent Prince Dorgon 多爾袞 (1612–1650) to promptly adopt the new calendar that the Jesuit missionary Johann Adam Schall von Bell (1592–1666) calculated according to Tychonic mathematical astronomy but to refuse Schall's request to dismiss the Astronomical Bureau officials who resisted giving up the Great Concordance (*Datong* 大統) system of calendar making.[36] This chapter ends by showing that, although some old astronomer families were suppressed and some withdrew from the Astronomical Bureau, family networks remained an important channel through which Schall could recruit new members for the Bureau and find suitable individuals to learn his New Western Method (*Xiyang xinfa* 西洋新法).

Chapter 4 examines how the Kangxi Calendar Dispute (*Kangxi lizheng* 康熙曆爭) (1664–1669) impacted the organization of the Astronomical Bureau and the demography of the hereditary astronomer families. After temporarily returning to the Great Concordance system of calendar making between 1665 and 1668, which was then referred to as the Old Method (*Gufa* 古法), the Qing court reinstalled the New Western Method and Jesuit astronomers to the Astronomical Bureau. However, as this chapter reveals, the Jesuits never regained the same controlling power over the Astronomical Bureau that Schall once had. The supporters of the Old Method remained in the Astronomical Bureau. As such, He Luoshu 何雒書 and his son He Junxi 何君錫, two leading supporters of the Old Method, were able to keep their high offices gained during the dispute, thus laying the foundation for their descendants to grow into the most influential hereditary family in the Qing Astronomical Bureau.

Chapter 5 focuses on the interactions between the Kangxi and Yongzheng emperors and the He family. In particular, it shows how these two emperors utilized the mathematical talents of He Junxi's sons—the famous court astronomers He Guozong, He Guozhu 何國柱, and He Guodong 何國棟—and manipulated their careers. The He brothers, whose talents and loyalty could be guaranteed by their father's service records, became the Kangxi emperor's favorite candidates for testing his vision of mathematics. However, the Yongzheng emperor, who was famous for his tremendous attention to administrative affairs, grew concerned about the expansion of the He family's powers. Within years of the Yongzheng emperor's accession, the fortunes of the He brothers declined precipitously.

Chapter 6 completes the discussion of the Yongzheng emperor and the He family presented in the previous chapter with a detailed study of the circumstances surrounding the solar eclipse of 1730. On the one hand, ministers and officials from all regions eulogized the emperor and denied that the Astronomical Bureau's prediction of the 1730 eclipse was a failure. On the other, the He family, Jesuit missionaries, the Astronomical Bureau officials, and even the Yongzheng emperor knew beforehand that the prediction was likely to fail. In the end, all Bureau officials, missionaries included, were forced into silence. Only the Yongzheng emperor, who staged a political performance, benefited from this incident.

Chapter 7 investigates the roles of astronomers and their family interests in the imperial state's management of reproducing astronomical knowledge. The first case studied here is the new compilation project of astronomical treatises that took place in the early Qianlong reign. Rather than representing a voluntary initiative from the Jesuits, this chapter argues that the project arose from hereditary astronomer families' need to obtain the mathematical knowledge that their Jesuit colleagues in the Astronomical Bureau had shrouded in secrecy since 1730. The rest of the chapter is devoted to a comparison between the mathematics program of the late Yongzheng reign and the College of Mathematics founded in the early Qianlong reign. The attempt to add mathematics into the curriculum of general education failed, and the Yongzheng mathematics program was terminated after just four years. It was replaced with the College of Mathematics, which aimed to recruit newcomers for the Astronomical Bureau and did not conflict with the hereditary astronomer families' interests.

Chapter 8 explains some of the patterns and strategies that hereditary astronomer families exhibited during their long careers at the Astronomical Bureau. It describes how members of the same families often clustered in one section of the Astronomical Bureau until they overcrowded that section and new members had to be reallocated to a different section. It then investigates the personal concerns and family interests that motivated some officials to choose to remain in the Astronomical Bureau as opposed to accepting higher positions in different government institutions. This chapter ends by describing some symptomatic features that declining astronomer families often exhibited.

Chapter 9 shows the importance of the administrators and the administrative system in the history of the Astronomical Bureau. European missionaries' continual loss of status in the Qing court resulted in their complete withdrawal from the Astronomical Bureau in 1826. By then, the Astronomical Bureau and the College of Mathematics had become stagnant and the periodical examination system had become formulaic. However, the stagnation gradually changed after May 1824, when the Daoguang emperor named Jingzheng 敬徵 (1785–1850), who was famous for his administrative ability rather than his knowledge of astronomy or mathematics, as superintendent of these two institutions.[37] Aggressively utilizing the existing periodical examination system, Jingzheng ousted the old and incompetent He family from the Astronomical Bureau. New and proficient astronomer families arose. By the time Jingzheng retired from public service in 1845, the Bureau had repaired its astronomical instruments and had updated the constants used in the calendar-making process.

This book focuses more on Han Chinese than non-Han astronomer families for two reasons. First, because the majority of the members and their families found were Han Chinese, their records can be comprised into a relatively complete storyline. Second, early in the research process, it became apparent that administrative laws hampered the formation of non-Han astronomer families. The Qing dynasty maintained the social and legal divisions between bannermen (*qi ren* 旗人), the members of the social and military organization Eight Banners (*Ba qi* 八旗), and the conquered Han commoners (*Han ren* 漢人). The members of the Eight Banners were further divided into three ethnic categories—Manchu, Mongol, and military Han (*Han jun* 漢軍)—and endowed with different levels of legal privilege.[38] Section 4.2 of Chapter 4 is devoted to an assessment of the impacts that the ethnic categories had on Astronomical Bureau officials' career paths.

Based on the archival records, it is evident that throughout the Qing period, the Astronomical Bureau astronomers closely followed the traditional yet non-mandatory custom of using the same pattern of naming the newborns of the same generation. For instance, He Guozong and his brothers and cousins all had the character *guo* 國 in their names. Although there are not always enough surviving records to clarify the exact relations among the Bureau astronomers, their urge to express the bond among themselves and their belonging to certain genealogical groups are undeniable. In fact, both the ambiguity and belonging reflected the ways that their contemporaries perceived these astronomers. They might come to know or at least suspect that a Bureau astronomer was from a certain family but could not determine his exact relation to that family unless they became his acquaintance. Therefore, this book uses the term *family* rather freely to denote a group of Bureau astronomers with the same surname as long as some name patterns can be found among them. As such, this dissertation does not supplement or serve as a substitute for the genealogy of astronomer families. Rather, it examines the historical representation of the hereditary astronomer families.

While some hereditary astronomer families served the Qing dynasty until its last days, the narration of this book stops around the time that the He family left the Astronomical Bureau. Rather than presenting a complete survey of the history of the Astronomical Bureau, it highlights the historical events that best reflect the characteristics of the hereditary astronomer families of the Qing Astronomical Bureau and their interactions with the imperial state. This book ends with a conclusion that discusses the contributions that its research findings can make to the methodology and historiography of the history of astronomy in the Qing dynasty.

Notes

1 In the Qing dynasty, the civil service ranking hierarchy was divided into nine levels, with rank one being the highest level in the hierarchy and rank nine the lowest (see more in Chapter 2, Section 2.3). The Supervisor of the Winter Office ranked at the sixth level, thus a position low down rather than near the top in the whole hierarchy of the bureaucratic system.
2 Bao's age is calculated according to his résumé mentioned later in the same paragraph, in which Bao states that he was 46 *sui* 歲 at the time of the audience. *Sui* is the Chinese traditional way of age reckoning, according to which newborns start at one *sui* and one more *sui* is added to the age at the beginning of every new calendar year. However, it should be noted that officials did not always report their ages honestly to the government. Therefore, these calculations would better be understood as approximations.
3 In this book, the most appropriate translation of *li* 曆 will often be "calendar." However, this will not always be the case. Thus, for instance, when *Datong li* 大統曆 refers to the detailed instructions and sets of tables that enabled the staff of the Astronomical Bureau to carry out the calculations of the movements and positions of the sun, moon, and planets needed to predict the sequence on months, seasons on which the calendar was based, together with the predictions of planetary conjunctions and both solar and lunar eclipses that it was their duty to provide, *Datong li* must be rendered as "Great Concordance [astronomical] system," rather than "Great Concordance calendar." On this, see Christopher Cullen, *Heavenly Numbers: Astronomy and Authority in Early Imperial China* (Oxford: Oxford University Press, 2017), 24.
4 Except for those in the Astronomical Bureau, the book follows the translation convention of administrative posts given in Charles O. Hucker, *A Dictionary of Official Titles in Imperial China* (Taipei: Southern Materials Center, 1985).
5 QGLL 13: 189. All translations are mine.
6 QGLL 13: 189–90.
7 IHP 023895.
8 This book uses Ruan Yuan 阮元 et al., *Chouren zhuan huibian* 疇人傳彙編 (Taipei: Shijie shuju, 1982) as the reference to the series of works mentioned here. It includes the *Biographies of Mathematicians and Astronomers* (*Chouren zhuan* 疇人傳) compiled and published by Ruan Yuan in 1799, the *Sequel to the Biographies of Mathematicians and Astronomers* (*Chouren zhuan xubian* 疇人傳續編, 1840) by Luo Shilin 羅士琳, *The Third Addition to the Biographies of Mathematicians and Astronomers* (*Chouren zhuan sanbian* 疇人傳三編, 1886) by Zhu Kebao 諸可寶, *Records of the works of Modern Mathematicians and Astronomers* (*Jindai chouren zhushu ji* 近代疇人著述記, 1884) by Hua Shifang 華世芳, and *The Fourth Addition to the Biographies of Mathematicians and Astronomers* (*Chouren zhuan sibian* 疇人傳四編, 1898) by Huang Zhongjun 黃鍾駿. For He Guozong, Mei Juecheng, and Minggantu, see Ruan, *Chouren zhuan*, 518–22, 485–90, and 623–27.
9 Yunlu 允祿 et al., *Yuzhi lixiang kaocheng* 御製曆象考成 [1754], SKQS 790: 5–7.
10 On the development of mathematics in the Kangxi period, see, for instance, Catherine Jami, *The Emperor's New Mathematics: Western Learning and Imperial Authority during the Kangxi Reign (1662–1722)* (New York: Oxford University Press, 2012) and Han Qi's 韓琦 works listed in bibliography.
11 For the early generations of the Bao family, see Chapter 3, Section 3.3.
12 Huang Bolu 黃伯祿, *Zhengjiao fengbao* 正教奉褒 [1884], in *Zhongguo Tianzhujiao shiji huibian* 中國天主教史籍彙編 ed. Chen Fangzhong 陳方中 (Taipei: Furen daxue chubanshe, 2003), 520–5. See also Chapter 4, Section 4.1.
13 For the Rites Controversy, see David E. Mungello, ed., *The Chinese Rites Controversy: Its History and Meaning* (Nettetal: Steyler Verlag, 1994). For the testimony, see Nicolas Standaert, *Chinese Voices in the Rites Controversy: Travelling Books,*

12 *Introduction*

Community Networks, Intercultural Arguments (Roma: Institutum Historicum Societatis Iesu, 2012), 138–46, 327–34. For Bao and other astronomer families' involvement in the Rites Controversy, see Huang Yi-Long 黃一農, "Beihulue de shengyin—jieshao Zhongguo Tianzhujiaotu dui 'liyi wenti' taidu de wenxian" 被忽略的聲音—介紹中國天主教徒對「禮儀問題」態度的文獻, *Tsinghua xuebao* 清華學報 25, no. 2 (1993): 149, 152–3; Han Qi 韓琦, "Fengjiao tianwenxuejia yu 'Liyi zhi zheng' (1700–1702)" 奉教天文學家與'禮儀之爭' (1700–1702), in *Xiangyu yu duihua: Mingmo Qingchu Zhongxi wenhua Jiaoliu guoji xueshu yiantaohui wenji* 相遇與對話：明末清初中西文化交流國際學術研討會文集, ed. Zhuo Xinping 卓新平 (Beijing: Zongjiao wenhua chubanshe, 20;03), 392–3.

14 Bao Duo 鮑鐸 and Bao Quan 鮑銓 are the last two possible Bao family members to serve in the Astronomical Bureau that the author has found. Bao Duo was a Student Astronomer in 1807, and he advanced to Erudite by 1812. Bao Quan was a Student Astronomer of the Section of Heavenly Sign around 1814. For Bao Duo, see IHP 170472; Qinghua daxue tushuguan kejishi ji guwenxian yanjiusuo 清華大學圖書館科技史暨古文獻研究所, ed., *Qingdai Jinshenlu Jicheng* 清代縉紳錄集成 (Beijing: Daxiang chubanshe, 2008), 6: 608 and 8: 416. For Bao Quan, see Fang Hao 方豪, *Zhongxi jiaotongshi* 中西交通史 (Shanghai: Shanghai renmin chubanshe, 2008), 2: 508–11.

15 For Tan Tai, see Ruan, *Chouren zhuan,* 665–9. On the meanings of *Chou* 疇 and *Chou ren* 疇人, see Tan Tai 談泰, "Chouren jie" 疇人解, in *Chouren zhuan huibian* 疇人傳彙編 (Taipei: Shijie shuju, 1982), 1–4.

16 Ibid., 2–3.

17 Ruan, *Chouren zhuan*, 91–109.

18 Joseph Needham and Wang Ling, *Science and Civilisation in China, Vol. 3: Mathematics and the Sciences of the Heavens and the Earth* (Cambridge, UK: Cambridge University Press, 1959), 101–2.

19 Li Yan 李儼, *Zhongguo Suanxueshi* 中國算學史 (Beijing: Shangwu yinshuguan, 1998), 44–5.

20 Ruan, *Chouren zhuan*, 107.

21 Ibid., 627.

22 See Jami, *Emperor's New Mathematics*, 307, for a brief introduction to Minggantu's achievements. For a more complete introduction, see Jianjin Luo, "Ming Antu and His Power Series Expansions," in *Seki, Founder of Modern Mathematics in Japan: A Commemoration on His Tercentenary*, ed. Eberhard Knobloch, Hikosaburo Komatsu, and Dun Liu (Tokyo: Springer Japan, 2013).

23 Yunlu, *lixiang kaocheng*, 790: 6.

24 Minggantu 明安圖 and Chen Jixin 陳際新, *Geyuan milü jiefa* 割圓密率捷法, XXSK 1045: 1–2.

25 The highest position in the Astronomical Bureau, Director, was at the fifth level (out of nine) of the civil service hierarchy.

26 The Qing court maintained a State Historical Archive (*Guoshi guan* 國史館) to preserve and to write its own history. The *Draft History of the Qing* (*Qingshi gao* 清史稿) was compiled in the 1910s and 1920s, mainly based on the documents left by the Qing State Historical Archive. The compilation is widely regarded as unsuccessful for the many errors it contains. The *History of the Qing Empire* (*Qing guoshi, Jiayetang chaoben* 清國史，嘉業堂鈔本) was directly copied from the documents preserved in the Qing State Historical Archive. This research uses both sets of documents but relies more heavily on the *History of the Qing Empire*.

27 Since the second update performed in the Qianlong reign, compilers have kept the main body of the laws in the *Collected Statutes* but have moved the minor regulations and precedents to a separate work: the *Collected Statutes and Precedents of the Great Qing* (called *Da Qing huidian zeli* 大清會典則例 in the Qianlong reign and *Da Qing huidian shili* 大清會典事例 in the Jiaqing and Guangxu reigns).

28 Qu Chunhai 屈春海, "Qingdai Qintianjian ji Shixianke zhiguan nianbiao" 清代欽天監暨時憲科職官年表, *Zhongkuo keji shiliao* 中國科技史料 18, no. 3 (1997): 45–71.
29 Shi Yumin 史玉民, "Qing Qintianjian Tianwenke zhiguan nianbiao" 清欽天監天文科職官年表, *Zhongkuo keji shiliao* 中國科技史料 21, no. 1 (2000): 34–47.
30 Ibid., 35–6.
31 One type of routine memorials that Shi Yumin used were those written to submit the *Weather Records* (*Qingyulu* 晴雨錄) on the first day of the second month every year.
32 Neige daku dang'an 內閣大庫檔案, Institute of History and Philology of Academia Sinica, Taipei, http://archive.ihp.sinica.edu.tw/mctkm2/index.html (accessed 2014–20).
33 Qin Guojing 秦國經, ed., *Qingdai guanyuan lüli quanbian* 清代官員履歷檔案全編, 30 vols. (Shanghai: Huadong shifan daxue chubanshe, 1997).
34 Qingdai gongzhongdang zouzhe ji junjichudang zhejian quanwen yingxiang ziliaoku 清代宮中檔奏摺及軍機處檔摺件全文影像資料庫, National Palace Museum, Taipei, http://npmhost.npm.gov.tw/tts/npmmeta/GC/indexcg.html (accessed 2014–20); Ren Mengqiang 任夢強, ed., *Qingdai lizhi shiliao* 清代吏治史料, 103 vols. (Beijing: Xianzhuang shuju, 2004).
35 Wu Han 吳晗, ed., *Chaoxian Lichao shilu zhong de Zhongguo shiliao* 朝鮮李朝實錄中的中國史料, 12 vols. (Beijing: Zhonghua shuju, 1980).
36 For the life of Johann Adam Schall von Bell, see Rachel Attwater, *Adam Schall, a Jesuit at the Court of China, 1592–1666*, adapted from the French of Joseph Duhr (Milwaukee: Bruce Publishing, 1963); Alfons V äth, *Johann Adam Schall von Bell SJ: Missionar in China, kaiserlicher Astronom und Ratgeber am Hofe von Peking, 1592–1666* [1933] (Nettetal: Steyler Verlag, 1991). For the Tychonic astronomical theory introduced by the Jesuits, see Keizo Hashimoto, *Hsü Kuang-Ch'i and Astronomical Reform: The Process of the Chinese Acceptance of Western Astronomy, 1629–1635* (Osaka: Kansas University Press, 1988).
37 For biographical information of Jingzheng, see "Xiangbaiqi Manzhou Jingzheng lülice" 廂白旗滿州敬徵履歷冊, Da Qingguo renwu liezhuan ji shiguandang zhuanbao zhuangao 大清國人物列傳及史館檔傳包傳稿, No. 702002053(6), National Palace Museum Library, Taipei.
38 In most cases, the ethnic categories agreed with the members' ethnic origins. Military Hans were mainly composed of the descendants of Han Chinese who had lived in Manchuria and became allies of Manchu conquerors.

Bibliography

Abbreviations for Archival and Published Sources

IHP: Neige daku dang'an 內閣大庫檔案. Institute of History and Philology of Academia Sinica, Taipei. http://archive.ihp.sinica.edu.tw/mctkm2/index.html

QGLL: *Qingdai guanyuan lüli dang'an quanbian* 清代官員履歷檔案全編, edited by Qin Guojing 秦國經. 30 vols. Shanghai: Huadong shifan daxue chubanshe, 1997.

SKQS: *Yingyin wenyuange sikuquanshu* 景印文淵閣四庫全書. 1500 vols. Taipei: Taipei shangwu yinshuguan, 1986.

XXSK: *Xuxiu sikuquanshu* 續修四庫全書. 1800 vols. Shanghai: Shanghai guji chubanshe, 2002.

Other Sources

Huang Bolu 黃伯祿. *Zhengjiao fengbao* 正教奉褒 [1884]. In *Zhongguo Tianzhujiao shiji huibian* 中國天主教史籍彙編, 445–575, edited by Chen Fangzhong 陳方中. Taipei: Furen daxue chubanshe, 2003.

Minggantu 明安圖 and Chen Jixin 陳際新. *Geyuan milü jiefa* 割圜密率捷法. XXSK 1045.
Qinghua daxue tushuguan kejishi ji guwenxian yanjiusuo 清華大學圖書館科技史暨古文獻研究所, ed. *Qingdai Jinshenlu Jicheng* 清代縉紳錄集成. 95 vols. Beijing: Daxiang chubanshe, 2008.
Qin Guojing 秦國經, ed. *Zhongguo diyi lishi dang'anguan cang Qingdai guanyuan lüli dang'an quanbian* 中國第一歷史檔案館藏清代官員履歷檔案全編. 30 vols. Shanghai: Huadong shifan daxue chubanshe, 1997
Ren Mengqiang 任夢強, ed. *Qingdai lizhi shiliao* 清代吏治史料. 103 vols. Beijing: Xianzhuang shuju, 2004.
Ruan Yuan 阮元 et al. *Chouren zhuan huibian* 疇人傳彙編. 2 vols. Taipei: Shijie shuju, 1982.
Wu Han 吳晗, ed. *Chaoxian Lichao shilu zhong de Zhongguo shiliao* 朝鮮李朝實錄中的中國史料. 12 vols. Beijing: Zhonghua shuju, 1980.
"Xiangbaiqi Manzhou Jingzheng lülice" 廂白旗滿州敬徵履歷冊. Da Qingguo renwu liezhuan ji shiguandang zhuanbao zhuangao 大清國人物列傳及史館檔傳包傳稿, No. 702002053(6), National Palace Museum Library, Taipei.
Yunlu 允祿 et al. *Yuzhi lixiang kaocheng* 御製曆象考成, SKQS 790: 5–7.

Secondary Sources

Attwater, Rachel. *Adam Schall, a Jesuit at the Court of China, 1592–1666*. Adapted from the French of Joseph Duhr. Milwaukee: Bruce Publishing, 1963.
Cullen, Christopher. *Heavenly Numbers: Astronomy and Authority in Early Imperial China*. Oxford: Oxford University Press, 2017.
Fang Hao 方豪. *Zhongxi jiaotongshi* 中西交通史. Vol. 2. Shanghai: Shanghai renmin chubanshe. 2008.
Han Qi 韓琦. "Fengjiao tianwenxuejia yu 'liyi zhi zheng' (1700–1702)" 奉教天文學家與 '禮儀之爭' (1700–1702). In *Xiangyu yu duihua: Mingmo Qingchu zhongxi wenhua jiaoliu guoji xueshu yiantaohui wenji* 相遇與對話—明末清初中西文化交流國際學術研討會文集, edited by Zhuo Xinping 卓新平, 381–99. Beijing: Zongjiao wenhua chubanshe, 2003.
Hashimoto, Keizo. *Hsü Kuang-Ch'i and Astronomical Reform: The Process of the Chinese Acceptance of Western Astronomy, 1629–1635*. Osaka: Kansai University Press, 1988.
Huang Yi-Long 黃一農. "Beihulue de shengyin—jieshao Zhongguo Tianzhujiaotu dui 'liyi wenti' taidu de wenxian" 被忽略的聲音—介紹中國天主教徒對「禮儀問題」態度的文獻. *Tsinghua xuebao* 清華學報 25, no. 2 (1995): 137–60.
Hucker, Charles O. *A Dictionary of Official Titles in Imperial China*. Taipei: Southern Materials Center, 1985.
Jami, Catherine. *The Emperor's New Mathematics: Western Learning and Imperial Authority during the Kangxi Reign (1662–1722)*. New York: Oxford University Press, 2012.
Li Yan 李儼. *Zhongguo Suanxueshi* 中國算學史. Beijing: Shangwu yinshuguan, 1998.
Luo, Jianjin. "Ming Antu and His Power Series Expansions." In *Seki, Founder of Modern Mathematics in Japan: A Commemoration on His Tercentenary*, edited by Eberhard Knobloch, Hikosaburo Komatsu, and Dun Liu, 299–310. Tokyo: Springer Japan, 2013.
Mungello, David E., ed. *The Chinese Rites Controversy: Its History and Meaning*. Nettetal: Steyler Verlag, 1994.

Needham, Joseph, and Wang Ling. *Science and Civilisation in China, Vol. 3: Mathematics and the Science of the Heavens and the Earth*. Cambridge: Cambridge University Press. 1959.

Qu Chunhai 屈春海. "Qingdai Qintianjian ji Shixianke zhiguan nianbiao" 清代欽天監暨時憲科職官年表. *Zhongkuo keji shiliao* 中國科技史料 18, no. 3 (1997): 45–71.

Shi Yumin 史玉民. "Qing Qintianjian Tianwenke zhiguan nianbiao" 清欽天監天文科職官年表. *Zhongkuo keji shiliao* 中國科技史料 21, no. 1 (2000): 34–47.

Standaert, Nicolas. *Chinese Voices in the Rites Controversy: Travelling Books, Community Networks, Intercultural Arguments*. Roma: Institutum Historicum Societatis Iesu, 2012.

Väth, Alfons. *Johann Adam Schall von Bell SJ: Missionar in China, kaiserlicher Astronom und Ratgeber am Hofe von Peking, 1592–1666* [1933]. Nettetal: Steyler Verlag, 1991.

2 The Organization of the Qing Astronomical Bureau

This chapter describes the organization and functions of the Qing Astronomical Bureau on an institutional level. Writing an institutional history for the Qing Astronomical Bureau needs a completely different book, and it is not the purpose of this chapter to provide even a condensed version. Early in the research process, it became apparent that a clear understanding of the Bureau's organization and each official's position in the Bureau are fundamental to analyzing the Qing state papers related to the Astronomical Bureau. Aiming at removing such difficulties for the readers, this chapter will summarize the organizational regulations relevant to the Astronomical Bureau from the level of the bureau to its subordinated sections and then to the individual officials.

2.1 The Bureau

The most essential duty of the Astronomical Bureau was to produce annual calendars for the dynasty. The Qing Empire, as its predecessors, regarded calendar publication as a state-monopolized business. As a means of displaying the empire's authority, every year on the first day of the tenth month the court held a grand ceremony to promulgate next year's calendar.[1] All government institutions at the capital sent representatives to attend the ceremony to receive their copies of the new calendars. For instance, the Ministry of Rites (*Libu* 禮部) alone needed several hundred copies of the calendars to be distributed to Korean and Annam kingdoms; being vassal states of the Qing, they were not allowed to make calendars themselves.[2] In total the Astronomical Bureau had to have more than 67,000 copies of the new calendars in Chinese, Mongol, and Manchu languages ready before the promulgation ceremony.[3] As a result, the computation of the new calendars had to be finished even earlier. The statutory laws required the Astronomical Bureau to submit the sample calendar in Chinese to the emperor on the first day of the second month.[4] After the emperor approved, the sample was translated into the Manchu and Mongol languages and reproduced. The reproduced copies were then dispatched to each province on the first day of the fourth month so that the provincial government could start preparing the new calendars.[5]

DOI: 10.4324/9781003008255-2

Organization of Qing Astronomical Bureau 17

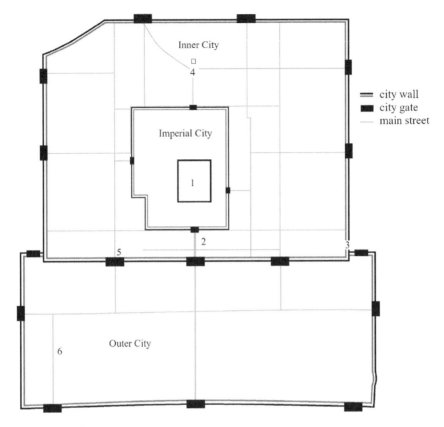

1. Forbidden city
2. Main office of the Astronomical Bureau
3. Observatory
4. Watch tower
5. *Xuanwumen* Jesuit residence
6. Muslim community

Figure 2.1 Map of Qing Beijing, 1644–1900. Created by the author.

Unlike the Ming dynasty, which maintained a branch of the Astronomical Bureau in Nanjing, the entire Qing Astronomical Bureau was in Beijing. The Bureau had three major workplaces (see Figure 2.1). The first was the main office (*yamen* 衙門), which was located in the block of central government institutions between and slightly to the east of the Gate of Heavenly Peace (*Tianan men* 天安門) and the Gate of the Great Qing (*Da Qing men* 大清門). Within the main office were various rooms of subordinated sections and storages that preserved records, documents, and printing blocks of astronomical treatises. It was in the main office that most bureaucratic affairs were conducted, including calendar calculation and production.[6]

The second major workplace was the observatory (*guanxiangtai* 觀象臺) located at the southeast corner of the Beijing city wall. A small team of officials was on duty at the observatory at all times so that the Bureau could record all celestial anomalies and immediately interpret them for the monarch.[7]

The third was the Drum Tower (*Gu lou* 鼓樓) located at the north end of the central axis of the Inner City. The *Collected Statutes of the Great Qing* prescribes that the Astronomical Bureau should keep track of time by monitoring a multilevel water clock or burning incense at the watch tower (*qiao lou* 譙樓), but it does not mention exactly where this watch tower was.[8] Nonetheless, records from the local history of Beijing indicate that the Astronomical Bureau had used the Drum Tower for timekeeping and announced the time to the public in Beijing from there since the Ming era.[9]

In addition to the aforementioned routine work, the Astronomical Bureau was responsible for various kinds of temporary assignments. The most frequent assignment was to announce the time at court ceremonies and imperial palaces.[10] The most important one, however, was the responsibility of finding auspicious burial grounds for the imperial family. Bureau officials sent on field trips for [tomb] site evaluation were often called geomantic officials (*xiangdu guan* 相度官, literally "officials for evaluation and measurement").[11] They might have to stay there as long as the construction works needed their advice.[12]

Probably to make the various kinds of services that the Astronomical Bureau could provide—time keeping, astronomical interpretation, divination, and so on—readily available, the statutory laws required that any imperial trip had to include some Astronomical Bureau officials. The statutory laws even required embassies for bestowing honorary titles on vassal states to include Astronomical Bureau officials. However, this requirement had not been closely followed after the Kangxi emperor questioned the Bureau officials' usefulness in an embassy and permitted it to be dropped.[13] Finally, the court used Astronomical Bureau officials for geographical surveys. This was not a task prescribed by the statutory laws. Nonetheless, in the rare case that the court needed experts for drawing up new maps or surveying river courses, it utilized the mathematical specialty of the Astronomical Bureau officials.

For most of the Qing era, the Astronomical Bureau was a middle-ranking but autonomous institution. Its directors were at the fifth level (of nine) of the civil service hierarchy, the same as the dean of the Imperial College of Physicians (*Taiyiyuan* 太醫院).[14] In the Ming dynasty, the Ministry of Rites was responsible for selecting Astronomical Bureau officials for promotion and sending their background information to the Ministry of Personnel (*Libu* 吏部) for scrutiny.[15] The first years of the Qing followed the same procedures, but the role of the Ministry of Rites was gradually reduced. From 1658, the examinations to select the Bureau officials for promotions were held jointly by the Astronomical Bureau and the Ministry of Rites. In 1671, the court officially separated the Astronomical Bureau from the Ministry of Rites. From then on, whenever a position became available in the Astronomical Bureau, the Bureau directorate could nominate the candidates directly and then sent their background information to the Ministry of Personnel for scrutiny before asking the emperor to make a final decision.[16] If the Ministry of Personnel found the nomination improper because it violated existing regulations, the Bureau directorate could petition the emperor directly.[17]

The administrative regulations of the Astronomical Bureau had been adjusted several times during the Qing dynasty to stimulate the staff's learning. Every three years, the Qing bureaucratic system held a grand-scale job review called the Metropolitan Inspection (*jingcha* 京察) for central government officials or the Great Reckoning (*daji* 大計) for provincial officials. In 1667, the Metropolitan Inspection was extended to the Astronomical Bureau officials.[18] However, the way that Metropolitan Inspection graded an official's performance in four aspects—integrity (*shou* 守), governing (*zheng* 政), ability (*cai* 才), and age (*nian* 年)—did not seem suitable for evaluating a staff member of the Astronomical Bureau. A routine memorial submitted in 1753 pointed out, "the only thing that should be considered is how well [an Astronomical Bureau official] has learned mathematics."[19] Thereafter, the four-aspect grading system was abolished, and the Bureau Directors were required to write short comments on their subordinates in the Metropolitan Inspection report. On the other hand, examination performance gradually took a more important role in determining a person's career progression in the Astronomical Bureau. In 1745, a triennial examination that aimed at rewarding the most learned officials and punishing the worst was added to the Bureau administrative system.[20] The implementation of the periodical examination slackened in some periods, but after the first decade of the Daoguang reign (in the 1820s), a person's promotion became largely dependent on his performance in periodical examinations.[21]

2.2 The Sections

The Qing Astronomical Bureau inherited from its predecessor a structure divided into four sections (*ke* 科) according to different areas of duties. However, the adoption of the New Method soon made the Muslim Section (*Huihui ke* 回回科) lose its status (see later). After the Muslim Section was officially abolished in 1657, the Bureau maintained the division of three sections until the end of the dynasty.

2.2.1 The Calendar Section

The Calendar Section got its name, *li ke* 曆科, from its duty of making three kinds of state calendars. But before introducing these calendars, it should be noted that the character *li* 曆 was identical to the second character of the Qianlong emperor's Chinese name, Hongli 弘曆. When Hongli ascended the throne in October 1735, *li* immediately became taboo and nobody was permitted to use this character on any occasion. Thereafter the civil calendar (*min li* 民曆, sometimes called the "people's calendar") was renamed from *shixian li* (時憲曆, Timely Modeling calendar) to *shixian shu* 時憲書 (literally "Timely Modeling book") and the Calendar Section became *shixian ke* 時憲科 (Timely Modeling Section). Even the calendar promulgation ceremony had to abandon its traditional name, *banli* 頒曆 (Promulgating the calendar), and was renamed *bansuo* 頒朔 (Promulgating the first days of months).

Among the calendars calculated by the Calendar Section, the civil calendar was the one most widely distributed and used. While the calendar surely had to be recalculated every year, the arrangement of its contents hardly changed throughout the Qing dynasty. It always included a list of the number of days in every month, dates of the 24 solar terms (*jie qi* 節氣) together with predictions of eclipses, hours of the rising and setting of the sun and moon, and daily divination of whether it was favorable or unfavorable to conduct certain kinds of affairs.[22] The divination included 37 kinds of affairs for the calendar used by the common people and 67 for the monarch. For example, some affairs common to both the commoners and the monarch were ancestor worship, marriage, meeting friends, baths, and hair cutting, while the ones specific for the monarch were sending troops to the front and dispatching ambassadors.[23] The broad range of affairs covered by divination indicates the calendar's great influence on daily life. The complicated calculations needed for finishing the various entries on the calendar led the Calendar Section to become the section in the Bureau with the largest number of staff members. When fully staffed, it had 96 officials and trainees—more than the other two sections combined.

Besides the civil calendar, the Calendar Section produced two other kinds of calendars which needed intensive calculations of planetary orbits. The calendar of Latitude-Longitude Degrees of Seven Governors (*Qizheng jingwei chandu shixian li* 七政經緯躔度時憲曆), often shortened as the Seven Governors calendar (*Qizheng li* 七政曆), provided the daily celestial coordinates of the seven (classical) planets—the sun, the moon, and the five planets—with notes of additional information such as when the planets would be visible and whether they were in retrograde motion. The Seven Governors calendar was also distributed in the calendar promulgation ceremony but only in a small number and limited to the high nobles and officials.[24] This was probably because the astronomical data provided by the Seven Governors calendars could be used for astrology. The calendar of Encroachments (close approaches and conjunctions) of the Moon and the Five Planets (*Yue wuxing lingfan shixian li* 月五星凌犯時憲曆) was in the same vein.[25] Encroachments (*lingfan* 凌犯) were celestial phenomena so critically related to the ruling house and the court that, except the emperor, nobody should investigate its astrological interpretation. Thus every year the Calendar Section produced only one copy of the Encroachments calendar and submitted it to the emperor in the last month of the year.[26]

Calculating upcoming eclipses was another critical duty of the Calendar Section. By the Qing era, the cause of eclipses was no longer a mystery, but the traditional Rescue Ritual (*jiuhu* 救護) for saving the sun or the moon was still performed at the state and provincial capitals. The Calendar Section's ability to predict solar eclipses accurately was particularly important for maintaining the symbolic connection between the sun and the emperor. The Calendar Section had to submit its prediction to the emperor five months before every solar or lunar eclipse. The prediction included time, duration, and magnitude of the eclipse.[27] Notably, the Ming Astronomical Bureau only calculated eclipses for the capital region. But the Qing Astronomical Bureau, except during the time of Yang Guangxian's directorship (see Chapter 4, Section 4.1), provided predictions not only for the state capital Beijing but also for all provincial capitals.[28]

2.2.2 The Section of Heavenly Signs

The Section of Heavenly Signs (*Tianwen ke* 天文科) was in charge of observing celestial phenomena and promptly delivering their interpretations to the Son of Heaven (*Tianzi* 天子)—namely, the emperor. The officials of the Section of Heavenly Signs were on rotation to conduct nonstop observation of the sky in every direction. If any unusual natural phenomenon occurred, such as a meteor, comet, or abnormally strong wind or rain, the Section of Heavenly Signs had to report it to the emperor immediately with a divinatory interpretation. Indeed, there were some occasions when the emperor scolded the Astronomical Bureau for failing to report in time.[29] On the first day of the second month, the Section of Heavenly Signs had to submit to the emperor the *Weather Records* (*Qingyulu* 晴雨錄) composed of daily observation records from the previous year.[30]

2.2.3 The Water Clock Section

Time keeping was the least technically demanding service that the Astronomical Bureau provided to the court, and this responsibility fell on the Water Clock Section (*Louke ke* 漏刻科). The Water Clock Section had a team of 12 members at the watch tower on rotation for operating the water clock and announcing the time to Beijing residents. Another team of seven was responsible for keeping track of the time by burning incense in the inner court. In addition, most court ceremonies needed the Water Clock Section officials for telling the time. Because these tasks required little skill and knowledge, most of them were assigned to the lowest-level trainees of the section.[31]

The other tasks of the Water Clock Section fell into two categories: selecting auspicious days (*zou ri* 諏日) and selecting auspicious sites (*ze di* 擇地). Before holding a court ceremony or event, the court always consulted the Water Clock Section for selecting an auspicious day.[32] For some routine ceremonies such as worshiping the imperial ancestors, the Water Clock Section had to select the proper days and hours two years ahead and inform related institutions.[33] Most state construction projects needed consultations from the Water Clock Section. The projects could be as grand as building a palace or as small as replanting a tree in front of an imperial tomb.[34] Besides choosing an auspicious day for starting construction work, the Water Clock Section officials had to make sure that the building was located at an auspicious spot and faced a favorable direction.[35] Although the Water Clock Section officials' civil service ranks were low, they frequently received special rewards for their contribution to the state construction projects.[36]

2.2.4 The Muslim Section

In the Ming era, the Muslim Section and Muslim astronomical system served the Astronomical Bureau mainly in two aspects. First, instead of relying on the Great Concordance system alone to calculate the coming solar and lunar eclipses, the court used the predictions from the Muslim astronomical system as a second opinion to reduce the risks of not holding the Rescue Ritual in time.[37] Second, the Muslim astronomical system was used to calculate the Encroachments calendar because the Great Concordance system lacked the ability to calculate the latitudes of planets.[38]

The fate of the Muslim Section was sealed soon after the New Western Method became the official method of calendar making for the Qing dynasty in September 1644. In November 1644, the court forbade the Muslim Section from submitting future predictions "with the purpose of disturbing the New Method" (*yi luan xin fa* 以亂新法).[39] In June 1646, the court declared that it no longer needed the Encroachments calendar calculated according to the Muslim astronomical system.[40] Although there are records showing that some Muslim officials stayed in the Bureau well into the 1660s, the Muslim Section was officially abolished in 1657.[41]

2.3 The Posts

During the Ming-Qing transition, the Astronomical Bureau changed its mathematical astronomy system and adjusted the organizational structure, but it hardly affected the officials' titles and job contents. This section introduces the posts of the Astronomical Bureau from the lowest level to the highest one. Although the posts of Directors and Vice-Directors are included here, the composition of the Bureau directorate needs more elaboration and will be analyzed again in the next section.

A brief introduction to the rank system in the Qing dynasty is necessary before proceeding. As in previous dynasties, the Qing bureaucratic system placed officials into a nine-level ranking hierarchy. Each level (*pin* 品) was subdivided into two categories: *zheng* 正 ("regular" denoted by A) and *cong* 從 ("associate" denoted by B). Officials of rank 1A—namely, the regular category of the first level (*zheng yi pin* 正一品)—were the most important and prestigious, while those who ranked at 9B, the associate category of the ninth level (*cong jiu pin* 從九品), were at the bottom level of the hierarchy. There were also some government positions that were considered too insignificant to be assigned any rank. The entry-level positions of the Astronomical Bureau—Student Astronomers and Yin-Yang Students—were two such positions.

2.3.1 Student Astronomer and Yin-Yang Student

The entry-level position of the Calendar Section and the Section of Heavenly Signs was Student Astronomer (*Tianwensheng* 天文生). According to the *Collected*

Table 2.1 Personnel quotas for Student Astronomers

	Manchu	Mongol	Military Han	Han
1644–1666				66
1666–1670				160
1670–1675	48		32	160
1675–1725	16		8	80
1725–1792	16 (shared with Mongol)		8	80
1792–1912	12	4	8	80

Sources: QHD KX 7749–50; QHDZL QL 625: 131; QHDSL GX 813: 305–6.

Statutes, the Qing court initially gave the Astronomical Bureau a quota of 66 Han Chinese Student Astronomers and increased it to 160 in 1666. Banner Student Astronomers were not added to the Bureau until 1670 and the initial quota was 80 (six Manchus and four military Hans per banner). In 1675, the quota of Han Student Astronomers was reduced to 80 and banner Student Astronomers 24 (two Manchus and one military Han per banner).[42] When the College of Mathematics was founded in 1725, special regulation was made for its Mongol graduates to allow them to use the quota of Manchu Student Astronomers.[43] This regulation was refined in 1792; among the 16 posts shared by Manchus and Mongols, 4 were allotted to Mongols and 12 to Manchus. Thereafter, the quotas of Student Astronomers stayed the same until the end of the dynasty.[44]

Within the Qing bureaucratic system, a Student Astronomer was considered as a student or a trainee (*sheng* 生) rather than an official (*guan* 官). They were given monthly stipends but generally were not assigned any civil service rank. Nonetheless, Student Astronomers were allowed to wear the same official robes and decorations as those at the lowest civil service rank (9B) when attending public ceremonies.[45] In 1723, Manchu Student Astronomers' monthly stipends were raised to the level of rank-nine officials. The next year, on the grounds of fairness, the Bureau was allowed to choose 24 Han Student Astronomers to elevate their monthly stipends to the same level of Manchu Student Astronomers.[46] These 24 Han Student Astronomers were often referred to as Fed-by-salary (*Shifeng* 食俸) Student Astronomers, while the rest 56, whose monthly stipends stayed the same as before, as Fed-by-grain (*Shiliang* 食糧) Student Astronomers.

The Water Clock Section had a position lower than Student Astronomer called Yin-Yang Student (*Yinyangsheng* 陰陽生), or Yin-Yang Person (*Yinyangren* 陰陽人) in the Shunzhi and early Kangxi reigns.[47] This was a position reserved for Han Chinese. Yin-Yang Students were in charge of the simplest works at the Astronomical Bureau: keeping track of and announcing the time by monitoring the water clock and incense burning.[48] Probably because of the minimal amount of knowledge and skill needed for their jobs, Yin-Yang Students were placed below Student Astronomers and paid less than Fed-by-grain Student Astronomers.[49] Throughout the Qing dynasty, the Astronomical Bureau was allowed a quota of ten Yin-Yang Students.[50]

All three sections had unofficial junior personnel called apprentice students (*yiyesheng* 肄業生). Apprentice students were newcomers to the Astronomical Bureau. By contrast, those who were from hereditary astronomer families were called hereditary students (*shiyesheng* 世業生 or *shiye zidi* 世業子弟, literally means descendants from the families that followed the same craft generation after generation). There is no record to show that apprentices students and hereditary students were ever paid. They had to pass entrance examinations to become Student Astronomers of the Calendar Section and the Section of Heavenly Signs or Yin-Yang Students of the Water Clock Section.[51] Because there is no surviving record to show the contents of the examination, it is impossible to assess how difficult it was to pass the examination. In the early Qing era, there seemed to be no rigid regulation of how the Astronomical Bureau recruited its unofficial apprentice students and how many apprentice students it could have. These were not standardized until July 1756.[52]

2.3.2 Erudite

After serving some years and passing periodical examinations to prove his ability, a Student Astronomer could be elevated to the position of Erudite (*Boshi* 博士). An Erudite was an official with rank 9B. Treating Erudites as officials rather than as trainees implied that the state considered Erudites accomplished astronomers. Although the *Collected Statutes of the Great Qing* prescribes no specific duty to each individual Erudite, other sources show that proficient Erudites were important assistants to senior colleagues. On occasion, state documents include names of the Erudites who made significant contributions to the tasks of the Bureau.

2.3.3 Calendar Manager, Astronomical Observer, and Timekeeper

The *Collected Statues of the Great Qing* did not prescribe specific duties to Calendar Managers (*Sili* 司曆, or *Sishu* 司書), but some evidence suggests that Calendar Managers were responsible for supervising the production process of the calendars.[53] Until 1675, there were two posts of Calendar Managers. Afterward, only one post remained, and it became the only middle-level position between Erudites and the Supervisors of the Calendar Section.[54] Ranking merely at 9A, a Calendar Manager would be better considered a position for the most senior or proficient Erudite rather than a position with the responsibility to supervise other officials (see Table 2.2 and Figure 2.2). Like Erudites and Student Astronomers, a Calendar Manager was required to take the periodical examination to prove the steady progress of his professional knowledge. Note that the position of Calendar Manager was reserved for Han officials.

While Astronomical Observer (*Jianhou* 監候) was a rank 9A position in the Section of Heavenly Signs reserved for Han officials, Timekeeper (*Sichen* 司晨) of the Water Clock Section was ranked at 9B and given to military Han officials only. The *Collected Statues of the Great Qing* did not prescribe specific duties to Astronomical Observers and Timekeepers. Probably their statuses were similar to Calendar Manager, except that they were positions in different sections. Like Calendar Managers, Astronomical Observers and Timekeepers were required to attend the triennial examination.

2.3.4 Supervisor of the Five Offices

In the Calendar Section, Han and banner officials both were given five posts of the highest-ranking positions of Supervisors. However, their duties were not the same. Han Supervisors were in charge of computing the state calendars, arguably the most critical and technically demanding work in the Astronomical Bureau, while banner Supervisors were responsible for translating and verifying the contents of the calendars.[55] Probably because of these five Han Supervisors' important role in the Bureau, each of them was given a distinct title—Supervisor of the Spring Office (*Chunguanzheng* 春官正), Supervisor of the Summer Office (*Xiaguanzheng* 夏官正), Supervisor of the Autumn Office (*Qiuguanzheng* 秋官正), Supervisor of the Winter Office (*Dongguanzheng* 冬官正), and Supervisor of the Middle Office (*Zhongguanzheng* 中官正). Manchu and Mongol Supervisors were given a uniform title: Supervisor of the Five Offices (*Wuguanzheng* 五官正), while the military Han Supervisor was always called the Supervisor of the Autumn Office (*Hanjun qiuguanzheng* 漢軍秋官正). The head of the Muslim Section (*Huihui ke* 回回科) was also called the Supervisor of the Autumn Office.[56]

The civil service ranks of Han and banner Supervisors deserve more attention. Only the *Collected Statutes* compiled in the Qianlong reign records that Han and banner Supervisors were of the same rank.[57] The other four editions of the *Collected Statutes* state that Han Supervisors ranked slightly higher than banner Supervisors. Han Supervisors ranked at 6A, the same as a Vice-Director's rank, while banner Supervisors ranked at 6B. The Qing bureaucratic system in general gave banner and Han officials the same ranks.[58] Thus, the difference between Han and banner Supervisors' ranks could be another acknowledgment of Han Supervisors' critical role in the Astronomical Bureau.

2.3.5 Observatory Manager and Water Clock Manager

The heads of the Section of Heavenly Signs and the Water Clock Section were the Observatory Manager (*Lingtailang* 靈臺郎) and the Water Clock Manager (*Qiehuzheng* 挈壺正), respectively.[59] The Observatory Manager was of rank 7B, below the Supervisor of the Five Offices but higher than the Recorder (see later). The Water Clock Manager, however, ranked lower than the Recorder at merely 8B (see Table 2.2).

Nonetheless, the following example illustrates the importance of Han Water Clock Managers in fulfilling the court's expectation of the Astronomical Bureau. In August 1744, the Astronomical Bureau had to nominate two candidates to succeed a vacant post of Vice-Director. According to the administrative regulations, the two most senior officials among the Supervisors of the Five Offices, Observatory Managers, Recorders, and Water Clock Managers were the legitimate candidates. However, the Bureau directorate nominated a Water Clock Manager and a Water Clock Section Erudite. The Ministry of Rites opposed the nomination because the other candidates had more years of service, but the Bureau directorate begged the Qianlong emperor to grant an exception. The directorate argued that "because geomantic selection (*fengshui xuanze* 風水選擇) was the most important work of our bureau" and because the construction project of preparing the future imperial grave had just begun, an official who was proficient in selecting auspicious sites and times was needed.[60] The directorate suggested that experts from the Water Clock Section would fill the vacant post of Vice-Director better than the ones from the Calendar Section or the Section of Heavenly Signs. The emperor immediately approved the Bureau directorate's suggestion and sent the new Vice-Director from the Water Clock Section to continue the construction project right away. Even the routine audience for making the final decision between the two candidates was omitted.[61]

2.3.6 Director and Vice-Director

From 1644 to 1826, the Qing court employed a series of European missionaries as Directors of the Astronomical Bureau.[62] However, only the first one, Johann Adam Schall, had full administrative power over Astronomical Bureau affairs. Between 1665 and 1668, there was no European missionary at the Bureau.[63] When Manchu Director and Vice-Director were added to the Astronomical Bureau in 1665, the Qing court initially gave them ranks higher than their Han Chinese counterparts.[64] This difference was eliminated in 1670, around the time that European a missionary was back in the Bureau. Henceforth, the Astronomical Bureau Director was of rank 5A and the Vice-Director 6B, regardless of whether these positions were destined for Europeans, Han Chinese, or Manchus.

Until European missionaries withdrew from the Qing Astronomical Bureau in 1826, the highest position that a Han official could obtain in the Astronomical Bureau was Vice-Director, not Director. This was because the Kangxi emperor did not create a new position for European Director in 1669 but ordered that the European Director should fill the Han Director's quota.[65] The number of Vice-Directors of each ethnic group changed over time. For example, the Astronomical Bureau had two Manchu, one Western, and two Han Vice-Directors until 1753. Afterward, the compositions of Vice-Directors changed to one Manchu, one Han, and two Westerners.[66] When there were two Vice-Directors from the same ethnic group, the senior one was called the *Zuo jianfu* 左監副, and the junior one, *You jianfu* 右監副.

2.3.7 Recorder and Scribe

Recorder (*Zhubu* 主簿) was a middle-level administrative position at the Astronomical Bureau. There was one post for a Han and one for a Manchu. Recorders were responsible for maintaining the day-to-day operations of the Astronomical Bureau, corresponding with other institutions, and drafting memorials to the

Table 2.2 Civil service ranks of Qing Astronomical Bureau officials, mid-Kangxi reign

Rank	Administration Office	Calendar Section	Heavenly Signs Section	Water Clock Section
5A	Director 監正			
6A	Vice-Director 監副	Han Supervisor of the Five Offices 漢五官正		
6B		Manchu Supervisor of the Five Offices 滿洲五官正		
7B			Observatory Manager 靈臺郎	
8A	Recorder 主簿			
8B				Water Clock Manger 挈壺正
9A		Calendar Manager 司曆	Astronomical Observer 監候	
9B		Erudite 博士	Erudite 博士	Erudite 博士	Timekeeper 司晨
None	Scribe 筆帖式	Student Astronomer 天文生	Student Astronomer 天文生	Student Astronomer 天文生	Yin-Yang Person 陰陽人

Source: QHD KX, 183–208.

Note: Except for the Supervisors of the Five Offices, Han and Manchu officials of the same title were bestowed the same civil service ranks.

emperor. Preserving the wood blocks used for printing the mathematical treatises published by the court was also part of a Recorder's duties. So many administrative affairs were under their supervision that Recorders had a separate subunit called the Recorders' Office (*Zhubuting* 主簿廳) within the main Bureau office.[67]

Scribes (*Bitieshi* 筆帖式) were licensed bannermen who were responsible for document translation and processing in government institutions. Scribes were divided into different categories according to their abilities in translation and transcription, and they obtained their qualifications by passing corresponding examinations held by the Ministry of Personnel. Those who passed the translation examination enjoyed higher status than the ones who only passed the transcription examination.[68] It is noteworthy that although Scribes in theory were employees of the Astronomical Bureau, they were assigned to the Astronomical Bureau without having to pass an entrance examination as did Student Astronomers, and

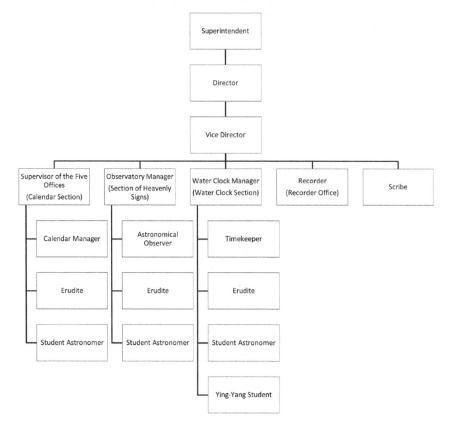

Figure 2.2 Organization structure of Qing Astronomical Bureau, after 1745. Created by the author.

they were not required to study mathematics and astronomy during their service at the Astronomical Bureau. After serving for a certain period, scribes would be transferred to other government institutions.

2.3.8 *Official Astrologer*

According to the *Rites of Zhou* (*Zhou li* 周禮), the *Baozhangshi* 保章氏 was an ancient official responsible for astronomical observation and prognostication.[69] In the Tang dynasty, *Baozhangzheng* 保章正 was used as the title for the Astronomical Bureau official in charge of training the Student Astronomers of the Calendar Section.[70] In the Ming Astronomical Bureau, *Baozhangzheng* was responsible for keeping a log of unusual celestial phenomena and determining their divinatory interpretations.[71] As such, *Baozhangzheng* will henceforth be translated to Official

Astrologer in this book. The Qing court, however, eliminated the position of Official Astrologer in 1675.[72] Because the elimination happened before the earliest *Collected Statutes of the Great Qing* was finished, it is not clear which duties had been assigned to the Official Astrologer in the early Qing. All we know is that there were two posts of Official Astrologer in the Calendar Section, and it was placed below the Supervisor of the Five Offices and above Calendar Manager.[73]

2.4 Superintendents and the Directorate

The position of Superintendent, referred to as Grand Minister Concurrently Managing Bureau Affairs (*Jianguan jianshi dachen* 兼管監事大臣) or Grand Minister Managing Bureau Affairs (*Guanli jianshi dachen* 管理監事大臣) in the *Collected Statutes of the Great Qing*, was a later addition to the organization of the Astronomical Bureau.[74] In the first century of the Qing dynasty, the highest position at the Astronomical Bureau was Director. But in April 1745, a Manchu Directors' continuous malfeasance frustrated the Qianlong emperor. He ordered Le'ersen 勒爾森, a Manchu nobleman and the Right Vice Minister of the Rites (*Libu you shilang* 禮部右侍郎), and He Guozong, then the Left Vice Censor-in-chief of the Censorate (*Duchayuan zuo fudu yushi* 都察院左副都御史), to "concurrently manage the affairs of Bureau Directors" (*jianguan jianzheng shi* 兼管監正事).[75] While the title given to Le'ersen and He seems similar to that of Schall, the first *de facto* Western Director of the Bureau, their natures were different and deserve more explanation.

From late 1644 to early 1665, Schall was the only one in the Astronomical Bureau to have a title closer to the directorship. He administered the Bureau under the title of "Managing the Astronomical Bureau" (*guan Qintianjian* 管欽天監), "Managing the Affairs of Bureau Director" (*guan jianzheng shi* 管監正事), or "In Charge of the Seal and Affairs of the Astronomical Bureau" (*zhang Qintianjian inwu* 掌欽天監印務).[76] Although there were two Han Vice-Directors, their names seemed to appear only on routine memorials related to divination, in which Schall, as a Jesuit missionary, did not want to be involved.[77] For instance, when memorializing the monarch that the new annual calendar was ready for his approval, Schall listed only his name and no one else's.[78] This suggests that Schall alone was in charge of the Astronomical Bureau.

However, the composition of the Astronomical Bureau's directorate was rather different when the Qianlong emperor added Le'ersen and He Guozong to it in 1745. At the time the Astronomical Bureau had a Manchu Director, a Western Director, two Manchu Vice-Directors, two Han Vice-Directors, and a Western Vice-Director.[79] When memorializing the monarch regarding the Bureau affairs, all Directors and Vice-Directors had to sign their names.[80] This indicates that Western missionaries' domination in Astronomical Bureau's administration had been greatly reduced.

Moreover, the Qianlong emperor's imperial order was not a temporary measure to replace an incompetent Manchu Director with two courtiers who were capable enough to take up a second job. It began a new practice of placing the

Astronomical Bureau under the superintendence of trusted ministers handpicked by the emperor. Sources show that later on the vacant directorship left by the incompetent Manchu Director was filled by a banner Supervisor of the Five Offices.[81] Thus, instead of taking up any quota from existing directorate, Le'ersen and He Guozong became additional members of the directorate. After He Guozong lost his post in the Astronomical Bureau in 1757, the number of Grand Ministers Managing Bureau Affairs was reduced to one.[82] Nonetheless, in routine memorials, the grand minister always headed the directorate roster. Whenever the Astronomical Bureau failed to satisfy the emperor, the Grand Minister Managing Bureau Affairs was always punished with the rest of the Bureau directorate. As such, the Grand Minister Managing Bureau Affairs in the mid- and late Qing era was a superintendent whose status was not equivalent to, but higher than that of the Directors.

The Grand Minister Managing Bureau Affairs held the superintendence of the Astronomical Bureau as a concurrent job, and his social and political status depended more on his concurrent position and title at the court than on the job at the Astronomical Bureau. Except for the first and only Han superintendent He Guozong, Manchu superintendents were not known for their distinct knowledge in mathematics or astronomy. Unlike Bureau officials who earned their positions with a specialty in mathematics, the grand minister was given the extra duty of supervising the Astronomical Bureau mainly because the emperor trusted his administrative ability.

Manchu directorships and the superintendency are two important devices that the Qing rulers added to control the Astronomical Bureau. The superintendent, in particular, became an indispensable agent for the monarch, who most of the time had neither the knowledge nor the motivation to care about the administrative details of the Astronomical Bureau. Chapter 9 analyzes the administrative reformation led by superintendent Jingzheng 敬徵 in the Daoguang reign (1821–1850), which resulted in the technical and knowledge renewals of the Astronomical Bureau.

Notes

1. QHDSL GX 803: 75–81.
2. QHD GX 718.
3. Calculated according to the numbers cited by Director Jin'ai 進愛 in 1740. IHP 019954.
4. QHD GX 718.
5. Ibid.
6. For a more detailed description, see Shi Yumin 史玉民, "Qing Qintianjian yashu weizhi ji xieyu guimo" 清欽天監衙署位置及廨宇規模, *Zhongkuo keji shiliao* 中國科技史料 24, no. 1 (2003).
7. QHD GX 751.
8. Ibid., 757.
9. Yu Minzhong 于敏中 et al., *Rixia jiuwen kao* 日下舊聞考 [1785–1787] (Beijing: Beijing guji chubanshe, 2000), 2: 870; Wu Changyuan 吳長元, ed., *Chenyuan shilue* 宸垣識畧 [1788] (Beijing: Beijing guji chubanshe, 2000), 109–10.

10 QHD GX 757.
11 QHD KX 7763. *Xiangdu* 相度 here is used as a term equivalent to geomancy because of the evaluation and measurement process needed before determining a site's auspiciousness.
12 QHD GX 757.
13 QJZ KX (BJ), B005742.
14 QHDSL GX 798: 346.
15 MHD WL 792: 639.
16 QHD KX 7737–8.
17 See, for example, IHP 051696.
18 QHD KX 442.
19 QHDZL QL 620: 255.
20 IHP 216304.
21 NPM 060148.
22 Chinese methods of calendar making, the Great Concordance system included, divide the time of a solar year between two winter solstices (*dong zhi* 冬至) into 24 equal periods. Each of these 24 dividing moments, called solar terms (*jie qi* 節氣), has a traditional and unique name. For example, spring equinox is called "*chun fen*" 春分, and summer solstice "*xia zhi*" 夏至. The New Western Method introduced by the Jesuits does not change the traditional names of solar terms but the method to calculate them is different. Instead of dividing the solar year into equal time intervals, the New Western Method divides the ecliptic into 24 equal 15-degree intervals. Because the sun does not travel with a constant apparent velocity, solar terms calculated according to the New Western Method are different from those calculated according to the Great Concordance system. For the role of solar terms in the dispute between the New Western Method and the Great Concordance system in the early Kangxi reign, see Pingyi Chu, "Scientific Dispute in the Imperial Court: The 1664 Calendar Case," *Chinese Science* 14 (1997): 10–24.
23 QHD GX 748.
24 Ibid., 718.
25 Renamed to the calendar of the Mutual Distances of the Moon and the Five Planets (*Yue wuxing xiangju shixian li* 月五星相距時憲曆) in 1731. QHDZL QL 625: 141.
26 QHD GX 719.
27 Ibid.
28 The practice of including predictions for provincial capitals began with Schall's prediction for the solar eclipse of September 1, 1644. See Väth, *Johann Adam Schall*, 157–8.
29 See SL 4: 359 for one such incident that took place in June 1668.
30 QHD GX 719.
31 Ibid., 757.
32 Ibid.
33 Ibid., 719.
34 IHP 173768.
35 QHD GX 757.
36 QHD KX 7763; QHD YZ 15712.
37 Thatcher Elliott Deane, "The Chinese Imperial Astronomical Bureau: Form and Function of the Ming Dynasty *Qintianjian* from 1365 to 1627" (Ph.D. diss., University of Washington, 1989), 274–5. According to modern simulation, the Great Concordance system outperformed the Muslim system in calculating the time and duration of eclipses. But the Muslim system did better in calculating the magnitude of eclipse, which was a critical factor in determining whether a Rescue Ritual should be held or not. See Li Liang 李亮, Lu Lingfeng 呂凌峰, and Shi Yunli 石云里, "*Huihui lifa jiaoshi jingdu zhi fenxi*" 《回回曆法》交食精度之分析, *Ziran kexueshi yanjiu* 自然科學史研究, 30, no. 3 (2011): 312–16.

38. Shi Yunli 石云里, Li Liang 李亮, and Li Huifang 李輝芳, "Cong *Xuande shinian yue wuxing lingfan* kan Huihui lifa zai Mingchao de shiyong" 從《宣德十年月五星凌犯》看回回曆法在明朝的使用, *Ziran kexueshi yanjiu* 自然科學史研究 32, no. 2 (2013): 156–64.
39. QHD KX 7751.
40. Ibid. The Qing court abolished the Encroachments calendar between 1646 and 1657. Johann Adam Schall et al., "Xiyang xinfa lishu, Zoushu" 西洋新法曆書奏疏, in *Mingmo Qingchu Tianzhujiao shi wenxian xinbian* 明末清初天主教史文獻新編, ed. Zhou Yan 周岩 (Beijing: Guojia tushuguan chubanshe, 2013), 1336.
41. QHD KX 7751.
42. Ibid., 7749–50. The fluctuation of the quota of Student Astronomers in the 1660s and 1670s probably was related to the court's decision to return to the Great Concordance system between 1665 and 1668. See Chapter 4, Section 4.1.
43. QHDZL QL 625: 131.
44. QHDSL GX 813: 305–6.
45. QHD KX 7749.
46. QHDZL QL 621: 579–80. It is not clear if military Han Student Astronomers' monthly stipends were also raised.
47. QHD KX 7750.
48. QHD GX 757.
49. Yin-Yang Students and Fed-by-grain Student Astronomers were paid the same amount of monetary stipend, which was one tael and five maces per month, but while Fed-by-grain Student Astronomers received seven *dou* 斗 of rice per month, Yin-Yang Students received only three *dou* per month. QHDSL GX 813: 306.
50. QHD GX 757.
51. Ibid., 744.
52. NPM 403012106. See Chapter 7, Section 7.3.
53. Some records show that Calendar Managers were punished for misconducts relating to the calendar production process. See, for example, the 1702 case of Bao Yingqi 鮑英齊 in Chapter 4, Section 4.1 and the 1816 case of Fang Luheng 方履亨 in Chapter 9, Section 9.4.
54. QHD KX 132.
55. QHDSL GX 813: 307.
56. QHD KX 131–2, 7751.
57. QHD QL 619: 50.
58. QHD KX 177.
59. QHD GX 751, 756.
60. IHP 051696. *Fengshu* 風水, literally means "wind-water," is a traditional practice of Chinese geomancy.
61. Ibid.
62. European missionaries temporarily lost the directorship between 1665 and 1668. See Section 4.1.
63. See Chapter 4, Section 4.1.
64. In 1665, Manchu Director ranked at 4 and Vice-Director 5. Their ranks were elevated to 3 and 4 in 1667, and then reduced to 5A and 6B, respectively, in 1670. QHD KX 183, 187.
65. QHD YZ 161.
66. QHDZL QL 620: 90.
67. QHD GX 744.
68. Scribes were divided into different categories according to the different levels of examinations in translation and transcription that they had passed. Those who passed the translation examinations enjoyed higher status than the ones who only passed the transcription examinations. See Ye Gaoshu 葉高樹, "Fanyi kaoshi yu Qingchao qiren de rushi xuanze" 繙譯考試與清朝旗人的入仕選擇, *Taiwan shida lishi xuebao* 臺灣師

大歷史學報 no. 52 (2014): 101–2; Mark C. Elliott, *The Manchu Way: The Eight Banners and Ethnic Identity in Late Imperial China* (Stanford: Stanford University Press, 2001), 151–2, 204.
69 Zheng Xuan 鄭玄 et al., *Zhouli zhushu* 周禮注疏, SKQS 90: 316, 490–2; Needham and Wang, *Science and Civilisation*, 190.
70 Chen Xiaozhong 陳曉中 and Zhang Shuli 張淑莉, *Zhongguo gudai tianwen jigou yu tianwen jiaoyu* 中國古代天文機構與天文教育 (Beijing: Zhongguo kexue jishu chubanshe, 2012), 77–80.
71 Zhang Tingyu 張廷玉 et al., *Ming shi* 明史 (Beijing: Zhonghua shuju, 2000), 1207.
72 QHDSL GX 813: 304.
73 This is deduced from the order of official titles shown on the rosters of the Timely Modeling calendars.
74 For the invention and design of superintendency in the Qing central government, see Beatrice S. Bartlett, *Monarchs and Ministers: The Grand Council in Mid-Ch'ing China, 1723–1820* (Berkeley: University of California Press, 1991). For Grand Minister Managing Bureau Affairs, see QHD QL 619: 817, QHD JQ 2763, QHD GX 718.
75 SL 12: 41–2. For Le'ersen and He Guozong's titles, see IHP 021541.
76 For example, see IHP 006498, 038713, 036556, and 091676.
77 IHP 087784, 091801.
78 IHP 006498, 091676.
79 QHD QL 619: 817.
80 IHP 090156, 127466.
81 Qu, "Qingdai Qintianjian," 55–6.
82 For He Guozong's loss of the superintendency, see *Qing guoshi*, 6: 484. See also Chapter 8, Section 8.1. For the change of the number of Grand Ministers Managing Bureau Affairs, see Qu, "Qingdai Qintianjian," 56–7.

Bibliography

Abbreviations for Archival and Published Sources

CKSB: *Jindai Zhongguo shiliao congkan sanbian* 近代中國史料叢刊三編, edited by Shen Yunlong 沈雲龍. 850 vols. Taipei: Wenhai chubanshe, 1982.
IHP: Neige daku dang'an 內閣大庫檔案. Institute of History and Philology of Academia Sinica, Taipei. http://archive.ihp.sinica.edu.tw/mctkm2/index.html
MHD WL: *Da Ming huidian* 大明會典 [1587]. XXSK 789–92.
NPM: Qingdai gongzhongdang zouzhe ji junjichudang zhejian quanwen yingxiang ziliaoku 清代宮中檔奏摺及軍機處檔摺件全文影像資料庫. National Palace Museum, Taipei. http://npmhost.npm.gov.tw/tts/npmmeta/GC/indexcg.html
QHD GX: *Qinding Da Qing huidian* 欽定大清會典 [1899]. XXSK 794.
QHD JQ: *Qinding Da Qing huidian (Jiaqing chao)* 欽定大清會典 (嘉慶朝) [1818]. CKSB 631–40.
QHD KX: *Da Qing huidian (Kangxi chao)* 大清會典 (康熙朝) [1690]. CKSB 711–30.
QHD QL: *Qinding Da Qing huidian* 欽定大清會典 [1764]. SKQS 619.
QHD YZ: *Da Qing huidian (Yongzheng chao)* 大清會典 (雍正朝) [1732]. CKSB 761–90.
QHDSL GX: *Qinding Da Qing huidian shili* 欽定大清會典事例 [1899]. XXSK 798–814.
QHDZL QL: *Qinding Da Qing huidian zeli* 欽定大清會典則例 [1764]. SKQS 620–5.
Qing guoshi, Jiayetang chaoben 清國史嘉業堂鈔本. 14 vols. Beijing: Zhonghua shuju, 1993.
QJZ KX (BJ): *Qingdai qijuzhuce, Kangxi chao* 清代起居注冊, 康熙朝. Edited by Zou Ailian 鄒愛蓮. 32 vols. Beijing: Zhonghua shuju, 2009.

SKQS: *Yingyin wenyuange sikuquanshu* 景印文淵閣四庫全書. 1500 vols. Taipei: Taipei shangwu yinshuguan, 1986.
SL: *Qing shilu* 清實錄. 60 vols. Beijing: Zhonghua shuju, 1985.
XXSK: *Xuxiu sikuquanshu* 續修四庫全書. 1800 vols. Shanghai: Shanghai guji chubanshe, 2002.

Other Sources

Schall, Johann Adam et al. "Xiyang xinfa lishu, Zoushu" 西洋新法曆書奏疏. In *Mingmo Qingchu Tianzhujiao shi wenxian xinbian* 明末清初天主教史文獻新編, edited by Zhou Yan 周岩, 1235–363. Beijing: Guojia tushuguan chubanshe, 2013.
Wu Changyuan 吳長元, ed. *Chenyuan shilue* 宸垣識畧 [1788]. Beijing: Beijing guji chubanshe, 2000.
Yu Minzhong 于敏中 et al. *Rixia jiuwen kao* 日下舊聞考 [1785–1787]. 4 vols. Beijing: Beijing guji chubanshe, 2000.
Zhang Tingyu 張廷玉 et al. *Ming shi* 明史. Beijing: Zhonghua shuju, 2000.
Zheng Xuan 鄭玄 et al. *Zhouli zhushu* 周禮注疏. SKQS 90.

Secondary Sources

Bartlett, Beatrice S. *Monarchs and Ministers: The Grand Council in Mid-Ch'ing China, 1723–1820*. Berkeley: University of California Press, 1991.
Chen Xiaozhong 陳曉中, and Zhang Shuli 張淑莉. *Zhongguo gudai tianwen jigou yu tianwen jiaoyu* 中國古代天文機構與天文教育. Beijing: Zhongguo kexue jishu chubanshe, 2012.
Chu, Pingyi. "Scientific Dispute in the Imperial Court: The 1664 Calendar Case." *Chinese Science* 14 (1997): 7–34.
Li Liang 李亮, Lu Lingfeng 呂凌峰, and Shi Yunli 石云里. "*Huihui lifa* jiaoshi jingdu zhi fenxi" 《回回曆法》交食精度之分析. *Ziran kexueshi yanjiu* 自然科學史研究 30, no. 3 (2011): 306–17.
Needham, Joseph, and Wang Ling. *Science and Civilisation in China, Vol. 3: Mathematics and the Science of the Heavens and the Earth*. Cambridge: Cambridge University Press, 1959.
Qu Chunhai 屈春海. "Qingdai Qintianjian ji Shixianke zhiguan nianbiao" 清代欽天監暨時憲科職官年表. *Zhongkuo keji shiliao* 中國科技史料 18, no. 3 (1997): 45–71.
Shi Yumin 史玉民. "'Xifa' chuan Chao kao (shang) (xia)" '西法'傳朝考(上) (下). *Guangxi minzu xueyuan xuebao (ziran kexue ban)* 廣西民族學院學報 (自然科學版) 10 (2004) 1: 30–8 and 2: 42–8.
Shi Yunli 石云里, Li Liang 李亮, and Li Huifang 李輝芳. "Cong *Xuande shinian yue wuxing lingfan* kan Huihui lifa zai Mingchao de shiyong" 從《宣德十年月五星凌犯》看回回曆法在明朝的使用. *Ziran kexueshi yanjiu* 自然科學史研究 32, no. 2 (2013): 156–64.
Väth, Alfons. *Johann Adam Schall von Bell SJ: Missionar in China, kaiserlicher Astronom und Ratgeber am Hofe von Peking, 1592–1666* [1933]. Nettetal: Steyler Verlag, 1991.
Ye Gaoshu 葉高樹. "Fanyi kaoshi yu Qingchao qiren de rushi xuanze" 繙譯考試與清朝旗人的入仕選擇. *Taiwan shida lishi xuebao* 臺灣師大歷史學報 no. 52 (2014): 95–132.

3 From the Old Method to the New Method

3.1 Hereditary Astronomer Families in the Ming Dynasty

In China, calendar making had long been a state monopoly. The effects of this tradition were paradoxical. On the one hand, the imperial state's need to produce accurate calendars and astronomical predictions stimulated the development of mathematical astronomy. A new dynasty might seek out those who were capable of improving methods of calendar making and sometimes rewarded them handsomely. As a result, calendrical mathematics became an advanced area of study. On the other hand, the connection between the calendar and the prestige of a dynasty made the study of mathematical astronomy a sensitive issue. Publishing unauthorized calendars was strictly prohibited, but even theoretical study of this needed to be conducted carefully. Astronomical observation, for instance, could be a dangerous activity for a commoner, as the imperial state might interpret it as a malicious attempt to detect messages from heaven that the Son of Heaven, the emperor, did not always want to reveal to his subjects. In the same vein, when a dynasty had obtained a calendar-making system that was satisfactorily accurate, it did not necessarily want to share all the details of that system with its subjects for fear of losing its superior knowledge in calendar making.[1]

It was probably on the basis of such views that in 1373 the Hongwu 洪武 emperor (r. 1368–1398), founding emperor of the Ming dynasty (1368–1644), added working at the Astronomical Bureau to the other mandatory hereditary occupations he had established, such as military service. Willing or not, the families that happened to work at the Astronomical Bureau at the time were forced to stay with the Bureau forever. "The staff members of the Astronomical Bureau are forever forbidden to emigrate," the Hongwu emperor decreed. "Their descendants shall study only astronomy and the calculation method for calendar making. They are not allowed to learn other professions."[2] The punishment for not obeying this imperial order was severe: "Those who do not learn will be banished to the Southern Ocean."[3] Because of the Hongwu emperor's decree, astronomical science became a profession confined to a small number of families working for the Astronomical Bureau. While some families were permanently commissioned to the task of making the official calendar, people not belonging to those families had no way of entering the profession of imperial astronomer.

DOI: 10.4324/9781003008255-3

As a side effect, the Ming court saw no need to maintain the College of Mathematics (*Suanxue* 算學) as previous dynasties had done.[4] The recruitment and training of future imperial astronomers were conducted within hereditary astronomer families. It was not until 1519 that the Ming court began to regulate the training of the Astronomical Bureau. According to the regulations, the Astronomical Bureau should select teachers from its own staff and at the end of a year, under the supervision of the Ministry of Rites, should hold an examination to check the staff members' progress in their studies. If they made no progress, the teachers should be punished along with the students.[5] However, these regulations did not clearly define what the punishments should be. Although confirmation of these findings requires more evidence from the archival materials, the effectiveness of this teaching and examination system is questionable.

In contrast to the abolition of the College of Mathematics, the official status and organization of the Astronomical Bureau were preserved. After some initial adjustments, the Bureau officials' ranks were permanently fixed in 1392, with the highest position, Director, placed at rank 5A.[6] There are at least two factors that contributed to this preservation. First, the imperial state needed a calendar that was not just accurate but also authoritative. It was desirable to the imperial state to have a calendar produced by a government institution rather than by civilian families. In fact, to strengthen its authority, at the end of every annual calendar was a roster of 11 Astronomical Bureau officials: five Supervisors of the Calendar Section, one Observatory Manager, two Official Astrologers, one Water Clock Manager, and two Calendar Managers. Second, having an official status was more convenient for the Astronomical Bureau in terms of interacting with other government institutions. The Astronomical Bureau had duties other than calendar making. It was in charge of managing the state observatory, and its staff had to attend many court ceremonies. Even if the imperial state allowed some disorganization within the Astronomical Bureau, it had to give the Bureau a clear official status and bestow proper civil service ranks to its major staff members.

The *Collected Statutes of the Great Ming* (*Da Ming huidian* 大明會典, or *Ming Statutes*) provides more details on the organization of the Ming Astronomical Bureau. The Ming dynasty updated the *Ming Statutes* several times. Table 3.1 shows the personnel quotas in the Astronomical Bureau recorded in the last two updated editions of the *Ming Statutes*. The Zhengde 正德 edition (completed in 1509) was published only slightly past the midpoint of the dynasty's lifespan, thus it did not include any information on the changes to the organizational or administrative regulations that took place in the later period of the dynasty. The last update of the *Ming Statutes* was the Wanli 萬曆 edition published in 1587. In theory, it may provide more information about the late Ming period for understanding the Astronomical Bureau during the Ming-Qing transition. However, some numbers from the 1587 edition are problematic. For instance, the 1587 edition states that the quota of Official Astrologers had been reduced from two to one.[7] But a quick survey of the rosters attached to the annual calendars between 1586 and 1643 proves that there were always two Official Astrologers in the late Ming Astronomical Bureau.[8] The 1587 edition states that there was only one Clepsydra Erudite

(*Louke boshi* 漏刻博士), but this was also unlikely to be true because a different paragraph describes that a certain court ceremony required two Clepsydra Erudites to be present.[9] Similarly problematic is the statement that the last three posts of Muslim Erudites had been eliminated. If that had been true the Astronomical Bureau would have had no Muslim officials at all.[10] But as the following sections will show, plenty of archival records from the early Qing dynasty show that the Muslim officials not only existed in the Astronomical Bureau until the end of the Ming dynasty but well into the beginning of the Qing Kangxi reign.

Further insight can be obtained from the numbers and personnel quotas of Astronomical Bureau officials recorded in Johann Adam Schall's reorganization plan of the Bureau in March 1645 (see Table 3.2).[11] The records in this reorganization plan show that the quotas were distributed relatively evenly among the four sections, with every section having eight or nine officials. However, the reorganization plan also notes that while the Calendar Section was only given a quota of three Instruction Erudites (*Jiaoxi boshi* 教習博士), it in fact employed 17. This indicates that the official quotas did not always reflect the actual number of people employed in the late Ming Astronomical Bureau. It is also noteworthy that Instruction Erudite (of the Calendar Section and the Section of Heavenly Signs) and Erudite (of the Water Clock Section) are not titles seen in the *Ming Statutes*

Table 3.1 Personnel quotas and civil service ranks for late Ming Astronomical Bureau officials

Title	Quota		Rank
	Zhengde edition (1509)	Wanli edition (1587)	
Director	1	1	5A
Vice-Director	1	2	6A
Supervisor of the Five Offices	5	5	6A
Observatory Manager	8	4	7B
Official Astrologer	2	1	8A
Recorder	1	1	8A
Water Clock Manager	2	1	8B
Calendar Manager	2	2	9A
Astronomical Observer	2	2	9A
Timekeeper (*Sichen* 司辰)	2	2	9B
Clepsydra Erudite (*Louke boshi* 漏刻博士)	7	1	9B
Muslim Erudite	3	0	

Sources: MHD ZD 617: 39–40, 122–8; MHD WL 789: 74, 181–6.

Note: The posts belonging to the Nanjing branch of the Astronomical Bureau are not included. No information on the posts of Student Astronomer and Yin-Yang Person is provided in the sources.

Table 3.2 Numbers of Astronomical Bureau officials reported by Schall in 1645

Title	Number
Director	1
Vice-Director	2
Recorder	1
Calendar Section	
Supervisor of the Five Offices	5
Official Astrologer	2
Calendar Manager	2
Instruction Erudite (*Jiaoxi boshi* 教習博士)	17
Section of Heavenly Signs	
Observatory Manager	4
Astronomical Observer	2
Instruction Erudite	3
Water Clock Section	
Water Clock Manager	2
Timekeeper (*Sichen* 司晨)	3
Erudite	3
Muslim Section	
Supervisor of the Autumn Office	1
Water Clock Manager	1
Erudite	6
Student Astronomer	23

Source: Johann Adam Schall et al., *Xiyang xinfa lishu, Zoushu* 西洋新法曆書奏疏, in *Mingmo Qingchu Tianzhujiao shi wenxian xinbian* 明末清初天主教史文獻新編, ed. Zhou Yan 周岩 (Beijing: Guojia tushuguan chubanshe, 2013), 1289–90.

(see Table 3.1). We are not sure if they had officially replaced the title of Clepsydra Erudite or Schall, the author of the reorganization plan, used them conveniently to indicate these officials' responsibilities. Similarly, for reason unclear to us, the reorganization plan replaced the title *Sichen* 司辰 seen in the *Ming Statutes* with *Sichen* 司晨, and *Sichen* 司晨 became the official title of Timekeeper in the Qing era.

Nonetheless, the 1587 edition of the *Ming Statutes* supplies important information regarding Student Astronomers in the late Ming period. The 1645 reorganization plan states that there was not a fixed quota for Student Astronomers in the Ming Astronomical Bureau.[12] The 1589 edition of the *Ming Statutes* does not include a count of Student Astronomers in the personnel quotas of officials, perhaps because Student Astronomers were considered trainees rather than officials. It, however, contains a regulation added in 1570 that set the quota of grain stipends given to Student Astronomers. The regulation allowed the Calendar Section to have 75 Student Astronomers; the Section of Heavenly Signs, 80; the Water Clock Section, 35; the Muslim Section, 50; and the Yin-Yang Persons working at the watch tower, 40.[13] It seems reasonable to assume these were the number of Student Astronomers and Yin-Yang Persons at the Bureau. In fact, the above number of Student Astronomers of the Section of Heavenly Signs was consistent with the number mentioned in a memorial written by Johann Adam Schall in 1655, in which he stated that the Section of Heavenly Signs was allowed to have 80 Student Astronomers in the Ming period.[14]

A comparison with the Qing Astronomical Bureau calls into question whether the Ming Astronomical Bureau indeed needed so many Student Astronomers and Yin-Yang Persons to maintain its operation. After the Qing dynasty was established, the Astronomical Bureau retained roughly the same numbers of officials but employed only 66 Student Astronomers and 10 Yin-Yang Persons.[15] By contrast, the late-Ming Astronomical Bureau employed 190 Student Astronomers for the three main sections and 40 Yin-Yang Persons, and there were 40 additional Student Astronomers in the Muslim section, whose astronomical system was only used for comparison and not for publishing. It seems that the entry-level employees hired by the Ming Astronomical Bureau far exceeded the Bureau's need to maintain its operation. This surely is an indication of corruption in the appointment process.[16] On the other hand, it is a cost that the Ming court had to pay in order to maintain the Bureau's mandatory hereditary system. The Hongwu emperor's decree in 1373 was essentially equivalent to forcing some families to accept the permanent commission of working for the Astronomical Bureau. To maintain such a commission system, the court was obliged to supply those families' basic living expenses. It seems that this obligation was fulfilled by maintaining a pool of Student Astronomers that was larger than actually needed and paying them monthly grain stipends.

Nonetheless, it is unlikely that the Hongwu emperor's decree was implemented literally. The increase in family members over each generation should have made it impractical to keep all descendants in the profession, because there simply would not have been enough vacant positions in the Astronomical Bureau for them. Some regulations added in a later period indicate that the mandatory requirement of inheriting the profession of imperial astronomers had largely become a birthright for obtaining a job at the Astronomical Bureau. For example, when a Student Astronomer retired at the age of 60 years, one of the sons of his principal wife (*dinan* 嫡男) was allowed to take his place. Whenever an examination was held to fill the vacant posts of Student Astronomers, sons of principal wives had priority over other relatives from the astronomer families to obtain the positions.[17]

By the end of the sixteenth century, the Great Concordance system of calendar making no longer could provide satisfactory astronomical predictions.[18] However, most imperial astronomers did not seem to have the will or ability to carry out a calendar reform. In the second year of the Chongzhen 崇禎 reign (1629), the Astronomical Bureau's prediction of a solar eclipse failed again. Supervisor of the Summer Office Ge Fengnian 戈豐年 and other officials at the Astronomical Bureau defended themselves:

> The Great Concordance calendar used by our bureau was established by Director Yuantong 元統 when the dynasty was founded. Actually, it was the

Season Granting calendar (*Shoushi li* 授時曆) created by Prefect Guo Shoujing 郭守敬 and others in the Yuan dynasty. In the past 260 years, calendar officials computed according to the calendrical system and never made any change because we dared not and could not do so. Any hasty change has the risk of causing the deviation to deteriorate more. . . . Merely eighteen years after Shoujing had created the calendrical system, there was an incident that a lunar eclipse did not take place as predicted. [Three years later,] the computation missed a lunar eclipse again. . . . Even Shoujing could do nothing [to improve the system], because he had reached the limit of wisdom and skills and could not progress any further. *If the creator of the system could only offer so much, we, who only know how to follow the system step-by-step, of course could not do better.*[19]

Ge Fengnian was from a prominent astronomer family of the Astronomical Bureau. According to the *Genealogy of the Ge Family* (*Geshi zongpu* 戈氏宗譜), the north Zhili branch of the Ge family could trace their ancestors to a pair of brothers, Ge Ning 戈凝 and Ge Sheng 戈昇, who moved from Wujin, Jiangsu 江蘇武進 to Xian District of North Zhili Province (Pei Zhihli Xian xian 北直隸獻縣, a region located in the east of the modern Hebei Province) in the early Ming period to take up government jobs.[20] Ge Jiugong 戈九功, a great-grandson of Ge Ning, became an Astronomical Bureau Erudite.[21] From then on, every generation of the Ge family had some members who worked for the Astronomical Bureau.[22] By further comparing the records of *Genealogy of the Ge Family* Bureau officials with the rosters of the Great Concordance calendars (see Appendix B), we can reconstruct the lineage of Ge Bureau officials (see Figure 3.1). By the end of the Ming dynasty, the Ge family produced three Directors, one Vice-Director, five Supervisors of the Five Offices, two Calendar Managers, and two Official Astrologers.[23] The large number of family members working at the Bureau and occupying high offices of the Calendar Section strongly suggests the possibility that the Ge family would have liked to preserve their positions in the Bureau by continuing to employ the Great Concordance system.

Nevertheless, it is wrong to assume that all astronomer families and individuals were against calendar reform. For instance, the Zhou 周 family, no less prominent than the Ge family, seemed to hold a rather liberal view on calendar reform. After the end of the sixteenth century, several plans to amend the Great Concordance system were suggested.[24] In December 1610, the Astronomical Bureau made an inaccurate prediction of a solar eclipse. This led the Ministry of Rites to suggest that recruiting experts of calendar to work with Astronomical Bureau officials was necessary for improving the calendrical system.[25] In response, Supervisor of the Five Offices Zhou Ziyu 周子愚 recommended Nicolò Longobardo (1559–1654) and Sabatino de Ursis (1575–1620) to the emperor, "It is desirable to have Confucian officials who know the calendrical system to lead the Astronomical Bureau officials so that all the books brought by them [the Westerners] could be translated and used to amend the incompleteness of our treatises."[26] Zhou Ziyu personally

From the Old Method to the New Method 41

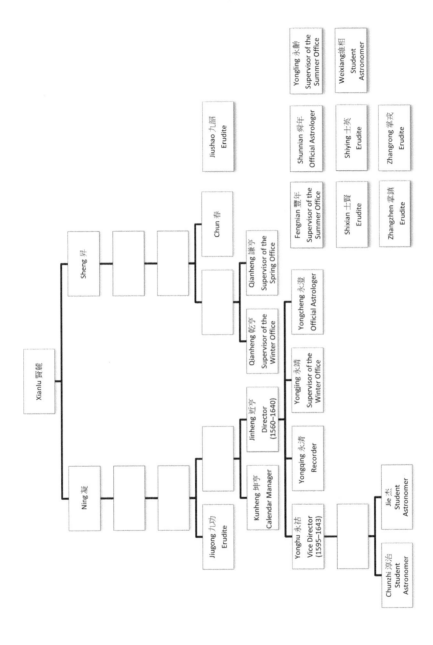

Figure 3.1 Reconstructed family tree of the Ges. Created by the author.

42 *From the Old Method to the New Method*

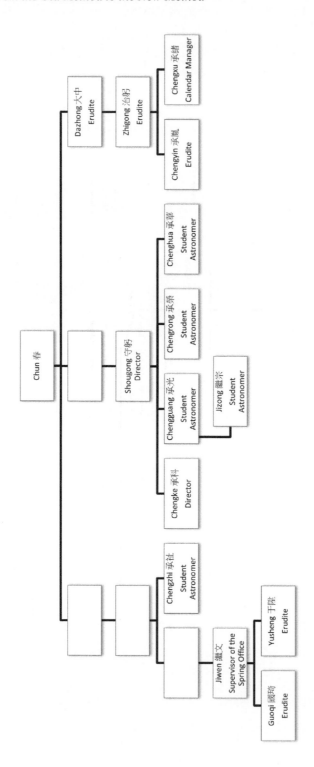

Figure 3.1 (cont.)

assisted de Ursis to write the *On the Gnomon* (*Biaodu shuo* 表度說). He wrote in the preface of the *On the Gnomon*:

> Our Chinese Astronomical Bureau is equipped with the gnomon. However, without a treatise to explain it, we cannot not thoroughly understand its principles and put it to a good use. I saw the method [of using the gnomon] in great Western masters' treatises. Therefore I requested Master Long Jinghua 龍精華 [Nicolò Longobardo] to translate the treatise to supplement our fundamental canons and to complement our calendar-making principles. Master Long agreed and let his friend Master Xiong yougang 熊有綱 [Sabatino de Ursis] give me oral instructions [on the contents of the treatise], which I elaborated into this treatise. . . . The treatises that Western masters brought to our country are of great variety and each is extremely profound. We Chinese should circulate and translate each of them, as what has been done to this treatise.[27]

In a memorial submitted to the Tianqi 天啟 emperor (r. 1621–1627) in 1623, Zhou Ziyu, then the Director of the Astronomical Bureau, emphasized the importance of translating the Westerners' treatises and stated: "According to what I know, Westerners excel in studying the principles of the calendar."[28] Two years later, he again personally took up the job assisting Johann Adam Schall to write the *Eclipse Measurement* (*Ce shi* 測食).[29] Zhou Ziyu's supportive view of integrating Western and Chinese methods of calendar making seemed to have been well known in the court. In the memorial that successfully persuaded the Chongzhen emperor (r. 1628–1644) to set up a Calendar Department (*Li ju* 曆局) for researching the New Western Method (*Xiyang xinfa* 西洋新法) of calendar making, Vice Minister of Rites Xu Guangqi 徐光啟 (1562–1633) reminded the emperor that "In the fortieth year of the Wanli reign (1612), Director Zhou Ziyu had suggested that integrating all [methods] into one was necessary in order to obtain consultations [of improving the official calendar]."[30]

Zhou Yin 周胤, possibly a relative of Zhou Ziyu, appeared favorable, too.[31] After the Calendar Department was opened, Zhou Yin, then the Supervisor of the Autumn Office, dutifully took turns with other Bureau officials to go to the Calendar Department to learn the New Method and to help with the calculation. When Xu Guangqi sent from his deathbed his last memorial to the emperor in 1633 with regard to the business of the Calendar Department, he stated that Zhou Yin and eight other officials from the Astronomical Bureau "have been diligent learning [the New Method]. They should be rewarded after completing their studies."[32] Two years later, Li Tianjing 李天經 (1579–1659), the successor of Xu Guangqi, also wrote to the emperor: "For several months, together with the Astronomical Bureau Director Zhang Shoudeng 張守登 and Vice-Directors Ge Chengke 戈承科 and Zhou Yin, we have modestly examined [the New Method] without prejudice."[33]

By the late Ming period, serving at the Astronomical Bureau had been transformed from a mandatory profession to an inheritable family interest. On the one hand, the law that prohibited the descendants of the astronomer families of the Astronomical Bureau from transferring to other professions was no longer strictly implemented. For example, the genealogical records of the Ge family show many members passed the civil service examinations and became high courtiers or provincial officials.[34] On the other hand, there was no incentive for these families to completely give up the posts at the Astronomical Bureau reserved for them. The Ming court made little effort to reform the organization of the Astronomical Bureau, and it hesitated in replacing the traditional calendrical system with a new one, particularly a foreign one. As a result, the court repeatedly held competitions for predicting upcoming eclipses between different methods of calendar making. Yet, the Great Concordance system supported by the old astronomer families remained the official method of calendar making until the end of the dynasty. It was not until the Qing rulers settled in Beijing and inherited the personnel and government institutions of the Ming that a calendar reform was finally carried out.

3.2 Imperial Regent and Jesuit Missionary

Beginning at the turn of the seventeenth century, Jesuits followed the tactics of Matteo Ricci (1552–1610) in trying to extend their missionary work in Ming China.[35] Ricci arrived in Macao in 1582. After some years of failure, he found that he could attract Chinese attention effectively through a change in social status. Instead of shaving his head bald like a Buddhist monk, he wore the clothes of a Confucian scholar and tried to behave like the gentry.[36] He constantly showcased advanced scientific knowledge and gave away fancy mechanical presents from Europe, such as clocks and telescopes.[37] By means of these measures, in 1601, he finally obtained permission to enter the capital, Beijing, as an expert in calendar making.[38] In late 1605, Ricci and other Jesuit missionaries purchased a house near the Gate of Declaring Military Power (*Xuanwu men* 宣武門), the western gate on the south wall of the Inner City, as their residence and rebuilt part of the house into a small chapel (see Figure 2.1). This chapel, now colloquially known as the "South Church" (*Nantang* 南堂), became the foundation for the Jesuit China mission.[39] Ricci stayed in Beijing until his death in 1610 and he became the first Jesuit buried there.[40]

Establishing a permanent base in Beijing was only the first step. Subsequently, the Jesuit mission's progress slowed down. By the time Ricci came to Beijing, the Ming court was already badly in need of a calendar reform. Nonetheless, it was still almost three decades before Xu Guangqi, one of the most important figures for the founding of Chinese Catholicism, won approval for setting up the Calendar Department for researching the New Western Method. Under Xu's patronage, Jesuit missionaries and their Chinese converts at the Calendar Department prepared astronomical treatises and instruments based on the Tychonic system of mathematical astronomy.[41] Unfortunately, Xu died in 1633 and his replacement at the Calendar Department, Li Tianjing, was less influential politically.[42] The Calendar Department tried to establish the New Method's credibility by repeatedly challenging the Astronomical Bureau to predict solar and lunar eclipses. The results, according to later documents, seemed always to favor the New Method.[43] But the Chongzhen emperor hesitated to give up the Great Concordance system that had been used to calculate the calendar since the founding of his dynasty. Instead of a complete switch to the New Western Method, the emperor hoped that the Astronomical Bureau officials could conciliate the New Method with the Great Concordance system.[44] The Jesuits' efforts to convince the Chongzhen emperor to adopt the Western Tychonic system of mathematical astronomy were almost in vain.

Finally, in 1643 the Chongzhen emperor decreed, "If the New Method again closely predicts the next eclipses, make it [take the place of] the Great Concordance system that the whole world shall use."[45] By this time, Ricci's most important successor, Johann Adam Schall von Bell, had already been living in Beijing for almost 15 years. Perhaps the residents of Beijing knew the small Jesuit Christian chapel and heard some Bible stories, but very few of them knew the meaning of the Christian dating system that numerated this year as "the Year of the Lord 1643." To the Chinese, the proper way to numerate the year used the reign title of the current emperor. Therefore, the Chinese under the Ming Emperor's regime, Beijing residents included, would call this year the sixteenth year of the Chongzhen reign. It is unknown whether the Chongzhen emperor would have kept his promise to adopt the New Method or command another conciliation of the New Method and the Great Concordance system, as he was dead within a year. Schall and other Beijing residents would soon have to change the way they numerated the year.

For those ruled by the rapidly growing Qing Empire in Manchuria, the year that the Chongzhen emperor died was not called the seventeenth of the Chongzhen reign but the first year of the Shunzhi 順治 reign. The Qing Empire was founded in 1636, and Shunzhi was the reign title for its second emperor, Fulin 福臨.[46] The Qing had not been able to expand their territory south beyond the Great Wall, but the uprising against the Chongzhen emperor brought it a great opportunity. In the third month of the year (April 1644), the Chongzhen emperor committed suicide after the rebel forces of Li Zicheng 李自成 (1606–1645) broke into the Imperial City Beijing.[47] Dorgon 多爾袞 (1612–1650), regent for the child Shunzhi emperor (r. 1644–1661), was indeed a highly efficient leader.[48] He quickly marched Qing forces into China and defeated Li.[49] In two months' time, Beijing was under Dorgon's control.[50] Soon Dorgon arranged to have Fulin and the court relocated from Manchuria to the Forbidden City. On the first day of the tenth month (October 30, 1644), Fulin was declared the new sovereign of China.[51] On the same day, the Qing dynasty published the new official calendar printed with the Qing emperor's reign title, Shunzhi.[52]

During this chaotic period, Schall took certain courageous and crucial decisions. He stayed in Beijing to protect the church properties against robbers and Li Zicheng's rebel forces.[53] When the newly arrived Qing forces ordered all Beijing residents to move out of the north city in three days in order to make room for the Qing armies, Schall immediately went to the temporary office of the Grand Secretariat (then known as the Palace Academy, *Neiyuan* 內院) to petition for exception.

Schall reasoned that he was not a Han Chinese but a missionary from afar and that an abrupt moving would damage the printing blocks crucial to the upcoming calendar reform.[54] The next day, the Grand Secretariat granted Schall's petition on behalf of Dorgon and forbade the Qing army to disturb Schall's chapel.[55]

Schall's brave and timely actions probably caught Dorgon's attention. Soon Dorgon decided to adopt Schall's new calendar. In July 1644, Dorgon announced that he would send some ministers to observe the upcoming solar eclipse on the first day of the eighth month (September 1, 1644) along with Schall and the Astronomical Bureau officials.[56] Ostensibly, this observation, as those of the Ming Chongzhen reign, was to compare the accuracy of Schall's New Method of calendar making with that of the old Great Concordance system. But, in fact, Dorgon already showed his preference for the New Method in the announcement of the comparison test:

> The old calendar has accumulated errors while the New Western Method has repeatedly shown its accuracy. I knew about these. [Schall's] memorial includes [the predictions of] the beginning and ending times and shapes of the solar eclipse. It also gives different eclipse magnitudes and durations for observer in different provinces. It is already obvious that his calculation is detailed and carefully executed.[57]

Days after the announcement, Dorgon again showed his preference for Schall's New Method by telling the Astronomical Bureau officials to discard their sample calendar. Dorgon dictated that the new calendar, called the Timely Modeling (*shixian* 時憲) calendar, had to be computed according to the New Method. Meanwhile, Dorgon told Schall, "The necessary calendar should all be computed according to the New Method completely. Speed up the preparation for the sample calendar and submit it to the Ministry of Rites."[58] Dorgon even began to discuss some revisions of the calendar's format with Schall.[59] With a new ruler so enthusiastic about Schall's calendar, the Astronomical Bureau officials knew that the Great Concordance system's days were numbered. On August 26, 1644, six days before the observation of the solar eclipse, the Astronomical Bureau high officials sent the following to Dorgon:

> The discrepancy of the Old Method has gradually worsened while the New Method repeatedly demonstrated in tests that it matches closely [with observed results]. . . . We have no other opinion about making all the calendar of the next year according to new format and calculating the orbits of five planets according to the New Method. We beg you to acknowledge and implement these.[60]

After the eclipse, the ministers sent by Dorgon reported that the results closely matched the prediction of the New Western Method, while both the Great Concordance and the Muslim systems showed considerable errors.[61]

When the Han Chinese received the new calendar, they noticed that its front cover was printed with a different phrase, "According to the New Western Method" (*yi Xiyang xinfa* 依西洋新法).[62] This phrase was more than an acknowledgment of Schall's contribution to the new calendar. It was so significant that two decades later, it would become critical evidence in accusing Schall and the Astronomical Bureau officials of treason. While the new reign title would tell the Han Chinese that they were now under a new Manchu emperor, the new phrase told them that the traditional Chinese method of calendar making had been replaced by a better one from the West. The new dynasty used the phrase to demonstrate its authority. Without further delay, the traditional yet outdated calendar was to make way for a new, more accurate one, despite its foreign origin. Moreover, the new calendar declared the new dynasty's trust in the superiority of Western mathematical astronomy provided by Jesuit missionaries. As the declaration boosted the social status of Schall and his Jesuit colleagues, it would help the Jesuit China mission.

However, a more careful reading of Schall and Dorgon's discussions of the new calendar's format reveals that Schall did not get everything he wanted. Schall requested that Dorgon let him remove the roster of the Astronomical Bureau officials customarily attached to the end of the calendar (see Figure 3.2). He argued, "The submitted calendar is completely made according to the New Method. It is not calculated by the Astronomical Bureau officials."[63] Schall emphasized that he and his Calendar Department labored day and night to verify each step of their calculations, but the Astronomical Bureau officials made no significant contribution. The only use of those officials was to copy the entries on auspicious and inauspicious days for various activities, which "were not based on measurement and none of them needs to be calculated." Nevertheless, Dorgon did not approve Schall's request: "Since it is an old custom, the list shall still be appended after Schall's name."[64] Dorgon's concern went beyond undeserved credit for the Astronomical Bureau officials. As a conqueror, Dorgon wanted to take over the people and institutions left by the Ming instead of completely brushing them aside. He was willing to adopt the New Method and acknowledge Schall's contribution but that was not equivalent to abolishing the old institution of the Astronomical Bureau. To ensure the new format of the calendar was what he wanted, Dorgon ordered a sample calendar from the Astronomical Bureau to be submitted to him as a reference.[65]

Without Dorgon's full support, the power struggle between Schall and the Astronomical Bureau dragged on. After the test of solar eclipse, Dorgon ordered the Ministry of Rites, along with the Office of Scrutiny for Rites (*Li ke* 禮科), to hold an examination to determine which Astronomical Bureau staff members had learned the New Method well enough to stay.[66] Schall, who surely was the one best qualified to evaluate Astronomical Bureau staff members' knowledge of the New Method, was not among the examiners. But rather than being a sign of distrust to Schall, Dorgon's order probably was based on the Ming regulations that placed the examinations and promotions of the Astronomical Bureau officials under the supervision of the Ministry of Rites.[67] However, this gave the

48 *From the Old Method to the New Method*

Figure 3.2 Ming Great Concordance calendar, the fifteenth year of the Yongle reign (1417).

Left, front cover. The statement in the right box declares that the Astronomical Bureau alone has the imperial permission to make and print the calendar. Piracy will lead to the death penalty, and informers will be rewarded with 50 taels of silver.

Bottom, last two pages. The leftmost 11 columns were the titles and names of the Astronomical Bureau officials.

Courtesy of the National Central Library, Taiwan.

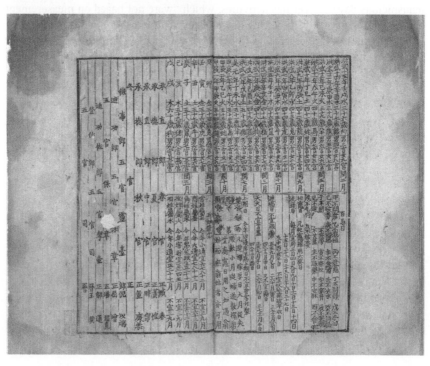

Ministry of Rites another chance to take sides with the Astronomical Bureau. In a palace memorial submitted to Dorgon four days before the scheduled date of the examination, Schall described that he was threatened at the Ministry of Rites.[68] He wrote:

> In the *chen* 辰 hour (7:00–9:00) of the eighteenth day of this month (September 18, 1644), at the instigation of the Astronomical Bureau officials, the Ministry of Rites suddenly summoned me to its office. An interpreter then told me that holding an examination for the Astronomical Bureau officials was not an urgent thing to do at this critical moment. If it causes any delay to the publication of the calendar, it will completely be my fault. Many of his words were so ridiculous that I could not bear to hear. Without giving me any chance to explain, they scolded me and sent me back. . . . I never imagine that at such an advanced age I would have to prostrate in a public office and to be coerced repeatedly by low-ranking petty officials. How can I still have the honor to create the laws [of calendar making] for future generations and to make them part of this prosperous era?[69]

Despite Schall's graphical description, Dorgon only reiterated his decision to adopt the New Method but did not punish anyone from the Ministry of Rites and Astronomical Bureau.[70]

It turns out that the examination was held as scheduled, but instead of giving a test on astronomical knowledge or calculation ability, the high officials of the Ministry of Rites and the Office of Scrutiny for Rite merely interviewed the examinees to observe if they appeared capable to learn the New Method.[71] In the report to Dorgon, the Ministry of Rites cited the Astronomical Bureau officials and Student Astronomers' argument as an explanation that they were not ordered to learn the details of the New Method until this month; thus, except the three officials who had been learning from Schall, none of them should be expected to be able to pass an examination on the New Method in such short period of time.[72] As a result, the Ministry of Rites suggested giving 45 officials and 18 Student Astronomers belonging to the three major sections a three-month extension before they were tested again, and replacing two officials, who appeared too old to learn the New Method, by young members from their families. Only three officials and 14 Student Astronomers, who either did not attend this examination or were regarded too ignorant, were dismissed immediately. As for the Muslim Section, the Ministry of Rites claimed that the Muslim Section was not related to the issue of switching from the Old Method to the New Method. Thus, the Ministry of Rites suggested that the five Muslim officials should all be allowed to stay so that the Muslim system could continue serving as a reference to the state astronomical system. Five out of the eight Muslim Student Astronomers, however, should be dismissed immediately, and the rest three should be made to learn the New Method.[73] Dorgon accepted all suggestions from the Ministry of Rites and allowed the majority of Astronomical Bureau staff members to keep their jobs, at least until the next examination was held.

In contrast, Schall saw a complete replacement as the right solution. By the end of the three-month extension, Schall wrote another palace memorial to Dorgon:

> Now that more than half of the extension period has passed, [the Bureau officials and students] still fool around. Their indolence can be known from this. Moreover, the younger ones do not even know anything about the Old Method. How can they possibly concentrate on learning the New Method? If I teach them [the New Method], I am afraid not only that my efforts will be wasted but also that they will steal and alter the [New] Method. If so, the dispute will never end. I repeatedly think this over and feel that I cannot teach them the New Method rashly. . . . I beg Your Majesty to make a decisive verdict to cut off the residue so that the New Method can be transmitted to eternity.[74]

There is no record to show that Dorgon had responded to this memorial.

On the other hand, at the end of November 1644, Dorgon ordered the Ministry of Rites to have Schall submit an evaluation of the contributions of Astronomical Bureau and Calendar Department officials.[75] Schall sent a list of 21 people classified into three groups according to their contributions (see Table 3.3). On the list, only three were from the Astronomical Bureau. These three officials had long been cooperative with the Calendar Department and eager to learn the New Method. The other 18 people were all Schall's disciples at the Calendar Department. Schall intended his list to tell Dorgon that he did not want to retain current Astronomical Bureau staff. Nevertheless, the Ministry of Rites once again took the Astronomical Bureau's side. After more than 20 days' delay, the Ministry of Rites delivered Schall's list to Dorgon along with another list of contributors from the Astronomical Bureau.[76] Because some of his officials had diligently proofread the format of the calendar, the Astronomical Bureau Director claimed, "We dare not obliterate their toil."[77]

By the time Schall's and the Ministry of Rites' recommendation lists reached Dorgon, Dorgon had decided to place the Astronomical Bureau under Schall's direction. On December 24, 1644, Dorgon decreed:

> [Regarding] the official seal of the Astronomical Bureau, let Tang Ruowang [Schall] be in charge of it. All Bureau staff are subordinated to Ruowang. Anything relating to submitting calendars [for imperial reviews], astrology, and geomancy, they had to act according to the Seal-holding Official's order. No transgression is allowed.[78]

This decree equated to make Schall the Director of the Astronomical Bureau. Schall immediately memorialized that he had no intention to become an official, not to mention to become the Seal-holding Official of the Astronomical Bureau.[79] Dorgon refused to retract the appointment. On January 3, 1645, Dorgon gave Schall the power to rectify Bureau regulations and to impeach indolent subordinates directly.[80]

Table 3.3 Schall's disciples in Ming Calendar Department and Astronomical Bureau, 1644

Name	Grade given by Schall	
Bao Yingqi 鮑英齊	2	Calendar Department
Huang Hongxian 黃宏憲	1	Calendar Department
Jiao Yingxu 焦應旭	3	Calendar Department
Jia Liangqi 賈良琦	2	Supervisor of the Middle Office
Li Hua 李華	3	Calendar Department
Li Zubai 李祖白	1	Calendar Department
Liu Youqing 劉有慶	2	Supervisor of the Autumn Office
Liu Yunde 劉蘊德	3	Calendar Department
Song Fa 宋發	1	Calendar Department
Song Kecheng 宋可成	2	Calendar Department
Song Keli 宋可立	3	Calendar Department
Sun Youben 孫有本	2	Calendar Department
Wu Zhiyan 武之彥	3	Calendar Department
Xu Huan 徐瑛	2	Calendar Department
Yin Kai 殷鎧	2	Calendar Department
Zhang Sheng 掌乘	2	Calendar Department
Zhang Youzhuan 掌有篆	3	Calendar Department
Zhu Guangda 朱光大	1	Calendar Department
Zhu Guangxian 朱光顯	2	Erudite
Zhu Guangyin 朱光蔭	3	Student Astronomer
Zhu Xingshu 朱廷樞	1	Calendar Department

Source: IHP 038804.

Table 3.4 Organization of Qing Astronomical Bureau proposed by Schall in 1645

Title	Quota
Seal-holding Official	1
Director	1
Vice-Director	1
Recorder	1
Calendar Section	
Supervisor of the Five Offices	5
Vice Supervisor of the Five Offices	5
Official Astrologer	2
Calendar Manager	2
Copyist	10
Section of Heavenly Signs	
Observatory Manager	4
Astronomical Observer	2
Instructor Erudite	6
Water Clock Section	
Water Clock Manager	2
Timekeeper	3
Erudite	1
Student Astronomer	20

Source: Schall, *Xiyang xinfa lishu*, 1289–90.

It seems that at the time Schall was able to reform the Astronomical Bureau as he saw fit. Indeed, by the end of February 1645, the Grand Secretariat had approved the new organization and personnel quotas of the Astronomical Bureau proposed by Schall (Table 3.4).[81] A comparison with the old Bureau organization inherited from the Ming period (Table 3.2) shows Schall's vision for the new Astronomical Bureau. First, the Muslim Section would be abolished. Second, the Calendar Section would have five additional posts called Vice Supervisors of the Five Offices (*Wuguanfu* 五官副), and its 17 Eruncites would be replaced by 10 Copyists (*Shanxie guan* 繕寫官). Third, the numbers of Eruncites in the other two sections would also be adjusted. The Section of Heavenly Signs would have three additional Eruncites, which made for a total of six Eruncites. The Water Clock Section, in contrast, would have its Eruncites reduced from three to two.[82]

In early March, Schall held a four-day examination for Astronomical Bureau and Calendar Department staff members to determine who qualified for staying in his Astronomical Bureau. Before holding the first day's examination, Schall dismissed all Muslim staff by informing them that their section would be eliminated. He then proceeded to test the Calendar Department staff. Schall was satisfied by their knowledge of the New Method and passed them all. The second day, Schall tested the Calendar Section officials. From Table 3.2, we know that at the time the Calendar Section had 26 officials. But only two officials, Liu Youqing and Jia Liangqi,[83] could answer the questions adequately enough to pass the test. To give the rest officials a second chance, Schall asked them to elaborate on their knowledge about the Old Method. Still, only five officials showed that they could calculate the eclipses.[84] At the end of the day, Schall passed Liu, Jia, and these five officials, and failed the other 19 officials. However, "in afraid of betraying the court's virtues of [showing them] preferential tolerance," Schall chose five officials from the failed ones and allowed them to stay in the Bureau on the condition that they transferred to other sections or were demoted to Student Astronomers. The third day, Schall tested Student Astronomers and dismissed seven from them, including five who absented themselves from the examination. The final day of the examination, Schall dismissed four officials belonging to the Section of Heavenly Signs and the Water Clock Section.[85] In sum, out of approximately 55 officials and 23 Student Astronomers serving at the Astronomical Bureau, Schall intended to have 26 officials and 7 Student Astronomers dismissed and to have the other 5 officials demoted. Moreover, in the memorial to propose the rearrangement of Astronomical Bureau personnel based on the examination results, Schall suggests that Director Ge Chengke 戈承科, Vice-Director Zhou Yin 周胤, and Recorder Ge Yongqing 戈永清 should be discharged immediately for they had been leading subordinates into indolence and did not qualify for commanding those who had contributed to the New Method.[86]

Facing the crisis of losing their jobs, the Astronomical Bureau officials reacted fiercely.[87] They went around spreading the rumor that Schall had been too arrogant and jealous to teach them the true knowledge of the New Method wholeheartedly and that Schall had accepted bribes. Within days, the Bureau officials won the Ministry of Rites to their sides and Schall was made to stand a trial. It did not

Table 3.5 Numbers of Astronomical Bureau officials, 1658

Title	Number
Director	1
Vice-Director	2
Manchu translators	6
Recorder	1
Calendar Section	
Supervisor of the Five Offices	5
Official Astrologer	2
Calendar Manager	2
Erudite	26
Section of Heavenly Signs	
Observatory Manager	3
Astronomical Observer	1
Erudite	3
Water Clock Section	
Water Clock Manager	2
Timekeeper	1
Erudite	7
Muslim Section	
Supervisor of the Autumn Office	1
Erudite	4

Source: Schall, *Xiyang xinfa lishu*, 1336–7.

take too long for Schall to clear up the false accusations added upon him.[88] However, Schall's reorganization plan for the Bureau was largely canceled. A small number of accusers were removed from the Bureau, but as we shall see later, most Bureau officials and students were allowed to stay, regardless of whether they had failed the March examination or not.[89] When the court requested the Bureau to report the numbers of its employees in 1658, the organization of the Astronomical Bureau (see Table 3.5) recorded in Schall's memorial looks more like that in the late Ming period (Table 3.2) than what he had proposed in 1645 (Table 3.4).[90]

The Jesuits hoped that the New Method would replace the Chinese system of calendar making rather than supplement it. Their goal was to conduct missionary work, not merely to assist the Chinese in their calendar making. Thus they would not rest easy when the Chongzhen emperor repeatedly expressed the desire to conciliate the New and Old Methods or to assimilate the New Method to the Great Concordance system. If the Chongzhen emperor felt bound to the traditional system, Dorgon probably had different thoughts. As a foreign conqueror, Dorgon was not obligated to follow all the traditions of the conquered. He discarded the Great Concordance system because it was no longer adequate to serve the imperial privilege and obligation of producing the annual calendar. If a non-Chinese method of calendar making could reinforce the Qing conquest of China, nothing held back Dorgon from adopting it.

Table 3.6 Endorsers of Schall's *Response to Concerns over the Notes on Civil Calendar*

Names	Title
Bao Yinghua 鮑英華	Erudite
Bao Yingqi 鮑英齊	Erudite, rank 8B
Du Ruyu 杜如預	Water Clock Manager, Honorary Director
Ge Guoqi 戈國琦	Erudite
Ge Jiwen 戈繼文	Calendar Manager, rank 8A
He Qiyi 何其義	Erudite, rank 8B
Huang Gong 黃鞏	Observatory Manager
Jia Liangqi 賈良琦	Supervisor of the Middle Office, rank 4A
Jiao Yingxu 焦應旭	Erudite, rank 8B
Li Guangda 李光大	Erudite, rank 8B
Li Zubai 李祖白	Supervisor of the Summer Office, rank 5A
Liu Youqing 劉有慶	Senior Vice-Director, rank 4A
Liu Youtai 劉有泰	Official Astrologer, rank 7A
Si Ergui 司爾珪	Erudite, rank 8B
Song Fa 宋發	Supervisor of the Autumn Office, rank 5A
Song Kecheng 宋可成	Supervisor of the Spring Office, rank 5B
Sun Youben 孫有本	Erudite, rank 8B
Xue Wenbing 薛文炳	Erudite, rank 8B
Yang Hongliang 楊弘量	Water Clock Manager
Yin Kai 殷鎧	Calendar Manager
Zang Wenxian 臧文顯	Erudite, rank 7B
Zhang Sheng 掌乘	Recorder, rank 6B
Zhang Guangxiang 張光祥	Erudite, rank 7A
Zhang Qichun 張其淳	Observatory Manager
Zhang Wenming 張問明	Official Astrologer
Zhou Shichang 周士昌	Erudite, rank 8B
Zhou Yin 周胤	Junior Vice-Director, rank 4A
Zhu Guangxian 朱光顯	Supervisor of the Winter Office, rank 5A

Source: Johann Adam Schall, *Minli puzhu jiehuo* 民曆鋪註解惑, XXSK 1040: 2–3.

Still, Dorgon attempted to reconcile the conquered and the conquerors. He considered more than whether the Astronomical Bureau officials had indeed contributed to the new calendar. What he intended was to show his new subjects that the Astronomical Bureau, the only state institution legally responsible for interpreting heavenly signs, endorsed the Qing. Consequently, he would not let Schall remove the roster of Astronomical Bureau officials from the calendar. Dorgon adopted Schall's New Method, but Schall would have to reconcile the Calendar Department and the Astronomical Bureau for Dorgon.

3.3 New and Old Astronomer Families in the Shunzhi Reign

The decade of the Shunzhi emperor's personal rule saw Schall reach the peak of his career as a Qing courtier. On December 31, 1650, Regent Dorgon died unexpectedly in a hunting trip.[91] At the time, the Shunzhi emperor was not yet 13 years old, but he quickly consolidated power and commenced personal rule.[92] Schall's connection with the imperial house grew stronger.[93] The young emperor, in particular, regarded Schall as a trusted elderly friend. He enjoyed visiting Schall's church in less formal settings and often spent hours talking with Schall on topics ranging from the theory of solar eclipse to the Astronomical Bureau staff's progress.[94] By the time the Shunzhi emperor passed away on February 1, 1661, Schall was bestowed the first level of civil service rank.[95]

Schall's success in the court may lead one to overlook the obstacles that he had to deal with when managing the Astronomical Bureau. For instance, as late as 1655, Schall still had difficulty in recruiting a full staff for the Section of Heavenly Signs. To boost morale, Schall memorialized the Shunzhi emperor to present special rewards to Observatory Manager Li Zhigui 李之貴 and two Manchu officials in charge of translating the calendar. Furthermore, he stated:

> Even if the Section [of Heavenly Signs] cannot have the quota of recruiting eighty Student Astronomers as in the Ming era, it should be allowed to add sixteen men to make the total twenty. Moreover, compared to eighty, twenty merely makes up a quarter of the trainees needed. The lesser the number of trainees, the heavier the work they have to do. . . . Previously, according to decision of the Ministry [of Rites], the quota of Student Astronomers was only allowed to increase by eight. . . . Now that more than seven months has passed . . . because the monthly grain stipend of six *dou* 斗 is not enough for sustaining a living, nobody has come forward to take this job. Even though this winter is fiercely cold, there are only four Student Astronomers available to take turns for going up to the observatory.[96]

While the Ming court allowed the Section of Heavenly Signs to hire 80 Student Astronomers, the early Shunzhi reign cut it down to merely four. Even the Ministry of Rites finally agreed to triple the quota of Student Astronomer to 12, Schall had to complain to the emperor again that nobody was willing to take such a low-ranking and miserably paid position. Moreover, the Astronomical Bureau had been deeply poisoned by factionalism and mutual distrust among its staff. This was the aftereffect of the severe power struggle between the Calendar Department and the Astronomical Bureau during the late Ming period. The new dynasty merged these two institutions, but Dorgon did not allow Schall to discharge the staff left over from the Ming dynasty. These rivals were stuck working together.

About a year after the end of the Shunzhi reign, Schall published the *Response to Concerns over the Notes on Civil Calendar* (*Minli puzhu jiehuo* 民曆鋪註解惑).[97] As the highest administrator of the Astronomical Bureau, Schall had dutifully produced the annual calendar for the Qing Empire for almost two decades. As a missionary, however, he faced challengers in the Jesuit order denouncing his calendar, which provided advice on the choice of days for various activities calculated according to Chinese divinatory theories, for promulgating superstition.[98] Perhaps to make the *Response to Concerns* more convincing, Schall attached a list of 28 endorsers from the Astronomical Bureau to the preface (see Table 3.6).

Recall that when Dorgon chose Schall to produce the state calendar in 1644, Schall did not want the Astronomical Bureau officials' names to appear on his new calendar. Eighteen years later, Schall proudly displayed the endorsement from an impressive number of high officials of the Astronomical Bureau. Moreover, while Schall's disciples clustered in the Calendar Section, the endorsers came from three major sections of the Astronomical Bureau. Both Water Clock Managers, Yang Hongliang 楊弘量 and Du Ruyu 杜如預, endorsed Schall's treatise, as did the Observatory Managers, Huang Gong 黃鞏 and Zhang Qichun 張其淳. The endorser list appears to show that Schall had firm control of the Astronomical Bureau.

A closer examination of the endorser list shows that the majority of the Astronomical Bureau high officials had affiliated with Schall since the Ming era, particularly the Calendar Department officials. Compare Tables 3.3 and 3.6. The names of Vice-Director Liu Youqing 劉有慶, Recorder Zhang Sheng 掌乘, and the Calendar Section Supervisors—Song Kecheng 宋可成, Li Zubai 李祖白, Jia Liangqi 賈良琦, Song Fa 宋發, and Zhu Guangxian 朱光顯—appear in both. This means that they were among Schall's disciples who worked on Qing China's first official calendar.[99] They were from the Ming Calendar Department, except that Jia Liangqi and Liu Youqing were from the Astronomical Bureau. Nonetheless, Jia and Liu had been cooperative with the Calendar Department and had diligently learned the New Method since the late Ming era. Ranked below them in the Shunzhi Astronomical Bureau were Calendar Manager Yin Kai 殷鎧 and Erudites Jiao Yingxu 焦應旭, Bao Yingqi 鮑英齊, and Sun Youben 孫有本. Their names also appeared in Schall's recommendation list to Dorgon (Table 3.3).

Comparing the *Response to Concerns* to a different historical document, the *Register of Metropolitan Officials According to the Shunzhi Imperial Screen* (*Shunzhi yuping jinggua zhimingce* 順治御屏京官職名冊) reveals different aspects of the Shunzhi Astronomical Bureau.[100] The *Register of Metropolitan Officials* originated with the Ming practices of keeping a special screen in the imperial palace. With a map of the whole country painted on the screen's background, each official's name was pinned to the screen on a piece of paper. When officials changed posts, their names were switched on the screen. Therefore, the screen served as a convenient register of officials. The *Register of Metropolitan Officials*, which was used for the following analysis, comes from the roster printed by the Ministry of Personnel in late 1660 to update the imperial screen.[101] Printed less than two years before the *Response to Concerns*, it includes records of all Astronomical Bureau officials at the time. Unlike the preface of the *Response to Concerns*, which contains only the endorsers' names, the *Register of Metropolitan Officials* includes all officials' places of origin, educational background, and most importantly the dates that they obtained their current positions. The *Response to Concerns* is critical in reconstructing how Schall ran the Astronomical Bureau. For instance, the *Register of Metropolitan Officials* contains records of four Muslim Erudites but no mention of the Muslim Supervisor of the Autumn Office, Wu

Mingxuan 吳明炫. It indicates that despite Wu Mingxuan's discharge from the Astronomical Bureau, the Muslim Section remained.[102]

Several observations can be obtained from the *Register of Metropolitan Officials*. First, although the Astronomical Bureau converted to the New Method, family networks remained an important channel through which the Astronomical Bureau recruited apprentices. Several new officials listed in the *Register of Metropolitan Officials* were from the families of Chinese Christians who learned the New Method from the Jesuits during the Ming era. Bao Yingqi, Schall's old Ming-era Calendar Department disciple, valued his Astronomical Bureau career enough that his younger brother Bao Yinghua 鮑英華 joined the profession and became an Erudite in October 1658.[103] Liu Biyuan 劉必遠, who became Erudite in February 1655, was Liu Youqing's nephew.[104] Liu Youtai 劉有泰, Liu Youqing's younger brother and Liu Biyuan's father, was one of the endorsers of the *Response to Concerns* (see Table 3.6). However, for reason unclear, his name is not seen in the *Register of Metropolitan Officials*. Nevertheless, we know from other sources that Liu Youtai was one of the five Calendar Section officials who failed the test on the New Method but was able to show their ability in calculating eclipses according to the Old Method in the examination held in March 1645.[105] Liu Youtai's name was not in Schall's list submitted to Dorgon; therefore, he probably did not start learning the New Method from Schall until Schall took over the Bureau. It seems that Liu Youtai soon mastered the New Method. He became an Official Astrologer in 1658 and the Supervisor of the Middle Office in February 1663.[106]

Second, the old astronomer families at the Astronomical Bureau survived the loss of prestige after Schall's takeover. Zhou Yin 周胤, one of the high officials that Schall suggested being removed from the Bureau immediately in 1645, kept his position as the Junior Vice-Director.[107] The *Register of Metropolitan Officials* sees four other Calendar Section Erudites with the surname Zhou.[108] Among them, Zhou Yin and Zhou Shichang 周士昌 endorsed the *Response to Concerns*.[109] For the Ge family, some members appear to have left the Astronomical Bureau; so that only three officials, Ge Jiwen 戈繼文, Ge Guoqi 戈國琦, and Ge Shiying 戈士英 appear on the *Register of Metropolitan Officials*.[110] However, Ge Jiwen and Ge Guoqi seemed to have adjusted to Schall's administration so well that the former received a promotion to Calendar Manager in July 1646 while the latter became an Erudite in December 1655.[111] Both endorsed the *Response to Concerns* (see Table 3.6). Ge Shiying advanced from Yin-Yang Person to Erudite of the Water Clock Section in 1660; he probably was not considered important enough to endorse the *Response to Concerns*.

By contrast, although the Zuo 左 family stayed in the Qing Astronomical Bureau, none of its members endorsed Schall's *Response to Concerns*. The Zuo family might have been more resistant to Schall's reformation than the Zhou and Ge families. When the first qualifying examination was held in September 1644 to determine who could stay in the Astronomical Bureau, two young Zuos, Zuo Chengsi 左承嗣 and Zuo Chengye 左承業, did not bother to take the examination.¹¹² Certainly, not every member of a family thinks the same and not everyone thought like Zuo Chengsi and Zuo Chengye. As the *Register of Metropolitan Officials* shows, Zuo Yudeng 左允登 and Zuo Yuhe 左允和 became Erudites in the Ming era, and they stayed in Schall's Astronomical Bureau. Furthermore, Zuo Youqing 左有慶, who might be a younger Zuo family descendant, was raised from Student Astronomer to Erudite in December 1653—presumably because of his knowledge of the New Method.¹¹³ Nonetheless, no Zuo endorsed Schall's treatise. The absence of the surname Zuo in the *Response to Concerns* suggests that more than 18 years after Schall's New Method became the norm for calendar making, resistance to Schall's administration persisted among some Astronomical Bureau staff.

Blame for the Astronomical Bureau's factionalism does not rest with the old Ming astronomer families alone. The *Register of Metropolitan Officials* shows a sharp difference in career development between two groups of the Astronomical Bureau staff. The first group consisted of officials who had become Student Astronomers in the Ming era. This group hardly received any promotion after Schall became the head of the Astronomical Bureau. The *Register of Metropolitan Officials* has records for 28 Calendar Section Erudites, 13 of which had similarly frozen careers. They all entered the Astronomical Bureau as Student Astronomers and had advanced to Erudites by April 1645. However, they were still Erudites when the *Register of Metropolitan Officials* published their records in April 1660. These officials were leftovers from the Ming era, and their expertise in the Great Concordance system was useless for Schall's Astronomical Bureau. Although they were allowed to keep their jobs, their careers were dead.

The second group of officials was those who entered the Astronomical Bureau as Confucian students (*rushi* 儒士) after Schall's takeover. *Rushi* was not an official degree or title but a label that Schall constantly used for his disciples since he ran the Ming Calendar Department. This group consisted of Schall's disciples, and many of them had advanced to higher positions of the Astronomical Bureau before the *Register of Metropolitan Officials* was published. For instance, Zhang Sheng 掌乘 became a Recorder in July 1646; Song Fa 宋發, the Supervisor of the Autumn Office in July 1646; and Yin Kai 殷鎧, a Calendar Manager in October 1658.¹¹⁴

A memorial submitted by the Ministry of Personnel in February 1663 further illustrates how promotion opportunities bypassed the leftover Ming officials and gave favor to Schall's adherents:

> According to the consultation given by the Astronomical Bureau to the Ministry of Rites, the vacancy left by Liu Youtai 劉有泰 after he was promoted from Official Astrologer (*Baozhangzheng* 保章正) to the Supervisor of the Middle Office (*Zhongguanzheng* 中官正) should be filled by Calendar Manager (*Sili* 司曆) Yin Kai 殷鎧. The vacancy of Calendar Manager should be filled by the Calendar Section Erudite Bao Yingqi 鮑英齊, and the vacancy of Erudite by Erudite Candidate Liu Yunde 劉蘊德, who is on the grain stipend of a Confucian student for assisting Bureau officials.¹¹⁵

A promotion in the Astronomical Bureau did not come often. It usually had to wait until some high official died or retired because of serious illness. The above chain of promotions was triggered by the possible death of Jia Liangqi 賈良琦 in late 1662.[116] Among those who obtained promotions, we have mentioned that Liu Youtai was Chinese Christian Liu Youqing's younger brother and that Yin Kai and Bao Yingqi were Schall's disciples from the Ming era. Liu Yunde, the last official in this chain of promotion, was also a disciple that Schall brought to the Astronomical Bureau (see Table 3.3). Liu Yunde's name was not included in the *Register of Metropolitan Officials* or the *Response to Concerns*, probably because he had lost the position of Erudite in late 1655 for "violating the deadline of delivering decrees" (*banzhao weixian* 頒詔違限).[117] The promotion of 1663 completely rehabilitated Liu. He became the Vice-Director in 1671 and continued serving the Astronomical Bureau until 1676.[118] It is noteworthy that although Liu was not a Christian when he worked at the Bureau, he joined the Society of Jesus in 1684 and was ordained to the priesthood in 1688.[119]

Another group that was absent from the endorsers of the *Response to Concerns* was the Muslim Section. Muslim astronomers' astronomical system and the Chinese Great Concordance system had coexisted without conflict in the Ming Astronomical Bureau for more than two centuries. The adoption of the New Method threatened not only the Muslim astronomical system but also the careers of Muslim astronomers. According to the transitional measure proposed by the Ministry of Rites in 1644, five Muslim officials were allowed to stay, but five of the eight Muslim Student Astronomers were dismissed.[120] Among the discharged was Wu Mingyao 吳明耀, a brother of Wu Mingxuan 吳明炫, the Muslim Section Supervisor of the Autumn Office.[121] Moreover, the three remaining Muslim Student Astronomers were ordered to convert to the New Method. Without Student Astronomers devoted to learning the Muslim astronomical system, the end of the Muslim Section was inevitable. After losing the competition of predicting the solar eclipse of September 1, 1644, the Muslim Section was forbidden to submit future eclipse predictions. In 1646, the court announced that the Muslim Encroachments calendar was no longer needed. In 1652, the Muslim Section was forbidden to report its reading of summer celestial signs.[122] Before Wu Mingxuan was ousted from the Bureau in April 1654, the Muslim Section already lost its status in Astronomical Bureau.[123]

Wu Mingxuan, a tenacious fighter for Muslim interests, was not ready to give up. In May 1657, Wu submitted a memorial to the Shunzhi emperor. In addition to criticizing Schall's New Method, Wu hoped that the emperor could take the Muslim Section's long history of service into consideration. Wu argued that Chinese dynasties had employed his ancestral families from the Far West as Astronomical Bureau officials because of their expertise in calendar making for 1,059 years. They had the independent expertise to compute planetary orbits and interpret celestial signs. Wu begged the Shunzhi emperor to restore him to the Astronomical Bureau "so that my Section can be preserved, and its unique learning can be transmitted [to future generations]."[124] June 1657 saw another eclipse prediction competition between Wu's Muslim method and Schall's New Method, but the result was inconclusive. In September 1657, the visibility of Mercury became the critical test between Wu's and Schall's methods. Wu failed miserably, however, not so much because of poor calculation but because his Muslim colleagues at the observatory retracted their testimony during the trial.[125]

Under Schall, mastering the New Method become the means to develop a career at the Astronomical Bureau. After 1653, a new group of Erudites emerged. Zuo Youqing 左有慶, a descendant of the old Zuo family, and Xu Hu 徐瑚, probably a brother of Schall's early disciple Xu Huan 徐煥, both became Erudites in November 1653. Understandably, not everyone welcomed such reform. It was not hard for a fresh, new Student Astronomer to begin learning with the New Method, but it was not as easy for those who had already devoted years to the study of the Great Concordance or the Muslim system. Almost half of the Erudites who were experts in the outdated Great Concordance system received no promotion after Schall ascended to the top of the Astronomical Bureau. That is the likely reason why only five of the 13 Calendar Section Erudites endorsed Schall's *Response to Concerns*. Dissatisfaction among the older staff accumulated. Wu Mingxuan's resistance in 1657 was just the beginning. After the death of Schall's greatest supporter, the Shunzhi emperor, in February 1661, Schall and the New Method soon faced a severe challenge.

Notes

1 For the official character of Chinese astronomy and the close association between the calendar and state power, see Needham and Wang, *Science and Civilisation*, 186–94.
2 MHD ZD 618: 723.
3 Ibid.
4 The earliest state-level College of Mathematics was set up in the Sui 隋 dynasty (581–618). See Li, *Zhongguo Suanxueshi*, 43–7; Thomas H.C. Lee, *Education in Traditional China, a History* (Leiden: Brill, 2000), 515–25.
5 MHD WL 792: 639–40.
6 Deane, "The Chinese Imperial Astronomical Bureau," 202–5, 212–8.
7 MHD WL 789: 74.
8 Ming Qintianjian 明欽天監, *Da Ming Datong li* 大明大統曆 [1368–1644] (Taipei: National Central Library), Microfilms, 305.3 06315–38; Beijing tushuguan chubanshe guji yingyinshi 北京圖書館出版社古籍影印室, *Guojia tushuguancang Mingdai Datongliri huibian* 國家圖書館藏明代大統曆日彙編, 6 vols.
9 MHD WL 792: 638.
10 Ibid., 789: 74.
11 Schall, *Xiyang xinfa lishu*, 1289–90. For Schall's reorganization plan, see section 3.2.
12 Schall, *Xiyang xinfa lishu*, 1290.
13 MHD WL 792: 639. For a more detailed discussion on the numbers of Student Astronomers and Yin-Yang Persons throughout the Ming period, see Deane, "The Chinese Imperial Astronomical Bureau," 220–5.
14 IHP 036556–3. See Chapter 2, Section 2.3.1 for the change of the numbers of Student Astronomers throughout the Qing period.
15 QHD KX 7749, 7763.
16 Deane, "The Chinese Imperial Astronomical Bureau," 220–3.
17 MHD WL 792: 640.
18 Zhang, *Ming shi*, 347.

19 Xu Guangqi 徐光啟 et al., "Zhili yuanqi" 治曆緣起, in *Chongzhen lishu fu Xiyang xinfa lishu zengkan shizhong* 崇禎曆書 附西洋新法曆書增刊十種, ed. Pan Naihui 潘鼐匯 (Shanghai: Shanghai guji chubanshe, 2009), 1549–50.
20 Ge Dingyi 戈定一, ed., *Luoyang Geshi zongpu shiliujuan* 洛陽戈氏宗譜十六卷 (Jiangsu: Wenxintang, 1949), 2: 15–16, 15: 6–7. Shanghai Library, 923668–83. https://jiapu.library.sh.cn/#/jiapu:STJP003477 (accessed January 2022).
21 Ibid., 2: 15.
22 Ibid., 2: 15–40, 15: 128–41.
23 Among the six Supervisors of the Five Offices shown in figure 3.1, Gen Jiwen did not become the Supervisor of the Spring Office until the Qing Kangxi reign (see chapter 4, section 4.1). The other five obtained their positions in the Ming era.
24 See, for example, an unapproved suggestion from Supervisor of the Middle Office Zhou Lian 周濂. Zhang, *Ming shi*, 349–56. It is not clear if Zhou Lian and Zhou Ziyu 周子愚 mentioned below were from the same family.
25 Zhang, *Ming shi*, 356; *Mingshenzong shilu* 明神宗實錄, vols. 96–112 of *Ming shilu* 明實錄 (Taipei: Zhongyang yanjiuyuan lishiyuyan yanjiusuo, 1955), 9012–14.
26 Zhang, *Ming shi*, 356, 5668. Zhou was included in Ruan Yuan's *Biographies of Mathematicians and Astronomers* for this recommendation. See Ruan, *Chouren zhuan*, 387. For Nicolò Longobardo and Sabatino de Ursis, see Louis Pfister, *Notices biographiques et bibliographiques sur les Jésuites de l'ancienne mission de Chine, 1552–1773* (Shanghai: Imprimerie de la Mission catholique, 1932–34), 58–66 and 103–6.
27 Zhou Ziyu 周子愚, preface to *Biaodu shuo* 表度說, by Sabatino de Ursis, in *Tianxue cuhan* 天學初函, ed. Wu Xiangxiang 吳湘湘 (Taipei: Taiwan xuesheng shuju, 1965), 2534–6.
28 "Xichao chongzhongji" 熙朝崇正集, in *Xichao chongzhongji Xichao ding'an (wai-sanzhong)* 熙朝崇正集 熙朝定案 (外三種), ed. Han Qi 韓琦 and Wu Min 吳旻 (Beijing: Zhonghua shuju, 2006), 25–6.
29 Johann Adam Schall, "Ce shi" 測食, in *Chongzhen lishu fu Xiyang xinfa lishu zengkan shizhong* 崇禎曆書 附西洋新法曆書增刊十種, ed. Pan Naihui 潘鼐匯 (Shanghai: Shanghai guji chubanshe, 2009), 1948, 1954.
30 Xu Guangqi 徐光啟, *Xu Guangqi ji* 徐光啟集, ed. Wang Zhongmin 王重民 (Beijing: Zhonghua shu ju, 1962), 327–8. This memorial was drafted by Xu and submitted under the name of the Ministry of Rites. See ibid., 329–30. Although Zhou Ziyu did become the Director of the Astronomical Bureau by 1623, he was still the Supervisor of the Winter Office or Vice-Director in 1612. Xu Guangqi probably mixed up Zhou's participation in the discussion of improving the calendrical system between the end of 1610 and 1612 with Zhou's suggestion on integrating Western and Chinese methods in 1623. On Xu Guangqi's role in late-Ming astronomical reform, see Hashimoto, *Hsü Kuang-Ch'i*.
31 Also known as Zhou Yun 周允 in documents dated after 1722.
32 Xu, *Xu Guangqi ji*, 428.
33 Xu, "Zhili yuanqi," 1639.
34 Ge, *Luoyang Geshi*, 15: 128–41.
35 For general introductions to Matteo Ricci's life and influence on the Jesuits' China mission, see Jonathan D. Spence, *The Memory Palace of Matteo Ricci* (New York: Penguin, 1985); Nicolas Standaert, "Jesuit Corporate Culture as Shaped by the Chinese," in *The Jesuits: Cultures, Sciences and the Arts, 1540–1773*, ed. John W. O'Malley et al. (Toronto: University of Toronto Press, 1999), 352–63; R. Po-Chia Hsia, *A Jesuit in the Forbidden City: Matteo Ricci, 1552–1660* (New York: Oxford University Press, 2012); Matteo Ricci and Nicolas Trigault, *China in the Sixteenth Century: The Journals of Matthew Ricci: 1583–1610*, trans. Louis J. Gallagher (New York: Random House, 1953).

36 Ricci and Trigault, *China in the Sixteenth Century*, 275–6.
37 For the importance of using science as a missionary tool, see the chapter of "Mathematics and Converts" in Ricci and Trigault, *China in the Sixteenth Century*, 325–31.
38 Standaert, "Jesuit Corporate Culture," 358–60.
39 Officially named the Cathedral of the Immaculate Conception, the chapel has been augmented, destroyed, and rebuilt several times during the Ming and Qing era. It was colloquially called the South Church because of its geographical location of the four historical Catholic churches. Cha Shih-Chieh 查時傑, "Tang Ruowang yu Beijing Nantang" 湯若望與北京南堂, *Taida lishi xuebao* 臺大歷史學報, no. 17 (1992): 287–314.
40 Hsia, *A Jesuit in the Forbidden City*, 245–86. Ricci was buried in Tenggong Zhalan 滕公柵欄. In the ensuing years, Ricci's burial ground was developed into a Jesuit cemetery. Lin Hua 林華 et al., *Lishi yihen: Limadou ji Ming Qing xifang chuanjiaoshi mudi* 歷史遺痕: 利瑪竇及明清西方傳教士墓地 (Beijing: Zhongguo renmin daxue chubanshe, 1994), 1–20.
41 Hashimoto, *Hsü Kuang-Ch'i*, 28–52.
42 Ibid., 69–71.
43 Xu, "Zhili yuanqi," 1581–752.
44 Zhang, *Ming shi*, 347–8.
45 Xu, "Zhili yuanqi," 1752.
46 In 1616, the Jurchen tribal leader Nurhaci announced the foundation of the Later Jin (Hou Jin 後金) dynasty. Hong Taiji, the most powerful son of Nurhaci, became the second khan of Later Jin when Nurhaci died in September 1626. Hong Taiji continued the expansion of the Later Jin. In May 1636, Hong Taiji officially changed the dynastic name from Later Jin to Qing and proclaimed himself emperor. Hong Taiji was succeeded by his son Fulin. Frederic Wakeman, Jr., *The Great Enterprise: The Manchu Reconstruction of Imperial Order in Seventeenth—Century China* (Berkeley: University of California Press, 1985), 23–86, 157–224.
47 Zhang, *Ming shi*, 223.
48 Hong Taiji's death in September 1643 triggered the power struggle among his brothers and sons. Dorgon, a half-brother of Hong Taiji and an outstanding military leader, was one of the strong competitors for the throne. As a settlement, Fulin, a six-year-old son of Hong Taiji, was enthroned, and Dorgon became one of the two prince-regents (*shezheng wang* 攝政王). Dorgon rapidly mastered administrative affairs and outpowered the other prince-regent. Wakeman, *The Great Enterprise*, 297–300.
49 Ibid., 301–11.
50 Dorgon and his army entered Beijing on June 6, 1644. SL 3: 57. Dorgon encountered almost no resistance from the capital's inhabitants, who probably were confusion about who their new ruler would be. Wakeman, *The Great Enterprise*, 315–8.
51 SL 3: 91–2.
52 Ibid., 92.
53 Väth, *Johann Adam Schall*, 144–7.
54 For the petition Schall submitted to the Grand Secretariat, see Johann Adam Schall et al., "Zoushu" 奏疏, in *Chongzhen lishu fu Xiyang xinfa lishu zengkan shizhong* 崇禎曆書 附西洋新法曆書增刊十種, ed. Pan Naihui 潘鼐匯 (Shanghai: Shanghai guji chubanshe, 2009), 2045–6.
55 Väth, *Johann Adam Schall*, 147–8; Schall, *Zoushu*, 2046; An Shuangcheng 安雙成, trans. and ed., *Qingchu xiyang chuanjiaoshi Manwen dang'an yiben* 清初西洋傳教士滿文檔案譯本 (Zhengzhou: Daxiang chubanshe, 2014), 38.
56 SL 3: 64.
57 IHP 006903; Schall, *Zoushu*, 2049.
58 IHP 185043–010; Schall, *Zoushu*, 2049–51.
59 Schall, *Zoushu*, 2052–3.

60 Ibid., 2056.
61 Ibid., 2058–9.
62 Only the calendar printed in Chinese had the phrase "According to the New Method" on its front cover, the calendar in Manchu did not. See An, 30, for the report for the trials held during the Calendar Dispute. According to Ferdinand Verbiest, Schall did not include this phase on the sample calendar he submitted. It was Dorgon who gave the order to add it to the cover of the calendar. See Ferdinand Verbiest, "Budeyi bian" 不得已辨, in *Tianzhujiao dongchuan wenxian* 天主教東傳文獻, ed. Wu Xiangxiang (Taipei: Taiwan xuesheng shuju, 1964), 348–9.
63 IHP 185043–9.
64 Ibid.
65 Ibid.
66 IHP 185045–13.
67 MHD WL 792: 639.
68 This memorial was submitted on September 19, 1644, the day after Schall was threatened at the Ministry of Rites. The examination was set to hold on September 22.
69 Zhongguo diyi lishi dang'anguan 中國第一歷史檔案館, ed., *Qing zhongqianqi xiuang Tianzhujiao zaihua huodong dang'an shiliao* 清中前期西洋天主教在華活動檔案史料 (Beijing: Zhonghua shuju, 2003), 4–6.
70 Ibid., 1.
71 Schall, *Zoushu*, 2063–4.
72 These three were Jia Liangqi 賈良琦, Liu Youqing 劉有慶, and Zhu Guangxian 朱光顯. See Table 3.3.
73 Ibid.
74 IHP 117453.
75 Schall, *Zoushu*, 2071.
76 A comparison between the report written by Schall and the palace memorial submitted by the Ministry of Rites shows the difference of contents and the dates. See IHP 038804 and Schall, *Zoushu*, 2071–3.
77 IHP 038804.
78 Schall, *Zoushu*, 2079.
79 Ibid., 2080–2.
80 Ibid., 2082.
81 Schall, *Xiyang xinfa lishu*, 1290.
82 Ibid., 1289–90.
83 Liu Youqing and Jia Liangqi had been learning the New Method from Schall (see Table 3.3). But probably because at the time Liu Youqing was the Supervisor of the Autumn Office and Jia Liangqi the Supervisor of the Middle Office, they were not tested on the first day but with the rest Calendar Section officials on the second day.
84 These five were Liu Youtai 劉有泰, Ge Yongjing 戈永靖, Zou Yunhe 左允和, Li Xuemo 李學謨, and Ge Jiwen 戈繼文.
85 Schall, *Xiyang xinfa lishu*, 1290–1.
86 Ibid., 1291–2.
87 See Väth, *Johann Adam Schall*, 161 and Schall's memorial included in Schall, *Xiyang xinfa lishu*, 1293–4 for this incident.
88 Schall submitted a memorial to propose the rearrangement of Astronomical Bureau personnel on March 9, 1645. In another memorial submitted on March 13, Schall mentions that he had confronted the accusers face to face at the trial and cleared up his own fame. Ibid., 1292, 1294.
89 Väth, *Johann Adam Schall*, 161. See also Section 3.3.
90 Schall, *Xiyang xinfa lishu*, 1336–7.
91 SL 3: 405.
92 Wakeman, *The Great Enterprise*, 896–8.

93 Schall built a strong connection with the Shunzhi emperor's mother, Empress Dowager Xiaozhuang (1613–1688). See Väth, *Johann Adam Schall*, 174–6. Also see Chapter 4, Section 4.1 for Empress Dowager Xiaozhuang's saving Schall from being executed.
94 Väth, *Johann Adam Schall*, 181–206.
95 Zhao Erxun 趙爾巽 et al., *Qingshi gao* 清史稿 (Beijing: Zhonghua shuju, 1976), 10020.
96 IHP 036556–3.
97 Johann Adam Schall, *Minli puzhu jiehuo* 民曆鋪註解惑, XXSK 1040: 2. For the contents of the *Minlipuzhu jiehuo*, see Huang Yi-Long 黃一農, "Tang Ruowang *Xinli xiaohuo* yu *Minli puzhu jiehuo* ershu lueji" 湯若望《新曆曉或》與《民曆鋪註解惑》二書略記, *Guoli Zhongyang tushuguan guankan* 國立中央圖書館館刊, New 25, no. 1(1992): 151–8.
98 Väth, *Johann Adam Schall*, 267–94.
99 IHP 038804.
100 "Shunzhi yuping jingguan zhimingce" 順治御屏京官職名冊, in *Wenxian congbian* 文獻叢編, nos. 27, 28 (Beijing: National Palace Museum, 1935).
101 Ibid., 27: 1.
102 Ibid., 28: 16.
103 Ibid., 28: 14.
104 Ibid., 28: 15. For Liu Youqing and Liu Biyuan's relationship, see SL 4: 220; An, *Qingchu xiyang*, 95–6.
105 Schall, *Xiyang xinfa lishu*, 1291.
106 An, *Qingchu xiyang*, 74, 86–7.
107 Schall, *Xiyang xinfa lishu*, 1291.
108 Zhou Shichang 周士昌, Zhou Shitai 周士泰, Zhou Shicui 周士萃, and Zhou Tong 周統. "Shunzhi yuping," 28: 14–15.
109 Schall, *Minli puzhu*, 2–3.
110 "Shunzhi yuping," 28: 14, 16.
111 Ibid., 28: 14.
112 Schall, *Zoushu*, 2063–5.
113 "Shunzhi yuping," 28: 15.
114 Ibid., 28: 14.
115 IHP 091306.
116 Qu, "Qingdai Qintianjian," 49. The last time Jia's name appeared on the official calendar was the second year of Kangxi. Therefore, Jia should have left his post between late 1644 and February 1645.
117 IHP 005601. This was probably related to the statutory laws that required embassies for bestowing honorary titles on vassal states to include Astronomical Bureau officials. See Chapter 2, Section 2.1.
118 Qu, "Qingdai Qintianjian," 49–50.
119 Pfister, *Notices biographiques*, 402–3.
120 IHP 185045–05.
121 Wu Mingxuan 吳明炫 also appears as Wu Mingxuan 吳明烜 in documents published after 1662 to avoid the naming taboo of the Kangxi emperor. Huang Yi-Long 黃一農, "Wu Mingxuan yu Wu Mingxuan—Qingchu yu xifa kangzheng de yidui Huihui tianwenjia xiongdi?" 吳明炫與吳明烜—清初與西法相抗爭的一對回回天文家兄弟？ *Dalu zazhi* 大陸雜誌 84, no. 4 (1992): 137–60.
122 QHD KX 7751.
123 Huang, "Wu Mingxuan," 145.
124 SL 3: 853.
125 Huang Yi-Long 黃一農, "Qingchu Tianzhujiao yu Huijiao tianwenjia jian de zhengdou" 清初天主教與回教天文家間的爭鬥, *Jiuzhou xuekan* 九州學刊 5, no. 33 (1993): 55–9.

Bibliography

Abbreviations for Archival and Published Sources

CKSB: *Jindai Zhongguo shiliao congkan sanbian* 近代中國史料叢刊三編, edited by Shen Yunlong 沈雲龍. 850 vols. Taipei: Wenhai chubanshe, 1982.
IHP: Neige daku dang'an 內閣大庫檔案. Institute of History and Philology of Academia Sinica, Taipei. http://archive.ihp.sinica.edu.tw/mctkm2/index.html
MHD WL: *Da Ming huidian* 大明會典 [1587]. XXSK 789–92.
MHD ZD: *Ming huidian* 明會典 [1509]. SKQS 617–18.
QHD KX: *Da Qing huidian (Kangxi chao)* 大清會典 (康熙朝) [1690]. CKSB 711–30.
SKQS: *Yingyin wenyuange sikuquanshu* 景印文淵閣四庫全書. 1500 vols. Taipei: Taipei shangwu yinshuguan, 1986.
SL: *Qing shilu* 清實錄. 60 vols. Beijing: Zhonghua shuju, 1985.
XXSK: *Xuxiu sikuquanshu* 續修四庫全書. 1800 vols. Shanghai: Shanghai guji chubanshe, 2002.

Other Sources

An Shuangcheng 安雙成, trans and ed. *Qingchu xiyang chuanjiaoshi Manwen dang'an yiben* 清初西洋傳教士滿文檔案譯本. Zhengzhou: Daxiang chubanshe, 2014.
Ge Dingyi 戈定一, ed. *Luoyang Geshi zongpu shiliujuan* 洛陽戈氏宗譜十六卷. 16 vols. Jiangsu: Wenxintang, 1949. Shanghai Library. 923668–83. https://jiapu.library.sh.cn/#/jiapu:STJP003477
Ming Qintianjian 明欽天監. *Da Ming Datong li* 大明大統曆 [1368–1644]. Taipei: National Central Library, Microfilms, 305.3 06315–38.
Mingshenzong shilu 明神宗實錄. Vol. 96–112 of *Ming shilu* 明實錄. Taipei: Zhongyang yanjiuyuan lishiyuyan yanjiusuo, 1966.
Ricci, Matteo, and Nicolas Trigault. *China in the Sixteenth Century: The Journals of Matthew Ricci: 1583–1610*. Translated by Louis J. Gallagher. New York: Random House, 1953.
Ruan Yuan 阮元 et al. *Chouren zhuan huibian* 疇人傳彙編. 2 vols. Taipei: Shijie shuju, 1982.
Schall, Johann Adam. *Minli puzhu jiehuo* 民曆鋪註解惑 [1662]. XXSK 1040: 1–16.
———. *Ce shi* 測食 [1625]. In *Chongzhen lishu fu Xiyang xinfa lishu zengkan shizhong* 崇禎曆書 附西洋新法曆書增刊十種, edited by Pan Naihui 潘鼐匯, 1941–1965. Shanghai: Shanghai guji chubanshe, 2009.
Schall, Johann Adam et al. "Zoushu" 奏疏. In *Chongzhen lishu fu Xiyang xinfa lishu zengkan shizhong* 崇禎曆書 附西洋新法曆書增刊十種, edited by Pan Naihui 潘鼐匯, 2041–89. Shanghai: Shanghai guji chubanshe, 2009.
———. "Xiyang xinfa lishu, Zoushu" 西洋新法曆書奏疏. In *Mingmo Qingchu Tianzhujiao shi wenxian xinbian* 明末清初天主教史文獻新編, edited by Zhou Yan 周岩, 1235–363. Beijing: Guojia tushuguan chubanshe, 2013.
Shunzhi yuping jingguan zhimingce 順治御屏京官職名冊. In *Wenxian congbian* 文獻叢編, nos. 27, 28. Beijing: National Palace Museum, 1935.
Verbiest, Ferdinand. "Budeyi bian" 不得已辨. In *Tianzhujiao dongchuan wenxian* 天主教東傳文獻, edited by Wu Xiangxiang 吳湘湘, 333–470. Taipei: Taiwan xuesheng shuju, 1964.
Xichao chongzhongji 熙朝崇正集. In *Xichao chongzhongji Xichao ding'an (wai san zhong)* 熙朝崇正集 熙朝定案 (外三種), edited by Han Qi 韓琦 and Wu Min 吳旻, 1–42. Beijing: Zhonghua shuju, 2006.

Xu Guangqi 徐光啟. *Xu Guangqi ji* 徐光啟集. Edited by Wang Zhongmin 王重民. 2 vols. Beijing: Zhonghua shuju, 1962.

Xu Guangqi 徐光啟 et al. "Zhili yuanqi" 治曆緣起. In *Chongzhen lishu fu Xiyang xinfa lishu zengkan shizhong* 崇禎曆書 附西洋新法曆書增刊十種, edited by Pan Naihui 潘鼐匯, 1545–752. Shanghai: Shanghai guji chubanshe, 2009.

Zhang Tingyu 張廷玉 et al. *Ming shi* 明史. Beijing: Zhonghua shuju, 2000.

Zhao Erxun 趙爾巽 et al. *Qingshi gao* 清史稿. 48 vols. Beijing: Zhonghua shuju, 1976.

Zhongguo diyi lishi dang'anguan 中國第一歷史檔案館, ed. *Qing zhongqianqi xiuang Tianzhujiao zihua huodong dang'an shiliao* 清中前期西洋天主教在華活動檔案史料. 4 vols. Beijing: Zhonghua shuju, 2003.

Zhou Ziyu 周子愚. Preface to *Biaodu shuo* 表度說 [1614] by Sabatino de Ursis. In *Tianxue cuhan* 天學初函, edited by Wu Xiangxiang 吳湘湘, 2523–618. Taipei: Taiwan xuesheng shuju, 1965.

Secondary Sources

Cha Shih-Chieh 查時傑. "Tang Ruowang yu Beijing Nantang" 湯若望與北京南堂. *Taida lishi xuebao* 臺大歷史學報, no. 17 (1992): 287–314.

Deane, Thatcher Elliott. "The Chinese Imperial Astronomical Bureau: Form and Function of the Ming Dynasty *Qintianjian* from 1365 to 1627." Ph.D. diss., University of Washington, 1989.

Hashimoto, Keizo. *Hsü Kuang-Ch'i and Astronomical Reform: The Process of the Chinese Acceptance of Western Astronomy, 1629–1635*. Osaka: Kansas University Press, 1988.

Hsia, R. Po-Chia. *A Jesuit in the Forbidden City: Matteo Ricci, 1552–1610*. New York: Oxford University Press, 2012.

Huang Yi-Long 黃一農. "Tang Ruowang *Xinli xiaohuo* yu *Minli puzhu jiehuo* ershu lueji" 湯若望《新曆曉或》與《民曆鋪註解惑》二書略記. *Guoli Zhongyang tushuguan guankan* 國立中央圖書館館刊 New 25, no. 1 (1992): 151–8.

———. "Wu Mingxuan yu Wu Mingxuan—Qingchu yu xifa kangzheng de yidui Huihui tianwenjia xiongdi?" 吳明炫與吳明烜—清初與西法相抗爭的一對回回天文家兄弟? *Dalu zazhi* 大陸雜誌 84, no. 4 (1992): 145–9.

———. "Qingchu Tianzhujiao yu Huijiao tianwenjia jian de zhengdou" 清初天主教與回教天文家間的爭鬥. *Jiuzhou xuekan* 九州學刊 5, no. 33 (1993): 47–69.

Lee, Thomas H.C. *Education in Traditional China, a History*. Leiden: Brill, 2000.

Li Yan 李儼. *Zhongguo Suanxueshi* 中國算學史. Beijing: Shangwu yinshuguan, 1998.

Lin Hua 林華 et al. *Lishi yihen: Li Madou ji Ming Qing xifang chuanjiaoshi mudi* 歷史遺痕: 利瑪竇及明清西方傳教士墓地. Beijing: Zhongguo renmin daxue chubanshe, 1994.

Needham, Joseph, and Wang Ling. *Science and Civilisation in China, Vol. 3: Mathematics and the Science of the Heavens and the Earth*. Cambridge: Cambridge University Press, 1959.

Pfister, Louis. *Notices biographiques et bibliographiques sur les Jésuites de l'ancienne mission de Chine. 1552–1773*. 2 vols. Shanghai: Imprimerie de la Mission catholique, 1932–4.

Qu Chunhai 屈春海. "Qingdai Qintianjian ji Shixianke zhiguan nianbiao" 清代欽天監暨時憲科職官年表. *China Historical Materials of Science and Technology* 中國科技史料 18, no. 3 (1997): 45–71.

Spence, Jonathan D. *The Memory Palace of Matteo Ricci*. New York: Penguin, 1985.

Standaert, Nicolas. "Jesuit Corporate Culture as Shaped by the Chinese." In *The Jesuits: Cultures, Sciences and the Arts, 1540–1773*, edited by John W. O'Malley, Gauvin Alexander Bailey, Steven J. Harris, and T. Frank Kennedy, 352–63. Toronto: University of Toronto Press, 1999.

———. *Chinese Voices in the Rites Controversy: Travelling Books, Community Networks, Intercultural Arguments*. Roma: Institutum Historicum Societatis Iesu, 2012.

Väth, Alfons. *Johann Adam Schall von Bell SJ: Missionar in China, kaiserlicher Astronom und Ratgeber am Hofe von Peking, 1592–1666* [1933]. Nettetal: Steyler Verlag, 1991.

Wakeman, Frederic, Jr. *The Great Enterprise: The Manchu Reconstruction of Imperial Order in Seventeenth—Century China*. 2 vols. Berkeley: University of California Press, 1985.

4 Kangxi Calendar Dispute

Between 1665 and 1668, the Qing court abandoned the New Western Method of calendar making that it had used for two decades and returned to the traditional Great Concordance calendar. While this incident, which we shall refer to as the Kangxi Calendar Dispute (*Kangxi lizheng* 康熙曆爭), might seem a short and temporary delay to the assimilation of European mathematics in Qing China, it forever changed the constitutions of the Astronomical Bureau.[1] Some of the oldest Han astronomer families that had worked for the Astronomical Bureau since the Ming era left after the Calendar Dispute. Muslim astronomers also lost their last few posts in the Bureau. By contrast, the Qing court added banner officials to the Bureau to learn mathematical astronomy and to share the administrative responsibility that had been monopolized by one European missionary in the Shunzhi reign. Despite the fact that the New Western Method was reinstalled as the official astronomical system of calendar making in late 1668, this chapter shows that the Kangxi emperor did not give his decisive endorsement to the New Method until 1676. Moreover, it shows that the Great Concordance system was not regarded as completely hopeless until 1688 when the Kangxi emperor finally decided to suppress its supporters.

4.1 A Failed Attempt to Return to the Great Concordance System

The Kangxi Calendar Dispute began when the Kangxi emperor was still too young to rule in person and the Qing Empire was ruled by a regency council. The regency council revised several Shunzhi policies, but Schall's status at the court and the relationship to the imperial house seemed intact. For instance, the Shunzhi emperor gave Schall a distinct honor by ordering him to adopt a grandson. After the Shunzhi emperor died, the regency council extended this honor by granting Schall's adopted grandson admission to the Imperial College (*Guozi jian* 國子監).[2] However, in September 1664, the regency council accepted an accusation from Yang Guangxian 楊光先 (1597–1669), one of the most aggressive advocates of the Great Concordance system, and began a lengthy trial of Schall and his colleagues.[3] Eight months later, the court found Schall and his colleagues guilty of almost every accusation Yang had made.[4] By mid-1665, the regency council had appointed Yang the Director of the Astronomical Bureau and given him the responsibility of making the state calendar. Although it was too late to recalculate the calendar for the coming year according to the Great Concordance system, the court decided that the phrase "According to the New Western Method" (*yi Xiyang xinfa* 依西洋新法) should be removed from the calendar cover.[5] Schall was only saved from execution by a timely earthquake and the negotiation from Grand Empress Dowager, the Kangxi emperor's grandmother.[6] He died a year later under house arrest.[7] Schall's most important disciples, the Supervisors of the Calendar Section—Song Kecheng, Li Zubai, Liu Youtai, Song Fa, and Zhu Guangxian—were beheaded. Their family members were stripped of all properties and banished to distant places. The same punishment even extended to family members of deceased officials such as Liu Youqing and Jia Liangqi.[8]

Yang Guangxian continued to persecute the rest of Schall's adherents after he became the Director of the Astronomical Bureau. Calendar Manager Bao Yingqi, who had worked with Schall since the Ming era, was banished to Ningguta 寧古塔, a remote town on the northeast border, under accusation of receiving bribes when purchasing paper used for printing the calendars.[9] While the Calendar Section suffered the most, the other two sections were fared only slightly better. Water Clock Managers Yang Hongliang and Du Ruyu lost their jobs but were able to escape the death penalty because of their past contributions in constructing several imperial tombs.[10] Observatory Managers Zhang Qichun and Li Guangxian 李光顯 found themselves promoted to Director and Vice-Director, respectively, at the beginning of the purge, because all the officials above them were ousted. Li managed to keep his post throughout the Calendar Dispute. Zhang, however, soon was demoted to Senior Vice-Director after Yang accused the Section of Heavenly Signs of fabricating observation results to favor the New Method (see Section 4.3).[11] By the end of 1666, Zhang Qichun's name had disappeared from records.[12] Around the same time, three other Erudites of the Section of Heavenly Signs—Huang Gong 黃鞏, Huang Chang 黃昌, and Li Guanghong 李光宏—also lose their jobs because of Yang's impeachments.[13] By the time the Kangxi emperor discharged Yang from the directorship in 1669, more than 20 officials had been purged from the Astronomical Bureau.[14]

Yet, the attempt to return to the Great Concordance system failed for several reasons. First, Yang did not have the mathematical knowledge required for calendar making and said so himself during the trials against Schall. Yang testified, "[I] only know the principles of calendar but not the mathematics of the calendar." When one minister asked him to evaluate three illustrations of solar eclipses, he testified again, "I have not studied the methods of calculating eclipses. I really do not know [how to evaluate them]."[15] Yang repeatedly tried to convince the regency council that he was not qualified for the directorship.[16] The regents forced the job on him anyway. Yang soon memorialized again and described his difficulty in learning mathematics: "There are only slightly more than forty fundamental rules for calculating calendars, but it has been four months since I was appointed [to a post at the Astronomical Bureau] and I still can not remember them all."[17] While Yang might have exaggerated his aging and bad memory to avoid responsibility,

Table 4.1 Officials purged from the Astronomical Bureau during the Kangxi Calendar Dispute

Names	Title
Bao Yinghua 鮑英華	Calendar Manager
Bi Lianqi 畢璉器	Manchu Department Director
Du Ruyu 杜如預	Water Clock Manager
Hao Benchun 郝本純	Erudite
Huang Gong 黃鞏	Observatory Manager
Huang Chang 黃昌	Erudite, Section of Heavenly Signs
Li Guanghong 李光宏	Erudite, Section of Heavenly Signs
Li Zubai 李祖白	Supervisor of the Summer Office
Liu Biyuan 劉必遠	Erudite, Calendar Section
Liu Youtai 劉有泰	Supervisor of the Middle Office
Ou Jiwu 歐繼武	Erudite, Water Clock Section
Si Ergui 司爾珪	Erudite, Water Clock Section
Song Fa 宋發	Supervisor of the Autumn Office
Song Kecheng 宋可成	Supervisor of the Spring Office
Song Keli 宋可立	Erudite, Calendar Section
Yang Hongliang 楊弘量	Water Clock Manager
Yin Kai 殷鎧	Official Astrologer
Zang Yuqing 臧餘慶	Observatory Manager
Zhang Huafeng 張化鳳	Erudite
Zhang Wenming 張問明	Official Astrologer
Zhou Yin 周胤	Senior Vice-Director
Zhu Guangxian 朱光顯	Supervisor of the Winter Office

Sources: "Li bu ti gao" 禮部題稿, in *Xichao chongzhongji Xichao ding'an (wai san zhong)* 熙朝崇正集 熙朝定案 (外三種) ed. Han Qi 韓琦 and Wu Min 吳旻 (Beijing: Zhonghua shuju, 2006), 399–407; Huang Bolu 黃伯祿, *Zhengjiao fengbao* 正教奉褒 [1884], in *Zhongguo Tianzhujiao shiji huibian* 中國天主教史籍彙編 ed. Chen Fangzhong 陳方中 (Taipei: Furen daxue chubanshe, 2003), 523–4.

it would be amazing to the officials of the Astronomical Bureau that their new Director did not even know the most fundamental rules of calendar making.

Indeed, a problem no less serious than Yang's incompetence in mathematical astronomy was that he was unable to mobilize support within the Astronomical Bureau, particularly the support from the families that used to specialize in the Great Concordance system. In his famous treatise attacking the New Method and Christianity, *I Have No Alternative* (*Budeyi* 不得已), Yang complained about the offspring of old astronomer families:

> I have no alternative but to look forward to the officials who inherited the traditional profession of Xi 羲 and He 和.[18] However, they are young and all have betrayed the craft handed down in the family. They take the enemy as their fathers. [like dogs] wagging their tails at the feet of the bandits, they turn back to bark at their own ancestors."[19]

After becoming the Director, Yang complained again:

> How excited and encouraged the calendar officials of Xi and He should be! Now they will demonstrate their ambition, so that they can repay the emperor's great consideration of readopting their family craft. However, they have different thought. . . . Those who know all about calculating eclipses and planetary orbits pretend that they have not practiced those methods for a long time, and it is not possible to review them immediately. Those who know one or two of those methods pretend to know none at all. Today an examination was held to choose the ones to fill the posts of Supervisors of the Five Offices at the Calendar Section. However, the Calendar Section did not ask critical calculation questions about the eclipse but trivial ones. They intended to aim for a temporary promotion while being able to shrink from their responsibility in the future with the excuse of not knowing anything.[20]

According to Yang's complaints, the old astronomer families were not as excited as he was about the reinstallation of the Great Concordance system and appeared uninterested in giving their full support to Yang.

The case of Ge Jiwen provides some insight into the hesitation of the old astronomer families in supporting Yang. Ge Jiwen was the same branch of the Ge family as the last Ming Astronomical Bureau Director Ge Chengke (see Chapter 3, Section 3.1). On the one hand, unlike other Erudites whose careers stalled after Schall's takeover because they were from old astronomer families, Ge Jiwen advanced from Erudite to Calendar Manager in July 1646.[21] How well Ge Jiwen had learned the New Method surely is questionable. Yet his descendants, in order to keep advancing in Schall's Astronomical Bureau, probably had decided to abandon the Old Method and to devote themselves to learning the New Method. By the end of 1656, Ge Jiwen's son Ge Guoqi 戈國琦, earned the position of Erudite from Schall.[22] When the Calendar Dispute broke out, Ge Jiwen and his family members might indeed have not practiced the old Great Concordance system for years.

On the other hand, although Ge became the Supervisor of the Spring Office shortly after Yang's coup, the responsibility of calendar calculation might have seemed terrifyingly heavy to him and his family. Ge obtained his new position because his colleagues recently lost their heads. A career at the Astronomical Bureau used to be stable and secure, but now one might lose property and even life simply because he had followed a calculation system that the court pronounced it wrong. Even Director Yang repeatedly told the emperor that working for the Astronomical Bureau would eventually cost him his life.[23] How was it possible that officials like Ge Jiwen would feel secure enough to cooperate with Yang? Ge could not know if the court would again decide one day to replace the Great Concordance system and punish its supporters. No wonder Ge Jiwen and the other Calendar Section officials were cool to Yang and the return of the Great Concordance system.

Unlike Schall, who was able to bring in his own team of specialists in the New Method to the Astronomical Bureau, Yang was incapable of gathering help from outsiders. To be sure, the imperial regents let Yang bring in new people to the Astronomical Bureau. In 1666, the number of Han Student Astronomers was increased from 66 to 160, and the number of Erudites was also increased by two.[24] The court also supplied Yang with rare materials and peculiar instruments needed for implementing the ancient method of Watching for the Ethers (*Houqi* 候氣), which he believed could improve the Great Concordance system.[25] But Yang could not deliver any practical result and his calendars met with complaints, particularly among the Manchus, since the first one promulgated in October 1666.[26] By 1668, even the young Kangxi emperor, who had assumed the personal rule in August 1667, noticed the unsatisfactory status of the Astronomical Bureau.[27] In December 1668, Yang admitted during an inquiry initiated by the emperor's order that he had not been able to find adequate experts in the theory of Watching for the Ethers. Yang requested to be discharged on the grounds of illness, but the court reckoned that he was just trying to avoid responsibility. The emperor quickly approved the court's suggestion to reject Yang's request.[28] Apparently, Yang had little credibility left in the court. The public was not particularly fond of Yang too. In *I Have No Alternative*, Yang Guangxian complained that the earthquake that interrupted Schall's execution made the Beijing residents praise Schall as a "true saint."[29] By contrast, people easily believed every street rumor that ridiculed him.[30]

One of the few helpers that Yang gathered was Muslim astronomer Wu Mingxuan, who surely hoped his contributions would help to restore the Muslim Section's status in the Astronomical Bureau. In the Ming times, the Muslim method had been used to calculate the Encroachments calendar.[31] Under Yang's recommendation, Wu Mingxuan was back to the Astronomical Bureau by spring 1666 to take up the responsibility of preparing the Encroachments calendar.[32] The Encroachments calendar of the sixth year of Kangxi (1667) submitted to the emperor in the end of December 1666 saw Wu listed as the Vice-Director Jointly Managing the Bureau Affairs (*Jiangfu tongli jianwu* 監副同理監務).[33] This title suggests that Wu was also given some administrative power. However, for reasons not recorded in survival documents, Wu's name disappeared from the next two years' Encroachments calendar; it is not clear whether he had been involved in preparing the Encroachments calendar in this period.[34] In August 1668, Wu submitted a memorial to express his views on improving the unsatisfactory status of official calendars.[35] That differences existed between the different versions of calendars based on the old system and the Seven Governors calendar calculated by the Muslim Section, Wu argued, was an example showing that the old Great Concordance system was not without errors.[36] He suggested to have experts in calendrical systems from all "four sections," (the three main sections and the Muslim Section) work on correcting the official calendars. Wu also asked for new astronomical instruments, including an earthquake detector needed for divination.[37] The court, under the emperor's decree to consider Wu's memorial carefully, concluded in early October that Wu's Seven Governors calendar was more accurate than the ones calculated according to the old systems. Because it was too late to change the civil calendar for the next year (1669), which had already been in the final stage of mass production, the court suggested to give Wu the responsibility of calculating the calendar of the ninth year of the Kangxi reign (1670) and to give Astronomical Bureau staff, Muslim officials included, a period of four years for perfecting the official method of calendar making.[38] The emperor approved all the suggestions and further decreed that Wu should submit a copy of his civil calendar and the Seven Governors calendar of the next year for examination.[39]

By the end of 1668, the Kangxi emperor had found the person to entrust with the affairs of calendar making: Jesuit missionary Ferdinand Verbiest (1623–1688).[40] On December 25, 1668, four grand ministers sent by the emperor visited the Jesuits residence in private before the dawn. They asked Verbiest, who was identified by the other two Jesuits as being a distinguished mathematician, to examine if the civil calendar for the next year (1669) made by the Astronomical Bureau contained any errors. Verbiest's speedy and clear answers pleased the ministers before they return to report to the emperor.[41] The next day, Verbiest and the other two Jesuits, Yang Guangxian, Wu Mingxuan, Manchu Director of the Astronomical Bureau, were all summoned to a meeting at the Palace Academy. Aimed at determining the most accurate mathematical astronomical system, the meeting turned out to be favorable to the Jesuits. The four ministers who had visited the Jesuits the preceding day questioned Yang on the calendrical errors that Verbiest had pointed out to them. The Manchu Director of the Astronomical Bureau stated plainly that he favored a return to the New Method, which had already shown its superiority in the first two decades of the dynasty. Finally, Wu was made to admit that the calendars he had submitted to the emperor might contain errors, even though Wu had not claimed the calendars were perfect and the emperor had agreed to give him four years to improve them (see earlier).[42] After the meeting, all participants were granted an imperial audience, in which the Kangxi emperor accepted Verbiest's proposal that a trial of predictions of the length of a gnomon's shadow at noon would show which astronomical system was the most accurate.[43] The trial prediction was repeated for three days in a row, and Verbiest successfully demonstrated the superiority of the New Method.[44] Pleased by the result, the emperor further ordered Verbiest to examine Wu's calendars in detail.[45] A month later, Verbiest finished this imperial assignment by submitting a 36-page dossier of the mistakes in Wu's calendars.[46]

The downfall of Yang Guangxian and Wu Mingxuan now was inevitable, but it took the court some time to determine Verbiest's position and title. Yang was dismissed in early March 1669.[47] Later he was sentenced to death, but the emperor pardoned him because of his advanced age.[48] Wu was allowed to stay as the Vice-Director on the condition that he would repent and cooperate with Verbiest.[49] But when the Manchu Bureau Director impeached Wu again in July 1669, the emperor dismissed Wu and had him sent to the Ministry of Punishments (*Xingbu* 刑部).[50] Soon after Yang was dismissed, the court made Verbiest the Vice-Director of the Astronomical Bureau. Unwilling to compromise his identity as a Jesuit missionary, Verbiest repeatedly declined a formal court appointment but promised that he would do his best to manage all astronomical affairs.⁵¹ In July 1669, the emperor finally accepted Verbiest's refusal of formal office.⁵² A year later, the emperor decreed that because astronomical affairs currently were managed by Verbiest, there was no need to find someone else to fill in the vacancy of Han Bureau Director left by Yang's discharge in March 1669.⁵³ This decree made Verbiest the de facto Director of the Astronomical Bureau.

In September 1669, the court restored Schall's title and civil service rank and returned the chapel and property to the Jesuits.⁵⁴ But the rehabilitation of Chinese Christian astronomer families did not come as soon. Purged officials were given back their original jobs if they were still alive, but for those who were already dead, their families did not receive any compensation. In fact, the officials received the confiscated properties only after the emperor ordered a thorough reinvestigation of the cases because Verbiest had submitted a memorial on behalf of Erudites Bao Yinghua and Bao Xuan 鮑選 in August 1671.⁵⁵ In the memorial, Yinghua and Xuan claimed that their brother Bao Yingqi, who was still banished, had been an innocent victim of Yang Guangxian's false accusation. The Ministry of Punishment refused to admit any wrongdoing in this case. Bao received a pardon only after the application of a special regulation regarding accomplished Student Astronomers.⁵⁶ Bao Yingqi eventually became the Vice-Director of the Astronomical Bureau, and his descendants continued to serve the Bureau until the beginning of the nineteenth century.⁵⁷

By contrast, some old families like the Ge decided to withdraw from the Bureau. Ge Jiwen's name disappeared from historical records after Wu Mingxuan criticized him for miscalculation in October 1668.⁵⁸ It is not clear whether Ge Jiwen happened to die around the time, retired voluntarily, or lost his job because of Wu's attack. The surname Ge never again appeared among the high officials of the Qing Astronomical Bureau. After the generation of Ge Guoqi 戈國琦 and Ge Yusheng 戈于陞 (a. 1685), both were Erudite and sons of Ge Jiwen, no other Ge family member seemed to work for the Astronomical Bureau.⁵⁹ Similarly, there is no record of the Zuo 左 family, which still had several members at the Astronomical Bureau in the Shunzhi reign, after the Calendar Dispute was concluded.

In the end, Dorgon's policy of not dismissing astronomers trained in the Great Concordance system seems to have been continued. Wu Mingxuan, the Muslim astronomer ousted from the Bureau by Jesuit missionary, fought fiercely for the Muslim calendrical system and the few official positions traditionally reserved to his community. Most members of the old astronomer families, however, would abandon the craft handed down in the family or bear with stagnant careers rather than risk their lives and family properties. Like Dorgon, the Kangxi emperor did not dismiss Bureau officials who supported the Great Concordance system during the Calendar Dispute. The following chapters will show that some descendants of those officials would become officials who played important roles not only in the Astronomical Bureau but also in the development of Qing imperial mathematics. Before returning to this storyline, the next section examines the permanent mark left by the Calendar Dispute: the reorganization of the Astronomical Bureau.

4.2 Ethnically Based Reorganization

The Calendar Dispute made the Qing court aware that its ignorance of astronomy could cause political and social instability. When Yang Guangxian's charge against Schall was still under investigation, the persecutors reported, "Astronomy is so profound that it is difficult to make matters clear."[60] Hitherto the Astronomical Bureau only had a small number of Scribes for translating calendars and documents. These Scribes did not participate in the highly specialized works performed by non-banner Bureau officials.[61] At a critical juncture like the Calendar Dispute, the court must have found that Scribes, who lacked the knowledge and hands-on experience about astronomical affairs, could provide little technical insights. Shortly after, the court began to discuss the necessity of adding more Manchu officials to the Astronomical Bureau. The discussion was finalized in 1665 and banner officials were added to every section of the Astronomical Bureau. It was decided that banner officials should be added to every section of the Astronomical Bureau. By July 1665, the reorganization of the Astronomical Bureau was largely finalized.[62]

Tables 4.2–4.6 show the personnel quotas of the Astronomical Bureau at different times according to different versions of the *Collected Statutes of the Great*

Table 4.2 Personnel quotas of Astronomical Bureau, 1690

Title	Rank	Manchu	Mongol	Military Han	Han	Total
Director	5A	1			1	2
Vice-Director	6A	2			2	4
Supervisor of the Five Offices	6A				5	5
Supervisor of the Five Offices	6B	2		1		3
Observatory Manager	7B	3		1	4	8
Recorder	8A	1			1	2
Water Clock Manger	8B	2			2	4
Calendar Manager	9A				1	1
Astronomical Observer	9A				1	1
Timekeeper	9B			1		1
Erudite						
Calendar	9B	3		1	17	21
Heavenly Signs	9B	3			2	5
Water Clock	9B				6	6
Student Astronomer		16		8	80	104
Yin-Yang Person					10	10
Scribe		12	2	6		20
Total		45	2	18	132	197

Sources: QHD KX 131–3, 183–200, 7737, 7749–50, 7752, 7759, 7762–3.

76 *Kangxi Calendar Dispute*

Table 4.3 Personnel quotas of Astronomical Bureau, 1732

Title	Rank	Manchu	Mongol	Han Military	Han	Total
Director	5A	1			1	2
Vice-Director	6A	2			2	4
Supervisor of the Five Offices	6A				5	5
Supervisor of the Five Offices	6B	2	2	1		5
Observatory Manager	7B	3		1	4	8
Recorder	8A	1			1	2
Water Clock Manger	8B	2			2	4
Calendar Manager	9A				1	1
Astronomical Observer	9A				1	1
Timekeeper	9B			1		1
Erudite						
Calendar	9B	3		1	17	21
Heavenly Signs	9B	3			2	5
Water Clock	9B				6	6
Student Astronomer		16		8	80	104
Yin-Yang Student					10	10
Scribe		12	2	6		20
Total		45	4	18	132	199

Sources: QHD YZ 161–4, 227–43, 3287, 15497, 15513–4, 15671, 15711–4.

Table 4.4 Personnel quotas of Astronomical Bureau, 1764

Title	Rank	Manchu	Mongol	Han Military	Westerner	Han	Total
Superintendent							
Director	5A	1		1			2
Vice-Director	6A	1		2		1	4
Supervisor of the Five Offices	6B	2	2	1		5	10
Observatory Manager	7B	3		1		4	8
Recorder	8A	1				1	2
Water Clock Manger	8B	2				2	4
Calendar Manager	9A					1	1
Astronomical Observer	9A					1	1
Timekeeper	9B			1			1
Erudite							
Calendar	9B	3		2		16	21
Heavenly Signs	9B	3				2	5
Water Clock	9B					6	6
Student Astronomer							
Calendar		12		8		42	62
Heavenly Signs		2				32	34
Water Clock		2				6	8
Yin-Yang Student						10	10
Scribe		11	4	2			17
Total		43	6	15	3	129	196

Sources: QHD QL 619: 50, 619: 817.

Table 4.5 Personnel quotas of Astronomical Bureau, 1818

Title	Rank	Manchu	Mongol	Han Military	Westerner	Han	Total
Superintendent							
Director	5A	1			1		2
Vice-Director	6A	1			2	1	4
Supervisor of the Five Offices	6A					5	5
Supervisor of the Five Offices	6B	2	2	1			5
Observatory Manager	7B	2	1	1		4	8
Recorder	8A	1				1	2
Water Clock Manger	8B	1	1			2	4
Calendar Manager	9A					1	1
Astronomical Observer	9A					1	1
Timekeeper	9B			1			1
Erudite							
Calendar	9B	4	2	1		15	22
Heavenly Signs	9B					2	2
Water Clock	9B			1		7	8
Student Astronomer							
Calendar		8	4	8		43	63
Heavenly Signs		2				31	33
Water Clock		2				6	8
Yin-Yang Student						10	10
Scribe		11	4	2			17
Total		36	13	15	3	129	196

Sources: QHD JQ 219–222, 2763, 2873, 2897, 2919, 2922.

Table 4.6 Personnel quotas of Astronomical Bureau, 1899

Title	Rank	Manchu	Mongol	Han Military	Han	Total
Director	5A	1			1	2
Vice-Director	6A	2			2	4
Supervisor of the Five Offices	6A				5	5
Supervisor of the Five Offices	6B	2	2	1		5
Observatory Manager	7B	2	1	1	4	8
Recorder	8A	1			1	2
Water Clock Manger	8B	1	1		2	4
Calendar Manager	9A				1	1
Astronomical Observer	9A				1	1
Timekeeper	9B			1		1
Erudite						
Calendar	9B	4	2	1	15	22
Heavenly Signs	9B				2	2
Water Clock	9B			1	7	8
Student Astronomer						
Calendar		8	4	8	43	63
Heavenly Signs		2			31	33
Water Clock		2			6	8
Yin-Yang Student					10	10
Scribe		11	4	2		17
Total		36	14	15	131	196

Sources: QHDSL GX 798: 325–58, 393–4.

Qing (*Da Qing huidian* 大清會典). Although the personnel quotas and the organization of the Bureau had been kept stable till the end of the dynasty, there are two minor adjustments deserve our attention. First, as we can see from Table 4.2, while military Hans were also given a certain number of posts in the Bureau, Mongols initially had only a quota of two Scribes after the 1665 reorganization. In 1693, two posts of Supervisor of the Five Offices destined to Mongols were added to the Bureau.[63] After the College of Mathematics was founded in 1725, administrative regulations were further modified to absorb graduated Mongol Mathematics Students into the Astronomical Bureau (see later).[64]

Second, while Table 4.2 shows that the Astronomical Bureau had Manchu and military Han Student Astronomers, they in fact were not added to the Bureau until 1670.[65] When the Bureau was reorganized in 1665, the prerequisite for a newly added banner official was excellent knowledge of both the Manchu and Chinese languages; no previous knowledge in mathematics or astronomy was required. Moreover, he was allowed to skip the trainee stage of being a Student Astronomer and started with the position of Erudite directly. Doubtlessly, a banner official could become a capable astronomer during his long stay at the Astronomical Bureau, but that did not seem to be the main intention of the court. Rather than having bannermen take over Han official's works, what the court cared about was to have Han astronomers closely watched over.

Before long the Qing rulers found that spying on astronomers' works would be an impossible task without mathematical knowledge. In October 1670, the Kangxi emperor reflected after the Calendar Dispute was mostly settled. He decreed:

> Astronomy is critical [to the dynasty]. It is necessary to have proper people selected and to have them concentrate on studying so that they can completely master it. Select them from Official Students and have them study with Han Student Astronomers. If any of them can master [the knowledge of astronomy], he can obtain one of the vacancies in the Astronomical Bureau by passing the examination. Relevant ministries should devise an exact scheme on how to select the students and to make them learn [astronomy]. Memorialize the conclusion to me.[66]

The Kangxi emperor's decree shows his realization that merely installing banner officials in the Astronomical Bureau could not solve the intellectual crisis or prevent it from happening again. Banner officials had to have sufficient astronomical knowledge before they could control the Astronomical Bureau. To stabilize Manchu rule, the imperial state had to have some bannermen trained in astronomy. The emperor approved the ministers' deliberation that each banner should select six Manchu and four military Han Official Students as Student Astronomers.[67] On September 8, 1676, the emperor even issued a specific edict that "in the case of transferring [from the Astronomical Bureau] to other ministries or bureaus, the post shall only be given to those who have studied. Those unwilling to learn are absolutely prohibited from transferring out of the Astronomical Bureau."[68] Although five years later, the number of banner Student Astronomers was reduced to two Manchus and one military Han per banner, banner Student Astronomers became a permanent fixture in the Astronomical Bureau.[69]

Nonetheless, a banner Bureau official's career path was different from that of a Han official. The key factor responsible for the difference was the administrative regulations based on different ethnic groups' career mobility. Since the earliest *Collected Statutes of the Great Qing* compiled in the Kangxi reign, the regulations for selecting Manchu and Han officials had been divided into two separate chapters.[70] The fact that the chapter regulating Manchu officials' promotion is further divided into three sections—Manchu, Mongol, and military Han—suggests that different ethnic groups followed distinct career ladders. Whenever a vacancy appeared in an institution, the first thing to consider was the candidate's ethnicity. Talent and job performance certainly were important. However, a person only needed to compete with the candidates from the same ethnic groups.

Comparing the career ladder of Han officials with that of the other three ethnic groups makes this important difference more obvious. Figures 4.1 to 4.4 illustrate the possible career ladders for officials belonging to different ethnic groups as regulated in the 1899 edition of the *Collected Statutes*.[71] Figures 4.1, 4.2, and 4.3 show that the career path of a banner official—no matter if he was a Manchu, a Mongol, or a military Han—transverses all three sections. For instance, in Figure 4.1, a Manchu Student Astronomer from the Section of Heavenly Signs could become an Erudite at the Calendar Section. After that, instead of becoming a Calendar Manager or Astronomical Observer, he would become a Water Clock Manager, a position that required a very different set of knowledge and he had no previous training. Similarly, Figure 4.2 shows that every Mongol official began in the Calendar Section, and then the state-designed career path would bring him to the post of Water Clock Manager. He would then become an Observatory Manager and finally the Supervisor of the Five Offices at the Calendar Section.[72] In contrast, Figure 4.4 shows that a Han official would most probably stay within the same section for his entire career at the Astronomical Bureau.[73] It is noteworthy that although this edition of the *Collected Statutes* was compiled near the end of the dynasty, the career progressions for Bureau officials from earlier period have been found to be consistent with the regulations used to construct the above career ladders. For example, the 1680s saw Manchus Asali 阿薩禮 and Gemei 戈枚 advanced from Observatory Managers to Supervisors of the Five Offices.[74] Sources related to banner Water Clock Managers are rarely seen, but there is a record from 1727 to show that a Manchu Water Clock Manager, Subanli 蘇頒禮, was promoted to the post of Observatory Manage.[75] For military Hans, the case of Wang Zhaolong 王兆龍 closely matches the career ladder illustrated in Figure 4.3. Wang, originally a military Han Official Student, became a Student Astronomer in 1699. He was made a Timekeeper in 1704 and then an Observatory Manager in 1708. In 1714, Wang advanced to the Supervisor of the Autumn Office, the highest position a military Han could obtain in the Astronomical Bureau.[76]

80 *Kangxi Calendar Dispute*

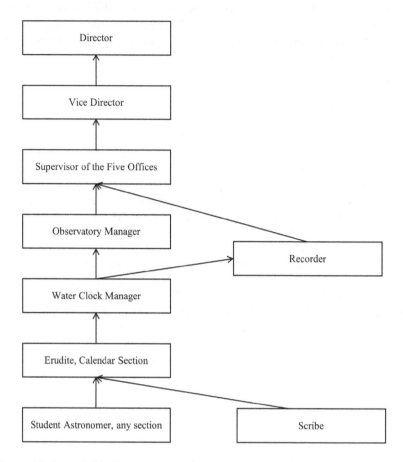

Figure 4.1 Career ladder for a Manchu official at the Astronomical Bureau. Adapted from QHDSL GX 798: 339–40.

The peculiar design of the career ladders suggests that the court did not expect banner officials to acquire the same level of knowledge and skills as Han officials did. The following case shows that the emperor's expectation of banner officials' mathematical knowledge was indeed less strict than that of the Han officials. In 1689, the Ministry of Personnel nominated two candidates, Chang'e 常額 and Sanbao 三保, to the position of Manchu Vice-Director. The Kangxi emperor decreed that they should take an examination. The examination had two parts: translation and calendar calculation. Chang'e, the first candidate, scored poorly in both parts and his computation of an upcoming eclipse had a startling error of nine days. The Kangxi emperor, therefore, gave the vice-directorship to the second candidate, Sanbao.[77] However, he did not punish Chang'e, then the Supervisor of the Five Office, for his poor knowledge of calendar calculation. Two years later,

Kangxi Calendar Dispute 81

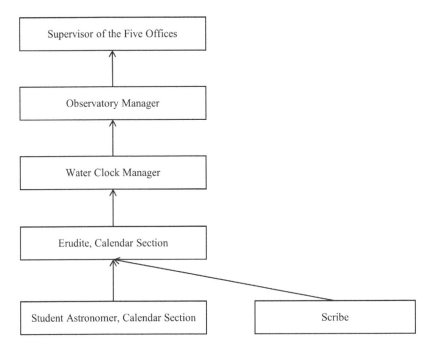

Figure 4.2 Career ladder for a Mongol official at the Astronomical Bureau. Adapted from QHDSL GX 798: 339.

Chang'e became the Vice-Director. By 1696, Chang'e was made the Manchu Director and he remained in this position until 1709.[78]

Although after October 1670 bannermen who entered the Astronomical Bureau had to start as Student Astronomers, the number of banner Student Astronomers was significantly fewer than that of the Han Student Astronomers (see Table 2.1). The Section of Heavenly Signs and the Water Clock Section each had only two Manchu Student Astronomers and no Mongols or military Hans. The Calendar Section, at first sight, appeared to have a sufficiently large number of banner Student Astronomers. It had 20 banner Student Astronomers and 43 Han Student Astronomers. However, the quota of banner Student Astronomers was equally divided among the eight banners.[79] Therefore, every banner could only send one Manchu and one military Han to be Student Astronomers in the Calendar Section.

The small number of banner Student Astronomers had two effects. First, working at the Astronomical Bureau might appear more attractive to banner Student Astronomers because they, in general, did not have to wait as long as Han Student Astronomers did to become Erudites. A successful banner official could finish his service at the Astronomical Bureau while still young enough to begin a second career with greater prospects. Second, the limited quota given to each banner made the formation of long-lasting hereditary astronomer families difficult. Even if a child of a banner astronomer had learned mathematics from his father, the

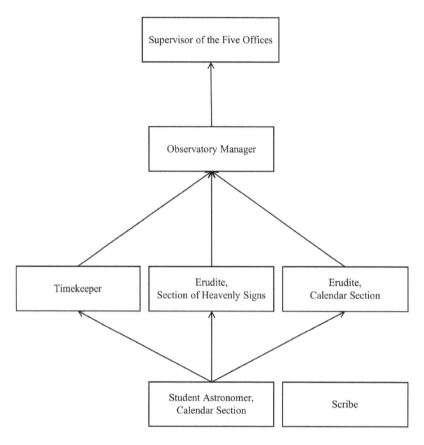

Figure 4.3 Career ladder for a military Han official at the Astronomical Bureau. Adapted from QHDSL GX 798: 340.

Bureau might not have a position available for him. It would also be difficult for a banner astronomer to send several children to work for the Astronomical Bureau and thus make being an imperial astronomer a family craft.

The quota system placed upon bannermen was kept until the end of the dynasty. It suggests that the court indeed expected banner officials to oversee rather than take over Han colleagues' works. If Han astronomers were encouraged to devote themselves not just as individuals, but also as a family to pass on their knowledge and skills for the imperial state, banner Bureau officials' duties were to oversee the Han astronomers' loyalty.

4.3 The Emergence of the He Family

During the Kangxi Calendar Dispute, one of the most influential hereditary astronomer families emerged. This section describes how the He family, which was

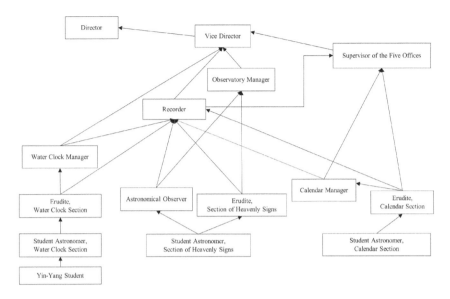

Figure 4.4 Career ladder for a Han official at the Astronomical Bureau. Adapted from QHDSL GX 346–55.

relatively insignificant in the late Ming and Qing Shunzhi Astronomical Bureau, navigated the Calendar Dispute, distinguished itself, and attracted imperial attention. After the Calendar Dispute, the Kangxi emperor continued to utilize the He family members' expertise in calendar making to counterbalance Jesuit missionaries' control of the Astronomical Bureau. Although the emperor eventually decided to completely abandon the Old Method, the He family forever changed its fortune.

Due to the scarcity of sources, much of the He family's status in the Ming period has to be left to speculation.[80] A search in the rosters of the existing Great Concordance calendars found only two officials with the surname He.[81] One is Observatory Manager He Xian 何暹 between 1557 and 1566, and the other is Calendar Manager He Wenlong 何文龍 between 1597 and 1604.[82] Nothing else about He Xian and He Wenlong is known, and there is no direct evidence to confirm whether they were the ancestors of the Hes working at the Qing Astronomical Bureau. However, one cannot rule out the possibility that He Wenlong's descendants might still have been working at the Astronomical Bureau when the Manchus marched into Beijing and became the new rulers of China, because the Ming dynasty ended merely four decades after He Wenlong's name last appeared on the Great Concordance calendar. On the other hand, even if his descendants continued working at the Astronomical Bureau, they were hardly in a position to be critically involved in the competition between the systems of calendar-making. This was because the Calendar Department led by Xu Guangqi did not open until 1629, and none of He Wenlong's descendants reached a position high enough to be included in the calendar's roster. Indeed, although the memorials submitted by Xu Guangqi and Li Tianjing often contained detailed lists of the Astronomical Bureau officials who participated in the calculation or observation of solar eclipses, the surname He did not ever appear among them.[83]

In fact, the presence of the He family in the late Ming Astronomical Bureau would be in question if the *Register of Metropolitan Officials* did not contain records of the following three officials: He Qiyi 何其義, He Luoshu 何雒書, and He Luotu 何雒圖. According to the *Register of Metropolitan Officials*, these three He officials were all from Zhejiang 浙江 and began their services at the Bureau as Student Astronomers. Among them, He Luotu was the latest to obtain the position of Erudite; he was not promoted to Erudite until the twelfth year of the Shunzhi reign (1655), more than a decade after Schall took over the Astronomical Bureau.[84] Hence, Luotu must have learned the New Method well enough to win the position of Erudite by passing the qualifying examinations that Schall administered. However, Luotu's record did not provide any clue as to whether he entered the Astronomical Bureau before or after Schall became the *de facto* Director. In contrast, He Qiyi and He Luoshu's records indicate that as of the third month of the second year of the Shunzhi reign (April 1645), they were already Calendar Section Erudites.[85] We have seen in Chapter 3, Section 3.2, Schall held the examination in early March for Astronomical Bureau and Calendar Section staff members, but his reorganization plan was largely canceled because of Bureau official's fierce reaction. Thus, the next month, April 1645, was the time that Schall and the Grand Secretariat finalized the reorganization of the Astronomical Bureau officials. Considering the long period that a Student Astronomer had to wait before advancing to the position of Erudite, He Qiyi and He Luoshu must have joined the Astronomical Bureau by the end of the Ming dynasty.

However, evidence for the connection between the Ming He family from Zhejiang and Qing He family from Daxing 大興 has to be found elsewhere. According to the *Biographies of Mathematicians and Astronomers,* He Guozong 何國宗, the most successful descendant of the Qing He astronomer family, was from the Daxing County of the Shuntian Prefecture (*Shuntian fu Daxing xian* 順天府大興縣) and the He family took on the profession of astronomy generation after generation (*shiye tianwen* 世業天文).[86] A statement in the *History of the Qing Empire* shows that He Guozong and his brother He Guozhu 何國柱 were "sons of the Supervisor of the Five Offices of the Astronomical Bureau, He Junxi 何君錫."[87] But the name He Junxi is not seen in the *Register of Metropolitan Officials*.

Later documents further clarify the relationship between He Qiyi, Luoshu, Luotu, and the He family of the Qing period. The *List of Successful Civil Service Candidates* (*Dengkelu* 登科錄) was a non-governmental publication aiming to provide the reader a quick survey of new civil service degree obtainers' biographical information, including their ancestries for three generations (great-grandfather, grandfather, and father).[88] By comparing different publishers' *List of Successful Civil Service Candidates* of 1712, the year that He Guozong became a Metropolitan Graduate (*jinshi* 進士), we can confirm that the names of Guozong's great-grandfather, grandfather, and father were Qiren 其仁, Luoshu 雒書, and Junxi 君錫, respectively.[89] Among them, we have seen He Luoshu listed in

Register of Metropolitan Officials as an Erudite (see earlier). Thus, at least from the generation of He Luoshu, Guozong's grandfather, the He family had been working at the Astronomical Bureau and must have been living in the nearby areas of Beijing. Unlike the Ming dynasty which forbade imperial astronomers' descendants to abandon their family profession, there is no document to show that the Qing court ever imposed similar restrictions to astronomer families. It would be reasonable for He Luoshu and He Junxi to cultivate some of their descendants to become civil servants. Therefore, after the Ming ended, He Luoshu and He Junxi must have changed the place of their house registration to the Daxing County of the Shuntian Prefecture so that their descendants could take the civil service examination in local Beijing instead of in their ancestral hometown in Zhejiang.[90] As a result, not only He Guozong took the civil service examination and obtain his degrees as a resident of Daxing but also the He family became known as an astronomer family of Daxing.[91]

The familial relations between the above He family members can be further reconstructed. Consider the Ming law's requirement that only descendants of astronomer families could obtain posts at the Astronomical Bureau. It is possible that He Qiren and Qiyi were Wenlong's sons and that He Luoshu entered the Astronomical Bureau because his father Qiren used to work there. Luoshu and Luotu must have been of the same generation, but it is uncertain whether they were brothers or cousins. On the other hand, while there is still no direct evidence to prove the proceeding assertions, it is certain that He Guozong's family had started working in the Astronomical Bureau since his grandfather or even his great-grandfather's generation (see Figure 4.5).

Among the three He family members working at the Astronomical Bureau during the Ming-Qing transition, Luotu appeared to have converted to the New Western Method. But how did Qiyi and Luoshu, who still testified as "Erudites of the Old Method" during the trial of Calendar Dispute, adapt to the Qing court's adoption of the New Method?[92] The Qing court's adoption of the New Method might have disheartened Qiyi and Luoshu. As colleagues of the Ming Astronomical Bureau, they spent years or even decades learning mathematical astronomy for making the state calendar. Before they could use their knowledge to pursue higher rankings and fortunes, the Ming dynasty ended and the new Manchu rulers decided to adopt a completely different astronomical system. He Qiyi and He Luoshu did not lose their jobs after Schall's takeover, but their expertise became obsolete. The fact that their *Register of Metropolitan Officials* records were never updated suggests that they remained in the same position of Erudite throughout the Shunzhi reign.

He Qiyi and He Luoshu took different approaches to counter career stagnation. It is not known how well He Qiyi learned the New Method. However, because Qiyi endorsed Schall's *Response to Concerns*, it seems reasonable to assert that he maintained a peaceful relationship with Schall. Furthermore, the *Response to Concerns* shows that He Qiyi's civil service rank had been elevated to higher than an ordinary Erudite, placing him at the same status as Schall's disciples Bao Yingqi and Jiao Yingxu 焦應旭.[93] Higher civil rank brought an official a slight

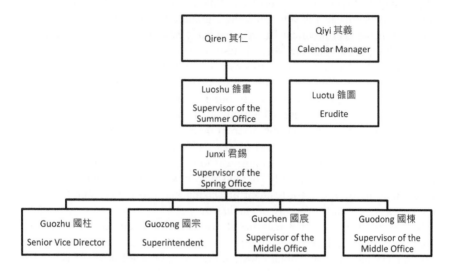

Figure 4.5 Early generations of the He family. Created by the author.

increase in salary and grain stipend. Although Schall seemed to advance only his own disciples to higher positions, he may have rewarded Erudites such as He Qiyi for their cooperation by elevating their civil ranks. Nonetheless, He Qiyi's cooperation with Schall could not have been very close. Otherwise, he would have been demoted or ousted from the Astronomical Bureau when Yang Guangxian became the Director and purged the adherents of Schall. When Yang Guangxian became the Astronomical Bureau Director and needed some lower-ranking officials to fill in the vacant positions in the Calendar Sections, he elevated He Qiyi to the position of Calendar Manager.[94] Qiyi remained in this position without further advancement until his career ended around 1677, by which time the Jesuits had held the leadership of the Astronomical Bureau for more than seven years.[95] He Qiyi's slow career advancement indicates that he might have chosen to keep a neutral attitude between rival fractions.

He Luoshu, to the contrary, seemed hostile to Schall and the New Method. He Luoshu's name appears not in the endorser list of Schall's *Response to Concerns* (see Table 3.6) but in Yang Guangxian's treatise *I Have No Alternative*. We may recall that Yang frankly admitted his ignorance of mathematical astronomy. If some insiders from the Astronomical Bureau had not assisted him, Yang would have been unable to calculate an eclipse prediction according to the Great Concordance system, not to mention comparing it with the New Western Method. The case of predicting the solar eclipse of January 16, 1665, exemplifies the importance of He Luoshu to Schall. This solar eclipse happened during the trial of the Calendar Dispute and provided a timely chance for comparing the accuracy of the New Western, Great Concordance, and Muslim methods. According to Väth's biography of Schall, Yang and his adherents submitted the prediction days

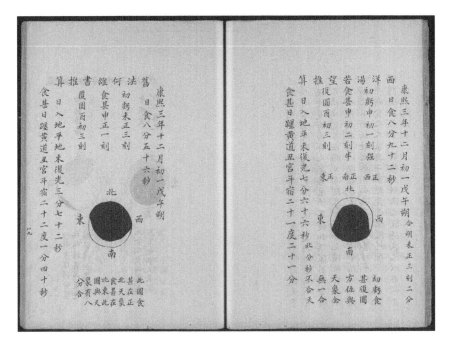

Figure 4.6 Schall's and He Luoshu's predictions of the 1665 solar eclipse in *I Have No Alternative*. *Right*, "Western [Method] Calculated by Tang Ruowang [Schall]." At the bottom is Yang Guangxian's comment: "None of the beginning, maximum, and ending positions of the eclipse agreed with celestial phenomenon." *Left*, "Old Method Calculated by He Luoshu." Yang Guangxian's comment: "Eighty percent of this illustration agreed with celestial phenomenon." Courtesy of the National Central Library, Taiwan.

before the solar eclipse and confidently proclaimed that they would be the winner. Unfortunately for them, the solar eclipse started at the time predicted by the New Western Method. The prediction of the Great Concordance turned out to be even worse than that of the Muslim method.[96] Yang was not scared off by this shameful failure. Instead, he wrote, "Verifying the Solar Eclipse by Celestial Phenomena" (*Rishi tianxiang yan* 日食天象驗) to rebut the success of Schall's prediction. Yang began by boldly advocating, "I would rather let China (*Zhong xia* 中夏) not have a good calendar method than let China have Westerners."[97] He then placed He Luoshu's and Schall's predictions of the solar eclipse of January 16, 1665 side by side with the observation results, compared each phase of the eclipse, and concluded that, in terms of the direction and proportion of the eclipse, He Luoshu's prediction was superior to Schall's (see Figures 4.6 and 4.7).[98]

He Luoshu's alliance with Yang Guangxian brought him rewards in terms of career development. Soon after becoming the Director, Yang Guangxian inspected the observatory with some high ministers. Upon examining the sundial, Yang scolded Li Guanghong, an Erudite of the Section of Heavenly Signs, for having purposely manipulated the instrument to favor Schall's prediction. Yang said, "If

88 *Kangxi Calendar Dispute*

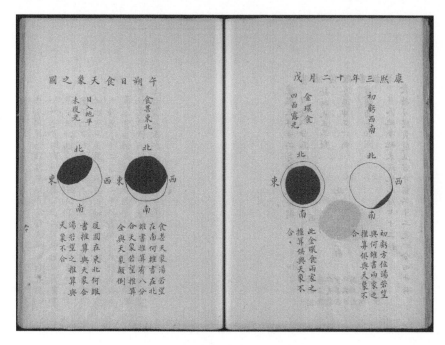

Figure 4.7 Yang Guangxian's observation of the solar eclipse of January 16, 1665, in *I Have No Alternative. Right to Left*: initial obscuration, annular eclipse, maximum obscuration, recovery. Yang comments at the bottom of the first two eclipse phases that both Schall's and He's calculations disagreed with the observation results. For the third one, maximum obscure, Yang comments that He's prediction was 80 percent agreed with the observation result, while Schall's was completely upside down. For the last phase, Yang comments that He's prediction agreed with the celestial phenomenon, while Schall's did not. Courtesy of the National Central Library, Taiwan.

the solar eclipse was measured on this tilted sundial, how would it be possible that Calendar Section Erudites He Luoshu and Ma Weilong 馬惟龍 did not lose [in the competition of predicting eclipses]?"[99] Within a year, Yang demoted Li Guanghong and dismissed several Erudites. Meanwhile, He Luoshu was elevated from Erudite to fill one of the vacancies left by the beheaded Supervisors of the Five Offices. In March 1669, the Kangxi emperor decided to reinstate the New Method and kicked Yang out of the Astronomical Bureau. He Luoshu, however, was not punished, and he remained the Supervisor of the Summer Office until 1684.[100]

While He Qiyi and He Luoshu illustrated how different choices could affect their careers, a more crucial figure to the future of the He family was He Qiyi's son, He Junxi 何君錫. He Junxi's name was not in the *Register of Metropolitan Officials*. Therefore, Junxi, at best, was a Student Astronomer at the end of the Shunzhi reign. It was also possible that He Junxi entered the Astronomical Bureau during the mass recruitment of Student Astronomers and Erudites for re-establishing the Great Concordance system in 1666 because of He Luoshu's recommendation.[101] Either way, by January 1667, he already became the Supervisor of the Winter Office.¹⁰² The fact that He Junxi's career advanced with surprising speed during the Calendar Dispute indicates that he, similar to his father, was an expert and advocate of the Great Concordance system. Later we shall see more evidence of He Junxi's adherence to the Old Method. Moreover, it turns out that the Kangxi emperor did not completely lose interest in the Great Concordance system when the Calendar Dispute ended in 1669.

Some evidence suggest that the New Western Method did not immediately convince the Kangxi emperor. First of all, it is noteworthy that the Kangxi emperor let He Luoshu remain the Supervisor of the Summer Office. The emperor's decision might be both political and intellectual. The Calendar Dispute stimulated the emperor's interest in mathematics, and he would eventually take mathematical lessons from the Jesuits.¹⁰³ However, at this time the emperor was probably not confident enough to make a final choice between the New and Old Methods. Politically, as long as the adherents of the Great Concordance system did not become troublemakers like Yang Guangxian or Wu Mingxuan, keeping them in the Astronomical Bureau could counterbalance the power of a European astronomer.

Beyond simply keeping Great Concordance experts employed in the Astronomical Bureau, the Kangxi emperor used them to initiate a new challenge to the New Western Method. In March 1675, the emperor instructed Manchu Vice-Director Antai 安泰 directly: "The Old Method shall not be abandoned. You can learn from He Junxi."¹⁰⁴ That the emperor pointed to He Junxi instead of He Luoshu implies not only that Junxi might have better knowledge of the Great Concordance system than anyone else in the Astronomical Bureau but also that the Kangxi emperor had paid great attention to the staff and ongoing affairs of the Astronomical Bureau. Moreover, the Kangxi emperor's decree must have been encouraging to the adherents of the Old Method. About six months later, He Luoshu informed Verbiest that the predictions for the solar eclipse of June 11, 1676 differed significantly between the Old and New Methods. Verbiest predicted that the eclipse magnitude would be merely 20 *wei* (0.02% of the diameter). He Luoshu's prediction, however, claimed that it would be five *fen* and 60 *miao* (56% of the diameter).¹⁰⁵ According to Verbiest's prediction, the court did not need to hold a Rescue Ritual (*jiuhu* 救護) on the day of eclipse, for the eclipse was barely visible.¹⁰⁶ But if He Lushu's prediction was right, the court would be greatly embarrassed for missing the Rescue Ritual for an eclipse that obscured more than half of the sun. Verbiest was confident in his New Western Method. He did not report He Luoshu's prediction to the emperor on the grounds that there was no need to prepare a Rescue Ritual for this eclipse.¹⁰⁷ But the adherents of the Old Method did not give up so easily. In March 1676, Antai directly requested the emperor to verify the accuracy of the Old Method by sending officers to provinces to observe the upcoming solar eclipse. This time, Verbiest felt the threat. He sent the emperor a copy of his prediction for every province and a long memorial to explain the astronomical principles of the solar eclipse.¹⁰⁸

On the day of the solar eclipse, a comparison test was performed on the observatory. According to an abridged version of Verbiest's memorial recorded in the *History of the Qing Empire*, the magnitude of this solar eclipse was less than one *fen* (10% of the diameter).[109] Apparently, as Verbiest commented, "The number deduced by the Old Method was wildly off target."[110] The observed magnitude also showed that a Rescue Ritual was indeed not necessary for this solar eclipse. Nonetheless, the visibility of the eclipse must have been larger than Verbiest's expectation for he admitted that "the New Method also appeared not completely close [to the observation]."[111]

To ensure his success was undoubted, Verbiest further explained the important effect of refraction in his memorial to the Kangxi emperor. Verbiest pointed out that this eclipse had taken place when the sun and moon were very close to the horizon, so that the effect of atmospheric refraction was an important factor. He claimed that as long as the observers were willing to take the effect of refraction into consideration, they would understand that the New Method, in fact, was accurate. The denser atmosphere near the horizon could refract a small object into a larger one, Verbiest explained, hence the magnitude of the eclipse might appear larger than it really was. This was why the observed magnitude of the eclipse was slightly larger than the prediction deduced from the New Method. Furthermore, the deviation depended on the density of the atmosphere, which unfortunately was forever changing and could not be deduced beforehand.[112]

A reasonable explanation of the deviation, to some extent, eased the burden of producing precise predictions for eclipses near the horizon. Whether the Kangxi emperor throughout agreed or understood Verbiest's explanation of the effect of refraction was not known, but his ability to explain the prediction's failure would have appealed to him. On the other hand, neither the *History of the Qing Empire* nor the *Veritable Records* mentions if He Luoshu and the other adherents of the Old Method had ever provided any explanation or refutation.[113] Probably they had not been able to. After reviewing Verbiest's memorial, the Kangxi emperor ordered "the relevant departments [to] take note of this [explanation]."[114] Three months later, in August 1676, the emperor's final verdict ended the last hope of the Great Concordance system:

> Previously, there were disputes over the rightness or wrongness of the New and Old Methods. Now the correctness of the New Method is known. The Manchu officials in your bureau, who have the duty to study astronomy and calendar making, shall be particularly diligent. From now on, only those who study well will be granted promotion. Those who do not study will not be granted any promotion.[115]

The He family was left to cope with the imperial verdict. The last time that the names of He Qiyi and He Luoshu appeared on the official calendar was in 1677 and 1685, respectively.[116] No further record about their later years has been found.

He Junxi would continue in the Astronomical Bureau for three more decades, but the Kangxi emperor made sure that he did not have a chance again to advocate the Old Method. On January 28, 1688, Ferdinand Verbiest died. Because the Kangxi emperor did not create a new office for Verbiest but let him use the quota reserved for Han Chinese, He Junxi, at the time the most senior Calendar

Section Supervisor, legally had the right to succeed to the directorship. The Ministry of Rites put He Junxi in the list of nominations with Vice-Director Bao Yingqi, a long-time adherent of Jesuit missionaries, and let the Kangxi emperor select between them. The emperor, however, chose neither; the post of Han Director went to another European missionary.[117] If the Kangxi emperor's choice meant only that he preferred a European Director to a Han Chinese, the following incident demonstrates his determination to suppress He Junxi. Less than three months after Verbiest's death, the Han Vice-Directorship became vacant, and He Junxi was again nominated to succeed the post. According to the records of April 10, 1688, in the *Imperial Diary*, the Kangxi emperor made the following specific comments with respect to He Junxi in front of several grand ministers:

> The Ministry of Personnel memorialized regarding the vacancy left by the Vice-Director of the Astronomical Bureau, Li Guanghong. The Ministry nominated He Junxi to fill that vacancy. The emperor decreed, "Previously I had He Junxi come to the palace and calculate a solar eclipse. Attempting to meddle, he absurdly presented me a result calculated according to the Old Method that the eclipse magnitude would be three *fen* [three-tenths of the diameter]. I know everything about the New and Old Methods, and I knew that his result was wrong. Therefore, I sent people to every place to observe the eclipse. According to current regulations, there is no need to submit a routine memorial if an eclipse is less than two *fen* [two-tenths of the diameter]. Indeed, after the eclipse, nobody memorialized me. From this incident, I know he is unacceptable. Find another person for this post.[118]

Whether He Junxi's abrupt recommendation of the Old Method happened before the solar eclipse of 1676 or another one was no longer important. These imperial words diminished He Junxi's hope of making further career advancement. He remained a Supervisor of the Calendar Section for the rest of his career at the Astronomical Bureau and never advanced beyond that position.

In the long run, He Junxi's career setback had only a temporary effect on the family fortune. He Luoshu and He Junxi lost the battle for advocating the Great Concordance system of calendar making, but they won for themselves and their family higher positions in the Astronomical Bureau. More importantly, He Junxi had impressed the Kangxi emperor with his mathematical expertise. The next chapter will show that, when the political tide turned against the Jesuits in later years, He Junxi's sons who inherited his mathematical talent would become imperial favorites and would advance the whole family to a more prosperous status.

Notes

1 For the Kangxi Calendar Dispute, see Catherine Jami, "Revisiting the Calendar Case (1664–1669): Science, Religion, and Politics in Early Qing Beijing," *The Korean Journal for the History of Science* 37, no. 2 (2015): 459–77; Ma Weihua 馬偉華, *Lifa, zongjiao yu huangquan: Ming Qing zhiji Zhongxi lifa zhizheng zaiyanjiu* 曆

法, 宗教與皇權: 明清之際中西曆法之爭再研究 (Beijing: Zhonghua shuju, 2019), 84–153; Chu, "Scientific Dispute," 7–34.
2. Huang, *Zhengjiao fengbao*, 501.
3. For the date that the regency council accepted Yang Guangxian's accusation, see Väth, *Johann Adam Schall*, 299; Yang Guangxian 楊光先, "Budeyi" 不得已, in *Tianzhujiao dongchuan wenxian xubian* 天主教東傳文獻續編, ed. Wu Xiangxiang 吳湘湘 (Taipei: Taiwan xuesheng shuju, 1966), 1080–1. For the life Yang Guangxian, see Huang Yi-Long 黃一農, "Yang Guangxian jiashi yu shengping kao" 楊光先家世與生平考, *Guoli bianyiguan guankan* 國立編譯館館刊 19, no. 2 (1990): 15–28.
4. An, *Qingchu xiyang*, 220–57. On the change of political atmosphere after the Shunahi emperor's death that led the regency council to remove Schall by means of Yang Guangxian's accusation, see Ma, *Lifa, zongjiao yu huangquan*, 99–100.
5. *Qing guoshi*, 4: 624; QHDZL QL 625: 139.
6. For the earthquake, see Väth, *Johann Adam Schall*, 313–6. For Grand Empress Dowager's intervention, see Huang, *Zhengjiao fengbao*, 503.
7. Huang, *Zhengjiao fengbao*, 503–4; Väth, *Johann Adam Schall*, 320.
8. An, *Qingchu xiyang*, 267–8.
9. Huang, *Zhengjiao fengbao*, 520–1.
10. SL 4: 220; An, *Qingchu xiyang*, 257.
11. For Li's demotion, see Huang, *Zhengjiao fengbao*, 514–15. For Yang's accusation, see Yang, "Budeyi," 1282–5.
12. The civil calendar of the sixth year of Kangxi (1667) lists Zhang as Senior Vice-Director, but the Encroachments calendar of the same year no longer sees his name. Qu, "Qingdai Qintianjian," 49; Zhou Weiqiang 周維強, "Yuancang Qingdai *Yue wuxing lingfan shixianli* chutan" 院藏清代《月五星凌犯時憲曆》初探, *Gugong wenwu yuekan* 故宮文物月刊 7, no. 413 (2017): 84–5.
13. Huang, *Zhengjiao fengbao*, 514–15.
14. Ibid., 523–4.
15. Yang, "Budeyi," 1264.
16. Yang memorialized four times in 1647, requesting to be released from the posts of Vice-Director and Director.
17. Ibid., 1268.
18. According to the *Canon of Yao* 堯典 in *Book of Document* 尚書, Yao 堯 commanded Xi 羲 and He 和 to observe the sky and to make a calendar. Kong Anguo 孔安國 et al., *Shangshu zhushu* 尚書注疏, SKQS 54: 35; Needham and Wang, *Science and Civilisation*, 186–8.
19. Yang, "Budeyi," 1197.
20. Ibid., 1285–7.
21. "Shunzhi yuping," 28: 14.
22. Ge, *Luoyang Geshi*, 2: 27; "Shunzhi yuping," 28: 14.
23. Yang, "Budeyi," 1275, 1277.
24. For the increase of Student Astronomers, see QHD KX 7749. The records related to the increase of Erudites are not seen in the earliest edition of the *Collected Statutes* published in the Kangxi reign, but they can be found in later editions. Because the number of Student Astronomers had been greatly increased, it seems reasonable to assume that the quota of Erudite had been increased at the same time. QHD YZ 163; QHDZL QL 620: 90.
25. SL 4: 379. For the role of the theory of Watching for the Ethers in the Kangxi Calendar Dispute, see Huang Yi-Long 黃一農 and Chang Chi-Cheng 張志誠, "Zhongguo chuantong houqishuo de yanjin yu shuaitui" 中國傳統候氣說的演進與衰頹, *Tsinghua xuebao* 清華學報 23, no. 2 (1993): 135–40.
26. Christopher Cullen and Catherine Jami, "Christmas 1668 and after: How Jesuit Astronomy Was Restored to Power in Beijing," *Journal for the History of Astronomy* 51, no. 1 (2020): 12.
27. Ibid., 13.

28 Ibid., 14.
29 Yang, "Budeyi," 1287–8.
30 Ibid., 1277–8.
31 Shi, Li, and Li, "Cong *Xuande shinian*," 156–64.
32 Zhao et al., *Qingshi gao*, 10022–3; *Xichao ding'an* 熙朝定案, in *Xichao chongzhongji Xichao ding'an (wai san zhong)* 熙朝崇正集 熙朝定案 (外三種), ed. Han Qi 韓琦 and Wu Min 吳旻 (Beijing: Zhonghua shuju, 2006), 80.
33 *Da Qing Kangxi liunian wuxing lingfan shixianli* 大清康熙六年五星凌犯時憲曆, Qingdai wenxian dangce quanwen yingxiang ziliaoku 清代文獻檔冊全文影像資料庫, National Palace Museum, Taipei, http://npmhost.npm.gov.tw/ttscgi/ttswebfile?@@A185F981B38629F0A856 (accessed May 2020).
34 Zhou, "*lingfan shixianli*," 84–5.
35 SL 4: 365.
36 At the time, the Bureau seemed to have two calendars based on the old system. One was calculated by the Supervisors of the Five Offices, including Ge Jiwen. The other one was calculated by Recorder Chen Yuxin 陳聿新. SL 4: 365, 4: 370.
37 SL 4: 365–6.
38 SL 4: 370, *Qing guoshi*, 4: 624.
39 Cullen and Jami, "Christmas 1668 and after," 13.
40 For Ferdinand Verbiest's life and works, see Noel Golvers, *The* Astronomia Europaea *of Ferdinand Verbiest, S.J. (Dillingen, 1687); Text, Translation, Notes and Commentaries* (Nettetal: Steyler Verlag, 1993); John W. Witek, ed., *Ferdinand Verbiest (1623–1688): Jesuit Missionary, Scientist, Engineer and Diplomat* (Nettetal: Steyler Verlag, 1994).
41 Cullen and Jami, "Christmas 1668 and after," 9–11.
42 Ibid., 15–18.
43 Ibid., 18.
44 For more details on the three shadow trials, see ibid., 21–8.
45 Ibid., 28.
46 Ibid., 30.
47 Huang, *Zhengjiao fengbao*, 507–8.
48 Ibid., 515.
49 Ibid., 508.
50 Ibid., 510.
51 Ibid., 508–9.
52 Ibid., 509–10.
53 *Xichao ding'an*, 84–5.
54 SL 4: 417.
55 Huang, *Zhengjiao fengbao*, 520–5.
56 Yao Yuxiang 姚雨薌 and Hu Yangshan 胡仰山, eds., *Da Qing lüli huitong xinzuan* 大清律例會通新纂, CKSB 211: 381–2. As in previous dynasties, if a Student Astronomer had already mastered the mathematical studies, he could exchange the banishment for reduced corporal punishment so that he could remain in Beijing and continue working for the Astronomical Bureau.
57 Qu, "Qingdai Qintianjian," 50–1; IHP 170472. See Appendix A for a reconstructed family tree for the Baos.
58 SL 4: 371.
59 Ge Yusheng and Ge Zhangzhen 戈掌鎮 were listed in a memorial written in January 1685 as Erudites, but Ge Yushen was a generation earlier than Ge Yusheng. See Antai 安泰 et al., *Qinding xuanze lishu* 欽定選擇曆書, 1685, and Figure 3.1.
60 An, *Qingchu xiyang*, 257, see also SL 4: 220.
61 See Chapter 2, Section 2.2.7.
62 QHDSL GX 798: 393.
63 QHD YZ 15513–4.
64 QHDZL QL 625: 131.

65 See Chapter 2, Section 2.3.1 for more details on the change of the numbers of Student Astronomers.
66 IHP 278678–22.
67 QHD KX 7749. Later the number of Han Student Astronomers was also reduced to 80.
68 IHP 091507.
69 QHD KX 7750.
70 For banner officials, see "Libu wu" 吏部五, QHD KX 209–74. For Han officials, see "Libu liu" 吏部六, QHD KX 275–346.
71 For banner officials, see "Libu yi" 吏部一, "QHDSL GX 798: 325–40. For Han officials, see "Libu er" 吏部二, QHDSL GX 341–6.
72 Some exceptions existed. Minggantu 明安圖 was a Mongol but he became a Vice-Director and then a Director.
73 It was possible for a Recorder from the Water Clock Section or the Section of Heavenly Signs to become one of the Supervisors of the Section of Calendar, but very few cases have been found.
74 Asali 阿薩禮, also appeared as Ashali 阿沙禮, was an Observatory Manager from 1677 to 1681, and a Supervisor of the Five Office from 1682 to 1684 before advancing to the position of Vice-Director. Gemei was an Observatory Manager from 1681 and 1684, and a Supervisor of the Five Office from 1685 and 1687 before becoming a Vice-Director. Shi, "Tianwenke," 37; Qu, "Qingdai Qintianjian," 50.
75 GYQX 11: 6143.
76 QGLL 12: 14.
77 QJZ KX (BJ), B012438.
78 Qu, "Qingdai Qintianjian," 50–1.
79 QHD KX, 7750.
80 Chang Ping-Ying 張秉瑩, "Shidai bianjuzhong de chouren jiazu—yi Mingmo Qingchu de Qingtianjian Hejia weili" 時代變局中的疇人家族—以明末清初的欽天監何家為例, *Hanxue yanjiu* 漢學研究 36, no. 2 (2018): 130–2.
81 Ming Qintianjian, *Da Ming Datong li*, microfilms, 305.3 06315–38, contains 48 calendars between 1617 and 1643. Beijing tushuguan chubanshe guji yingyinshi, *Guojia tushuguancang Mingdai Datongliri huibian*, contains 99 different years' calendars between 1446 and 1641.
82 For He Xian, see ibid., 3: 32, 98, 136, 168. For He Wenlong, see ibid., 4: 378–608.
83 These memorials were collected in Xu Guangqi 徐光啟 et al., "Zhili yuanqi" 治曆緣起, in *Chongzhen lishu fu Xiyang xinfa lishu zengkan shizhong* 崇禎曆書 附西洋新法曆書增刊十種, ed. Pan Naihui 潘鼐匯 (Shanghai: Shanghai guji chubanshe, 2009), 1545–752.
84 "Shunzhi yuping," 28: 14.
85 Ibid., 28: 15.
86 Ruan, *Chouren zhuan*, 518.
87 *Qing guoshi*, 4: 626.
88 The record of three-generation ancestry was usually referred to as *sandai lüli* 三代履歷.
89 *Kangxi wushiyinian dengkelu* 康熙五十一年登科錄, vol. 14 of *Zhongguo keju wenxian conglu* 中國科舉文獻叢錄 (Beijing: Quanguo suowei fuzhi zhongxin, 2010), 402; *Kangxi wushiyinian renchenke huishi yibaijiushiwuming sandai jinshi lüli* 康熙五十一年壬辰科會試一百九十五名三代進士履歷, disc 2 of *Dengkelu* 登科錄 (Tokyo: Kokuritsu kōbunshokan, 2012). For the comparison, see Chang, "Shidai bianjuzhong de chouren jiazu," 132–7. See Chapter 5, Section 5.1 for He Guozong's degree of Metropolitan Graduation.
90 A civil service examinee must satisfy the following requirements before he is allowed to take examination: (1) His grandfather and father have moved to the place of household registration (*ru ji* 入籍) for more than 20 years; (2) family graves, farmland, and residences are in the place of household registration; (3) the examinee has secured a letter of guaranty from local official's. QHD KX 2518–9.

91 He Guozong became a Provincial Graduate (*juren* 舉人) of the Shuntian Prefecture in 1708. Li Wei 李衛 et al., *Jifu tongzhi* 畿輔通志 [1735], SKQS 505: 606.
92 An, *Qingchu xiyang*, 50, 55.
93 Schall, *Minli puzhen*, 2–3.
94 *Da Qing Kangxi liunian wuxing lingfan shixianli*.
95 Qu, "Qingdai Qintianjian," 49–50.
96 Väth, *Johann Adam Schall*, 307–8.
97 Yang, "Budeyi," 1249.
98 Ibid., 1250–3.
99 Ibid., 1282–3. Ma Weilong used to be an Erudite of the Muslim Section. See "Shunzhi yuping," 28: 16.
100 Qu, "Qingdai Qintianjian," 49–50.
101 For the records of Student Astronomers and Erudites being added to the Astronomical Bureau, see QHD KX 7749 and QHD YZ 163. In "'Zili jingshen' yu lisuan huodong—Kang-Qian zhiji wenren dui Xixue taidu zhi gaibian ji qi Beijing" '自立精神'與曆算活動—康乾之際文人對西學態度之改變及其背景, *Ziran kexueshi yanjiu* 自然科學史研究 21, no. 3 (2002): 210–2, Han Qi claims that He Junxi was Yang Guangxian's disciple based on a letter written by Antoine Thomas. However, judging from the fact that Yang had to use He Luoshu's calculation in his treatise and that he had testified that he did not know the mathematics of the calendar, it is highly unlikely that Yang had taught He Junxi mathematics and calendar making. Instead, Antoine Thomas' letter probably means He Junxi became a Student Astronomer when Yang was the Director of the Astronomical Bureau.
102 He Junxi was listed as the Supervisor of the Winter Office in the Encroachments calendar of the sixth year of the Kangxi reign (1667), which was submitted to the emperor by the end of the previous year.
103 The Kangxi emperor began to learn mathematics and astronomy from Verbiest in May 1675. See Golvers, *The Astronomia Europaea*, 98–101, 260n89, 262n90; Jami, *Emperor's New Mathematics*, 74–8.
104 *Qing guoshi*, 4: 625. Cf. Zhao et al., *Qingshi gao*, 1666, omits the sentence "The Old Method shall not be abandoned."
105 *Xichao ding'an*, 124.
106 The Rescue Ritual was held only for eclipses whose magnitudes were greater than one *fen* (10% of the diameter). SL 4: 7744–5. See also Chapter 6, Section 6.1.
107 *Xichao ding'an*, 124.
108 Ibid., 123–5.
109 SL 4: 790. See *Xichao ding'an*, 125–7 for Verbiest's original memorial.
110 *Qing guoshi*, 4: 625, SL 4: 790.
111 Ibid.
112 *Xichao ding'an*, 125–7.
113 *Qing guoshi*, 4: 625, SL 4: 790.
114 *Xichao ding'an*, 127.
115 *Qing guoshi*, 4: 625; SL 4: 804.
116 Qu, "Qingdai Qintianjian," 50.
117 *Xichao ding'an*, 169.
118 QJZ KX (BJ), B011722–3.

Bibliography

Abbreviations for Archival and Published Sources

CKSB: *Jindai Zhongguo shiliao congkan sanbian* 近代中國史料叢刊三編, edited by Shen Yunlong 沈雲龍. 850 vols. Taipei: Wenhai chubanshe, 1982.

IHP: Neige daku dang'an 內閣大庫檔案. Institute of History and Philology of Academia Sinica, Taipei. http://archive.ihp.sinica.edu.tw/mctkm2/index.html
GYQX: *Guanyuan quanxuan shiliao* 官員銓選史料 of *Qingdai lizhi shiliao* 清代吏治史料, edited by Ren Mengqiang 任夢強. 34 vols. Beijing: Xianzhuang shuju, 2004.
QGLL: *Qingdai guanyuan lüli dang'an quanbian* 清代官員履歷檔案全編. Edited by Qin Guojing 秦國經. 30 vols. Shanghai: Huadong shifan daxue chubanshe, 1997.
QHD JQ: *Qinding Da Qing huidian (Jiaqing chao)* 欽定大清會典 (嘉慶朝) [1818]. CKSB 631–40.
QHD KX: *Da Qing huidian (Kangxi chao)* 大清會典 (康熙朝) [1690]. CKSB 711–30.
QHD QL: *Qinding Da Qing huidian* 欽定大清會典 [1764]. SKQS 619.
QHD YZ: *Da Qing huidian (Yongzheng chao)* 大清會典 (雍正朝) [1732]. CKSB 761–90.
QHDSL GX: *Qinding Da Qing huidian shili* 欽定大清會典事例 [1899]. XXSK 798–814.
QHDZL QL: *Qinding Da Qing huidian zeli* 欽定大清會典則例 [1764]. SKQS 620–5.
QJZ KX (BJ): *Qingdai qijuzhuce, Kangxi chao* 清代起居注冊, 康熙朝. Edited by Zou Ailian 鄒愛蓮. 32 vols. Beijing: Zhonghua shuju, 2009.
SKQS: *Yingyin wenyuange sikuquanshu* 景印文淵閣四庫全書. 1500 vols. Taipei: Taipei shangwu yinshuguan, 1986.
SL: *Qing shilu* 清實錄. 60 vols. Beijing: Zhonghua shuju, 1985.
XXSK: *Xuxiu sikuquanshu* 續修四庫全書. 1800 vols. Shanghai: Shanghai guji chubanshe, 2002.

Other Sources

An Shuangcheng 安雙成, trans and ed. *Qingchu xiyang chuanjiaoshi Manwen dang'an yiben* 清初西洋傳教士滿文檔案譯本. Zhengzhou: Daxiang chubanshe, 2014.
Antai 安泰 et al. *Qinding xuanze lishu* 欽定選擇曆書 [1685]. Taipei: National Central Library, Microfilm, 00515226.
Beijing tushuguan chubanshe guji yingyinshi 北京圖書館出版社古籍影印室, ed. *Guojia tushuguancang Mingdai Datongliri huibian* 國家圖書館藏明代大統曆日彙編. 6 vols. Beijing: Beijing tushuguan chubanshe, 2007.
Da Qing Kangxi liunian wuxing lingfan shixianli 大清康熙六年五星凌犯時憲曆. Qingdai wenxian dangce quanwen yingxiang ziliaoku 清代文獻檔冊全文影像資料庫. National Palace Museum, Taipei. http://npmhost.npm.gov.tw/ttscgi/ttswebfile?@@A185F981B38629F0A856
Ge Dingyi 戈定一, ed. *Luoyang Geshi zongpu shiliujuan* 洛陽戈氏宗譜十六卷. 16 vols. Jiangsu: Wenxintang, 1949. Shanghai Library. 923668–83. https://jiapu.library.sh.cn/#/jiapu:STJP003477
Huang Bolu 黃伯祿. *Zhengjiao fengbao* 正教奉褒 [1884]. In *Zhongguo Tianzhujiao shiji huibian* 中國天主教史籍彙編, 445–575, edited by Chen Fangzhong 陳方中. Taipei: Furen daxue chubanshe, 2003.
Kangxi wushiyinian dengkelu 康熙五十一年登科錄. Vol. 14 of *Zhongguo keju wenxian conglu* 中國科舉文獻叢錄. Beijing: Quanguo suowei fuzh zhongxin, 2010.
Kangxi wushiyinian renchenke huishi yibaijiushiwuming sandai jinshi lüli 康熙五十一年壬辰科會試一百九十五名三代進士履歷. Disc 2 of *Dengkelu* 登科錄. Tokyo: Kokuritsu kōbunshokan, 2012.
Kong Anguo 孔安國 et al. *Shangshu zhushu* 尚書注疏. SKQS 54: 1–450.
Li Wei 李衛 et al. *Jifu tongzhi* 畿輔通志 [1735]. SKQS 504–6.

Ming Qintianjian 明欽天監. *Da Ming Datong li* 大明大統曆 [1368–1644]. Taipei: National Central Library, Microfilms, 305.3 06315–38.
Qing guoshi, Jiayetang chaoben 清國史嘉業堂鈔本. 14 vols. Beijing: Zhonghua shuju, 1993.
Ruan Yuan 阮元 et al. *Chouren zhuan huibian* 疇人傳彙編. 2 vols. Taipei: Shijie shuju, 1982.
Schall, Johann Adam. *Minli puzhu jiehuo* 民曆鋪註解惑 [1662]. XXSK 1040: 1–16.
Shunzhi yuping jingguan zhimingce 順治御屏京官職名冊. In *Wenxian congbian* 文獻叢編, nos. 27, 28. Beijing: National Palace Museum, 1935.
Xichao ding'an 熙朝定案. In *Xichao chongzhongji Xichao ding'an (wai san zhong)* 熙朝崇正集 熙朝定案 (外三種), edited by Han Qi 韓琦 and Wu Min 吳旻, 43–200. Beijing: Zhonghua shuju, 2006.
Xu Guangqi 徐光啟 et al. "Zhili yuanqi" 治曆緣起. In *Chongzhen lishu fu Xiyang xinfa lishu zengkan shizhong* 崇禎曆書 附西洋新法曆書增刊十種, edited by Pan Naihui 潘鼐匯, 1545–752. Shanghai: Shanghai guji chubanshe, 2009.
Yang Guangxian 楊光先. "Budeyi" 不得已. In *Tianzhujiao dongchuan wenxian xubian* 天主教東傳文獻續編, edited by Wu Xiangxiang 吳湘湘, 1069–332. Taipei: Taiwan xuesheng shuju, 1966.
Yao Yuxiang 姚雨薌, and Hu Yangshan 胡仰山, eds. *Da Qing lüli huitong xinzuan* 大清律例會通新纂. CKSB 211–20.
Zhao Erxun 趙爾巽 et al. *Qingshi gao* 清史稿. 48 vols. Beijing: Zhonghua shuju, 1976.

Secondary Sources

Chang Ping-Ying 張秉瑩. "Shidai bianjuzhong de chouren jiazu—yi Mingmo Qingchu de Qingtianjian Hejia weili" 時代變局中的疇人家族—以明末清初的欽天監何家為例. *Hanxue yanjiu* 漢學研究 36, no. 2 (2018): 127–60.
Chu, Pingyi. "Scientific Dispute in the Imperial Court: The 1664 Calendar Case." *Chinese Science* 14 (1997): 7–34.
Cullen, Christopher, and Catherine Jami. "Christmas 1668 and after: How Jesuit Astronomy Was Restored to Power in Beijing." *Journal for the History of Astronomy* 51, no. 1 (2020): 3–50.
Golvers, Noel. *The* Astronomia Europaea *of Ferdinand Verbiest, S. J.: (Dillingen, 1687); Text, Translation, Notes and Commentaries*. Nettetal: Steyler Verlag, 1993.
Han Qi 韓琦. "'Zili jingshen' yu lisuan huodong—Kangqian zhiji wenren dui xixue taidu zhi gaibian ji qi beijing" '自立精神' 與曆算活動—康乾之際文人對西學態度之改變及其背景. *Ziran kexueshi yanjiu* 自然科學史研究 21, no. 3 (2002): 210–21.
Huang Yi-Long 黃一農. "Yang Guangxian jiashi yu shengping kao" 楊光先家世與生平考. *Guoli bianyiguan guankan* 國立編譯館館刊 19, no. 2 (1990): 15–28.
Huang Yi-Long 黃一農 and Chang Chi-Cheng 張志誠. "Zhongguo chuantong houqishuo de yanjin yu shuaitui" 中國傳統候氣說的演進與衰頹. *Tsinghua xuebao* 清華學報 23, no. 2 (1993): 125–47.
Jami, Catherine. *The Emperor's New Mathematics: Western Learning and Imperial Authority during the Kangxi Reign (1662–1722)*. New York: Oxford University Press, 2012.
———. "Revisiting the Calendar Case (1664–1669): Science, Religion, and Politics in Early Qing Beijing." *The Korean Journal for the History of Science* 37, no. 2 (2015): 459–77.

Ma Weihua 馬偉華. *Lifa, zongjiao yu huangquan: Ming Qing zhiji Zhongxi lifa zhizheng zaiyanjiu* 曆法，宗教與皇權：明清之際中西曆法之爭再研究. Beijing: Zhonghua shuju, 2019.

Needham, Joseph, and Wang Ling. *Science and Civilisation in China, Vol. 3: Mathematics and the Science of the Heavens and the Earth*. Cambridge: Cambridge University Press, 1959.

Qu Chunhai 屈春海. "Qingdai Qintianjian ji Shixianke zhiguan nianbiao" 清代欽天監暨時憲科職官年表. *Zhongkuo keji shiliao* 中國科技史料 18, no. 3 (1997): 45–71.

Shi Yumin 史玉民. "Qing Qintianjian Tianwenke zhiguan nianbiao" 清欽天監天文科職官年表. *Zhongkuo keji shiliao* 中國科技史料 21, no. 1 (2000): 34–47.

Shi Yunli 石云里, Li Liang 李亮, and Li Huifang 李輝芳. "Cong *Xuande shinian yue wuxing lingfan* kan Huihui lifa zai Mingchao de shiyong" 從《宣德十年月五星凌犯》看回回曆法在明朝的使用. *Ziran kexueshi yanjiu* 自然科學史研究 32, no. 2 (2013): 156–64.

Väth, Alfons. *Johann Adam Schall von Bell SJ: Missionar in China, kaiserlicher Astronom und Ratgeber am Hofe von Peking, 1592–1666* [1933]. Nettetal: Steyler Verlag, 1991.

Witek, John W., ed. *Ferdinand Verbiest (1623–1688): Jesuit Missionary, Scientist, Engineer and Diplomat*. Nettetal: Steyler Verlag, 1994.

Zhou Weiqiang 周維強. "Yuancang Qingdai *Yue wuxing lingfan shixianli* chutan" 院藏清代《月五星凌犯時憲曆》初探. *Gugong wenwu yuekan* 故宮文物月刊 7, no. 413 (2017): 74–85.

5 Emperors and the He Brothers

5.1 Imperial Empowerment

On the twenty-fifth day of the third month of the fifty-second year of the Kangxi reign (April 19, 1713), the emperor invited 1,846 senior civilians and officials, who came to Beijing from all over the country to celebrate his sixtieth birthday,[1] to a grand banquet held in front of the palace known as the Changchun Garden (*Changchun yuan* 暢春園). To show his appreciation and respect, the emperor personally attended the banquet and ordered junior members of the royal family to serve wine to these guests.[2] According to *The First Collection of the Imperial Birthday Ceremony* (*Wanshou shengdian chuji* 萬壽盛典初集), in which the proceedings of the birthday celebration were recorded in detail, among the guests sitting in the first row of the banquet was a 70-year-old official from the Astronomical Bureau called He Junxi 何君錫.[3] He Junxi spent his entire life working for the Astronomical Bureau, and he had reached the highest position in the Calendar Section four decades earlier.[4] However, because the Kangxi emperor did not appreciate his passion for the Old Method—namely, the Great Concordance system of calendar making—he never advanced into the Bureau directorate.

In contrast to He Junxi's stagnant career, imperial grace was currently shining on his sons. *The First Collection of the Imperial Birthday Ceremony* mentions three of He Junxi's sons: He Guozhu 何國柱, He Guozong 何國宗, and He Guodong 何國棟. In the paragraph that describes a special embassy to Korea, Calendar Manager He Guozhu was listed among the members handpicked by the emperor.[5] In another section, "Praises Written by Courtiers of the Studio for Cultivating the Youth (*Mengyangzhai* 蒙養齋)," He Guozong, a Hanlin Academician (*Hanlinyuan shujishi* 翰林院庶吉士), and He Guodong, a Provincial Graduate (*juren* 舉人, "selected person"), presented their poetry.[6] In the last decade of the Kangxi reign, the emperor himself led a team of young mathematicians to work on the assimilation of Western mathematical sciences. Guozhu, Guozong, and Guodong were among the earliest and principal members of that team. By the end of the Kangxi reign, the He brothers had shown promise in their careers and the future of the He family could not seem brighter. If career stagnation had ever disheartened He Junxi, the Kangxi emperor's appreciation of his sons' mathematical

DOI: 10.4324/9781003008255-5

talent might have been a considerable source of comfort in the last few years of his life.

The Kangxi emperor's favor toward the Jesuits declined after the mid-1700s. To a large part, the success of the Jesuit China mission during the late Ming and early Qing periods was due to the contribution of the Rules of Matteo Ricci (*Li Madou guiju* 利瑪竇規矩), which interpreted the sacrifices to ancestors as social rites that were wholly compatible with Christianity. However, not all missionaries agreed with such an interpretation, and the debates that were prevalent in China and Europe gradually evolved into the Rites Controversy (*Liyi zhi zheng* 禮儀之爭). In 1704, the papal court decided to forbid Chinese Christians to perform traditional rites and sent a legate to communicate this decision to the Kangxi emperor and Chinese Christians. The Kangxi emperor met with the papal legate several times between 1705 and 1706, but he was so irritated by the papal decree that the papal legate was expelled. This incident greatly undermined the emperor's trust in the Catholic mission and even the court Jesuits.[7] In a secret meeting that took place in November 1706, the Kangxi emperor told two of his closest courtiers, Li Guangdi 李光地 and Xiong Cilü 熊賜履:

> Did you know that the Westerners have become troublemakers? They even condemned Confucius. The reason that I have been treating them well is merely to utilize their skills. The calendric and mathematical skills [introduced by the Westerners] are indeed great. You both are scholars. When meeting with local officials and those who can understand the reasons, let them know my true intention.[8]

The Kangxi emperor had employed the Jesuits to make the state calendar for more than three decades, and he had personally acquired considerable mathematical knowledge from them. He studied intensively under Verbiest's direction for more than five months in 1675 and then from 1690 to the mid-1690s, under the mentorship of Joachim Bouvet (1656–1730) and Jean-François Gerbillon (1654–1707), Antoine Thomas (1644–1709), and Tomás Pereira (1645–1708).[9] The Kangxi emperor was famous for his interest in personally carrying out astronomical observations.[10] However, his growing suspicion of the Jesuits may well have motivated his interest in verifying the astronomical calculations they had produced.

Around mid-1711, the Kangxi emperor's suspicion turned into anger. While enjoying the summer retreat in Chengde, the emperor found that the time of the summer solstice he observed did not match with his calculation. He immediately sought explanations from the Jesuits, but their answers did not satisfy him.[11] To be sure, it is difficult to find the time of the solstice precisely by shadow observations, as the emperor attempted, because of the very slow change of the sun's noon altitude around the date of a solstice.[12] However, the emperor must have seen himself as a careful and experienced observer. The Jesuits' explanations for the possible causes of observational errors did not seem acceptable to him. Worse, the emperor thought the Jesuits' explanations were nothing but excuses for covering up their mistakes in calendars. In response to a palace memorial submitted by

Director Philippus Maria Grimaldi (1639–1712), Vice-Director Bernard-Kilian Stumpf (1655–1720), and Astronomical Bureau officials, the Kangxi emperor angrily wrote, "How despicable you are!"[13] The emperor did not keep the anger and distrust to himself. A few days later, he criticized the Jesuits on a palace memorial submitted by Hesu 和素, who had been in charge of delivering the communication between the emperor and Jesuit missionaries, "No matter how worried they are, this is their imperial calendar. At this time, they can be stubborn. Wait until I return to the imperial palace and [have them] calculate in front of me, probably [they will] know it [the results]."[14] In September 1711, he again wrote on a memorial submitted by Hesu, "Nowadays the Westerners' words have become inconsistent. All of you shall take precautions with them."[15] On November 25, 1711, Grimaldi requested the emperor to permit him to retire due to his old age. Although most Directors of the Astronomical Bureau remained in their posts until they died and Grimaldi was once a trusted courtier, the Kangxi emperor immediately approved the old man's request.[16] In what was likely a gesture of warning to the Jesuits, the Kangxi emperor publicly commented on the incident of the summer solstice:

> I have constantly paid attention to astronomy and the method of calendar making. The principles of the Western system are correct, but in the long run, detailed measurements are bound to have some errors. This summer solstice, the Astronomical Bureau memorialized me that it would occur at the seventh quarter of the *wu* hour 午正三刻 (12:45). I carefully measured the sun's shadow and [the summer solstice] was at the ninth minutes of the third quarter of the *wu* hour 午初三刻九分 (11:54). At this moment, the error is little, but I am afraid that several decades later, the accumulated error will become excessive. . . . This point was indeed proved, and it is not like the compositions written by scholars that shrink away from responsibility by empty words. Now let us wait and see how the coming winter solstice will be.[17]

It is unknown how well the Jesuits' prediction of the winter solstice satisfied the Kangxi emperor; however, by the end of the next winter, the Kangxi emperor had begun to take the whole issue of ensuring the imperial state had a reliable supply of mathematical knowledge into his own hands.

Between late 1711 and 1713, the Kangxi emperor organized a new group of mathematicians. He ordered the Ministry of Rites to hold special examinations to recruit court mathematicians, who later were referred to as 'personnel serving in mathematics' (*xiaoli suanfa renyuan* 效力算法人員).[18] There are not enough historical records to provide a clear understanding of exactly what the content of these examinations was. Nonetheless, according to Wang Hong 王玒, an official who had passed the examination, the examination took place in April 1712.[19] The Kangxi emperor also recruited mathematicians through his courtiers' personal network. For instance, as a result of Li Guangdi's recommendation, the Kangxi emperor summoned Chen Houyao 陳厚耀 (1648–1722) to Beijing in early 1708.[20] Mei Juecheng 梅瑴成, a grandson of Mei Wending 梅文鼎 (1633–1721),

the famous mathematician of the Qing period, was also summoned to join the group of personnel serving in mathematics in July 1712.[21]

The Kangxi emperor's personal involvement in the process of recruiting and training personnel serving in mathematics greatly elevated their social status. When the examination took place, the Kangxi emperor personally tested the examinees and chose 42 of them as personnel serving in mathematics.[22] To attend a test that was personally administered by the monarch was an honor similar to attending the final stage of the civil service examination, in which the monarch chose the essay questions and decided the ranks of those admitted. This process built a symbolic teacher-student relationship similar to that between the emperor and successful candidates of the examination. In the case of personnel serving in mathematics, the teacher-student relationship was more intimate than merely symbolic. In the summer of 1712, the emperor brought a small group of mathematicians to the Chengde Summer Palace (*Chengde bishu shanzhuang* 承德避暑山莊). According to the *History of the Qing Empire,*

> In the fifth month of the fifty-first year (June 1712), the emperor went to the Summer Palace. Suzhou Prefecture Instructor (*Suzhou fu jiaoshou* 蘇州府教授) Chen Houyao, Supervisor of the Five Offices of the Astronomical Bureau He Junxi's sons, Guozhu and Guozong, imperially chosen Official Student Minggantu and former Vice-Director [of the Astronomical Bureau] Chengde 成德 were ordered to go with him. They served and stayed in Kuangguan 曠觀 located inside the north gate of the palace. [The emperor] provided many treatises from imperial secret collection for them to study. From time to time the emperor personally went [to Kuangguan] to give his earnest teachings. He allowed them to ask questions directly as if [the emperor and they were] teacher and students.[23]

Having a whole empire to rule, the Kangxi emperor surely had very limited time to teach personnel serving in mathematics face to face. But no doubt they studied under the emperor's attentive guidance. They won a prestigious status for being the emperor's personal students. The Kangxi emperor's favor of the newly recruited personnel serving in mathematics must have been well known among his courtiers. In addition to the "Praises Written by Courtiers of the Studio for Cultivating the Youth," a drawing in *The First Collection* illustrating the imperial procession clearly shows that "fourteen Manchu and Han personnel serving in mathematics" gathered at a temple to pray for the emperor's longevity.[24] This suggests that the high ministers preparing for the grand celebration of the emperor's sixtieth birthday had thought the presence of personnel serving in mathematics a must and thus gave them a notable place.

Having gathered enough mathematicians around him, the Kangxi emperor commenced his project of compiling mathematical treatises. After the grand birthday celebration, the emperor again went to Chengde for summer retreat and brought with him some personnel serving in mathematics. In July 1713, the compilation of treatises on music and mathematics began at the Chengde Summer

Emperors and the He Brothers 103

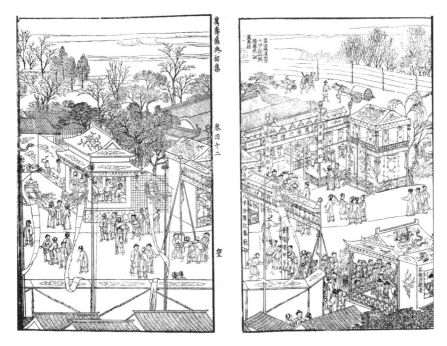

Figure 5.1 Personnel serving in mathematics in *The First Collection of the Imperial Birthday Ceremony*. Text at the upper left corner of the right page: 14 Manchu and Han personnel serving in mathematics sincerely chant the Longevity Sutra (*Wanshou jing* 萬壽經) at this Xinglong Temple (*Xinglong an* 興隆庵). Courtesy of the National Central Library, Taiwan.

Palace. The compilation project was further formalized after the emperor returned to Beijing. He assigned the Studio for Cultivating the Youth (*Mengyang zhai* 蒙養齋) in the imperial Changchun Garden as the compilation project's office, which was referred to, amongst other titles, as the Office of Compiling Mathematical Treatises (*Xiu suanshu chu* 修算書處).[25] Yinzhi 胤祉 (1677–1732), the third son of the Kangxi emperor, was the chief leader of the project. Personnel serving in mathematics were given another examination to select experts to staff the Office of Compiling Mathematical Treatises.[26] In the following years, the Kangxi emperor's passion about this compilation project showed no sign of declining. He corrected the draft submitted by the Office on a daily basis. Moreover, the emperor brought some personnel serving in mathematics with him whenever he went to the Chengde Palace so that the compilation project would not be interrupted.[27] In 1719, the special examinations in mathematics were held again. Twenty-eight new members were added to the Office of Compiling Mathematical Treatises to increase its capacity of calculation.[28]

After nine years of diligent work, the compilation project reached its final stage in July 1722.[29] The Office of Compiling Mathematical Treatises memorialized the Kangxi emperor that in addition to the first two finished treatises, the *Exact Meaning of the Pitch-pipes* (*Lülü zhengyi* 律呂正義) and the *Essence of Numbers and Their Principles* (*Shuli jingyun* 數理精蘊), the third and last treatise, the *Book on Calendrical Astronomy in Reverent Accord* (*Qinruo lishu* 欽若曆書), was currently in the final stage of proofreading and printing. The whole set of treatises, titled *Origins of Mathematical Harmonics and Astronomy* (*Lüli yuanyuan* 律曆淵源), would be completely finished in the coming spring.[30] The Kangxi emperor was very pleased with this accomplishment. He joyfully promised that he would write a preface for the treatise.[31] Unfortunately, the Kangxi emperor passed away on December 20, 1722.[32] He did not live to see the publication of the *Origins of Mathematical Harmonics and Astronomy*, nor did the Office of Compiling Mathematical Treatises ever receive the preface from him.[33]

In 1725, the Essence of Numbers and Their Principles and the *Book on Calendrical Astronomy in Reverent Accord* (renamed to *Thorough Investigation of Astronomical Phenomena, Lixiang kaocheng* 曆象考成) became the textbooks used in the Astronomical Bureau and the guidebooks for calendar making.[34] From then on, the staff members of the Astronomical Bureau did not have to learn directly from the Jesuits. Instead, they were able to learn from the Thorough Investigation of Astronomical Phenomena and the Essence of Numbers and Their Principles and claim the intellectual lineage from the Kangxi emperor instead of the Jesuits. The Jesuits still occupied some posts in the directorate of the Astronomical Bureau, but they became the colleagues of Han and banner officials as opposed to their teachers.

5.2 A Promising Start for the He Brothers

The compilation project led by the Kangxi emperor in the last decade of his rule changed the lives of many individuals and their families. The family of He Junxi and his sons best illustrates this point. Unlike in the Ming era, the descendants of the Qing Astronomical Bureau astronomer families could take any profession they liked. Preparing descendants for the career at the Astronomical Bureau was thus more of a choice than an obligation or mandate. It is quite understandable that, considering his own stagnant career, He Junxi would not want to tie his family's future completely to the Astronomical Bureau. He sent Guozhu to the Astronomical Bureau but let Guozong and Guodong pursue careers as regular government officials by taking the civil service examinations. If the Kangxi emperor had not wanted to cultivate a group of mathematicians and had noticed their mathematical talent, Guozong and Guodong's whole careers probably would not have had any connection with mathematics.

He Guozong was the most successful member of the He family. During a civil service career that lasted 50 years, he served three emperors as a high-ranking court official. Although Guozong never became one of the ministers who assisted the emperors daily in making the most critical political decisions, his specialty in mathematics continued to win the emperors' attention. Projects involving a geographical survey, for instance, were one important area in which the emperors made use of He Guozong's mathematical knowledge. The Yongzheng emperor sent him to inspect flooding in the Grand Canal and Yellow River, and the Qianlong emperor sent him to produce a map of newly conquered Xinjiang.[35] He Guozong's most indisputable value to the court was his administration of the publication of the imperial mathematical treatises. With the exception of the treatises written by the Jesuits, most early Qing official compilation projects of mathematical works were under He Guozong's supervision. He Guozong's excellent mathematical knowledge was undoubtedly the biggest contributory factor to his successful career.

However, He Guozong's original career goal was not related to mathematics. He did not intend to inherit He Junxi's profession as an astronomer at the Astronomical Bureau. According to two memorials written by He Guozong that mentioned his own age, He Guozong was born in 1687.[36] In 1708, when he was merely 22 years old, He Guozong obtained the degree of Provincial Graduate.[37] At such a young age, Guozong had plenty of opportunities to pass the top-level examination for the degree of Metropolitan Graduate and set his goal to become a high minister. Even if he failed, he could still become a District Magistrate (*Zhi xian* 知縣) or Instructor (*Jiao shou* 教授) at a Prefecture-level Confucian School.[38] Either way, Guozong could bring more fame and income to his family by staying in the system of regular civil servant than working for the Astronomical Bureau. On the other hand, because preparing for the civil service examination was tremendously demanding, it is highly unlikely that He Guozong had the time or energy to work at the Astronomical Bureau in his early years. Indeed, no record ever mentions that He Guozong had spent his youth studying or working at the Astronomical Bureau.

He Guozong's training and accomplishment in the civil service examination gave him access to an extended social circle and afforded him a more prestigious status than those who spent their entire working lives in the Astronomical Bureau. For instance, He Guozong became a well-known calligrapher; perhaps he developed the talent of calligraphy while preparing for the civil service examination. Mei Yi 梅釴, son of mathematician Mei Juecheng 梅瑴成, was known to have learned calligraphy from He Guozong.[39] He Guozong's status gave him the opportunity to learn calligraphy from Zhang Zhao 張照 (1691–1745), a grand minister and one of the most famous calligraphers during the Qing period, and to build up their friendship.[40] Such friendship not only was helpful to He Guozong's career in the Qianlong period but also passed on to their descendants. He Guozong's daughter, who was the wife of the seventieth generation Duke Yansheng (*Yansheng gong* 衍聖公, literally means Duke of Fulfilling the Sage), married her daughter to Zhang Zhao's son, Zhang Yingtian 張應田.[41]

He Guozong's career had progressed to a different direction by May 1712. In April 1712, the Kangxi emperor and his high ministers went through a long process of choosing Metropolitan Graduate degree candidates.[42] However, after diligently reading hundreds of examination essays written by Provincial Graduates, the emperor still felt that he had not found enough well-qualified candidates. He ordered the ministers to recommend and to re-examine the failed essays, "particularly those written by the Provincial Graduates working at the book compilation departments for some of them were very knowledgeable."[43] The purpose of the civil service examination was, after all, not to reward the best scholars but to select government officials who could best serve the emperor's needs. Therefore, it was perhaps through recommendations from courtiers like Li Guangdi, who knew the Kangxi emperor's intention to recruit a group of mathematicians and who had been closely involved in the process of grading the essays and choosing candidates, that He Guozong was given a special permission to take the palace examination (*dianshi* 殿試) alongside the other candidates.[44] He Guozong successfully passed the palace examination and earned the Metropolitan Graduate degree. Soon the emperor granted him more honor by admitting him to the Hanlin Academy (*Hanlinyuan* 翰林院).[45]

He Guozong was one of the earliest personnel serving in mathematics to receive the honorary civil service degrees from the emperor. Such an imperial honor indicates that the Kangxi emperor had decided to groom He Guozong to become one of the core members of mathematical projects and thus might not want him to spend further effort in preparing for the civil service examination. After He Guozong, Mei Juecheng was given the honorary Provincial Graduate degree in 1713 and two years later the honorary Metropolitan Graduate degree.[46] Wang Lansheng 王蘭生 (1679–1737), a young disciple of Li Guangdi and a specialist in phonology and music, was also awarded the Provincial Graduate degree in 1713.[47] Despite the fact that Wang failed the metropolitan examination in 1721, the Kangxi emperor allowed him to take the palace examination directly.[48] Both Mei Juecheng and Wang Lansheng passed the palace examination and became Hanlin Academicians. Unlike other personnel serving in mathematics who gained a temporary favorable status from the Kangxi emperor's personal empowerment, the high civil service degree ensured that He Guozong benefitted from a far better and more powerful career starting point, which afforded him many more chances to navigate the bureaucratic system. When the Kangxi emperor formally commenced the project of the *Origins of Mathematical Harmonics and Astronomy*, he made He Guozong the leader of the compilers by placing He Guozong right under Yinzhi and above all the other personnel serving in mathematics.[49]

He Guozhu and He Guodong were also personnel serving in mathematics. He Guozhu's name first appears with Guozong's on the records describing the Kangxi emperor's summer retreat to Chengde in 1712, in which they were referred to as "sons of the Supervisor of the Five Offices of the Astronomical Bureau, He Junxi."[50] But unlike Guozong and Guodong, Guozhu's name did not appear among the degree holders listed in the *General History of the Capital Region* (*Jifu tongzhi* 畿輔通志). This means that even if Guozhu had studied for the civil service examination, he did not obtain a degree higher than the District Graduate (*shengyuan* 生員). According to the contents of a decree issued by the Yongzheng emperor in 1723, which will be discussed further in the next section, we know that Guozhu is Guozong and Guodong's elder brother.[51] Thus, it is reasonable to assert that Guozhu followed in his father's footsteps to become an astronomer and had started working at the Astronomical Bureau in his youth. This way Guozhu could bring additional income to the family and help to pay for his younger brothers' studies.

Several pieces of evidence suggest that He Guozhu had distinct talent and ability. First, it is worth noting that Guozhu was not the only member of the He family who worked at the Astronomical Bureau around 1712. For instance, He Guochen 何國宸, another son of He Junxi, states in his official résumé that he became a Student Astronomer in 1704 and then a Calendar Section Erudite in 1710.[52] The fact that the Kangxi emperor picked Guozhu, not Guochen, to go to the Chengde Summer Palace suggests that Guozhu possessed mathematical ability superior to that of his brothers. Second, both the annual calendar published in 1713 and *The First Collection* list He Guozhu as a Calendar Manager.[53] Therefore, besides years of qualified work at the Astronomical Bureau, Guozhu must have successfully demonstrated his mathematical knowledge in calendar making to be awarded the post of Calendar Manager in 1712.[54] Third, according to the description of the special embassy to Korea in *The First Collection*, Guozhu was a Calendar Manager of civil service rank five, an unusually high rank equivalent to that of the Astronomical Bureau Director.[55] There is no known historical record to explain how He Guozhu acquired his rank. Nonetheless, it is reasonable to assert that his professional performance greatly exceeded requirements.

He Guozhu's embassy to Korea is worthy of further analysis. On the surface, it seems to be a routine embassy whose purpose was to demonstrate the Qing's authority over its tributary state Korea. As such, Qing state records do not mention what He Guozhu and the other members of the embassy had done during the trip. However, Korean records provide interesting insight into the real purpose of this embassy. The *Veritable Records of the Chosŏn Dynasty* (*Chaoxian Lichao shilu* 朝鮮李朝實錄) states that having a Calendar Manager included in the embassy was "something that never happened before."[56] Indeed, as early as 1682, the Kangxi emperor had doubted the usefulness of including an Astronomical Bureau official in a diplomatic embassy and allowed such a regulation to be neglected.[57] One wonders why 30 years later, the emperor suddenly recall this regulation and included a Calendar Manager to the embassy. It turns out that the emperor had a use of He Guozhu's mathematical expertise for geographical inspection. According to the *Veritable Records of the Chosŏn Dynasty*, the Qing embassy requested to see the map of Korea upon arriving in Seoul. The Korean court hesitated, concerned for its national security, yet this hesitation did not come as a surprise to the Qing embassy. The Qing ambassadors showed the Korean court a map of the entire Korean kingdom they had brought from China and demanded that the Korean courtiers provide a comparison.[58] He Guozhu probably did not draw the map brought from China, but he would undoubtedly have had the ability to compare the accuracy between two different maps. It is even possible that He Guozhu had performed similar assessments all the way along the route from Beijing to Seoul to verify the map's accuracy.

He Guozhu also met with Korean mathematicians and astronomers in a more relaxed atmosphere. In the beginning, the Qing ambassador introduced He Guozhu's mathematics as "the fourth best under heaven" and attempted to provoke competitions between both parties.[59] The mutual challenges continued for several days, but the rivalry served to strengthen the communication between Qing and Korean official astronomers. Soon after He Guozhu and the other Qing officials left, a Korean minister suggested that the next embassy to the Qing should include astronomer Hŏ Wŏn 許遠 because "when the Calendar Manager came here, Hŏ Wŏn learned mathematical methods and instruments [from him]."[60] Moreover, Hŏ Wŏn could remind He Guozhu of his promise that "after I go back [to Beijing], I will find the treatises and instruments that your country does not have and give them to you."[61] In the next chapter, we will see how the He family played an important role in the development of mathematical astronomy between the Qing and Korea until the mid-eighteenth century.

He Guozhu's performance during the Korea trip had so pleased the Kangxi emperor that he made an exceptional arrangement for Guozhu's career. On November 10, 1713, the Kangxi emperor told the Minister of Revenue (*Hubu shangshu* 戶部尚書):

> In your ministry, the calculation of monetary affairs and grain supply all rely on clerical subofficials. Their calculation only can give an approximation. Astronomical Bureau official He Guozhu currently serves me at the inner court. His mathematics is excellent. I will make him an official of your ministry. This arrangement shall be beneficial to the calculation of monetary affairs and grain supply. No matter if the affair is complicated or superfluous, he can understand it instantly. I cannot guarantee his personal integrity, but he seems a prudent and honest person. He shall be a Supernumerary Vice Department Director (*Ewai yuanwailang* 額外員外郎) until a vacancy arises. Have him work at both places [the Ministry of Revenue (*Hubu* 戶部) and the Astronomical Bureau] concurrently.[62]

The Kangxi emperor's words show that he thought mathematics should not be limited to calendar making and music. Finances and resource management of the government, for instance, could benefit from better execution of mathematical calculations, and a clear-minded mathematician could be a good official, even though he did not hold any civil service degree. Therefore, instead of turning the Studio for Cultivating the Youth into a permanent scientific research institution like the French Royal Academy of Sciences, the Kangxi emperor might have intentionally kept the Studio for Cultivating the Youth as a temporary organization so that after the mathematical treatises were finished, he could send his disciples to various positions in the government.[63] Probably due to his distinct ability in mathematics, the emperor chose He Guozhu as a test case.

Other records further prove the Kangxi emperor's interests in what a mathematician could contribute to the government. In March 1714, Guozhu applied for mourning leave, presumably over the death of his father because He Junxi's name disappeared from the state calendar's roster.[64] Because Guozhu held two jobs concurrently, the Ministry of Personnel asked the Kangxi emperor whether He Guozhu should take the normal mourning leave of three years as a Vice Department Director or the shortened mourning leave of three months that the regulations specially prescribed for officials of the Astronomical Bureau.[65] The Kangxi emperor replied:

> Have the Vice Department Director of the Ministry of Revenue He Guozhu take the mourning leave as a regular official. He is quite familiar with calculation. When the Ministry has accounting cases need verification, ask him to come to do the calculation. He Guozhu's household finance is fragile. Give him the salary as usual.[66]

Certainly, the emperor's words again show that he valued He Guozhu's mathematical ability and that he held the He family in high esteem. More importantly, the emperor's reply affirms that he did not want to interrupt the experiment of extending the use of mathematics into regular governmental institutions.

Unfortunately, the Kangxi emperor's ministers did not always share his interest in extending the use of mathematicians in the government. Zhao Shenqiao 趙申喬 (1644–1720), a famous incorruptible Confucian scholar, best illustrates this point.[67] When He Guozhu finished his mourning leave in November 1716 and was ready to return to work, the Kangxi emperor had to demand that Zhao Shenqiao, then the Minister of Revenue, produce a detailed report on why he did not appreciate having a mathematician such as He Guozhu serving at his ministry. The Kangxi emperor decreed the following:

> I gave He Guozhu exceptional promotion to Department Secretary (*Zhushi* 主事) because he is good at calculation. Previously, I had asked [the Minister of Revenue] Zhao Shenqiao whether such an arrangement was beneficial to the accounting tasks of the Ministry of Revenue. *Zhao Shenqiao said that in his ministry, everything related to monetary affairs and grain supply had to be calculated according to fixed rules. Other officials also know how to calculate and verify [the results]. There is no use for him.* Is it because He Guozhu has done something else wrong? Have Zhao Shenqiao answer my question and temporarily withhold the post that should be given to He Guozhu.[68]

Zhao Shenqiao could not pinpoint any fault He Guozhu had, but his attitude did not seem to change.[69] Months later, on another occasion of selecting officials, the Kangxi emperor bitterly complained:

> I sent a person good at calculation to your minister, hoping that he will be beneficial to the calculation of monetary affairs and grain supply. Zhao Shenqiao stubbornly refused to keep him and sent him back. Now you intend to put the blame [of using wrong people] to me by sending the candidates as many as the vacant positions needed to be filled. How is it possible that I consent?[70]

110 *Emperors and the He Brothers*

However, the Kangxi emperor did not give up. He sent He Guozhu to the Ministry of War (*Bingbu* 兵部).

Born in 1690, He Guodong was a younger brother of He Guozong.[71] It seems unlikely that Guodong had accompanied the Kangxi emperor to the Chengde Summer Palace in 1712 because the *History of the Qing Empire* does not mention him. Nonetheless, like his two brothers, Guodong's mathematical talent attracted the emperor's special attention. He also became one of the personnel serving in mathematics and worked at the Studio for Cultivating the Youth. In December 1714, Yinzhi suggested re-measuring the North Pole's altitude at various spots. The Kangxi emperor picked seven people from those who worked at the Studio for Cultivating the Youth for such tasks and He Guodong was given the responsibility to carry out the observations in Guangdong.[72]

Like Guozong, Guodong did not originally intend to work at the Astronomical Bureau and had instead commenced his career as a regular civil servant. Indeed, Guodong had a promising start to his career in civil service. He became a Provincial Graduate in 1713.[73] The Kangxi emperor did not give Guodong an honorary Metropolitan Graduate degree; however, this was probably because he had already given one to Guozong and did not want to treat the He brothers with excessive favor. The intense work involved in compiling the *Origins of Mathematical Harmonics and Astronomy* might have delayed Guodong's pursuit of the Metropolitan Graduate degree. But, as the following will show, the Provincial Graduate degree was high enough to set a solid foundation for He Guodong's career in civil service.

By August 1721, the compilation of the *Origins of Mathematical Harmonics and Astronomy* was largely finished, and the Kangxi emperor began the process of dispatching the personnel serving in mathematics who had been working at the Office of Compiling Mathematics Treatises since 1713 to new positions in the government.[74] To ensure his beloved disciples were rewarded handsomely, the Kangxi emperor decreed:

> All these people were handpicked by myself. I ordered them to learn mathematics and to work in the inner court. They are different from those serving at outer-court offices. Moreover, the Office of Compiling Mathematics Treatises is very strict. Whoever works there has to be very diligent. Grade the members listed on the memorial, discuss how to reward them, and then report back to me.[75]

These personnel serving in mathematics were divided into three grades according to their contribution. He Guodong was among the 11 people who received the highest grade.[76] By the end of the year, He Guodong became the Dingzhou Prefect (*Dingzhou zhifu* 汀州知府).[77] The importance of the Provincial Graduate degree can be further appreciated by comparing the position offered to He Guodong with the one afforded to Minggantu. Minggantu was also given the highest grade, but he held only the degree of District Graduate.[78] The position Minggantu obtained after leaving the Office of Compiling Mathematics Treatises was the Supervisor of the Five Offices at the Astronomical Bureau, which was of civil service rank 6B.[79] In contrast, a Prefect was of rank 4A, which was even higher than that of the Astronomical Bureau Director.[80] Not to mention that a Prefect could accumulate a significant fortune for He Guodong much easier and faster than a Bureau Director could.

When the Kangxi emperor died in December 1722, the future of the He brothers' careers looked promising. He Guozong was a Hanlin Academician. Guozhu was both a high official of the Astronomical Bureau and a middle-ranking official in the Ministry of War, and Guodong was a Prefect. The He family's strategy to send some members to work for the Astronomical Bureau while others pursued civil service degrees worked out well. Surely, the family's past service records had deepened the emperor's trust, and the mathematical knowledge that the family exhibited significantly expedited their career progression. However, the future of the He family and the brothers' careers would depend on the next emperor. In the rest of this chapter, we will see how the Yongzheng emperor, who ruled with a focus that differed with the preceding emperor, changed the He family's fortune.

5.3 The He Brothers Under the Yongzheng Emperor's Rule

The last two decades of the Kangxi reign were a time of severe competition between the royal princes for the throne. The intensive rivalry among his sons disheartened the Kangxi emperor. Immediately after returning from the summer retreat of 1712, the Kangxi emperor placed the Heir Apparent Yinreng 胤礽 (1674–1725) under permanent house arrest.[81] The aged Kangxi emperor managed to maintain social and political stability to the last day of his life, at which point he was succeeded by Yinzhen 胤禛 (1678–1735), his fourth son and later known as the Yongzheng 雍正 emperor.[82]

The influences of the struggle for the throne to the development of imperial mathematics in the Yongzheng reign surely is worthy of notice but should not be exaggerated. Most importantly, as already shown in the previous section, it was the Kangxi emperor, not Yongzheng, who disbanded personnel serving in mathematics. The Kangxi emperor's intention was to send the mathematicians he trained to serve in various government institutions. The Jesuits might have informed the Kangxi emperor about the European scientific research institutions, but the Mathematics Office at the Studio for Cultivating the Youth was a temporary organization for book compilation. It was founded due to the emperor's distrust to the Jesuits instead of taking up their advice. In short, Yinzhen's succession to the throne did not cause an immediate change in the imperial state's policy on mathematics and astronomy.

Nonetheless, the Yongzheng emperor acted cautiously in order to ensure that his competitors did not rise in fame and strength. In this case, the leader of the group of young and capable mathematicians was Yinzhi, one of the Yongzheng emperor's elder brothers. While the personnel serving in mathematics were dispatched to different local and central governmental institutions according to their individual contribution to the *Origins of Mathematical Harmonics and Astronomy*, the publication of the treatise itself was delayed. When the treatise was printed in 1724, its contents appeared to be intact, and the main compilers' names were listed with their new official titles. However, Yunlu 允祿 (1685–1767), a much younger yet trusted brother of the new emperor, was listed and referred to as the chief leader of the compilation project, and Yinzhi's name (already changed to Yunzhi 允祉) was moved to second place.[83] Through this act, the Yongzheng emperor clearly displayed his intention and authority. From then on, Yunlu replaced Yunzhi as the chief leader in mathematical projects that court mathematicians such as He Guozong and Jesuit missionaries worked on. Only by providing satisfactory service to the new emperor could He Guozong and the other disciples of the late Kangxi emperor continue their prosperous careers.

While the Kangxi emperor focused on the grand policy of imperial mathematics, Yongzheng paid more attention to the details of management. Historians of the Yongzheng period were mostly concerned with the ban on Christianity. In the aspect of Chinese sciences, this was roughly equivalent to terminating the importation of new knowledge and skills from Europe that had greatly stimulated scientific development in the early Qing dynasty. The rest of this chapter is concerned with a different aspect, not the external stimulation, but the internal bureaucratic administration. Using the He brothers as examples, this section focuses on the Yongzheng emperor's management of the group of young mathematicians. It will again demonstrate how the familial relations faired under a different monarch's alternative political focus.

The He brothers' career development in the early years of the Yongzheng reign might seem as great as it was in the last decade of the Kangxi reign. In February 1724, He Guozhu's position within the Astronomical Bureau reached the highest level a Han official could obtain at that time—that of Senior Vice-Director.[84] His post as a regular civil servant advanced, too. By December 1723, he was a Department Director of the Ministry of War (*Bingbu langzhong* 兵部郎中).[85] He Guozong's career also continued to advance as fast as any high degree-holder could wish. In February 1723, the Yongzheng emperor chose him as one of the Imperial Diarists (*Rijiang qijuzhu guan* 日講起居注官). This gave He Guozong plenty of opportunity to observe the monarch and his high ministers. By April 1725, He Guozong was appointed Secretary Concurrently the Vice Minister of Rites (*Neige xueshi jian libu shilang* 內閣學士兼禮部侍郎).[86] He Guodong seemed to be doing as well as his brothers Guozhu and Guozong. In December 1723, Guodong's superiors, Governor-General of Fujian and Zhejiang (*Min-Zhe zongdu* 閩浙總督) Mamboo 滿保 and Governor of Fujian (*Fujian xunfu* 福建巡撫) Huang Guochai 黃國材, felt that Guodong's job performance as the Dingzhou Prefect was so outstanding that he deserved a special recommendation. In a periodical review on all his subordinates, Mamboo described Guozhu as follows:

> He Guodong is capable and he abides by the laws. Minor officials and people respect and obey him. . . . [He Guodong and the other three] are all incorruptible and capable officials. Their names are attached to the list of

recommendations, although they have not yet fulfilled the requirement of holding offices for more than three years. Please consider having the relevant departments make a note of their excellence and grant them a special audience.[87]

However, the He brothers' fortune began to take a different turn. Soon after He Guozhu became the Senior Vice-Director of the Astronomical Bureau, the Yongzheng emperor began to limit the He family's expansion. In April 1724, the Ministry of Personnel submitted a routine memorial to the Yongzheng emperor requesting to promote He Guo'an 何國安 from Erudite to Water Clock Manager. The Yongzheng emperor rejected the request on the grounds that "it is improper to let He Guozhu's family occupy so many posts at the Astronomical Bureau."[88] Notice that the emperor did not ask his ministers to regulate the expansion of all astronomer families but specifically targeted at the He family. Such action signified that the He family was no longer in imperial favor. He Guo'an lose this promotion and there was no record to show that his career ever made further advancement. Moreover, almost none of the He family members in the Astronomical Bureau obtained any promotion until the end of the Yongzheng reign. Worst, the He family would soon lose its most powerful figure in the Astronomical Bureau.

Half a year after reaching the peak, He Guozhu's career as a civil servant came to an abrupt end under the accusation of having special connection with Yunti 允禵 (also known as Yinzhen 胤禎 or Yinti 胤禵), the Yongzheng emperor's younger brother and a strong competitor to the throne. In July 1724, Yunti's principal wife passed away. Soon after, the emperor received a report that Yunti refused to accept the burial site selected for his deceased wife on the grounds that it was an inauspicious place. Angered by his brother but probably trying to maintain a benevolent image, the emperor assigned He Guozhu to re-survey the burial sites. However, He Guozhu's training was on calendar making. Although he was the Senior Vice-Director of the Astronomical Bureau, he might know very little about geomancy. After surveying all the possible burial sites, Guozhu turned in a report that, according to the Yongzheng emperor's words, "did not examine [the sites] in detail but copied the phrases from previous records."[89] The emperor deduced that Guozhu might have accepted Yunti's request attempting to "give me a bad name after the burial by purposely burying her in an inauspicious place."[90] By the end of September 1724, Guozhu was discharged from both positions at the Astronomical Bureau and the Ministry of War.[91] He Guozhu became a scapegoat for the emperor's anger toward his own brother.

He Guodong also became a target of the Yongzheng emperor's suspicion. In July 1724, Mamboo received a secret message from the Yongzheng emperor: "I heard that He Guodong is too young and frivolous and not familiar with the affairs of Personnel Management. Is it really so?"[92] The emperor named not only He Guodong but several officials subordinate to Mamboo. However, Mamboo had made a special recommendation for He Guodong just months earlier; he hesitated about how to answer the emperor's question on He Guodong. Mamboo quickly responded to the emperor that, for various reasons, his impeachments to all but He Guodong had been, or would be, submitted to the proper departments. Then Mamboo wrote cautiously:

> It is true that He Guodong is not very experienced and capable because he is young and this is his first post. However, he is very determined to learn the proper ways. . . . Indeed, he does not take advantage of his position to do anything unethical. Could it be possible to allow me some more months to reinvestigate him? . . . I never had any special connection to He Guodong's family. I dare not favor him.[93]

Mamboo tried to avoid contradicting his previous recommendation on He Guodong and hoped his words would buy more time to reinvestigate not only He Guodong but also the Yongzheng emperor's real intention. Mamboo's declaration of his fairness is noteworthy, for he mentions not the individual He Guodong but the whole He family. It suggests that the He brothers' fame had spread among contemporaries and that the weight of the familial relations factored in the evaluation of a person.

Ironically, the Yongzheng emperor, who in the case of He Guo'an had worried about the overexpansion of the He family, now made a contradictory statement. The emperor once again wrote to Mamboo, this time stating that he was only concerned with a person's job performance, not with his familial relations:

> Do not wrongly impeach He Guodong simply because you heard about the case of He Guozhu. Not to mention that currently I have great use of He Guozong. I never considered whether they were brothers or even father and son. I only care if the individual person has done the right things or not. Handling it fairly is the way to win my appreciation.[94]

Rather than believing the emperor's words, Mamboo decided to impeach He Guodong. Mamboo submitted the impeachment on 6 November 1724, stating that He Guodong "has completely changed" from what he was in the previous year and that "now he does everything capriciously and impatiently." Mamboo claimed that the impeachment was necessary because "an impatient person like him should not be tolerated because he will bungle the local administration."[95]

It turns out that the Yongzheng emperor would use the case of Mamboo and He Guodong as a public demonstration that "in this way, all of you know that I have no prejudice."[96] After receiving Mamboo's impeachment, the Yongzheng emperor made public his previous communications with Mamboo and the reason why He Guozhu was discharged. He criticized that Mamboo's impeachment was nothing more than an improper effort to please him. "If He Guodong is indeed a disqualified official," the emperor commented, "Mamboo should say so frankly when I first asked him."[97] The emperor told his ministers how he thought the familial relations would work in this case: "once He Guodong heard that his elder brother He Guozhu was punished and that I had inquired [about him], he could only be frighten and thus work diligently and carefully."[98] Perhaps waiting to see how his strategy worked out, the Yongzheng emperor made no further reaction to Mamboo's impeachment in the next few months. In May 1725, the Yongzheng emperor consulted Huang Guochai, He Guodong's another superior, and finally decreed, "Since Huang Guochai claims that Prefect He Guodong neither has any voracious action nor any financial deficit, it is suitable to have He stay at his post. The appropriate ministry is to take note [on my verdict]."[99] Mamboo was punished by subtracting two levels of his extra civil rank.[100] He Guodong was allowed to keep his post, but only for a short time. By the end of 1726, He Guodong's career as Dingzhou Prefect ended.[101]

On the other hand, the Yongzheng emperor did have a use for He Guozong. In the same way as previous dynasties, the flood control of the Yellow River and the maintenance of the Grand Canal were crucial to the economic and social stability of the Qing. During the Kangxi emperor's six trips to South China, the inspection of flood preventive work was always an important part of his visit. He even personally conducted the geographical measurements to verify the correctness of his courtiers' suggestions on the construction work and to demonstrate his superior mathematical knowledge. The Yongzheng emperor did not have sufficient mathematical knowledge to carry out the same kind of performance. Therefore, the inspection of flood control work became a task similar to writing a preface for the *Origins of Mathematical Harmonics and Astronomy*: the Yongzheng emperor had to find someone else to do it for him. He Guozong, a court mathematician with sufficient classical training, was an obvious choice for the Yongzheng emperor. In May 1725, around the same time that he rejected Mamboo's impeachment of He Guodong, the Yongzheng emperor made He Guozong a Secretary (*Xueshi* 學士). Three months later, he ordered He Guozong to organize a small team of metropolitan officials to inspect the Canal and Yellow River in the Shandong and Henan area.[102] He Guozong was allowed to choose two assistants from the Astronomical Bureau officials and to bring whatever instruments he needed for the survey. He's team left Beijing on September 26, 1725. For several months, they traveled along the Canal and the Yellow River to survey the river course. The goal of He's team was to find methods to improve flood control and the traffic of the Canal while not hampering the farmers' need for irrigation. In February 1726, the emperor told the Grand Secretariat that He Guozong's reports on the situation of the Canal were very detailed and clear.[103] He's efforts seemed to have pleased the Yongzheng emperor.

However, the Yongzheng emperor had only revealed part of his thoughts about He Guozong. In fact, He Guozong's inspection tour did not proceed without problems. He Guozong's team seriously disagreed with Henan Governor (*Henan xunfu* 河南巡撫) Tian Wenjing 田文鏡, one of the most trusted favorites of the Yongzheng emperor.[104] In a secret memorial to the emperor, Tian bitterly criticized He for rushing to conclusions without listening to the local peoples' and officials' opinions on the construction work. Unlike the occasion when he pretended to be a just ruler in front of Mamboo, the Yongzheng emperor allowed Tian to know his distrust of He Guozong. "He Guozong and the others [of the team of river course inspection] originally were just despised low officials," the emperor said. "They were not appointed by me. I merely utilize their ability of inspection."[105] On a different occasion, the emperor warned He Guozong directly, "You [and the rest of the team] originally were just contemptible low officials. Do not forget diligence and caution even for a moment."[106] Eventually, the emperor decided to adopt Tian's suggestion on the flooding problem rather than He's because he believed that Tian, as a local governor, would produce more reliable observations and solutions.[107] In the next five years, the Yongzheng emperor kept He Guozong among the high courtiers and sent him to various flood-prevention projects. However, in May 1732, when Tian Wenjing once again accused He of making serious mistakes in previous surveys and claimed that these errors had caused terrible damage to local people, the Yongzheng emperor stripped He Guozong of all his titles and never employed him again.[108]

From 1713 to 1722, Guozhu, Guozong, and Guodong were rising stars in the officialdom. They won the Kangxi emperor's attention not only because they were assiduous and talented but also because they were from a family that had served the emperor for generations. Because the emperor's attitude toward the Jesuits itself had changed, the He family's past records of resisting Jesuit mathematics became a guarantee of He Guozong and his brothers' loyalty to the newly constructed imperial mathematics. He Guozong and his brothers thus enjoyed a more personal and trusting connection to the Kangxi emperor than other personnel serving in mathematics. It was not a coincidence that the Kangxi emperor made special career arrangements for them.

From 1723 to 1731, the Kangxi emperor's successor, the Yongzheng emperor, dissolved the prestigious status of the He brothers one by one. Lack of personal interest in mathematics did not hamper the Yongzheng emperor's ability to recognize the importance of it. However, the cautious emperor would not easily forget that the He brothers had been working closely for years with his rival in competition for the throne. He dismissed Guozhu and Guodong before utilizing Guozong's mathematical specialty. The sequential discharge of He Guozong in 1731 would have been a heavy blow to the He family. Just years earlier, He Junxi's plan to let some of his children pursue civil service degrees could not have seemed more successful; now it had devastatingly fallen apart. In the end, Guozhu, Guozong, and Guodong were all without official jobs. The He family would have to be supported by the other members who still worked at the Astronomical Bureau. These individuals are the focus of the next section.

5.4 The Yongzheng Emperor's Administrative Policy of the Astronomical Bureau

The Yongzheng emperor continued the Kangxi emperor's efforts to institutionalize imperial mathematics by rectifying the administration of the Astronomical Bureau. The Kangxi emperor was famous for his mathematical talent, but he tended to let the Astronomical Bureau take care of its own daily administration.

By contrast, the Yongzheng emperor's interest was not in mathematics but in the details of the administration of officialdom. The previous section has illustrated how the Yongzheng emperor's distrust led to the downfall of He Guozhu, Guodong, and finally Guozong. The Yongzheng emperor did not suppress other members servicing in mathematics. Mei Juecheng and Minggantu, for example, were left to continue their careers without disturbance. Therefore, the Yongzheng emperor's attitude toward the He brothers was one important aspect but not the totality of his managing policy on mathematics and mathematicians. It is necessary to further investigate the administration of the Astronomical Bureau in general and the adjustment induced by the Yongzheng emperor in particular. This section revisits the case of He Guo'an and analyzes the Yongzheng emperor's influence on the administration of the Qing Astronomical Bureau.

The memorial submitted to the Yongzheng emperor in March 1724 regarding the promotion of He Guo'an indeed appears as routine as any other ones did. After beginning the memorial with his full official title, Minister of Personnel Longkodo 隆科多 wrote:

> [We] sincerely memorialize for the issue of filling out an official's vacancy. We have delivered that the vacancy left by Shenxu 沈旭, who had been promoted from Water Clock Manager to Vice-Director, shall be filled by He Guo'an, an Erudite of the Water Clock Section, according to the suggestion from it [the Astronomical Bureau]. We sincerely memorialize and wait for Your Majesty's decree.[109]

Observe the limited role the emperor was supposed to play in the above personnel arrangement. The Astronomical Bureau and the Ministry of Personnel had already decided who should be given the position, and they provided the emperor with very little knowledge about how they reached the decision and who the chosen person was. They simply informed the emperor that He Guo'an was currently an Erudite of the Water Clock Section. No additional information was provided, such as He Guo'an's past job performance, personality, or ability, to help the emperor decide whether he should approve this personnel arrangement or not. If not for the similarity of their names, the Yongzheng emperor may not even have noticed that He Guo'an and He Guozhu were from the same family.

Although Water Clock Manager was a petty position and Longkodo had been so close to the emperor that "Uncle" (*Jiu jiu* 舅舅) was made part of his official title, the Yongzheng emperor wanted to retain full control of the bureaucratic system.[110] He replied to the Ministry of Personnel at length:

> [Your memorial suggests to] fill this vacancy of Water Clock Manager completely according to the recommendation from the Astronomical Bureau. Is the recommendation based on the seniority of candidates' service or the excellence of job performance? [Your memorial] includes no explanation. In addition, it is not proper to let He Guozhu's family occupy so many posts.

>From now on, the Ministry of Personnel shall carefully examine the officials recommended by the Astronomical Bureau before sending in the routine memorial on filling posts.[111]

It is noteworthy that the Yongzheng emperor did not order an investigation into the nomination process of He Guo'an. Whether He Guo'an himself might indeed be a qualified candidate for the position was not the only issue with which the Yongzheng emperor was concerned. Rather than treat this as a discrete incident, he saw it as a weakness in the administration system that had to be removed.

The Yongzheng emperor clearly intended to prevent potential malfeasances from occurring. His attention went beyond limiting the expansion of the He family. At the time in question, with the exception of He Guozhu, all other members of the He family were at the level of Erudite or Student Astronomer.[112] By contrast, in the early Kangxi era, three members of the He family served as high-level officials of the Calendar Section at the same time.[113] Therefore, it was not that the He family had already overly expanded that motivated the Yongzheng emperor to constrain them. However, He Guozhu was not an ordinary Senior Vice-Director; he concurrently held a directorship at the Ministry of War. His brothers, Guozong and Guodong, were also high officials. The He brothers' combined influence could easily place the He family in dominant positions in the Astronomical Bureau. Worse, similar situations could happen to any other lower-level bureaus in the government. If there were no proper mechanism to closely examine the process of distributing lower-level positions, such positions would soon be occupied by the friends and relatives of influential officials.

Later in the same year, the Ministry of Personnel again received a list of nominated officials from the Astronomical Bureau. This time, the Ministry of Personnel wrote a much longer and more detailed routine memorial to the emperor:

> My ministry requested the Astronomical Bureau to send in an evaluation of the candidates for promotion. Then my ministry went together with the Astronomical Bureau officials to interview the candidates and to decide the best and the second one. Along with the ones recommended by high-level court officials, their names are all listed on the routine memorial waiting for Your Majesty's decision. Please select one for each post from the two candidates or from high-level court officials' recommendations.[114]

Following this, the nomination process became more systematic and the emperor was more informed in detail. For a vacant position in the Astronomical Bureau, the Bureau and the Ministry of Personnel had to suggest two potential candidates and provide the emperor with a brief job evaluation together with personal information such as place of origin and age. Such information was far from comprehensive, but the point was that the presentation of an alternative candidate gave the emperor more power in the decision-making process. Even though, in most cases, the emperor chose the first candidate nominated by the Bureau, the uncertainty of the two-candidate system was an important showcase of imperial authority.

Audiences were another important means through which Yongzheng and other Qing emperors demonstrated their authority. During the Qing period, most personnel orders for granting government positions were finalized only after imperial audiences, unless the positions were regarded as too insignificant to deserve the emperor's attention. Due to the large number of audiences held every day, most of them were ceremonial and the emperor would simply approve the suggestions submitted by the Ministry of Personnel. However, diligent emperors, such as Yongzheng, aggressively utilized audiences to select qualified officials. There are plenty of examples in archival records that demonstrate how audiences could affect an individual's career. In November 1726, two Manchu posts of Observatory Managers became vacant and the Astronomical Bureau and the Ministry of Personnel presented the Yongzheng emperor with two candidates for each post. Usually, the Yongzheng emperor selected the first candidate suggested by the Ministry of Personnel. This time, however, after the audience, the emperor decreed that one of the first candidates was "not good enough," and he awarded the post to one of the second candidates.[115] In a case in April 1725, the Yongzheng emperor approved the Ministry of Personnel's suggestion to fill the vacant vice-directorship with the first candidate; however, he added a reminder: "[The second candidate] is too unqualified for any promotion. Never send him in [for the audience] again."[116] Apparently, the candidate's poor performance during the audience cost him not only his current promotion but also all future hope for career progression. Furthermore, a failed audience could lead the emperor to suspect the integrity of the officials involved in the nomination process. Feeling that the candidate for the Manchu Water Clock Manager was too unqualified after an audience given in September 1728, the Yongzheng emperor scolded the Minister of Personnel: "On what ground did [the Astronomical Bureau] select him as the first candidate? Your ministry has to fully investigate and memorialize me the results."[117] The emperor's reproach was a warning to the Ministry of Personnel and the Astronomical Bureau that they would be penalized if the investigation report did not satisfy the emperor.

To summarize, the Yongzheng emperor treated the Astronomical Bureau as a regular institution of the central government. He neither downplayed nor emphasized the technical expertise of the Astronomical Bureau, which he was not familiar with in any case. His focus was on the administration of its officials. Just as Jesuit astronomers continued to be named the Directors, Bureau officials continued to be allowed to bring their offspring to work for the Bureau. However, the situation that a powerful Director alone, such as Johann Adam Schall, could determine candidates for all the posts of the Astronomical Bureau was not something the Yongzheng emperor would tolerate.[118] By systematizing the administrative process, the Yongzheng emperor looked to prevent corruption and factions in the Astronomical Bureau.

Notes

1. The Kangxi emperor was born on the eighteenth day of the third month of the eleventh year of the Shunzhi reign (May 4, 1654); according to Chinese reckoning, this day was his first birthday. Thus, the Kangxi emperor's sixtieth birthday was the eighteenth day of the third month of fifty-second year of the Kangxi reign (April 12, 1713), though according to Western reckoning he was still 58 years old. The celebration of the sixtieth birthday in Chinese tradition can also be understood as celebrating the day of birth in the year of 60 *sui*. See the explanation of Chinese reckoning of *sui* in Chapter 1, Note 2.
2. SL 6: 513–4.
3. Wang Shen 王掞 et al., *Wanshou shengdian chuji* 萬壽盛典初集, SKQS 653: 196–9. The age requirement for being invited to the Kangxi emperor's grand banquet was 65. Afterward, He Junxi was bestowed special gifts for being over 70 years old.
4. Qu, "Qingdai Qintianjian," 49.
5. Wang, *Wanshou shengdian*, 653: 174.
6. Ibid., 654: 480–2.
7. Jami, *Emperor's New Mathematics*, 253–5.
8. Li Guangdi 李光地, *Rongcun yulu; Rongcun xuyulu* 榕村語錄 榕村續語錄, ed. Chen Zuwu 陳祖武 (Beijing: Zhonghua shuju, 1995), 643.
9. For the lives of Joachim Bouvet, Jean-François Gerbillon, Antoine Thomas, and Tomás Pereira, see Pfister, *Notices biographiques*, 381–4, 403–6, 433–7, and 443–9 respectively. For the mentorship, see Golvers, *The* Astronomia Europaea, 117; Jami, *Emperor's New Mathematics*, 74–8, 139, 141–4, 180; Han Qi 韓琦, "Kangxi shidai de shuxue jiaoyu ji qi shehui beijing" 康熙時代的數學教育及其社會背景, in *Faguo hanxue* 法國漢學 (Beijing: Zhonghua shuju, 2003), 8: 434–5.
10. For how the Kangxi emperor used the performance of astronomical observations to manipulate his courtiers, see both Han Qi 韓琦, "Junchen yu buyi zhijian: Li Guangdi zai Kangxi shidai de huodong ji qi dui kexue de yingxiang" 君臣與布衣之間：李光地在康熙時代的活動及其對科學的影響, *Tsinghua xuebao* 清華學報 26. no. 4 (1995): 421 and Catherine Jami, "Imperial Control and Western Learning: The Kangxi Emperor's Performance," *Late Imperial China* 23, no. 1 (2002): 28–49.
11. For a more detailed description of this incident, see Jami, *Emperor's New Mathematics*, 260–1; Shi Yunli 石云里, "Reforming Astronomy and Compiling Imperial Science in the Post-Kangxi Era: The Social Dimension of the *Yuzhi Lixiang Kaocheng Houbian* 御製曆象考成後編," *East Asian Science, Technology, and Medicine* 28 (2008): 49–51.
12. The author thanks Professor Christopher Cullen for providing this insight.
13. For the lives of Philippus Maria Grimaldi and Bernard-Kilian Stumpf, see Pfister, *Notices biographiques*, 372–5, 472–3. For the Kangxi emperor's inquiry about the summer solstice, see Zhongguo diyi lishi dang'anguan 中國第一歷史檔案館, ed., *Kangxichao Manwen zhupi zouzhe quanyi* 康熙朝滿文朱批奏摺全譯 (Beijing: Zhongguo shehui kexue chubanshe, 1996), 723–4. For Grimaldi and Stumpf's memorial, see ibid., 1675.
14. Ibid., 724.
15. Ibid., 741.
16. QJZ KX (TP), T10998.
17. Ibid., T11004–5. *Qing guoshi*, 625 and SL 6: 456 omit the last sentence about the coming winter solstice.
18. *Qing guoshi*, 4: 625–6.
19. QGLL 13: 532.
20. Jami, *Emperor's New Mathematics*, 257–9; Han Qi 韓琦, "Mengyangzhai shuxuejia Chen Houyao de lisuan huodong—jiyu *Chenshi jiasheng* de xinyangjiu" 蒙養齋數學家陳厚耀的曆算活動—基於《陳氏家乘》的新研究, *Ziran kexueshi yanjiu* 自然科學史研究 33, no. 3 (2014): 300, 303.

21 Ibid.; Zhongguo diyi lishi dang'anguan 中國第一歷史檔案館, ed., *Kangxichao Hanwen zhupi zouzhe huibian* 康熙朝漢文硃批奏摺彙編 (Beijing: Dang'an chubanshe, 1985), 4: 323.
22 *Qing guoshi*, 4: 626.
23 Ibid. Zhao et al., *Qingshi gao*, 1668, has similar record but with emphasis on Mei Juecheng.
24 Wang, *Wanshou shengdian*, 653: 598, 613.
25 Due to its temporary nature, this office did not seem to have a formal title. It was referred to as *Xiu suanshu chu* 修算書處 or *Suanshu guan* 算書館 because of its function of compiling the mathematical treatises, but also as *Suanxue guan* 算學館 when teaching and learning activities happened there were stressed. See Jami, *Emperor's New Mathematics*, 272 for a discussion on the nature of the Studio for Cultivating the Youth.
26 *Qing guoshi*, 4: 626; SL 6: 524, 531–2.
27 *Qing guoshi*, 4: 626.
28 Ibid.
29 Ibid.
30 Zhongguo diyi lishi dang'anguan, *Kangxichao Hanwen*, 8: 1042.
31 *Qing guoshi*, 4: 627; SL 10: 1197–8.
32 SL 6: 901–2.
33 SL 10: 1198. For the publication of the *Origins of Mathematical Harmonics and Astronomy*, see section 5.3.
34 *Qing guoshi*, 4: 627. Zhao et al., *Qingshi gao*, 1669, states that the *Thorough Investigation of Astronomical Phenomena* was conferred to the Astronomical Bureau in 1723. However, He Guozong mentions in a memorial that the *Book on Calendrical Astronomy in Reverent Accord* was not immediately put into practice after the Yongzheng emperor wrote the preface. A routine memorial submitted in 1726 on how to reward the members of the Office of Compiling Mathematical Treatises also mentions that the treatises were not completely finished until June 1724. See NPM 402020087 and GYGL 21: 12505.
35 SL 7: 520; SL 15: 150.
36 GYGL 19: 11079; IHP 023912–001.According to *Kangxi wushiyinian renchenke huishi yibai jiushiwuming sandai jinshi lüli*, disc 2 of *Dengkelu*, He Guozong was born on November 12, 1688. But in memorials submitted in 1726 and 1747, He Guozong states that he was 40 and 61 *sui* 歲 respectively. In Chinese tradition, a person's age is reckoned to be one *sui* at birth, and one more *sui* is added to the age at the beginning of every new calendar year. Thus, a calculation based on He Guozong's memorials indicates that He's birth year is 1687, because civil service examinees customarily reported ages one or more years lesser than their true ages, it is more likely that He Guozong was born in 1687 than in 1688. On the birth year of He Guozong, see Chang, "Shidai bianjuzhong de chouren jiazu," 135–6; Han Qi, "He Guozong shengnian shishi xiaokao" 何國宗生年史事小考, *Ziran kexueshi yanjiu* 自然科學史研究 35, no. 4 (2016): 487–8.
37 Li, *Jifu tongzhi*, 505: 606.
38 QHD KX 294–7.
39 Li Fang 李放, *Huangqing Shushi* 皇清書史, in *Liaohai Congshu* 遼海叢書 (Shenyang: Liaoningsheng xinhua shuju, 1985), 1454, 1504.
40 For Zhang Zhao's life see Zhao et al., *Qingshi gao*, 10493–5 and *Qing guoshi*, 6: 708–9. For the friendship between Zhang and He, see Liang Ji 梁驥, *Zhang Zhao jiaoyoukao* 張照交遊考 (Zhengzhou: Zhongzhou guji chubanshe, 2016), 212–3. The well-known story that He Guozong learned calligraphy from Zhang Zhao when they were both in prison, however, is unlikely to be true, because they were jailed in different time periods.
41 Kong Qingyu 孔慶餘, ed., *Kongshi dazong zhipu bufenjuan* 孔氏大宗支譜不分卷 (Qufu, 1873), 39. Shanghai Library, 918015. https://jiapu.library.sh.cn/#/

jiapu:STJP003759 (accessed January 2021). In the Qing era, the direct descendant of Confucius inherited the title of Duke Yansheng.
42 QJZ KX (TP), T11301–34.
43 Ibid., 11332.
44 Li, *Jifu tongzhi*, 505: 501; SL 6: 473.
45 SL 6: 475.
46 *Qing guoshi*, 6: 501.
47 For Wang's relation with Li and Wang's contribution to the mathematical project, see Jami, *Emperor's New Mathematics*, 247–8, 270, 276, 373–7.
48 Ruan, *Chouren zhuan*, 719.
49 SL 6: 524.
50 *Qing guoshi*, 4: 626; Zhao et al., *Qingshi gao*, 1668.
51 Zhongguo diyi lishi dang'anguan 中國第一歷史檔案館, ed., *Yongzhengchao Hanwen yuzhi huibian* 雍正朝漢文諭旨匯編 (Guilin: Guangxi shifan daxue chubanshe, 1999), 6: 159.
52 QGLL 11: 453.
53 Wang, *Wanshou shengdian*, 653: 174.
54 Qu, "Qingdai Qintianjian," 52.
55 Wang, *Wanshou shengdian*, 653: 174.
56 Wu, *Lichao shilu*, 4315.
57 QJZ KX (BJ), B005742.
58 Wu, *Lichao shilu*, 4318.
59 Horng Wann-Sheng 洪萬生, "Shiba shiji dongsuan yu zhongsuan de yiduan duihua: Hong Zhengxia vs. He Guozhu" 十八世紀東算與中算的一段對話：洪正夏 vs. 何國柱, *Hanxue yanjiu* 漢學研究 20, no. 2 (2002): 70.
60 Wu, *Lichao shilu*, 4321. For the meeting between He Guozhu and Hŏ Wŏn in Seoul, see Lim Jongtae, "Journeys of the Modest Astronomers: Korean Astronomers' Missions to Beijing in the Seventeenth and Eighteenth Centuries," *Extrême-Orient, Extrême-Occident* 36: 101–2.
61 Wu, *Lichao shilu*, 4321.
62 QJZ KX (TP), T12378–9.
63 On the relation between the Studio for Cultivating the Youth and European academies, see Jami, *Emperor's New Mathematics*, 271–2.
64 The last year that He Junxi's name appeared on the roster was the 1714 Timely Modeling calendar.
65 For the special mourning leave applied to the officials of the Astronomical Bureau, see QHDZL QL 620: 189.
66 QJZ KX (BJ), B013820. Italics mine.
67 Zhao et al., *Qingshi gao*, 9912–6; *Qing guoshi*, 6: 50–3.
68 QJZ KX (BJ), B015328–9. Italics mine.
69 Ibid., B015347.
70 Ibid., B015606–7.
71 QGLL 19: 275–6. He Guodong's birth year is calculated according to his own statement that he was 78 *sui* in March 1767.
72 SL 6: 571.
73 Li, *Jifu tongzhi*, 505: 606, 609; QGLL 19: 275.
74 Li Zhen 李珍, ed., *Dingli quanbian Xuzhen xinli* 定例全編 續增新例 [1723], Oki Collection, Library of the Institute for Advanced Studies on Asia, University of Tokyo, 1: 27.
75 QHD YZ 261.
76 Li, *Dingli quanbian*, 1: 28.
77 Hao Yulin 郝玉麟 et al., *Fujian tongzhi* 福建通志, SKQS 528: 40.
78 Li, *Dingli quanbian*, 1: 28; *Qing guoshi*, 12: 891.
79 Qu, "Qingdai Qintianjian," 53.

80 QHD YZ 226.
81 SL 6: 486.
82 See Feng Erkang 馮爾康, *Yongzheng zhuan* 雍正傳 (Taipei: Taiwan shangwu yinshuguan, 1992) for an overview of the life of the Yongzheng emperor.
83 Yunlu, *lixiang kaocheng*, 790: 5–7. Yunlu was originally named Yinlu 胤祿. Soon after Yinzhen took the throne, all his brothers, Yinzhi and Yinlu included, changed the first character of their names from Yin 胤 to Yun 允 to avoid naming taboo of the new emperor.
84 GYQX 1701.
85 GYGL 4: 2173.
86 SL 7: 466.
87 GYGL 5: 2465.
88 GYQX 1994.
89 Zhongguo diyi lishi dang'anguan, *Yongzhengchao Hanwen yuzhi*, 6: 159.
90 Ibid.
91 Zhongguo diyi lishi dang'anguan, *Yongzhengchao Hanwen zhupi*, 3: 412. The date of He Guozhu's discharge was deduced from the Yongzheng emperor's reply to Mamboo.
92 Ibid., 3: 128.
93 Ibid, 130.
94 Ibid., 412.
95 GYGL 12: 6994.
96 SL 7: 478.
97 Zhongguo diyi lishi dang'anguan, ed., *Yongzhengchao Hanwen yuzhi*, 6: 159.
98 Ibid.
99 GYGL 12: 6994, 6996.
100 GYGL 12: 7123.
101 Hao, *Fujian tongzhi*, 528: 403. As of July 1726, He Guodong was still the Dingzhou Prefect, see Zhongguo diyi lishi dang'anguan, *Yongzhengchao Hanwen zhupi*, 783.
102 SL 7: 520.
103 Ibid., 586.
104 For Tian Wenjing as the model governor during the Yongzheng reign, see Feng, *Yongzheng zhuan*, 551–5.
105 NPM 402006973.
106 NPM 402007513.
107 SL 7: 692.
108 SL 8: 392.
109 GYQX 1994.
110 See Feng, *Yongzheng zhuan*, 98–9, 104–5, and 120–4 for the significant of the title 'Uncle,' Longkodo's domination of the appointments of officials, and the Yongzheng emperor's purge of Longkodo.
111 Ibid.
112 Qu, "Qingdai Qintianjian," 53–4; Shi, "Tianwenke," 39.
113 Qu, "Qingdai Qintianjian," 49–50; Shi, "Tianwenke," 37–8.
114 GYQX 2986.
115 Ibid., 6949–50.
116 Ibid., 3826.
117 Ibid., 10261.
118 Fan Guoliang 樊國樑 describes Schall's prominence in the late Shunzhi reign that "all the seventy-plus positions of the Astronomical Bureau, the emperor allowed Ruowang [Schall's Chinese name] to decides them alone." Fan Guoliang 樊國樑, *Yanjing kaijiao lue* 燕京開教略 [1905], in *Zhongguo Tianzhujiao shiji huibian* 中國天主教史籍彙編 ed. Chen Fangzhong 陳方中 (Taipei: Furen daxue chubanshe, 2003), 363–4.

Bibliography

Abbreviations for Archival and Published Sources

CKSB: *Jindai Zhongguo shiliao congkan sanbian* 近代中國史料叢刊三編, edited by Shen Yunlong 沈雲龍. 850 vols. Taipei: Wenhai chubanshe, 1982.
GYGL: *Guanyuan guanli shiliao* 官員管理史料 of *Qingdai lizhi shiliao* 清代吏治史料, edited by Ren Mengqiang 任夢強. 54 vols. Beijing: Xianzhuang shuju, 2004.
GYQX: *Guanyuan quanxuan shiliao* 官員銓選史料 of *Qingdai lizhi shiliao* 清代吏治史料, edited by Ren Mengqiang 任夢強. 34 vols. Beijing: Xianzhuang shuju, 2004.
IHP: Neige daku dang'an 內閣大庫檔案. Institute of History and Philology of Academia Sinica, Taipei. http://archive.ihp.sinica.edu.tw/mctkm2/index.html
NPM: Qingdai gongzhongdang zouzhe ji junjichudang zhejian quanwen yingxiang ziliaoku 清代宮中檔奏摺及軍機處檔摺件全文影像資料庫. National Palace Museum, Taipei. http://npmhost.npm.gov.tw/tts/npmmeta/GC/indexcg.html
QGLL: *Qingdai guanyuan lüli dang'an quanbian* 清代官員履歷檔案全編. Edited by Qin Guojing 秦國經. 30 vols. Shanghai: Huadong shifan daxue chubanshe, 1997.
QHD KX: *Da Qing huidian (Kangxi chao)* 大清會典 (康熙朝) [1690]. CKSB 711–30.
QHD YZ: *Da Qing huidian (Yongzheng chao)* 大清會典 (雍正朝) [1732]. CKSB 761–90.
QHDZL QL: *Qinding Da Qing huidian zeli* 欽定大清會典則例 [1764]. SKQS 620–5.
QJZ KX (BJ): *Qingdai qijuzhuce, Kangxi chao* 清代起居注冊, 康熙朝. Edited by Zou Ailian 鄒愛蓮. 32 vols. Beijing: Zhonghua shuju, 2009.
QJZ KX (TP): Kurena 庫勒納 et al. *Qingdai qijuzhuce, Kangxi chao* 清代起居注冊, 康熙朝. 22 vols. Taipei: Lianjing chuban, 2009.
SKQS: *Yingyin wenyuange sikuquanshu* 景印文淵閣四庫全書. 1500 vols. Taipei: Taipei shangwu yinshuguan, 1986.
SL: *Qing shilu* 清實錄. 60 vols. Beijing: Zhonghua shuju, 1985.

Other Sources

Fan Guoliang 樊國樑. *Yanjing kaijiao lue* 燕京開教略 [1905]. In *Zhongguo Tianzhujiao shiji huibian* 中國天主教史籍彙編, 285–444, edited by Chen Fangzhong 陳方中. Taipei: Furen daxue chubanshe, 2003.
Hao Yulin 郝玉麟 et al. *Fujian tongzhi* 福建通志. SKQS 527–30.
Kong Qingyu 孔慶餘, ed. *Kongshi dazong zhipu bufenjuan* 孔氏大宗支譜不分卷. Qufu, 1873. Shanghai Library. 918015. https://jiapu.library.sh.cn/#/jiapu/STJP003759
Li Fang 李放. *Huangqing Shushi* 皇清書史. In *Liaohai Congshu* 遼海叢書, 1399–714. Shenyang: Liaoningsheng xinhua shuju, 1985.
Li Guangdi 李光地. *Rongcun yulu; Rongcun xu yulu* 榕村語錄 榕村續語錄. Edited by Chen Zuwu 陳祖武. Beijing: Zhonghua shuju, 1995.
Li Wei 李衛 et al. *Jifu tongzhi* 畿輔通志 [1735]. SKQS 504–6.
Li Zhen 李珍, ed. *Dingli quanbian Xuzhen xinli* 定例全編 續增新例 [1723]. Oki Collection. Library of the Institute for Advanced Studies on Asia, University of Tokyo.
Qing guoshi, Jiayetang chaoben 清國史嘉業堂鈔本. 14 vols. Beijing: Zhonghua shuju, 1993.
Ruan Yuan 阮元 et al. *Chouren zhuan huibian* 疇人傳彙編. 2 vols. Taipei: Shijie shuju, 1982.
Wang Shan 王掞 et al. *Wanshou shengdian chuji* 萬壽盛典初集 [1716]. SKQS 653–4.

Wu Han 吳晗, ed. *Chaoxian Lichao shilu zhong de Zhongguo shiliao* 朝鮮李朝實錄中的中國史料. 12 vols. Beijing: Zhonghua shuju, 1980.

Yunlu 允祿 et al. *Yuzhi lixiang kaocheng* 御製曆象考成 [1723]. SKQS 790.

Zhao Erxun 趙爾巽 et al. *Qingshi gao* 清史稿. 48 vols. Beijing: Zhonghua shuju, 1976.

Zhongguo diyi lishi dang'anguan 中國第一歷史檔案館, ed. *Yongzhengchao Hanwen zhupi zouzhe huibian* 雍正朝漢文硃批奏摺彙編. 40 vols. Nanjing: Jiangsu guji chubanshe, 1989.

———. *Kangxichao Manwen zhupi zouzhe quanyi* 康熙朝滿文朱批奏摺全譯. Beijing: Zhongguo shehui kexue chubanshe, 1996.

———. *Yongzhengchao Hanwen yuzhi huibian* 雍正朝漢文諭旨匯編. 10 vols. Guilin: Guangxi shifan daxue chubanshe, 1999.

Secondary Sources

Feng Erh-k'ang 馮爾康. *Yongzheng zhuan* 雍正傳. Taipei: Taiwan shangwu yinshuguan, 1992.

Han Qi 韓琦. "Junchen yu buyi zhijian: Li Guangdi zai Kangxi shidai de huodong ji qi dui kexue de yingxiang" 君主與布衣之間：李光地在康熙時代的活動及其對科學的影響. *Tsinghua xuebao* 清華學報 26, no. 4 (1995): 421–45.

———. "Kangxi shidai de shuxue jiaoyu ji qi shehui beijing" 康熙時代的數學教育及其社會背景. In *Faguo hanxue* 法國漢學, 8: 434–48. Beijing: Zhonghua shuju, 2003.

———. "Mengyangzhai shuxuejia Chen Houyao de lisuan huodong—jiyu *Chenshi jiasheng* de xin yangjiu" 蒙養齋數學家陳厚耀的曆算活動—基於《陳氏家乘》的新研究, *Ziran kexueshi yanjiu* 自然科學史研究 33, no. 3 (2014): 298–306.

———. "He Guozong shengnian shishi xiaokao" 何國宗生年史事小考, *Ziran kexueshi yanjiu* 自然科學史研究 35, no. 4 (2016): 487–8.

Horng Wann-Sheng 洪萬生. "Shiba shiji dongsuan yu zhongsuan de yiduan duihua: Hong Zhengxia Vs. He Guozhu" 十八世紀東算與中算的一段對話：洪正夏 vs. 何國柱. *Hanxue yanjiu* 漢學研究 20, no. 2 (2002): 57–80.

Jami, Catherine. "Imperial Control and Western Learning: The Kangxi Emperor's Performance." *Late Imperial China* 23, no. 1 (2002): 28–49.

———. *The Emperor's New Mathematics: Western Learning and Imperial Authority during the Kangxi Reign (1662–1722)*. New York: Oxford University Press, 2012.

Liang Ji 梁驥. *Zhang Zhao jiaoyoukao* 張照交遊考. Zhengzhou: Zhongzhou guji chubanshe, 2016.

Lim, Jongtae. "Journeys of the Modest Astronomers: Korean Astronomers' Missions to Beijing in the Seventeenth and Eighteenth Centuries." *Extrême-Orient Extrême-Occident* 36 (2013): 81–108.

Pfister, Louis. *Notices biographiques et bibliographiques sur les Jésuites de l'ancienne mission de Chine. 1552–1773*. 2 vols. Shanghai: Imprimerie de la Mission catholique, 1932–34.

Qu Chunhai 屈春海. "Qingdai Qintianjian ji Shixianke zhiguan nianbiao" 清代欽天監暨時憲科職官年表. *Zhongkuo keji shiliao* 中國科技史料 18, no. 3 (1997): 45–71.

Shi Yumin 史玉民. "Qing Qintianjian Tianwenke zhiguan nianbiao" 清欽天監天文科職官年表. *Zhongkuo keji shiliao* 中國科技史料 21, no. 1 (2000): 34–47.

Shi Yunli 石云里. "Reforming Astronomy and Compiling Imperial Science in the Post-Kangxi Era: The Social Dimension of the *Yuzhi Lixiang Kaocheng Houbian* 御製曆象考成後編." *East Asian Science, Technology, and Medicine* 28 (2008): 36–81.

6 The Solar Eclipse of 1730

In January 1730, near the end of the seventh year of his reign, the Yongzheng emperor made a public announcement in response to the Astronomical Bureau's prediction that a solar eclipse would occur on the first day of the sixth month of the coming year (July 15, 1730):

> Never did the anomaly of a solar eclipse occur since I ascended to the throne seven years ago. According to the memorial submitted by the Astronomical Bureau, on the first day of the sixth month of the *gengxu* 庚戌 year (1730), the sun will be obscured up to nine *fen* 分 and twenty-two *miao* 秒 [nine-tenths and twenty-two-thousandths of its diameter]. My heart is deeply frightened. I think that my faults in government or personnel affairs might be the cause. Maybe ministers and officials have not carefully fulfilled their duties with sincerity and respect, and civilians have not yet been able to communicate [their needs to the government] easily. Therefore, heaven sends this warning sign.[1]

While the Yongzheng emperor's announcement aimed to show his respect to heaven, this solar eclipse did indeed turn out to be a critical milestone in the history of mathematical astronomy in the Qing period. Before the eclipse occurred, the Qing state calendar was based on the Tychonic system. Afterward, it followed the Newtonian system.[2] Unlike the Kangxi Calendar Dispute that caused social and political turbulence, this change took place almost in secrecy.[3] In fact, Qing state documents left very few records about this incident. The next two chapters analyze the different concerns of the parties involved in the process of transforming the state calendar from the Tychonic to the Newtonian system, namely, the monarchy, the astronomer families, and the Jesuit missionaries who held the directorship at the Astronomical Bureau. Together, they shaped the state policy of managing and reproducing knowledge of calendar making in the Yongzheng and Qianlong reigns. This chapter focuses on each party's political priorities when the state calendar was secretly changed.

6.1 Challenges From Heaven

Since antiquity, Chinese people have regarded celestial phenomena as enciphered messages from heaven. Over time, the decryption of heavenly messages developed

DOI: 10.4324/9781003008255-6

into a special branch of knowledge that was known as *tianwen* 天文, which means "celestial language" or "heavenly signs." Nonetheless, anyone who dared to boast of his knowledge of *tianwen* or to interpret celestial phenomena in public could easily offend those in positions of authority.[4] In fact, even owning astronomical instruments constituted a crime at the time of the Qing dynasty.[5]

Of all the celestial phenomena, the one deemed most critical was the solar eclipse. According to *tianwen* interpretation, the sun represented the monarch, Son of Heaven, thus the solar eclipse represented a divine evaluation of the current emperor's personal ethics and rightness of government. An unexpected solar eclipse or an eclipse that exceeded the predicted magnitude was perceived to be a sign that heaven was angry at the earthly ruler's malfeasance and the public could, and would, take it as a sign that the dynasty was losing the heavenly mandate (*tian ming* 天命). If there were any celestial phenomena that an emperor would like to hide from his subjects, it was the solar eclipse. However, the solar eclipse was a phenomenon that all people under heaven could see with their own eyes and interpret as they wished. The emperor had no means of keeping this occurrence secret. The Yongzheng emperor's concern about the upcoming solar eclipse and the way in which it would be interpreted was well grounded. Although the cause of the eclipse was no longer a myth, the Yongzheng emperor had to handle his first solar eclipse carefully so that it did not threaten his regime.

As the government institution asked for assistance for the emperor in handling the eclipses, the Astronomical Bureau followed a sophisticated protocol that required not only astronomical knowledge but also political wisdom. According to the Qing statutes and survival records, the Astronomical Bureau had to communicate with the emperor at least three times for each eclipse. The first communication took place approximately five months before the eclipse, when the Astronomical Bureau had finished calculating various data about the upcoming event, including the time, duration, magnitude, and position of the eclipse.[6] Recall that Schall gave Dorgon a good first impression of the New Western Method because he calculated the eclipse for every province.[7] As they originated from an area outside the traditional Chinese territory, Qing rulers were particularly conscious that an eclipse prediction calculated for the capital would not predict its appearance as seen by residents of other areas. Therefore, unlike the Ming court which only calculated predictions based on the location of its capital, the Qing court required the Astronomical Bureau to produce predictions for every province. In this way, no matter how far the subjects lived from the political center, the imperial state could demonstrate its authority to them through the eclipse predictions produced by the Astronomical Bureau.

After the emperor reviewed the data provided by the Astronomical Bureau, the Ministry of Rites would notify the provinces that needed to hold the Rescue Ritual (*jiuhu* 救護) on the day of the eclipse. The Rescue Ritual was determined by the eclipse magnitude, which was defined as the fraction of the sun's diameter that was obscured by the moon.[8] In the Shunzhi and Kangxi reigns, the Rescue Ritual was held in a province if the predicted eclipse magnitude exceeded one-tenth.[9] Afterward, the requirement was reduced to three-tenths but was eventually changed back to one-tenth in 1749.[10] The Qianlong emperor explained the political concern behind this change in no uncertain terms:

> The occurrences of solar and lunar eclipses can be known from computation. According to the examples set by the *Spring and Autumn Annals* (*Chunqiu* 春秋),[11] only solar eclipses need to be recorded. My only concern is that a [celestial] phenomenon so obvious and bright will lead people to look up to it. Even among all celestial movements, [eclipses] occur frequently. They cannot be compared with the constantly shining fixed stars that cause no apprehension. They have to be dealt with sincerely.[12]

Not wanting to see his subjects irritated by a celestial phenomenon, the Qianlong emperor ordered the government officials to attend the Rescue Rituals as frequently as necessary. After all, keeping subjects content was crucial to maintaining political stability. Calculating the occurrences of the solar eclipse was only the foundation for dealing with the phenomenon. Political performances, such as the rituals and decrees that showed the emperor's sincerity to local officials, were necessary to pacify people's restlessness.

The Yongzheng emperor's decree of January 1730 was in the same vein. Perhaps the Astronomical Bureau's prediction had alarmed him because the magnitude of the expected eclipse would be close to that of a full eclipse. Instead of waiting to react to any damage after the eclipse occurred, the Yongzheng emperor hoped to prevent disturbances from happening in the first place. A routine notification from the Ministry of Rites about holding the Rescue Rituals was not sufficient. The Yongzheng emperor's decree in January 1730 constituted a warning to local officials that they should handle the coming eclipse with extra caution.

Between a month and two weeks before the eclipse, the Astronomical Bureau was required to send a reminder of the upcoming celestial event to the emperor.[13] This reminder was accompanied with an illustration of the eclipse. As Figure 6.1 shows, the illustration provided the emperor with information on the period during which the eclipse would be visible, how its shape would change, and when its magnitude would reach its maximum. Indeed, the illustrations produced by the Astronomical Bureau were sufficiently clear and detailed so as to give the emperor a remarkable experience of astronomical observation, as long as he was interested in that. Although the emperor did not attend the Rescue Ritual, he often kept the illustration of the eclipse that was submitted with the reminder for his own reference. This allowed the emperor to personally verify the Astronomical Bureau's calculation by observing the eclipse and comparing it with the illustrations.

On the day of the solar eclipse, all government bureaus sent representatives to the Rescue Ritual held at the Ministry of Rites. At the same time, the Ministry of Rites sent some officials to the observatory, where the dynasty's best astronomical

Figure 6.1 A solar eclipse prediction produced by the Astronomical Bureau, 1849. IHP 163354. Courtesy of the Institute of History and Philology, Academia Sinica.

instruments were located, to observe the eclipse with the Astronomical Bureau superintendent and Directors. Together they confirmed the accuracy of the Bureau's calculation. After the eclipse, the Astronomical Bureau submitted a final report to the emperor.

However, in contrast to the detailed and informative prediction submitted in previous communications, the final report from the Astronomical Bureau was short and not particularly technical. A typical report began with a declaration that the Astronomical Bureau superintendents and the representatives from the Ministry of Rites had dutifully gone to the observatory to observe the eclipse. Following the declaration was a brief summary of the observation results. It is noteworthy that the observation results rarely included the eclipse magnitude. Even the report for the 1730 solar eclipse, whose predicted magnitude so worried the Yongzheng emperor, did not include the actual measurement of eclipse magnitude.[14] The last part of the report was the divination of the eclipse, which was mainly based on the celestial positions of the eclipse, particularly the start and end positions relative to the constellations.[15] Clearly, the report's purpose was not to verify the accuracy of the prediction but to provide the monarch with the divination. However, there was no rigid set of rules or references employed to interpret the heavenly signs. It is very likely that the Astronomical Bureau officials would not risk their jobs and lives to write an offending divination report.

The Astronomical Bureau was not the only institution that was responsible for producing the final report. Any mismatch between the predicted eclipse and observed eclipse would not only expose the Astronomical Bureau officials to charges of incompetence but also threaten the dynasty's authority. Unless the difference between prediction and observation was too obvious to be concealed, neither the Astronomical Bureau nor the imperial state would be willing to admit its existence. Normally, the emperor always accepted the Astronomical Bureau's final report without any question. To be sure, the mismatch did not always go entirely unnoticed. For example, Supervising Censor (*Jishizhong* 給事中) Song Shu 宋澍, who had observed the solar eclipse that happened on August 28, 1802, with his naked eyes when attending the Rescue Ritual, accused the Astronomical Bureau of misprediction.[16] According to Song's own observation, the maximum magnitude of the eclipse did not even reach seven *fen* (70% of the diameter of the moon) and was therefore much less than the nine *fen* and 34 *miao* (93.4% of the diameter) predicted by the Astronomical Bureau. Song complained that such an error was too severe to be tolerated. The Jiaqing emperor forwarded the case for further investigation but eventually decreed that Song's impeachment was not sustained because "Princes, grand minsters, and the officials attending the Rescue Ritual at the capital saw it with their eyes and they all have no objection."[17] It is noteworthy that none of the metropolitan officials positively testified that the eclipse magnitude was in the range of the Astronomical Bureau's prediction. Those officials that did attend the Rescue Ritual reported that they did not hear anyone arguing that the eclipse was seven or nine *fen*, while those who stayed in offices claimed that they had been unable to clearly recognize the eclipse magnitude. All government members distanced themselves from this case, including the emperor. As long as the alleged inaccuracy of the eclipse prediction did not cause a political or social disturbance, the emperor had no objection to the Astronomical Bureau officials and other courtiers covering up their colleagues' mirror malfeasance.

The solar eclipse of 1730, however, presented a more severe challenge than the above protocol could completely subdue. It exposed the shocking fact that the *Thorough Investigation of Astronomical Phenomena* finished less than a decade ago had not helped to slow down the deterioration in the predictive accuracy of the Timely Modeling system. The next section will show that, in the early Yongzheng reign, the Timely Modeling system had become so obviously inaccurate that even neighboring Korea noticed the errors.

6.2 The Korean Astronomical Bureau and the He Family

In recent years, Korean sources have attracted increased attention from Qing history scholars.[18] Thanks for the fact that most Korean sources were written in classical Chinese, historians of Qing history need little additional training to begin utilizing them. In "An Eighteenth Century Sino-Korean Dialogue on Mathematics: He Guozhu vs. Hong Jung Ha," for example, Wann-Shang Horng analyzes He

Guozhu's level of mathematical knowledge by scrutinizing the *Gu Il Jip* 九一集, in which Korean mathematician Hong Jeong-Ha 洪正夏 recorded how his conversation with He Guozhu had occurred during He's embassy to Seoul.[19] He Guozhu and the other He family members participated in the majority of the compilation projects of the Qing official mathematical treatises, but they left no personal work. Anecdotes, such as the one in the *Gu Il Jip*, provide valuable insights into the connection between Chinese and Korean mathematicians. One of the goals of this section is to examine how, for generations, the He family played an important role in transmitting European mathematical astronomy to the Chosŏn dynasty (1392–1910) that ruled Korea.

Korean sources, such as the *Veritable Records of the Chosŏn Dynasty*, are crucial to this research. The Korean Chosŏn Kingdom was founded in the late fourteenth century by Yi Seonggye 李成桂 (1392–1398) and lasted until the end of the nineteenth century. Korea was a vassal state of the Ming and Qing dynasties. The unequal statuses between these two states are clearly delineated in the *Veritable Records of the Chosŏn Dynasty* entries. For instance, the Qing documents routinely recorded what benevolence the Qing court had bestowed to the Korean embassies coming to Beijing to pay respect to the Qing monarchs but rarely described what the Qing embassies had demanded of the Korean court. The *Veritable Records of the Chosŏn Dynasty*, however, recorded Qing ambassadors' extortions and insults in detail. They also included numerous records that disclosed the intelligence about the Qing that the Korean embassies had gathered. While the Qing state historians omitted or altered the records that could potentially embarrass their dynasty, Korean court historians had no need to do so for the Qing. The deterioration of the Timely Modeling calendar is one example of an incident in which the Korean records were of particular use.

From the mid-seventeenth century, the Qing Astronomical Bureau in Beijing had been an important channel through which Koreans could import European mathematical astronomy.[20] As a vassal state, the Korean court had no choice but to adopt the calendar promulgated by the Qing.[21]. However, Korean astronomers showed no signs of reluctance to comply with this requirement; rather, they learned the Timely Modeling calendar with eagerness. As early as June 1645, Schall's name appeared on the *Veritable Records of the Chosŏn Dynasty* as the producer of the new calendar.[22] Soon the Korean court decided to dispatch Astronomical Bureau officials with the regular emissaries to Beijing to gather more information about the New Western calendar, even though "The central state (*Zhong yuan* 中原) [China] forbids foreign countries to make calendars."[23] By March 1648, a Korean Astronomical Bureau official managed to meet with Schall. However, because collecting treatises on calendar making or learning them was strictly forbidden at that time, the Korean official only obtained brief oral instructions from Schall.[24] Nevertheless, by the early 1650s, Korean astronomers were fully versed in the techniques used to calculate the civil calendar.[25] However, the calculation of the seven governors—namely, the sun, moon, and five planets, would take much more time to master. Korean astronomers did not make a significant breakthrough until 1705, when Hŏ Wŏn 許遠, an Astronomical Bureau official, came to Beijing and managed to meet with He Junxi 何君錫. The instruction that He Junxi gave to Hŏ helped Korean astronomers to make profound progress in their understanding of the methods used to compute planetary motions. Finally, the Korean Astronomical Bureau knew how to calculate the Seven Governors calendar.[26]

The factors that caused this long delay are worthy of further analysis. The Korean Astronomical Bureau had reported that its officials only learned the method of calculating the solar orbit from Schall because "when questioning through written communication, words could not deliver the meanings effectively."[27] Korean and Chinese officials, to a certain degree, could communicate directly through writing without the need to involve an interpreter.[28] This statement, however, suggests that European missionaries could not effectively deliver their knowledge to Korean officials; this was probably because Schall and other missionaries had limited knowledge of written Chinese.

Furthermore, the difference in the background knowledge of mathematical astronomy might have been the cause of communication difficulties during the meeting of Korean officials and European missionaries. Korean astronomers were trained in traditional Chinese mathematics and the Great Concordance system of calendar making. He Junxi, too, was an expert in the Great Concordance system. His strong empathy toward the Great Concordance system even cost him his promotion to the Bureau directorate.[29] However, after the Kangxi emperor's decree of August 1676, He was required to learn the New Method.[30] By the time of the meeting with Hŏ Wŏn, He should have mastered the New Method. He's experience of converting from the Great Concordance system to the New Method could imply that he knew exactly what the Korean Astronomical Bureau officials needed and they could learn from He more effectively than from European missionaries.

The He family continued to be involved in the transmission of Western mathematical astronomy to Korea. We have seen that the Kangxi emperor chose He Guozhu to participate in a special embassy to Korea in 1713.[31] Beside Hong Jung Ha, the author of the *Gu Il Jip*, He Guozhu also met with Hŏ Wŏn. He Guozhu taught Hŏ Wŏn some calculation methods and promised, "I will find the books and instruments that your country does not have and send them to you when I return to Beijing."[32] Because of the friendship that had been established between Hŏ and the He family, the Yi court once again sent Hŏ to Beijing. Unfortunately, when Hŏ arrived in Beijing, He Guozhu was on mourning leave.[33] It is unclear whether the Calendar Manager that Hŏ met was He Guozhu or He's successor, Shao Yunlong 邵雲龍.[34] Regardless, Hŏ successfully obtained nine treatises on the calculation of eclipses and calendar making in addition to the six instruments for calculation and measurement.[35]

By the time the inaccuracy of the Timely Modeling system became obvious in the early Yongzheng reign, Korean astronomers had a good grasp of the New Method. They were confident enough to assert that the errors they observed were not due to mistakes in their own computation but in the calendar-making system. In November 1728, the Korean Astronomical Bureau found that "the computational system is not as good as it used to be. The predictions of twenty-four solar terms and the new and full moons become erroneous."³⁶ Six months later, the Korean Astronomical Bureau sent the Korean king a more detailed report:

> Since last year, the Qing civil calendar had many errors. This is because the celestial motion gradually accumulates difference. The Timely Modeling system uses the *wuchen* 戊辰 year of the Chongzhen reign (1628) as the starting point of calendar calculation. That was already one hundred and two years ago. Computation, measurement, revision, and correction are the general methods and recognized principles for maintaining [the accuracy of] the calendar. However, our country does not have the instruments needed for various measurements. We can only follow their collections and use their guidebooks.... We have no choice but to regularly send one Bureau official [to Beijing] to obtain whatever has been missing and to learn the usage [of the guidebooks]. Then we can calculate the seven governors completely by ourselves.³⁷

In November 1730, one ambassador told the Korean king before he left for Beijing:

> I worked at the Astronomical Bureau. I heard that our calendar-making method is based on the *Kangxi Thorough Investigation of Astronomical Phenomena* (*Kangxi lixiang kaocheng* 康熙曆象考成), and it has gradually become erroneous. Each year it has at least six or seven errors. I will bring a Bureau official so that we can obtain the method of calendar making.³⁸

As a result of the deterioration of the Timely Modeling calendar, Korean officials repeatedly requested that their king dispatch astronomers to Beijing to acquire new treatises and instruments.

The fact that the Korean astronomers kept coming up with questions on the accuracy of the Timely Modeling calendar, however, would have alarmed Qing Astronomical Bureau officials, particularly members of the He family, who had been in contact with Korean astronomers for decades. It is unlikely that the Qing Bureau officials had not yet noticed the deterioration of the calendrical system themselves. Rather, the arrival of Korean astronomers indicated that the deterioration had worsened to the extent that the discrepancies would soon be noticed elsewhere.

The Yongzheng emperor's lack of mathematical expertise did not mean that the Astronomical Bureau officials could easily manipulate him. In fact, it might be harder to make him understand the causes of the inaccuracy. Even if he understood, whether or not the emperor was willing to admit that the Timely Modeling system and the *Thorough Investigation*, compiled under the Kangxi emperor's leadership, were no longer reliable was another question. It is highly possible that a strict sovereign like the Yongzheng emperor would simply make imperial astronomers scapegoats and punish them for failing to provide an accurate prediction.

134 *The Solar Eclipse of 1730*

In November 1729, the Astronomical Bureau officials submitted their prediction, which was calculated according to a method that they already knew was inaccurate. Unless the officials knew how to correct the current system, they had no alternative but to wait in fear of the possible penalty and political consequences. Their future and the prosperity of their families depended on the Yongzheng emperor's judgment.

6.3 The Yongzheng Emperor's Political Performance

The prediction of the 1730 solar eclipse turned out to be a failure—but the failure was seen as a blessing. Shortly after the solar eclipse, officials' congratulations flew to the throne from all over the country. A palace memorial written by some metropolitan officials exemplified what people had seen on that day and how they had interpreted it:

> The eclipse began at the *wu* 午 hour (11:00). After the eclipse reached two *fen*, suddenly clouds covered and a heavy rain fell. After the clouds vanished and the rain stopped, the eclipse barely reached three *fen*. At the third *ke* 刻 of the *wei* 未 hour (13:45), the eclipse was three *fen*; yet the sun began to return to roundness. Everyone witnessed it. Everyone said that this was definitely a response from heaven to the emperor's honest self-reflection.[39]

Li Wei 李衛, the Governor of Zhejiang Province, submitted a similar palace memorial. The Ministry of Rites had informed him that in Hangzhou, the city where the provincial government was located, the eclipse magnitude would be seven *fen* and 19 *miao*.[40] However, according to Li and other local officials' observations, the magnitude was less than five *fen*, and the eclipse ended much earlier than had been predicted: "Not only did I witness [this phenomenon] very clearly, everyone in the city—officials, clerks, soldiers, commoners, monks, Daoist priests and others—did. Thousands of eyes witnessed it together."[41] Li concluded that the emperor's assiduousness and self-reflection must have reached heaven.

The way in which Li and other officials responded to the failed prediction is not difficult to understand. If the observation had minor deviations from the prediction, it could conventionally be ascribed to observer error. However, this time the deviation was so large that a different explanation had to be employed. Fortunately, an eclipse less severe than the prediction had long been regarded as an auspicious omen from heaven. Instead of questioning whether the Astronomical Bureau had miscalculated the eclipse, the officials decided to acknowledge this eclipse as a miraculous representation of the emperor's greatness.

For instance, Fujian Governor Gao Qizhuo 高其倬 expressed his views in detail in his palace memorial written two days after the solar eclipse. Gao first described that he had observed this unusual celestial phenomenon with hundreds of thousands of the commoners under his administration. He then reminded the emperor that, in previous generations, the phenomena that the sun did not eclipse as much as predicted were always caused by miscalculation or inaccurate measurements produced by the Astronomical Bureau. This time Gao claimed:

> However, the measurement and computational method used by our dynasty were drawn from the best parts of previous generations and then combined with Western mathematics. They had been further perfected by the Kangxi emperor's sagely wisdom given by heaven. For more than sixty years, all the measurements conducted in provinces and other countries did not have the slightest inaccuracy. None of the inaccurate methods used by previous generations can be compared to [the method of our dynasty].[42]

Gao's argument assumed that the computational method drawn up by the Kangxi emperor would be perfect and methodical. Therefore, this solar eclipse could be nothing but a miraculous heavenly sign. However, did the Yongzheng emperor also think that the Kangxi emperor's works were always correct and should not be challenged or modified?

This was not the first time that the Yongzheng emperor heard a similar argument. In 1725, Yunlu 允祿 and He Guozong submitted a list of ten suggestions related to the newly published treatise, the *Origins of Mathematical Harmonics and Astronomy*. One of their suggestions, in effect, requested the Yongzheng emperor to remove Ignaz Kögler (1680–1746) from the position of the Administrator of the Calendrical Methods (*zhili lifa* 治理曆法).[43] Yunlu's and He Guozong's argument was similar to Gao Qizhuo's. They claimed that the *Thorough Investigation of Astronomical Phenomena* composed by the Kangxi emperor would not possibly need any more administration. Thus, Ignaz Kögler's title and duties in the Astronomical Bureau should be changed. The Yongzheng emperor approved the majority of Yunlu and He's suggestions. However, instead of discharging Kögler from the Astronomical Bureau, the Yongzheng emperor appointed him as the Bureau Director. He Guozong's plan to remove Kögler from the Astronomical Bureau failed and the He family never obtained the Bureau directorship.

The Yongzheng emperor was a smart and sophisticated ruler. He knew the importance of showing respect for his father's authority. But at the same time, he would not let the courtiers use that respect to manipulate him. Probably feeling that Gao was trustworthy, the Yongzheng emperor left a brief response on his memorial: "These predictive numbers that the officials had received were from the old and inaccurate computational method."[44] This comment indicates that the Yongzheng emperor knew that the prediction had been miscalculated soon after or even before the solar eclipse occurred. Hence, it was not a lack of astronomical knowledge but a political concern as to whether it was proper to admit publicly that such an auspicious omen was nothing more than a miscalculation. With the exception of Gao, the emperor replied to the memorials that attributed the unusual phenomenon to the emperor's sincere self-reflection with a simple word: "viewed" (*lan* 覽). As such, while the Yongzheng emperor appeared uninterested in his officials' praises, he did not in fact deny them.

The Yongzheng emperor waited until the end of the month to stage the last political performance. He issued a lengthy decree regarding the miraculous solar eclipse.[45] The emperor began by naming two officials, both of whom had congratulated him for this miraculous eclipse, and announced that he had severely rebuked them for flattering him. Interestingly, the original memorial submitted by one of those two officials has survived. A quick examination shows that the emperor's only comment on the memorial was on the word "viewed."[46] In fact, as already mentioned, there is no evidence to indicate that the Yongzheng emperor had rebuked any official. Rather than a statement of facts, the emperor's announcement was nothing more than a political performance that was designed to demonstrate his humbleness.

It is from his father, the Kangxi emperor, that the Yongzheng emperor learned how to use the occasions of solar eclipses to stage proper political performances.[47] In his decree, the Yongzheng emperor claims that the Kangxi emperor had led him and his brothers to observe solar eclipses. He quotes the Kangxi emperor's decree on the eclipse of February 21, 1697: "Although people can calculate solar eclipse beforehand, since antiquity emperors all take it as a fearful warning because that is the way to respect heavenly omens and improve administrative affairs."[48] By issuing a decree half a year before the 1730 eclipse to call for suggestions on administration, the Yongzheng emperor followed in his father's footsteps to demonstrate the sovereign's respect for heaven. When dealing with a special occasion, for example, when the eclipse could not be observed because of poor weather, the Kangxi emperor also set the model for his successor. The Yongzheng emperor's decree mentions another solar eclipse, that happened on the first day of the fifty-eighth year of the Kangxi reign (February 19, 1712). The Yongzheng emperor vividly recalls that the Kangxi emperor canceled all New Year feasts and celebrations, fasted, and sent him and other brothers to the Ministry of Rites to participate in the Rescue Ritual.[49] It turned out that bad weather blocked the view of the solar eclipse. Days later, the Kangxi emperor addressed his courtiers:

> Although solar eclipses are due to occur, their magnitudes can be calculated. Moreover, this New Year Day was cloudy and slightly snowy, so [the eclipse] was not visible. But there were bound to be unclouded places in other provinces, and some people must have seen it. Not to mention it happened on New Year Day. We cannot but be cautious about personnel affairs, for they may have some deficiencies. All courtiers should consider and discuss attentively.[50]

What the Yongzheng emperor had learned from his father was that the monarch could not but be cautious about personnel affairs, and he must not risk losing his subjects' respect. Thus instead of easily taking the 1730 eclipse as a sign of approval from heaven, the Yongzheng emperor, like his father, would rather perform being a humble sovereign.

If, after the performance of being a humble sovereign, some officials still insisted that the observed eclipse magnitude was less than the prediction, the Yongzheng emperor taught them where to point the finger. "If the eclipse magnitude was indeed less than predicted," the emperor decreed, "then the Astronomical Bureau must have calculated it wrong."[51] In the 1802 case, the Jiaqing emperor ruled in favor of the Astronomical Bureau because Song Shu was the only individual to exhibit dissent. In the current case, however, the Yongzheng emperor was ready to sacrifice the Astronomical Bureau if his own performance did not satisfy the public. The threat to the Bureau officials could not be more terrifying. They had no choice but to act as cooperative assistants in this imperial political performance.

Around the time that he delivered the long decree, the Yongzheng emperor quietly approved the Astronomical Bureau Director Mingtu's 明圖 request to reform the calendar-making system. On August 11, 1730, Mingtu submitted a memorial regarding the inaccurate prediction his Bureau had made for the solar eclipse of July 15, 1730.[52] Mingtu's memorial suggests that the Astronomical Bureau not only knew that the prediction might be inaccurate but had already made a comparison between prediction and observation on the day of solar eclipse. Mingtu stated:

> The [pre-calculated] movements of the sun and the moon accumulate errors over time. Before long the [calculation] method has to be modified so that it can closely agree with the sky's movements. We courtiers have been sincerely following the *Imperially Composed Thorough Investigation of Astronomical Phenomena* to calculate the Timely Modeling and the Seven Governors calendars to promulgate throughout the empire. Recently, according to my Bureau's Director Dai Jinxian 戴進賢 [Ignaz Kögler] and Vice-Director Xu Maode 徐懋德 [Andreas Pereira],[53] comparison between calculation and observation had found minor errors. . . . As foolish as I am, without verification, I dare not memorialize you. Now, for the solar eclipse of the first day of the sixth month of the eighth year of the Yongzheng reign (July 15, 1730), we had gathered at the observatory and had conducted careful observations. The measured results did not match the pre-calculated magnitude.[54]

Mingtu concluded his memorial by begging the emperor to let Kögler and Pereira lead the work to rectify the system. His memorial was quickly approved by the emperor.[55] In January 1732, Mingtu presented new tables of the solar and lunar orbits (*richan yueli biao* 日躔月離表) made by the Jesuits.[56] These two tables were added to the *Thorough Investigation* as if they were merely updated reference tables. There is no sign that the calculation procedures used by Bureau official had changed. As a result, other officials in the Astronomical Bureau likely were unaware that the basis of the dynasty's official method of calendar making had effectively been changed from the Tychonic system to the Newtonian system.

It is noteworthy that allowing the theoretical basis of the state calendar-making system to be changed under such secrecy was unprecedented. Dorgon could promptly decide to adopt the New Western Method because it had been repeatedly tested in the previous dynasty. However, publicizing the deterioration of the existing calendar-making system well into the dynasty was almost equivalent to challenging the works of the sagely Kangxi emperor. The Yongzheng emperor himself had approved the publication of the *Thorough Investigation*. Later, under He Guozong and Yunlu's suggestion, he even had the declaration on the cover of the official calendar changed to "calculated according to the *Imperially Composed Thorough Investigation of Astronomical Phenomena*."[57] Even though an important modification to the increasingly unsatisfactory calendar-making system had been made, doing so could not be presented in a way that would benefit the Yongzheng emperor. In light of the potential political implications, it is highly likely that the Yongzheng emperor decided that the current calendar-making system should be modified silently, if not secretly.

Chinese Astronomical Bureau officials and mathematicians, such as He Guozong, kept their silence because of their involvement with the *Thorough Investigation*. They likely soon found out that the data used in calendar making had been modified. However, admitting that the *Thorough Investigation* had already become inaccurate would not be in their best interest. Worse still, the Chinese Bureau officials had not found a way to improve the basic structure of the system. Although the Yongzheng emperor did not immediately punish anyone for the inaccuracy of the 1730 eclipse, his trust in He Guozong and the other Chinese astronomers may have suffered. In May 1731, the Yongzheng emperor dismissed He Guozong from all official positions.[58] When the emperor started a new mathematical education program in 1734 (see Chapter 7, Section 7.2), he did not recall He Guozong to service.

Up to the Qianlong reign, Korean astronomers continued to seek help from He family members.[59] By the end of 1734, the Korean court had found out that the Qing had modified the data used in calendar making and had managed to obtain a copy of the new tables of the solar and lunar orbits.[60] The He brothers, however, seemed to have lost their value to the imperial state. He Guozong was about 48 years old when the Yongzheng emperor died in October 1735.[61] He was not yet too old to lose all ambitions for the future. For himself and for his family, He Guozong had to patiently wait a few more years and figure out a new way to sell his mathematical talent to the succeeding Qianlong emperor.

Notes

1 QJZ YZ, 3384–5.
2 For the Newtonian system introduced by the Jesuits into Qing China, see Nicole Halsberghe and Hashimoto Keizo, "Astronomy," in *Handbook of Christianity in China, Vol. 1: 635–1800*, ed. Nicolas Standaert (Leiden: Brill, 2001), 711–36; Keizo Hashimoto 橋本敬造, "Daenho no tenkai—*Rekisho kosei gohen* no naiyo nit suite" 橢圓法の展開—『曆象考成後編』の内容について, *Toho Gakuho (Kyoto)* 東方學報 42 (1971): 245–72.
3 On the importance and secrecy in this change of the astronomical systems, see Shi, "Reforming Astronomy," 36–81.
4 Yao and Hu, *Da Qing lüli huitong xinzuan*, 1485–6.
5 Ibid., 1437.
6 QHD GX 719.
7 IHP 006903.
8 See Appendix H.2.

9. QHD KX 7744–5
10. QHDZL QL 625: 141.
11. The *Spring and Autumn Annals* is the court chronicle of the state of Lu 魯 from 722 BC to 481 BC. It is one of the Five Classics (*wu jing* 五經), the set of the most important traditional Confucian canon.
12. Ibid.
13. QHD GX 719. The statutory laws only required the Astronomical Bureau to send the emperor a reminder. No precise deadline was set.
14. Zhongguo diyi lishi dang'anguan 中國第一歷史檔案館 and Beijing tianwenguan guguanxiangtai 北京天文館古觀象臺, eds., *Qingdai tianwen dang'an shiliao huibian* 清代天文檔案史料匯編 (Zhengzhou: Daxiang chubanshe), 136.
15. For example, see IHP 155895 for the divination on a lunar eclipse in 1670, and NPM 154748 for a lunar eclipse occurred in 1903.
16. SL 29: 368–9; IHP 223343.
17. IHP 223343.
18. For example, see Shi Yunli 石云里, Lu Lingfeng 呂凌峰, and Zhang Binglun 張秉倫, "Qingdai tianwen dang'an Zhong jiaoshi yubao shiliao zhi buyi" 清代天文檔案中交食預報史料之補遺, *Zhongkuo keji shiliao* 中國科技史料 21, no. 3 (2000): 270–81; Pingyi Chu, "Shouer daxue kuizhangge cang *Chongzhen lishu* jiqi xiangguan shiliao yanjiu" 首爾大學奎章閣藏《崇禎曆書》及其相關史料研究, *Kyujanggak* 34 (2009): 250–62; Guo Shirong 郭世榮, *Zhongguo shuxue dianji zi Chaoxian bandao de liuchuan yu yingxiang* 中國數學典籍在朝鮮半島的流傳與影響 (Jinan: Shandong jiaoyu chubanshe, 2009); Shi Yunli 石云里, "Zhong Chao liangguo lishi shang de tianwenxue jiaowang (yi)(er)" 中朝兩國歷史上的天文學交往(一)(二), *Anhui shifan daxue xuebao (ziran kexue ban)* 安徽師範大學學報 (自然科學版) 37 (2014) 1: 6–15 and 2: 108–13; Wann-Sheng Horng, "History of Korean Mathematics, 1657–1868: An Overview," in *A Delicate Balance: Global Perspectives on Innovation and Tradition in the History of Mathematics,* ed. David E. Rowe and Wann-Sheng Horng (Cham: Springer International Publishing, 2015), 363–93. For Korean scholars' contributions to the Qing-Chosŏn history by utilizing Chinese and Korean sources, see, for example, Lim, "Journeys of the Modest Astronomers," 81–109; Jun Yong Hoon 全勇勳, "Chosen ni okeru Jikenreki no juyo katei to sono shisoteki haikei" 朝鮮における時憲曆の受容過程とその思想的背景, *Toho Gakuho* (Kyoto) 東方學報 84 (2009): 302–281.
19. Horng, "Shiba shiji," 68–76.
20. For a survey of the transmission of Western astronomy from China to Korea, see Jun, "Chosen ni okeru," 302–81; Yunli Shi, "The *Yuzhi Lixiang Kaocheng Houbian* in Korea," in *The Jesuits, the Padroado and East Asian Science (1552–1773),* ed. Luís Saraiva and Catherine Jami (Hackensack, NJ: World Scientific Publishing, 2008); 205–29; Shi Yunli 石云里, "'Xifa' chuan Chao kao (shang) (xia)" '西法' 傳朝考 (上)(下), *Guangxi minzu xueyuan xuebao (ziran kexue ban)* 廣西民族學院學報 (自然科學版) 10 (2004) 1: 30–8 and 2: 42–8.
21. QHDSL GX 803: 77.
22. Wu, *Lichao shilu*, 3749.
23. Ibid., 3754.
24. Ibid., 3771.
25. Shi, "'Xifa' chuan Chao kao," 1: 31.
26. Jun, "Chosen ni okeru," 291n50; Lim, 86, 99, and 101; Shi, "Zhong Chao liangguo," 2: 109.
27. Wu, *Lichao shilu*, 3801.
28. Hŏ Wŏn stated that he learned from He Junxi by exchanging short letters or notes on small pieces of paper. See Lim, 101.
29. See chapter 4, section 4.3.
30. SL 4: 804.
31. See chapter 5, section 5.2.
32. Wu, *Lichao shilu*, 4321.

33 He Guozhu was on mourning leave from early 1714 to 1716 (see Chapter 5, Section 5.2).
34 Wu, *Lichao shilu*, 4329; Qu, "Qingdai Qintianjian," 52–3.
35 Wu, *Lichao shilu*, 4329.
36 Ibid., 4429.
37 Ibid., 4431.
38 Ibid., 4436.
39 Zhongguo diyi lishi dang'anguan 中國第一歷史檔案館, ed., *Yongzhengchao Manwen zhupi zouzhe quanyi* 雍正朝滿文朱批奏摺全譯 (Hefei: Huangshanshushe, 1998), 1984.
40 Zhongguo diyi lishi dang'anguan, *Yongzhengchao Hanwen zhupi*, 18: 878.
41 Ibid.
42 Ibid., 18: 840–1.
43 Zhongguo diyi lishi dang'anguan, *Yongzhengchao Hanwen zhupi*, 31: 490. This memorial seems to be the one Andreas Pereira referred to in his letter of November 20, 1732. See Guo Shirong 郭世容 and Li Di 李迪, "Putaoya chuanjiaoshi Xu Maode zai Qintianjian de tianwen gongzuo" 葡萄牙傳教士徐懋德在欽天監的天文工作, *Shandong keji daxue xuebao* 山東科技大學學報 13, no. 2 (2011): 23, and Han, "Zili Jingshen," 216. For Ignaz Kögler, see Pfister, *Notices biographiques*, 643–51.
44 Zhongguo diyi lishi dang'anguan, *Yongzhengchao Hanwen zhupi*, 18: 841.
45 SL 8: 280.
46 Zhongguo diyi lishi dang'anguan, *Yongzhengchao Hanwen zhupi*, 18: 821.
47 On the Kangxi emperor's using astronomical observations as political performance, see Jami, "Imperial Control," 28–49; Han, "Junchen yu buyi," 421. See also Chapter 5, Section 5.2.
48 SL 8: 281.
49 Ibid., 6: 762, 8:281.
50 Ibid., 6: 762. The Yongzheng emperor quoted an abridged version of this decree. Ibid., 8: 281.
51 Ibid.
52 Yunlu 允祿 et al., *Yuzhi lixiang kaocheng houbian* 御製曆象考成後編 [1742], *Yingyin Zhaizaotang siku quanshu huiyao* 景印摛藻堂四庫全書薈要 (Taipei: Shujie shuju), 270: 3. Note that Han Qi 韓琦 misidentifies Mingtu 明圖 as Minggantu 明安圖 in "'Shuli gezhi' de faxian—Jianlun shiba shiji Niudun xiangguan zhuzuo zai Zhongguo de chuanbo" 《數理格致》的發現—兼論 18 世紀牛頓相關著作在中國的傳播, *Zhongkuo keji shiliao* 中國科技史料 19, no. 2 (1998): 78. Mingtu was the Bureau Director between 1710 and 1739, whereas Minggantu did not become the Director until about 1759.
53 For Andreas Pereira, see Pfister, *Notices biographiques*, 652–4; Guo and Li, "Putaoya chuanjiaoshi," 18–24.
54 Yunlu, *kaocheng houbian*, 270: 3.
55 On this memorial's tactful wording and the emperor's approval, see Shi, "Reforming Astronomy," 37–9, 54.
56 IHP 011779.
57 QHDZL QL 625: 140; Zhongguo diyi lishi dang'anguan, *Yongzhengchao Hanwen zhupi*, 31: 491. This was one of the ten suggestions that He Guozong and Yunlu made in 1725 (see above).
58 GYGL 42: 24491.
59 The latest known contact between Korean astronomers and the He family happened in 1743 when a Korean Astronomical Bureau official met with He Guochen 何國宸 and Ignaz Kögler in Beijing. See Shi, "Zhong Chao liangguo," 2: 109. He Guochen was He Guozong's younger brother. See QGLL 11: 453.
60 Shi, "Zhong Chao liangguo," 2: 109; Shi, "'Xifa' chuan Chao kao," 1: 32.
61 For He Guozong's date of birth, see Note 36 in Chapter 5, Section 5.2. For the date of the Yongzheng emperor's death, see SL 8:954.

Bibliography

Abbreviations for Archival and Published Sources

CKSB: *Jindai Zhongguo shiliao congkan sanbian* 近代中國史料叢刊三編, edited by Shen Yunlong 沈雲龍. 850 vols. Taipei: Wenhai chubanshe, 1982.

GYGL: *Guanyuan guanli shiliao* 官員管理史料 of *Qingdai lizhi shiliao* 清代吏治史料, edited by Ren Mengqiang 任夢強. 54 vols. Beijing: Xianzhuang shuju, 2004.

IHP: Neige daku dang'an 內閣大庫檔案. Institute of History and Philology of Academia Sinica, Taipei. http://archive.ihp.sinica.edu.tw/mctkm2/index.html

NPM: Qingdai gongzhongdang zouzhe ji junjichudang zhejian quanwen yingxiang ziliaoku 清代宮中檔奏摺及軍機處檔摺件全文影像資料庫. National Palace Museum, Taipei. http://npmhost.npm.gov.tw/tts/npmmeta/GC/indexcg.html

QGLL: *Qingdai guanyuan lüli dang'an quanbian* 清代官員履歷檔案全編. Edited by Qin Guojing 秦國經. 30 vols. Shanghai: Huadong shifan daxue chubanshe, 1997.

QHD GX: *Qinding Da Qing huidian* 欽定大清會典 [1899]. XXSK 794.

QHD KX: *Da Qing huidian (Kangxi chao)* 大清會典 (康熙朝) [1690]. CKSB 711–30.

QHDSL GX: *Qinding Da Qing huidian shili* 欽定大清會典事例 [1899]. XXSK 798–814.

QHDZL QL: *Qinding Da Qing huidian zeli* 欽定大清會典則例 [1764]. SKQS 620–5.

QJZ YZ: *Yongzhengchao qijuzhuce* 雍正朝起居注冊. Edited by Zhongguo diyi lishi dang'anguan 中國第一歷史檔案館. 5 vols. Beijing: Zhonghua shuju, 1993.

SKQS: *Yingyin wenyuange sikuquanshu* 景印文淵閣四庫全書. 1500 vols. Taipei: Taipei shangwu yinshuguan, 1986.

SL: *Qing shilu* 清實錄. 60 vols. Beijing: Zhonghua shuju, 1985.

XXSK: *Xuxiu sikuquanshu* 續修四庫全書. 1800 vols. Shanghai: Shanghai guji chubanshe, 2002.

Other Sources

Wu Han 吳晗, ed. *Chaoxian Lichao shilu zhong de Zhongguo shiliao* 朝鮮李朝實錄中的中國史料. 12 vols. Beijing: Zhonghua shuju, 1980.

Yao Yuxiang 姚雨薌, and Hu Yangshan胡仰山, eds. *Da Qing lüli huitong xinzuan* 大清律例會通新纂. CKSB 211–20.

Yunlu 允祿 et al. *Yuzhi lixiang kaocheng houbian* 御製曆象考成後編 [1742]. *Yingyin Zhaizaotang siku quanshu huiyao* 景印摘藻堂四庫全書薈要. Vol. 270. Taipei: Shijie shuju, 1985.

Zhongguo diyi lishi dang'anguan 中國第一歷史檔案館, ed. *Yongzhengchao Hanwen zhupi zouzhe huibian* 雍正朝漢文硃批奏摺彙編. 40 vols. Nanjing: Jiangsu guji chubanshe, 1989.

———. *Yongzhenchao Manwen zhupi zouzhe quanyi* 雍正朝滿文朱批奏摺全譯. 2 vols. Hefei: Huangshan shushe, 1998.

Secondary Sources

Chu, Pingyi. "Shouer daxue kuizhangge cang Chongzhen lishu jiqi xiangguan shiliao yanjiu" 首爾大學奎章閣藏《崇禎曆書》及其相關史料研究. *Kyujanggak* 34 (2009): 250–62.

Guo Shirong 郭世榮. *Zhongguo shuxue dianji zi Chaoxian bandao de liuchuan yu yingxiang* 中國數學典籍在朝鮮半島的流傳與影響. Jinan: Shandong jiaoyu chubanshe, 2009.

Guo Shirong 郭世榮, and Li Di 李迪. "Putaoya chuanjiaoshi Xu Maode zai Qintianjian de tianwen gongzuo" 葡萄牙傳教士徐懋德在欽天監的天文工作. *Shandong keji daxue xuebao* 山東科技大學學報 13, no. 2 (2011): 18–24.

Halsberghe, Nicole, and Hashimoto Keizo. "Astronomy." In *Handbook of Christianity in China, Vol. 1: 635–1800*, edited by Nicolas Standaert, 711–36. Leiden: Brill, 2001.

Han Qi 韓琦. "Junchen yu buyi zhijian: Li Guangdi zai Kangxi shidai de huodong ji qi dui kexue de yingxiang" 君主與布衣之間：李光地在康熙時代的活動及其對科學的影響. *Tsinghua xuebao* 清華學報 26, no. 4 (1995): 421–45.

———. "*Shuli gezhi* de faxian—Jianlun shiba shiji Niudun xiangguan zhuzuo zai Zhongguo de chuanbo" 《數理格致》的發現—兼論18世紀牛頓相關著作在中國的傳播. *Zhongkuo keji shiliao* 中國科技史料 19, no. 2 (1998): 78–85.

———. "'Zili jingshen' yu lisuan huodong—Kangqian zhiji wenren dui xixue taidu zhi gaibian ji qi beijing" '自立精神'與曆算活動—康乾之際文人對西學態度之改變及其背景. *Ziran kexueshi yanjiu* 自然科學史研究 21, no. 3 (2002): 210–21.

Hashimoto, Keizo. "Daenho no tenkai—*Rekisho kosei gohen* no naiyo nit suite" 橢圓法の展開—『曆象成後編』の内容について. *Toho Gakuho (Kyoto)* 東方學報 42 (1971): 245–72.

Horng Wann-Sheng 洪萬生. "Shiba shiji dongsuan yu zhongsuan de yiduan duihua: Hong Zhengxia Vs. He Guozhu" 十八世紀東算與中算的一段對話：洪正夏 vs. 何國柱. *Hanxue yanjiu* 漢學研究 20, no. 2 (2002): 57–80.

———. "History of Korean Mathematics, 1657–1868: An Overview." In *A Delicate Balance: Global Perspectives on Innovation and Tradition in the History of Mathematics*, edited by David E. Rowe and Wann-Sheng Horng, 363–93. Cham: Springer International Publishing, 2015.

Jami, Catherine. "Imperial Control and Western Learning: The Kangxi Emperor's Performance." *Late Imperial China* 23, no. 1 (2002): 28–49.

Jun Yong Hoon 全勇勳. "Chosen ni okeru Jikenreki no juyo katei to sono shisoteki haikei" 朝鮮における時憲曆の受容過程とその思想的背景. *Toho Gakuho (Kyoto)* 東方學報 84 (2009): 302–281.

Lim, Jongtae. "Journeys of the Modest Astronomers: Korean Astronomers' Missions to Beijing in the Seventeenth and Eighteenth Centuries." *Extrême-Orient Extrême-Occident* 36 (2013): 81–108.

Pfister, Louis. *Notices biographiques et bibliographiques sur les Jésuites de l'ancienne mission de Chine. 1552–1773.* 2 vols. Shanghai: Imprimerie de la Mission catholique, 1932–34.

Qu Chunhai 屈春海. "Qingdai Qintianjian ji Shixianke zhiguan nianbiao" 清代欽天監暨時憲科職官年表. *Zhongkuo keji shiliao* 中國科技史料 18, no. 3 (1997): 45–71.

Shi Yunli 石云里. "'Xifa' chuan Chao kao (shang) (xia)" '西法'傳朝考(上)(下). *Guangxi minzu xueyuan xuebao (ziran kexue ban)* 廣西民族學院學報 (自然科學版) 10 (2004) 1: 30–8 and 2: 42–8.

———. "Reforming Astronomy and Compiling Imperial Science in the Post-Kangxi Era: The Social Dimension of the *Yuzhi Lixiang Kaocheng Houbian* 御製曆象考成後編." *East Asian Science, Technology, and Medicine* 28 (2008): 36–81.

———. "The *Yuzhi Lixiang Kaocheng Houbian* in Korea." In *The Jesuits, the Padroado and East Asian Science (1552–1773)*, edited by Luís Saraiva and Catherine Jami, 205–29. Hackensack, NJ: World Scientific Publishing, 2008.

———. "Zhong Chao liangguo lishi shang de tianwenxue jiaowang (yi)(er)" 中朝兩國歷史上的天文學交往(一)(二). *Anhui shifan daxue xuebao (ziran kexue ban)* 安徽師範大學學報 (自然科學版) 37 (2014) 1: 6–15 and 2: 108–13.

Shi Yunli 石云里, Lu Lingfeng 呂凌峰, and Zhang Binglun 張秉倫. "Qingdai tianwen dang'an Zhong jiaoshi yubao shiliao zhi buyi" 清代天文檔案中交食預報史料之補遺. *Zhongkuo keji shiliao* 中國科技史料 21, no. 3 (2000): 270–81.

Zhongguo diyi lishi dang'anguan 中國第一歷史檔案館 and Beijing tianwenguan guguanxiangtai 北京天文館古觀象臺, eds. *Qingdai tianwen dang'an shiliao huibian* 清代天文檔案史料匯編. Zhengzhou: Daxiang chubanshe, 1997.

7 Knowledge Reproduction

7.1 Amending the Timely Modeling System

In May 1737, Gucong 顧琮 (1685–1755), a Manchu nobleman and He Guozong's former colleague at the Studio for Cultivating the Youth (see Chapter 5, Section 5.1), submitted a memorial to warn the Qianlong emperor that a calendar crisis would impact the imperial state in the future if the court failed to take immediate remedial measures.[1] Gucong began by reviewing previous emperors' contributions to the state-monopolized business of calendar making. The dynasty's official method of calendar making, Gucong explained, was based on the *Books on Calendrical Astronomy According to the New Method* (*Xinfa lishu* 新法曆書) compiled under the leadership of Xu Guangqi in the late Ming on the basis of various Western mathematical treatises.[2] The texts, illustrations, and reference tables of the *Books* were often obscure and inconsistent. Because the respected Kangxi emperor had recruited a group of officials to research them in detail, a consistent work of calendar making, namely the *Thorough Investigation of Astronomical Phenomena* (*Lixiang kaocheng* 曆象考成), finally was able to come into existence. The Yongzheng emperor completed the improvement of calendar-making by having the *Thorough Investigation* published and put into practice. After all these eulogies on previous emperors, Gucong pointed out where the potential crisis lay. In the previous reign, under the excuse of maintaining the accuracy of calendar making, two new tables of the solar and lunar orbits, in effect, had already replaced those presented in the *Thorough Investigation*. However, Gucong stated:

> These tables come with neither explanation nor the computational method. According to my knowledge, the author of these tables was [the Astronomical Bureau] Director and Honorary Vice Minister of Rites, the Westerner Ignaz Kögler. Only the Westerner Andreas Pereira, Vice-Director, and the Supervisor of the Five Offices Granted the Salary of the Vice Department Director Minggantu know how to use these tables. *Except for these three, nobody understands them*. If [these tables] are not amended and clarified, how can they be transmitted to the future? Our descendants will have no way to deduce and to find [the computational method]. *It will turn out to be the same as if they had never been compiled.*[3]

DOI: 10.4324/9781003008255-7

Gucong's memorial exposed a shocking fact about the state-monopolized business of calendar making. The imperial state staffed the Astronomical Bureau with 200 employees, but now the success of the entire business was in fact determined by just three people. None but these three understood the two essential reference tables used to calculate the solar and lunar orbits. Two of them were European missionaries and the only Qing official might not know the theory required to update these reference tables. Even though Gucong did not explicitly spell out the risky situation that the dynasty found itself in, his warning was clear: if European missionaries died before transmitting related knowledge to the Chinese or if they decided to cease serving the Qing imperial state, the court would lose the ability to produce accurate calendars and astronomical predictions.

The Qianlong emperor took immediate action. He approved Gucong's suggestion to commence annotating the tables of solar and lunar motion and correcting the *Thorough Investigation*. In addition to appointing Ignaz Kögler the Director-General (*Zongcai* 總裁) and Andreas Pereira and Minggantu the Vice Director-Generals (*Fu zongcai* 副總裁) to supervise the project as Gucong had suggested, the emperor assigned the responsibility of coordinating the whole project to Gucong.[4] A month later, upon Gucong's request, Mei Juecheng and He Guozong were also made the Director-Generals of the project. Soon an office was set up within the Astronomical Bureau, and 31 Bureau officials were chosen to work on the project. Perhaps in order to ensure that the project was under more secure supervision, the emperor later named Yunlu as the project's Superintendent (*Zongli* 總理).[5]

In June 1738, the Qianlong emperor received a carefully constructed initial report from Yunlu and the Director-Generals. To avoid any possible accusation of disrespect for previous emperors, the report begins by eulogizing the *Thorough Investigation* by declaring, "Although the long period of time may produce deviation, and occasional adjustments [to the astronomical constants] become necessary, no other method [of calendar making] will surpass it."[6] Next, the report claims that Kögler and Pereira's new method was adopted from inventions that had recently been made in the West for "extending what Digu 第谷 (Tycho) had implied in his incomplete theory."[7] It then explains the three categories that the recent inventions fell. The first two recommended that the astronomical constants should be adjusted, and the third suggested that the planetary orbits should be modified from circular to elliptic. Yunlu and the Director-Generals then evaluated the benefits of adopting these inventions, "Although using elliptic orbit makes calculation more difficult, modifying old constants to match celestial motions is rather new and skillful."[8] Rather than directly pointing out the fact that switching from circular to elliptical orbits would be a dramatic theoretical innovation, they downplayed the importance of such a modification by placing it in the last category, describing it as nothing more than a slight increase in the difficulty associated with the calculation. At the end of the report, they suggested keeping the *Thorough Investigation* intact while putting the new theory and reference tables into a separate volume entitled the *Later Part of Thorough Investigation of Astronomical Phenomena* (*Lixiang kaocheng houbian* 曆象考成後編).[9]

Historians may see the compilation of the *Later Part* as a one-directional knowledge transmission process in which Jesuit missionaries taught while Qing astronomers learned. For instance, when evaluating the theoretical achievements of the *Later Part*, Guo Shirong 郭世榮 and Li Di 李迪 praised Kögler and Pereira by saying, "Although its theory has serious flaws, in China it is already a relatively advanced treatise based on Western astronomy and methods of calendar making." In contrast, Guo and Li asserted, He Guozong and Mei Juecheng "probably did not do any substantive scientific research work" and "only Minggantu's work is worthy of affirmation and praise."[10] Here, Guo and Li seem to suggest that Qing astronomers, with the exception of Minggantu, were more interested in sharing the credit of the project than in learning the new Western knowledge.

Nevertheless, the Jesuits' role in the knowledge transmission process should be carefully reexamined. Kögler and Pereira surely made the most significant contribution to the contents of the *Later Part*. If they refused to cooperate, the *Later Part* would not have come into existence. However, one should not forget that Kögler, Pereira, and the other Jesuit missionaries were recipients of the astronomical theories, not their original inventors. Jesuit teachings contributed greatly to the process of transmitting Western theories into China, but Jesuit astronomers were not the ones who had developed those theories. In this respect, they were not much different from Chinese astronomers, and both parties had their own considerations in relation to the diffusion of knowledge. The Jesuits selected and repacked the astronomical theories to be transmitted to the Chinese in the best possible way for missionary purposes. He Guozong and other Chinese astronomers, for their families' future prosperity, had to learn the new astronomical theory.

This section will therefore analyze the social and political contexts of the birth of the *Later Part*. It will describe the Qing astronomers' awareness of the need to take ownership of the knowledge and explain how they pushed the Jesuits into revealing the new astronomical theory that eventually brought the *Later Part* into existence. The main issues to consider here are what motivated Gucong to initiate such a project and whether Gucong's action indeed was a favor to the Jesuits. Based on the fact that Gucong only recommended one non-Western astronomer, Minggantu, in his first memorial, Guo and Li assert that Gucong might have displeased the Han astronomers by his choice, and thus might have been pressed to add Mei Juecheng and He Guozong to the team of Director-Generals.[11] However, the following arguments will show that Gucong more likely had consulted or had been persuaded by Han astronomers such as Mei Juecheng and He Guozong *before* proposing the project to the emperor.

First of all, it is noteworthy that Gucong was an outsider to the Astronomical Bureau. In February 1736, he became the Governor of Jiangsu but soon was forced to leave that position for mourning leave and he returned to Beijing. In May 1737, a month before submitting the project proposal to the Qing emperor, Gucong was temporarily assigned to the role of Assistant Minister of Personnel (*Xieban libu shangshu* 協辦吏部尚書).[12] His position and official responsibility were completely unrelated to the Astronomical Bureau and astronomy.

Second, the Jesuits did not need Gucong to act as their proxy. They themselves were the Directors of the Astronomical Bureau and the original authors of the tables of solar and lunar motions. If they had decided the time had come to break the silence and reveal the theory behind the two reference tables, the Jesuits could have memorialized the emperor directly. In March 1674, Ferdinand Verbiest memorialized and presented the *New Treatise on the Instruments at the Observatory* (*Xinzhi lingtai yixiang zhi* 新製靈臺儀象志) to the Kangxi emperor.[13] Later, in 1744, Kögler also memorialized the Qianlong emperor directly concerning an amendment to the *New Treatise on the Instruments at the Observatory*.[14] These examples show that as a Director of the Astronomical Bureau, Kögler had no need to use an outsider, such as Gucong, to initiate the project for the Jesuits.

On the other hand, Gucong was no stranger to Mei Juecheng and He Guozong. In 1711, Gucong had passed the examination held by the Kangxi emperor and become one of the personnel serving in mathematics.[15] In the next decade, Gucong studied and worked with the He brothers and Mei Juecheng at the Studio for Cultivating the Youth. Gucong must have done relatively well in mathematics, for his name was listed alongside that of Minggantu and He Guodong in the section of observers (*kaoce* 考測).[16] When the Kangxi emperor dispatched personnel serving in mathematics to various branches of the government, Gucong, like Minggantu and He Guodong, received the highest grade for his contribution to the compilation project of mathematical treatises.[17]

As an outsider, Gucong would only have known the detailed affairs of the Astronomical Bureau through private connections, such as those he may have had with his former colleagues. Although neither Mei Juecheng nor He Guozong worked at the Bureau around the time Gucong submitted his memorial to the Qianlong emperor, the He family had at least four members working at the Astronomical Bureau, including Supervisor of the Middle Office He Guochen 何國宸 and Calendar Manager He Junhui 何君惠.[18] The new tables of solar and lunar motions had been in place for five years.[19] If none of the He brothers or of the Astronomical Bureau officials, Minggantu included, could have figured out the theory beyond the tables, the situation was indeed worrisome. Under the Kangxi emperor's full support, the *Thorough Investigation* still took nine years to finish. The length of time involved may have provided Gucong with an insight into the difficulties that scholars encountered when attempting to absorb Western mathematical astronomy. Moreover, like He Guozong and Mei Juecheng, Gucong might have been influenced by the Kangxi emperor's growing distrust of the Jesuits.[20] He Guozong could easily take advantage of that distrust to convince Gucong to force the Jesuits to explain the theory in detail.

Gucong's involvement was critical for He Guozong and his family's future. Mastering mathematical astronomy was the key for an astronomer family's career success. However, the He family members in the late Yongzheng and early Qianlong reigns faced a situation similar to what their ancestors experienced in the Shunzhi reign. The family's future was in danger if the Jesuits continued to keep the secret of the new theory to themselves. Unfortunately, He Guozong had lost all official posts after 1731, while Guodong only held a part-time job as a

Mathematics Instructor (*Suanxue jiaoxi* 算學教習) at a Banner Official School; neither of them was in a suitable position to make any direct proposal to the emperor. In fact, the emperor might suspect the sincerity of Gucong's proposal if he recommended the unemployed He Guozong brothers in the first memorial. He Guozong and Mei Juecheng did not have enough political power to press Gucong, but they could have utilized past personal connections and Gucong's sympathy for the He family to command his attention and persuade him that proposing the project was in the best interest of the imperial state.

Like his father before him, He Guozong became the emperor's tool to counterbalance the Jesuit control of mathematical knowledge. His career as a civil servant restarted with the task of amending the Timely Modeling system. In the following few years, the Office of Amending the Timely Modeling System grew into a series of book compilation projects, all of which were completed under He Guozong's supervision. In 1744, the Qianlong emperor rehabilitated He Guozong by placing him at the third level of the civil service ranks.[21] The reward most important to the He family came in April 1745, when He Guozong was given the responsibility to "concurrently manage the affairs of the Astronomical Bureau Director" (*jianguan Qintianjian jianzheng shi* 兼管欽天監監正事).[22] Because the civil service ranks of He Guozong and Le'ersen 勒爾森, a Manchu Vice Minister of Rites who was assigned the same responsibility and title, were higher than the rest of the directorate, they virtually became the heads of the Astronomical Bureau. On the roster, Le'ersen and He Guozong always preceded other Bureau officials, including Manchu and European Directors.[23] Working for the Astronomical Bureau once again constituted a promising career for the He family. As the next chapter shows, by the mid-Qianlong period, the He family had established a dominant position in the Astronomical Bureau.

The power struggle within the Astronomical Bureau involved a continuous process of negotiation. Until the early Kangxi reign, writing new treatises and studying mathematical astronomy provided the means through which the Jesuits could attract Chinese astronomers.[24] The compilation of the *Origins of Mathematical Harmonics and Astronomy* changed this situation. From then on, imperial astronomers knew they should study the *Essence of Numbers and Their Principles* and the *Thorough Investigation* instead of Jesuit treatises and that they should follow the authority of the Kangxi emperor, not the Jesuits. Despite the fact that the Jesuits successfully demonstrated that they were the most expert astronomers by presenting the new solar and lunar tables to the Yongzheng emperor, their control of the Astronomical Bureau had substantially declined. Descendants of earlier Chinese Christians—for instance, Supervisor of the Winter Office Bao Qinhui— still worked at the Bureau. However, either the Jesuits did not trust them enough to teach them the new theory or members of the Chinese Christian families were no longer interested in learning from the Jesuits. Following Gucong's proposal, the Jesuits were compelled to cooperate. Afterward, Europeans in the Qing Astronomical Bureau were not much different from any other ethnic group. He Guozong was almost 60 years old when the *Later Part* was finished. He had helped his family get back on track in the profession of imperial astronomers. With the exception of continuing to supervise the studies and work of his family members, there was not much left for Guozong to do for the family. For the Jesuits, slowing down the decline of their status and prolonging their stay in the Qing court entailed maintaining a friendly relationship with He Guozong and the other imperial astronomers. The golden days of Jesuit missionaries' domination of the Qing Astronomical Bureau were over.

7.2 The Short-Lived Yongzheng Mathematics Program

Toward the end of his reign, the Yongzheng emperor seemed to have come to a similar realization as his father about mathematics. On June 13, 1733, the Yongzheng emperor told his Grand Secretariat:

> Ministries and bureaus all rely on clerical subofficials to calculate the accounting of monetary affairs and grain supply. Since few among the superior officials and Scribes thoroughly understand mathematics (*suan fa* 算法), it is hard to detect even if treacherous subofficial functionaries have fraudulent practices. Mathematics is one of the Six Arts (*liu yi* 六藝).[25] For those Scribes of all ministries and bureaus who are willing to learn mathematics on their spare time, order them to study and wait for the examination I will give three years later. Moreover, order Official Students and expectant appointees of Scribes to study too. If they are willing to take the examination, they are allowed to do so. I will give those who excelled at the examination additional grace and make a special use of them.[26]

This decree leads one to recall what the Kangxi emperor had stated when he assigned He Guozhu to the Ministry of Revenue in 1713 (see Chapter 5, Section 5.2), although they had different emphases. The Kangxi emperor stressed the beneficial aspect of mathematics in improving government accounting, while the Yongzheng emperor thought that mathematical knowledge was necessary to detect fraud and corruption. Nonetheless, they both recognized the usefulness of mathematics in administrative affairs. Furthermore, the above decree suggests that the Yongzheng emperor, after more than a decade of ruling, might have decided to follow in his father's footsteps to cultivate a new generation of civil servants whose mathematical talents could serve the imperial state beyond the Astronomical Bureau. Such a decree would be encouraging to those who hope to obtain civil service position with their mathematical expertise. However, the mathematical activities at the Studio for Cultivating the Youth had long been discontinued, and the Yongzheng emperor did not have his father's mathematical knowledge. He needed a new implementation plan to cultivate civil servants whose mathematical expertise would be utilized by the imperial state.

In 1734, Yunli 允禮 (also known as Yinli 胤禮, 1697–1738), a trusted younger brother of the Yongzheng emperor and Yunlu, obtained imperial permission to begin an ambitious mathematics program at the Eight Banners Official Schools. Each banner official school had to select at least 30 students who were "clever and keen" to participate in the mathematics program, and each school was assigned two Mathematics Instructors (called *Suanxue jiaozi* 算學教習 or *Suanfa jiaoxi* 算法教習).[27] Among these Mathematics Instructors, three have been found in archival documents. The first two, He Guodong and Zhaohai 照海, had been personnel serving in mathematics at the Studio for Cultivating the Youth; their careers will be further discussed in the next section. The third the Mathematics Instructor at the Plain Blue Banner Official School (*Zhenglanqi suanfa zhengjiaoxi* 正藍旗算法正教習) Bao Qinhui, then the Supervisor of the Winter Office.[28] Bao passed the special examination for recruiting additional members of the Office of Compiling Mathematical Treatises in 1719, and worked there until the Office was disbanded in June 1724.[29] The background of these three former colleagues at the Studio for Cultivating the Youth suggests that the Yongzheng emperor provided the Eight Banners Official Schools with highly qualified Mathematics Instructors. While Mathematics Instructors only came to the school every other day, the selected students studied mathematics for two to four hours every afternoon.[30] On average, each banner official school had around 70 or 80 students, meaning that nearly half of the students were enrolled in the mathematics program, and they spent almost half of the day studying mathematics. In sum, the mathematics program had 16 instructors and more than 240 students.[31] In comparison, the Astronomical Bureau had only 24 banner Student Astronomers and 80 Han Student Astronomers.

Although Yunli's proposal did not mention a specific goal for the program, what the Yongzheng emperor and Yunli arguably had in mind was to make mathematics a part of the general education for banner officers rather than to train specialists in mathematics or astronomy. Several facts support this assertion. First, as mentioned earlier, the scale of the mathematics program far exceeded the requirement for the number of Astronomical Bureau apprentices and students. Second, the difference between banner Student Astronomers and the students of the mathematics program was significant. The former were selected from Official Students. After being selected, they became Student Astronomers of the Astronomical Bureau and no longer studied at the Banner Official Schools. Those who were selected to participate in the mathematics program, however, stayed at their original Banner Official Schools. With the exception of the time set aside for mathematics studies, they followed the same curriculum—riding and archery, translation, and Chinese classical study—as the other students. The imperial state decided to select them to study mathematics not because mathematics seemed a better path for them, but because they were considered talented enough to take the additional course. Third, the administrative responsibility for the mathematics program was not given to the Directors of the Astronomical Bureau but to Chengde 成德, a Manchu high official who had studied at the Studio for Cultivating the Youth.[32] This arrangement ensured that both organizations operated independently from each other.

Unfortunately, this mathematics program lasted only five years. Only a year after its founding, the mathematics program lost its main initiator and supporter when the Yongzheng emperor died in October 1735. The new monarch, the Qianlong emperor (r. 1736–1795), did not seem to be interested in the idea of adding courses into the general curriculum for cultivating future government officials.

In June 1736, high ministers and the Qianlong emperor rejected Mei Juecheng's suggestions to include mathematics in the civil service examinations and give special rewards to those who excelled at answering mathematical questions.³³ Mei Juecheng himself did not leave any explanation for why he made these suggestions. But judging from the time he submitted the memorial, it is possible that Mei intended to remind the Qianlong emperor of the special mathematics examination promised by the Yongzheng emperor three years ago. As a courtier who owed his current social and political position to the Kangxi emperor's compilation project at the Studio for Cultivating the Youth, Mei must have known the importance of the special examination to those who wished to serve the court with their mathematical expertise. Regretfully, there was no way Mei or any court mathematicians could compel the monarch to implement what his deceased father had promised.

Without a clear purpose and reward, the Yongzheng mathematics program soon deteriorated into failure. In 1738, Sun Jiagan 孫嘉淦 (1683–1753), who was in charge of the Imperial College affairs, submitted a detailed plan for improving the Eight Banners Official Schools. One of his suggestions was to terminate the mathematics program. Sun claimed that the Official Schools should focus on producing future banner officers who were trained in translation and Chinese classical study. "Regarding the art of mathematics (*suan fa* 算法)," Sun argued, "its principles and numbers are meticulous and delicate, it is impossible for the youth to understand in a short period."³⁴ Under the current system, Official Students were distracted from their original goal and failed to acquire adequate mathematical knowledge. Sun stressed, "Mathematics is a business belonging to the Astronomical Bureau," and concluded that the teaching of mathematics should be carried out by the Astronomical Bureau, not by the Eight Banners Official Schools.³⁵ After having some ministers discuss Sun's suggestion, the Qianlong emperor agreed to transform the mathematics program into a specialist school.

The new specialist school, called the College of Mathematics (*Suanxue* 算學), officially commenced in December 1739.³⁶ The responsibility of managing the College of Mathematics was given to Chengde, who had been managing the mathematics program at the Banner Official Schools. Through Chengde's nomination, He Guozong and Mei Juecheng were assigned to assist the management of the College of Mathematics.³⁷ This nomination probably did not come as a surprise to them. We have seen in Section 7.1 that He Guozong and Mei Juecheng became the Director-Generals of the new compilation project of the *Later Part* in mid-1737 because their former colleague Gucong's recommendation. Chengde was their another colleague at the Studio of Cultivating the Youth. They could have befriended each other since they accompanied the Kangxi emperor to the summer palace in 1712.³⁸ He Guozong and Mei Juecheng undoubtedly qualified for their new appointments. However, the Qing court forever lost the vision of cultivating officials who were both scholars in classics and mathematicians, such as He Guozong and Mei Juecheng.

Although the Qing official records, such as The *Collected Statutes of the Great Qing*, always included the short-lived Yongzheng mathematics program when tracing the origin of the College of Mathematics, few records about it have

152   *Knowledge Reproduction*

survived.[39] Hence, historians often confuse it with the mathematical activities that took place at the Studio for Cultivating the Youth in the last decade of the Kangxi era or its successor, the College of Mathematics founded in the early Qianlong reign.[40] In fact, as the next section will show, the College of Mathematics bore little resemblance to the Yongzheng mathematics program. The latter was part of the general education provided for future banner officials, while the former aimed to produce mathematics specialists to work for the Astronomical Bureau. These differences reflect the Qing court's changing views on the purpose and range of public mathematics education.

7.3 College of Mathematics

Instead of being a new educational institution or program, the College of Mathematics functioned more like an addition to the Astronomical Bureau. Prior to the formation of the College of Mathematics, the recruitment and training of imperial astronomers were rather informal and unsystematic. As already described in previous chapters, The Qing court's swift decision to adopt the New Western Method did nothing to increase the attractiveness of a career as an imperial astronomer. Until the last years of the Shunzhi reign, Schall, the head of the Astronomical Bureau, still had difficulty finding staff. The Calendar Dispute that occurred in the first decade of the Kangxi reign only served to increase the Bureau's lack of appeal as a place to work. In that period, any Han Chinese who was willing and had the basic ability to learn astronomy was able to obtain the position of Student Astronomer without much difficulty. Indeed, when the earliest bannermen were added to the Bureau in 1665, they started as Erudites despite lacking previous experience in astronomy and mathematics.[41] The situation seemed to have gradually improved after the Kangxi emperor decreed in August 1676 that the Bureau officials could only earn promotion by mastering the New Method.[42] Although seeming to teach in an informal setting, Ferdinand Verbiest once claimed that he had 160 to 200 disciples in the Astronomical Bureau.[43] After the College of Mathematics was founded, its students, called Mathematics Students (*Suanxuesheng* 算學生), became a bottom layer below the Student Astronomers of the Astronomical Bureau. Newcomers to the Bureau were rerouted to the College of Mathematics first. Only after passing the graduation examination did they obtain the license of Student Astronomers.

Although this rerouting delayed the astronomers' career advancement, they did gain some rewards. Previously, most banner Student Astronomers started their career at the Astronomical Bureau with little experience in mathematics. They were required to remain with the Astronomical Bureau even if they made little progress in learning astronomy. After the College of Mathematics was founded, an Official Student who was considering a career at the Astronomical Bureau could transfer to the College of Mathematics, where he would receive lessons in mathematics and astronomy. His monthly student stipend and his rights to take the civil service examinations stayed the same. He could choose to transfer back to the official school if he felt that becoming an astronomer was not his destiny.[44]

The College of Mathematics also was beneficial to Han Chinese. At its founding, the College of Mathematics was given a quota of 36 Mathematics Students: 12 Manchus, six Mongols, six military Hans, and 12 Han Chinese.[45] This gave Han Chinese who was not from hereditary astronomer families but was interested in joining the Astronomical Bureau a new channel to enter the Astronomical Bureau. Before the founding of the College of Mathematics, such a Han Chinese newcomer would have to work and study at the Bureau as an informal (and probably unpaid) apprentice, called Astronomy Apprentices (*Yiye tianwensheng* 肄業天文生), until he passed the examination for becoming a Student Astronomer.[46] The Astronomical Bureau continued to recruit Astronomy Apprentices after the College of Mathematics was founded. But in 1745, the Astronomical Bureau decided that maintaining a separate program to train its own apprentices was redundant. It obtained imperial permission to let the Astronomy Apprentices of the Calendar Section and the Section of Heavenly Signs study at the College of Mathematics. Only the training of the Astronomy Apprentices who belonged to the Water Clock Section remained in the Bureau.[47] In 1756, the quota of Astronomy Apprentices was fixed at 30; among them, 24 were sent to study at the College of Mathematics and thus were often referred to as Apprentices at the College of Mathematics (*Suanxue yiyesheng* 算學肄業生).[48] The presence of the 12 Han Mathematics Students and 24 Apprentices at the College of Mathematics together constituted the most significant difference between the College of Mathematics and the Yongzheng mathematics program. The Yongzheng mathematics program was part of the public educational system for bannermen, which excluded Han Chinese. The College of Mathematics was an institution that aimed to recruit and train future officials for the Astronomical Bureau. Because the Astronomical Bureau needed bannermen and Han Chinese, the College of Mathematics was open to both. In fact, it had more Han Chinese students than banner students.

It is noteworthy that the benefits offered to Han Mathematics Students and to Astronomy Apprentices were different. Han Mathematics Students were basically treated as Official Students. They were granted monthly stipends and the privilege to wear the same robes and decorations as Official Students when attending official ceremonies.[49] Astronomy Apprentices, however, were not given any monthly stipend.[50] This is probably because Astronomy Apprentices were not regarded as formal students of the College of Mathematics but as apprentices of the Astronomical Bureau. Except for the monthly stipend, courses and periodical examinations were administered to Mathematics Students and Astronomy Apprentices (at the College of Mathematics) alike, and there seemed to be no difference in the academic requirements imposed on each group.[51] Before the College of Mathematics was founded, a Han Chinese student without a family history of serving the Astronomical Bureau would have to begin working and studying at the Astronomical Bureau as an informal apprentice. There was no standardized course for teaching him, and he would not receive any stipend until he passed the examination for the position of Student Astronomer. After the College of Mathematics was founded, a Han Chinese with sufficient mathematical knowledge could become a Mathematics Student, and in this capacity, he received a monthly stipend until he passed the graduation examination. If the person's mathematical knowledge was not yet sufficient to qualify him as a Mathematics Student, he could still become an Apprentice at the College of Mathematics, and in this capacity, he had access to the teaching at the College of Mathematics.

Although the College of Mathematics was under the management of one or two grand ministers directly appointed by the emperor, the individual in charge of its day-to-day teaching and administration was the Principal Instructor (*Zhujiao* 助教).[52] Under the Principal Instructor were two Instructors (*Jiaoxi* 教習) and three Teaching Assistants (*Xietong fenjiao* 協同分教).[53] The Principal Instructor was a respected position, not only because of the administrative responsibility involved but also because of the difficulty associated with obtaining the role. A teaching term at the College of Mathematics was five years. Thus, the vacancy of Principal Instructor did not arise often. Once the position was available, the Astronomical Bureau held an examination that all Erudites and Instructors could sit and the post of Principal Instructor was awarded to the individual who performed the best in the examination.[54] After fulfilling the five-year teaching term, the Principal Instructor surpassed other senior colleagues and became the Supervisor of the Five Offices at the Calendar Section as soon as a post was available. Thus, the post of Principal Instructor was a great opportunity for Bureau officials to make faster career advancement. One such case was that of He Guodong.

Just as the amendment of the Timely Modeling system restarted He Guozong's career, the founding of the College of Mathematics was critical to He Guodong's career. He Guodong seemed unable to obtain a decent position after he lost the position of Dingzhou Prefect in 1725. He likely had taught at the Eight Banners Official Schools' mathematics program. Therefore, when the program was reorganized into the College of Mathematics, he obtained one of the Instructorships.[55] After one teaching term of Instructor and one of Principal Instructor, He Guodong became the Supervisor of the Middle Office in 1751.[56] Such a position came with far less political power and financial benefits than the prefect's post that he held 25 years earlier. Nonetheless, it was so stable and easy that Guodong repeatedly requested an extension to his tenure. He did not transfer to another institution until 1767, at which point he was already 77 years old.[57]

He Guodong was not the only one to benefit from taking up a teaching position at the College of Mathematics. Zhaohai 照海 was a Provincial Graduate and one of the earliest personnel serving in mathematics. In December 1714, the Kangxi emperor sent He Guodong to Guangdong to measure the North Pole's altitude, while Zhaohai was sent to Zhejiang.[58] After the *Thorough Investigation* was finished, Zhaohai became a Vice Department Director at the Ministry of Works (*Gongbu yuanwailang* 工部員外郎).[59] The fact that Zhaohai and He Guodong both had to serve three additional years after finishing the first teaching term of Instructor indicates that Zhaohai, like He Guodong, had been discharged dishonorably in the previous reign.[60] In April 1748, Zhaohai finally obtained the post of Observatory Manager.[61] He stayed in this position for the next ten years.[62]

The posts of Instructor and Teaching Assistant did not bring as much career advantage as that of the Principal Instructor. The earliest two Instructors, He

Guodong and Zhaohai, obtained their positions because they previously had been the Mathematics Instructors at the Eight Banners Official Schools. After them, the Astronomical Bureau held examinations for Student Astronomers to select the Instructors for the College of Mathematics.[63] Unless he was a civil service degree holder, an Instructor was normally awarded with the post of Erudite in the Calendar Section or the Section of Heavenly Signs after finishing the teaching term. For example, Zhaohai obtained the post of Observatory Manager instead of Erudite because he held the Provincial Graduate degree. It might be the lower civil rank and the hardship of working at the observatory that led He Guodong to choose to work another five years as the Principal Instructor so that he could become one of the Supervisors at the Calendar Section. To ease Principal Instructor and Instructors' burden of teaching, Teaching Assistants were selected from senior or graduated Mathematics Students and Student Astronomers.[64] But the job of Teaching Assistants brought neither additional monthly stipends nor any promotion. For Teaching Assistants who were still Mathematics Students, they had to take periodical examinations with the rest of the Mathematics Students. The only benefit a Teaching Assistant obtained was that he would continue receiving the monthly stipend of Mathematics Student until he became a Student Astronomer.[65]

The official curriculum prescribed a five-year program for the students at the College of Mathematics:

> Mathematics Students' classwork should follow the *Imperially Composed Essence of Numbers and Their Principles,* divided into three sections of the Line (*xian* 線), the Area (*mian* 面), and the Solid (*ti* 體). Each section [should be learned] within a year. Seven Governors should be thoroughly understood within two years. New students begin with the Line section and proceed in order. [Their progress] should be noted in class registers so that [students'] proficiency and familiarity can be expected. There are quizzes every month and seasonal examinations in spring and autumn. At the end of the year, the College of Mathematics should hold grand examinations jointly with the Astronomical Bureau to distinguish industrious students from indolent ones and which one should be expelled or allowed to stay.[66]

The Line, Area, and Solid sections mentioned in the above official curriculums correspond to the three main sections from the second part, "Dividing into Groups to Put to Use" (*fentiao zhiyong* 分條致用), of the *Essence of Numbers and Their Principles.*[67] We do not know if the first part of the *Essence of Numbers and Their Principles* was ever studied by Mathematics Students or if it was regarded as a prerequisite for entering the College of Mathematics. On the other hand, a historical record shows that every Mathematics Student was provided with a set of mathematics textbooks, including the *Essence of Numbers and Their Principles,* the *Thorough Investigation of Astronomical Phenomena,* and the *Later Part of Thorough Investigation of Astronomical Phenomena,* to study during his stay at the College of Mathematics.[68] Thus, it seems reasonable to assume that after three years' learning from the *Essential Principles of Mathematics,* a student should spend his last two years at the College of Mathematics studying the *Thorough Investigation* and the *Later Part* so that they could learn the astronomical knowledge and calculation about the "Seven Governors," the sun, the moon, and the five planets.

Very few records describe exactly how the teaching activities were conducted at the College of Mathematics. Non-official documents from the mid- and late Qing period suggest that students might have been divided into three classes (*tang* 堂), a possible imitation of the Six Classes (*Liu tang* 六堂) system implemented in the Imperial College and were then assigned to different instructors.[69] Thus, Principal Instructor and Instructors each had their own classes of students to teach and were responsible for the progress of the students under their supervision.[70] Unlike the civil service examinations that were held according to a fixed schedule, the College of Mathematics and the Astronomical Bureau held entrance examinations whenever they accumulated a certain amount of vacancies.[71] The graduation examination was held every five years and all but the first-year students could take it. Thus, some Mathematics Students might have studied at the College for less than five years.[72]

In sum, the College of Mathematics founded in the early Qianlong era was the opposite of the Yongzheng mathematics program in almost every aspect. Its goal was relatively moderate yet clear: to train specialists who would work for the Astronomical Bureau. While the teaching activities of the Yongzheng mathematics program were conducted at the Eight Banners Official Schools, the College of Mathematics was given its own campus near the Astronomical Bureau.[73] Within the government organizational chart, the College of Mathematics was subordinated to the Imperial College. This affiliation made the College of Mathematics a state-level official school and gave its instructors and students certain benefits and social status. However, the College of Mathematics had its own campus, administrative system, channels of recruiting students, and curriculum. These two institutions, in fact, had very limited connections. On the other hand, the goal of the College of Mathematics was to be aligned with the Astronomical Bureau. Its teachers were chosen from the Bureau officials and its students aimed to enter the Bureau after graduation. Often the emperor assigned the management responsibilities of the College of Mathematics and the Astronomical Bureau to the same person. In the late Qing period, the Han Astronomical Bureau Directors often worked concurrently to assist the management of the College of Mathematics.

Notes

1. For Gucong's biography, see *Qing guoshi*, 6: 467–70. For Gucong's memorial, see Yunlu, *kaocheng houbian*, 270: 4–5. Gucong was one of the 42 examinees who passed the first examination for recruiting the personnel serving in mathematics held in April 1612. *Qing guoshi*, 4:626.
2. Here Gucong means the *Books on Calendrical Astronomy According to the New Western Method* (*Xiyang xinfa lishu* 西洋新法曆書). It was recompiled and renamed from the *Books on Calendrical Astronomy of the Chongzhen Reign* (*Chongzhen lishu* 崇禎曆書) compiled under the leadership of Xu Guangqi.
3. Yunlu, *kaocheng houbian*, 270: 4–5. Italics mine.

4 Ibid., 5.
5 Ibid., 5–7.
6 Ibid., 6.
7 Ibid.
8 Ibid., 7.
9 Ibid., 7–8.
10 Guo and Li, "Putaoya chuanjiaoshi," 22.
11 Ibid., 21. Catherine Jami holds the same view. See Jami, *Emperor's New Mathematics*, 378–9.
12 *Qing guoshi*, 6: 468.
13 Ferdinand Verbiest, *Xinzhi lingtai yixiang zhi* 新製靈臺儀象志, XXSK 1031: 647–9.
14 Yunlu 允祿 et al., *Qinding yixiang kaocheng* 欽定儀象考成, SKQS 793: 2–3.
15 *Qing guoshi*, 4: 625–6.
16 Yunlu, *lixiang kaocheng*, 790: 5–6.
17 Li, *Dingli quanbian*, 1: 28.
18 "Qianlong sannian zaijing wenzhi Hanguan fengmi ji zhiming huangce erjuan" 乾隆三年在京文職漢官俸米及職名黃冊二卷, in *Qingchu shiliao congbian* 清初史料叢編, ed. Luo Zhenyu 羅振玉, CKSB 33: 710–16, 797–803. He Junhui's name suggests that he belonged to the generation of He Guochen's father, He Junxi. Due to the age difference, He Junhui probably was not a younger brother of He Junxi but a cousin descending from He Luotu or He Qiyi.
19 IHP 011779.
20 Han, "Zili jingshen," 215–9. See also Chapter 5, Section 5.1.
21 IHP 023912.
22 *Qing guoshi*, 6: 484; SL 12: 42.
23 For example, see IHP 021541, 045891, and 023895.
24 Han, "Fengjiao tianwenxuejia," 382–84.
25 According to the classic *Rites of Zhou* (*Zhou li* 周禮), noblemen should be well-educated in the Six Arts: rites (*li* 禮), music (*yue* 樂), archery (*she* 射), chariotry (*yu* 御), calligraphy (*shu* 書), and mathematics (*shu* 數). SKQS 90: 253.
26 Zhongguo diyi lishi dang'anguan, *Yongzhengchao Hanwen yuzhi*, 8: 284; Feng, *Yongzheng zhuan*, 493.
27 Wenqing 文慶 et al., *Guozijian zhi* 國子監志, XXSK 751: 651; Wang Ping 王萍, "Qingchu lisuan yanjiu yu jiaoyu" 清初曆算研究與教育, *Zhongyang yanjiuyuan jindaishi yanjiusuo jikan* 中央研究院近代史研究所集刊 3 (1972): 370–5. Yunli's memorial recorded in QHDZL QL 625:130 names this position *Suanxue jiaozi* 算學教習, while other documents refer it as *Suanfa jiaoxi* 算法教習. Guozijian 國子監, *Qinding Guozijian zeli* 欽定國子監則例 [1822], 1043. According to the résumé written by Bao Qinhui, who actually held this post (see below), it seems the latter was the official title.
28 QGLL 13: 189.
29 GYGL 21: 12505–7; QGLL 13: 189–90.
30 Sources differ on the length of the mathematics course. QHDZL QL 625:130 and Sun Jiagan's 孫嘉淦 routine memorial state that mathematics courses "starts in the *wei* 未 hour (13:00–15:00) and stops in the *shen* 申 hour (15:00–17:00)" [*weishi qi shenshi zhi* 未時起申時止]. Sun's memorial further states that students should study mathematics "during this one double-hour" [*ci yishi zhong* 此一時中]. Thus, it seems to be a two-hour course from 13:00 to 15:00. Wenqing et al., *Guozijian zhi*, 752: 476. But according to the *Monograph of the Imperial College* [*Guozijian zhi* 國子監志] and the *Precedents of the Imperial College* [*Guozijian zeli* 國子監則例], the study of mathematics was "daily for the two double-hours of *wei* and *shen*" [*meiri wei shen liangshi* 每日未申兩時], then the course would be four hours long between (13:00–17:00). Wenqing et al., *Guozijian zhi*, 751: 651, 752: 475; Guozijian, *Qinding Guozijian zeli*, 1043.

31 Wenqing et al., *Guozijian zhi*, 752: 475.
32 *Qing guoshi*, 4: 626.
33 Yunlu, *kaocheng houbian*, 270: 3–4.
34 Wenqing et al., *Guozijian zhi*, 752: 476. In accordance with the Yongzheng emperor's edict of June 13, 1733 (see above), here I translate *suan fa* 算法 as 'mathematics,' though a literally translation of 'computational methods' may be closer to what Sun had in mind.
35 Ibid.
36 IHP 020636.
37 SL 10: 280–1.
38 *Qing guoshi*, 4: 626.
39 QHDZL QL 625: 130; QHDSL JQ 70: 4225–6; QHDSL GX 813: 299.
40 For the former, see Fang, *Zhongxi jiaotongshi*, 2: 519–20; Catherine Jami, "Learning Mathematical Sciences during the Early and Mid-Ch'ing," in *Education and Society in Late Imperial China, 1600–1900*, ed. Benjamin A. Elman and Alexander Woodside (Berkeley: University of California Press, 1994), 238. For the latter, see Li, *Zhongguo Suanxueshi*, 222–4.
41 SL 4: 229.
42 Ibid., 804.
43 Jami, "Learning Mathematical Sciences," 237–8.
44 Guozijian, *Qinding Guozijian zeli*, 1037–8, 1041–2.
45 Ibid., 1035.
46 IHP 129743.
47 Guozijian, *Qinding Guozijian zeli*, 1027.
48 IHP 133172.
49 Guozijian, *Qinding Guozijian zeli*, 1038.
50 QHDZL QL 625: 131.
51 IHP 129743.
52 SL 10: 281; Guozijian, *Qinding Guozijian zeli*, 1023. There was no official title or quota for the grand ministers assigned to manage the College of Mathematics.
53 Ibid., 1025–9.
54 SL 4: 804.
55 Wenqing et al., *Guozijian zhi*, 752: 204.
56 Qu, "Qingdai Qintianjian," 56.
57 QGLL 19: 275–6.
58 SL 6: 571.
59 Yunlu, *kaocheng houbian*, 270: 6.
60 IHP 051694; NPM 002237.
61 NPM 002237.
62 QGLL 29: 390; Shi, "Tianwenke," 39.
63 Guozijian, *Qinding Guozijian zeli*, 1035.
64 Wenqing et al., *Guozijian zhi*, 751: 652. IHP 119130.
65 Ibid.
66 Wenqing et al., *Guozijian zhi*, 751: 651–2. QHDZL QL 625: 131 has similar statement about curriculums but it does not specifically mention the *Essential of Numbers and Their Principles*.
67 For the contents of the Essential Principles of Mathematics, see Jami, *Emperor's New Mathematics*, 315–9.
68 IHP139389. In this memorial, the grand minister supervising the College of Mathematics sought permission to print extra copies of the *Essence of Numbers and Their Principles*, the *Thorough Investigation of Astronomical Phenomena*, and the *Later Part of Thorough Investigation of Astronomical Phenomena* for Apprentices at the College of Mathematics so that, the same as Mathematics Student, "Everyone is give mathematics treatises (*suan shu* 算書) to benefit his studying. When the studying period ends, [a student] should return all treatises."

69 Ronglutang 榮祿堂, ed., *Juezhi quanlan* 爵秩全覽 [1904], CKZB 130: 263.
70 See the case of Principal Instructor Zhang Deyuan 張德源 in Chapter 9, Section 9.2.
71 IHP 152974, 080794, 26237, 226534, 099857.
72 IHP 020636.
73 QHDZL QL 625: 130. The *Collected Statutes* states that the College of Mathematics should be given its own campus near the Astronomical Bureau but does not specify its exact location. According to an officer of the Central Observatory (*Zhongyang guanxiangtai* 中央觀象臺) who had participated the newly founded republic government's takeover of the Qing Astronomical Bureau in 1912, the Ministry of Education received three groups of houses from the Qing Astronomical Bureau: main office, observatory, and the College of Mathematics. The College of Mathematics was located on the Xi Jiaomin Xiang 西交民巷 and it had been used as the place to calculate the calendar. Later the Ministry of Education used the campus of the College of Mathematics to set up an all-girls high school. Chen Zungui 陳遵媯, *Zhongguo tianwenxue shi* 中國天文學史 (Shanghai: Shanghai renmin chubanshe, 2016), 1353.

Bibliography

Abbreviations for Archival and Published Sources

CKSB: *Jindai Zhongguo shiliao congkan sanbian* 近代中國史料叢刊三編, edited by Shen Yunlong 沈雲龍. 850 vols. Taipei: Wenhai chubanshe, 1982.
CKZB: *Jindai Zhongguo shiliao congkan sanbian* 近代中國史料叢刊正編, edited by Shen Yunlong 沈雲龍. 1000 vols. Taipei: Wenhai chubanshe, 1966.
GYGL: *Guanyuan guanli shiliao* 官員管理史料 of *Qingdai lizhi shiliao* 清代吏治史料, edited by Ren Mengqiang 任夢強. 54 vols. Beijing: Xianzhuang shuju, 2004.
IHP: Neige daku dang'an 內閣大庫檔案. Institute of History and Philology of Academia Sinica, Taipei. http://archive.ihp.sinica.edu.tw/mctkm2/index.html
NPM: Qingdai gongzhongdang zouzhe ji junjichudang zhejian quanwen yingxiang ziliaoku 清代宮中檔奏摺及軍機處檔摺件全文影像資料庫. National Palace Museum, Taipei. http://npmhost.npm.gov.tw/tts/npmmeta/GC/indexcg.html
QGLL: *Qingdai guanyuan lüli dang'an quanbian* 清代官員履歷檔案全編. Edited by Qin Guojing 秦國經. 30 vols. Shanghai: Huadong shifan daxue chubanshe, 1997.
QHDSL GX: *Qinding Da Qing huidian shili* 欽定大清會典事例 [1899]. XXSK 798–814.
QHDSL JQ: *Qinding Da Qing huidian shili (Jiaqing chao)* 欽定大清會典事例 (嘉慶朝) [1818]. CKSB 641–700.
QHDZL QL: *Qinding Da Qing huidian zeli* 欽定大清會典則例 [1764]. SKQS 620–5.
SKQS: *Yingyin wenyuange sikuquanshu* 景印文淵閣四庫全書. 1500 vols. Taipei: Taipei shangwu yinshuguan, 1986.
SL: *Qing shilu* 清實錄. 60 vols. Beijing: Zhonghua shuju, 1985.
XXSK: *Xuxiu sikuquanshu* 續修四庫全書. 1800 vols. Shanghai: Shanghai guji chubanshe, 2002.

Other Sources

Guozijian 國子監. *Qinding Guozijian zeli* 欽定國子監則例 [1822]. CKSB 487–90.
Li Zhen 李珍, ed. *Dingli quanbian Xuzhen xinli* 定例全編 續增新例 [1723]. Oki Collection. Library of the Institute for Advanced Studies on Asia, University of Tokyo.
"Qianlong sannian zaijing wenzhi Hanguan fengmi ji zhiming huangce erjuan" 乾隆三年在京文職漢官俸米及職名黃冊二卷. In *Qingchu shiliao congbian* 清初史料叢編, edited by Luo Zhenyu 羅振玉. CKSB 33: 639–810.

Qing guoshi, Jiayetang chaoben 清國史嘉業堂鈔本. 14 vols. Beijing: Zhonghua shuju, 1993.
Ronglutang 榮祿堂, ed. *Juezhi quanlan* 爵秩全覽 [1904]. CKZB 130.
Verbiest, Ferdinand. "Budeyi bian" 不得已辨. In *Tianzhujiao dongchuan wenxian* 天主教東傳文獻, edited by Wu Xiangxiang 吳湘湘, 333–470. Taipei: Taiwan xuesheng shuju, 1964.
Wenqing 文慶 et al. *Guozijian zhi* 國子監志 [1834]. 2 vols. XXSK 751: 425–769, 752.
Yunlu 允祿 et al. *Yuzhi lixiang kaocheng* 御製曆象考成 [1723]. SKQS 790.
———. *Qinding yixiang kaocheng* 欽定儀象考成 [1754]. SKQS 793: 1–450.
———. *Yuzhi lixiang kaocheng houbian* 御製曆象考成後編 [1742]. In *Yingyin Zhaizaotang siku quanshu huiyao* 景印摛藻堂四庫全書薈要. Vol. 270. Taipei: Shijie shuju, 1985.
Zhongguo diyi lishi dang'anguan 中國第一歷史檔案館, ed. *Yongzhengchao Hanwen yuzhi huibian* 雍正朝漢文諭旨匯編. 10 vols. Guilin: Guangxi shifan daxue chubanshe, 1999.

Secondary Sources

Chen Zungui 陳遵媯. *Zhongguo tianwenxue shi* 中國天文學史. 2 vols. Shanghai: Shanghai renmin chubanshe, 2016.
Fang Hao 方豪. *Zhongxi jiaotong shi* 中西交通史. Vol. 2. Shanghai: Shanghai renmin chubanshe, 2008.
Feng Erh-k'ang 馮爾康. *Yongzheng zhuan* 雍正傳. Taipei: Taiwan shangwu yinshuguan, 1992.
Guo Shirong 郭世榮, and Li Di 李迪. "Putaoya chuanjiaoshi Xu Maode zai Qintianjian de tianwen gongzuo" 葡萄牙傳教士徐懋德在欽天監的天文工作. *Shandong keji daxue xuebao*山東科技大學學報 13, no. 2 (2011): 18–24.
Han Qi 韓琦. "'Zili jingshen' yu lisuan huodong—Kangqian zhiji wenren dui xixue taidu zhi gaibian ji qi beijing" '自立精神' 與曆算活動—康乾之際文人對西學態度之改變及其背景. *Ziran kexueshi yanjiu*自然科學史研究 21, no. 3 (2002): 210–21.
———. "Fengjiao tianwenxuejia yu 'liyi zhi zheng' (1700–1702)" 奉教天文學家與 '禮儀之爭' (1700–1702). In *Xiangyu yu duihua: Mingmo Qingchu zhongxi wenhua jiaoliu guoji xueshu yiantaohui wenji* 相遇與對話—明末清初中西文化交流國際學術研討會文集, edited by Zhuo Xinping 卓新平, 381–99. Beijing: Zongjiao wenhua chubanshe, 2003.
Jami, Catherine. "Learning Mathematical Sciences during the Early and Mid-Ch'ing." In *Education and Society in Late Imperial China, 1600–1900*, edited by Benjamin A. Elman and Alexander Woodside, 223–56. Berkeley: University of California Press, 1994.
———. *The Emperor's New Mathematics: Western Learning and Imperial Authority during the Kangxi Reign (1662–1722)*. New York: Oxford University Press, 2012.
Li Yan 李儼. *Zhongguo Suanxueshi* 中國算學史. Beijing: Shangwu yinshuguan, 1998.
Qu Chunhai 屈春海. "Qingdai Qintianjian ji Shixianke zhiguan nianbiao" 清代欽天監暨時憲科職官年表. *Zhongkuo keji shiliao* 中國科技史料 18, no. 3 (1997): 45–71.
Wang Ping 王萍. "Qingchu lisuan yanjiu yu jiaoyu" 清初曆算研究與教育. *Zhongyang yanjiuyuan jindaishi yanjiusuo jikan* 中央研究院近代史研究所集刊 3 (1972): 365–75.

8 Maintaining a Familial Career

8.1 Specialization

By mid-1745, He Guozong had obtained the superintendency of both the College of Mathematics and the Astronomical Bureau.[1] He Guozong's new position placed him above European and Manchu Bureau Directors. Although European missionaries would stay with the Qing Astronomical Bureau until 1826, the extent to which they had the power to influence the Bureau and the court was diminishing. The hereditary astronomer families reached their heyday in the Qianlong and Jiaqing reigns, not in the sense of scientific achievements but in the degree of power and control that they had over the Astronomical Bureau.

He Guozong held the superintendency until May 1757, at which point the Qianlong emperor stripped him of all government positions following accusations that Guozong had behaved dishonorably by recommending his own brother, Guodong, in the Metropolitan Inspection.[2] While recommending one's own relatives was indeed improper, the emperor's punishment appears somewhat harsh. The system in the Astronomical Bureau differed from the rest of the bureaucratic system in that it did not forbid members of the same family from working in the same institution. As described in previous chapters, family members were actually encouraged to join the Bureau. In fact, what led to Guozong's discharge was not a single instance of misconduct, but rather a series of incidents that had occurred over the preceding months. The worst of these took place when the Qianlong emperor wrongly accused the Astronomical Bureau of failing to report the first thunder of the year on time. Following an investigation, the Astronomical Bureau was cleared of all charges. However, the emperor seemed to feel that his authority had been violated and that He Guozong should still be punished for attempting to cover up another department's mistake.[3]

Fortunately, the emperor's anger did not prevail. A month after He Guozong's discharge, the Qianlong emperor pardoned him on the grounds that "He Guozong has been idle and doing nothing at home. Mathematics (*suan fa* 算法), after all, is a specialty that his family has mastered generation after generation."[4] He Guozong lost the superintendency of the Astronomical Bureau and the College of Mathematics, but neither Guodong nor any other He family member was punished.[5] The He family's reputation as mathematics specialists saved Guozong,

DOI: 10.4324/9781003008255-8

162 *Maintaining a Familial Career*

Figure 8.1 Qing Timely Modeling calendar, the eighteenth year of the Qianlong reign (1753).

Left, front cover. The statement in the right box declares that "The Astronomical Bureau reverently follows the *Essential Principles of Mathematics* to make and print the Timely Modeling calendar and promulgates throughout the empire."

Bottom, official roster in the last two pages. Right page, Le'ersen 勒爾森 and He Guozong 何國宗 are listed in the first two columns from the right, followed by Manchu Director Tongtai 佟泰 and European Director Augustin von Hallerstein in the third and fourth columns, respectively. Left page, Among the five Supervisor of the Calendar Section, three were from the He family: He Guoqing 何國卿, He Guoxiu 何國秀, and He Guodong 何國棟.

Source: Courtesy of the National Central Library, Taiwan.

Guodong, and the whole family. By the time Guozong retired completely from public service in 1762, the He family was again flourishing, if not dominating, within the Astronomical Bureau.

The rosters appended to the Timely Modeling calendars testify to the He family's rise and fall throughout the Qing dynasty. Figure 8.2 shows the numbers of the He officials who appeared in the annual calendars throughout the Qing dynasty. There are three high points in Figure 8.2. The first one (Point A) occurred around 1675 and it corresponded to the rise of the earliest generation of the He family in the Kangxi Calendar Dispute. This rise was not sustained because the court no longer appreciated the He family's specialty in the Great Concordance system, and He Junxi was in the process of moving his descendants into the new profession of Confucian scholar; this is why the number of He officials listed in calendars gradually declined to zero after 1715. Although He Guozong and his brothers' success could have become a powerful support to the He family members who still remained in the Astronomical Bureau, the Yongzheng emperor's suppression limited the He family's expansion. However, after He Guozong was appointed to superintend the Astronomical Bureau in 1744, the He family gradually climbed to its second high point (Point B) in the early Qianlong era. During this period, three of Guozong's brothers or cousins—Guoxiu 國秀, Guoqing 國卿, and Guodong 國棟—advanced to Calendar Section Supervisors. The He family constantly held two posts, sometimes three, of the five Supervisors of the Five Offices reserved for Han Chinese.[6]

Until the end of the Jiaqing reign (1796–1820), the surname He frequently appeared on records related to the Calendar Section. Guozong's brothers and cousins—namely, members of the generation that had the character *guo* 國 in their names—retired by the mid-Qianlong reign. By that time, a new generation had worked at the Bureau long enough to enter its upper echelon. When Supervisor of the Middle Office He Guodong left the Bureau in 1767, his post was filled by He Tinglu 何廷祿.[7] Soon more names from the *ting* 廷 generation appeared on the roster of annual calendar: He Tingxu 何廷緒, He Tingxuan 何廷瑄, and He Tingxuan 何廷璿, to name but a few (see table 8.1) and the family climbed to its third high point (Point C in Figure 8.2).[8] Before the Qianlong emperor abdicated in favor of his son, the Jiaqing emperor, in February 1796, six more members from later generations of the He family had served as Supervisors of the Five Offices. Three of them advanced to Vice-Directors. In sum, this research found that more than 60 He family members served at the Astronomical Bureau between the Qianlong and Daoguang reigns (1736–1850).[9] Although the He family gradually went into decline during the late Jiaqing reign, it managed to produce four more Supervisors of the Five Offices and continued to hold at least one post of the Han Supervisors of the Five Offices until 1808.[10]

The He family built and maintained its status on the basis of the superior mathematical talent of its members. The earliest members earned their fame during the Kangxi Calendar Dispute by lending their knowledge and support to the opponents of the European Tychonic system. Decades later, He Guozong and his brothers became the core members of the Kangxi emperor's compilation project of the

164　*Maintaining a Familial Career*

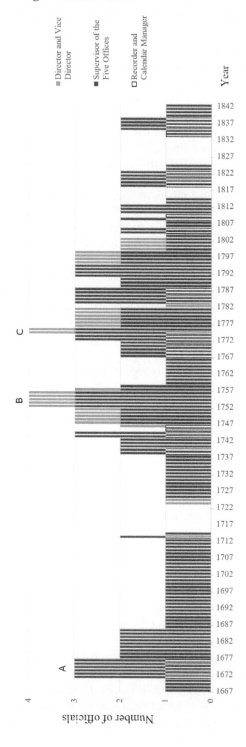

Figure 8.2 Numbers of He officials in the Timely Modeling calendars.
Source: Qu Chunhai 屈春海. "Qingdai Qintianjian ji Shixianke zhiguan nianbiao," *Zhongkuo keji shiliao* 中國科技史料 18, no. 3 (1997): 45–71. Created by the author.

Table 8.1 He officials appeared in the Timely Modeling calendars

Name	Title	Period
He Luoshu 何雒書	Supervisor of the Summer Office	1667–1685
He Junxi 何君錫	Supervisor of the Winter Office	1671–1710
	Supervisor of the Spring Office	1711–1713
He Qiyi 何其義	Calendar Manager	1671–1677
He Guozhu 何國柱	Calendar Manager	1713
	Vice-Director	1723–1724
He Guochen 何國宸	Supervisor of the Middle Office	1725–1744
He Junhui 何君惠	Calendar Manager	1738–1739
	Supervisor of the Spring Office	1740–1744
He Guoxiu 何國秀	Calendar Manager	1743–1744
	Recorder	1745–1746
	Supervisor of the Summer Office	1747–1758
He Guozong 何國宗	Director	1746–1757
He Guoqing 何國卿	Supervisor of the Spring Office	1747–1756
He Guodong 何國棟	Supervisor of the Middle Office	1752–1767
He Tingxu 何廷緒	Recorder	1767–1768
He Tinglu 何廷祿	Supervisor of the Middle Office	1768–1773
	Vice-Director	1774–1775
He Tingxuan 何廷璿	Calendar Manager	1769–1773
	Supervisor of the Middle Office	1774–1775
	Vice-Director	1776–1782
He Tingxuan 何廷瑄	Supervisor of the Winter Office	1772–1781
He Bangjun 何邦俊	Supervisor of the Summer Office	1775–1778
He Tingying 何廷瑛	Supervisor of the Spring Office	1778–1794
	Vice-Director	1795–1802
He Tingchen 何廷琛	Recorder	1783–1787
He Tingzan 何廷瓚	Supervisor of the Summer Office	1783–1805
He Yuanhao 何元浩	Supervisor of the Middle Office	1796–1798
He Yuanfu 何元富	Recorder	1804–1805
	Supervisor of the Middle Office	1806–1808
He Yuantai 何元泰	Recorder	1809
	Supervisor of the Summer Office	1810–1814
He Yuanhai 何元海	Supervisor of the Winter Office	1810–1812
He Yuanzi 何元滋	Calendar Manager	1818–1822
He Yuanying 何元瀛	Supervisor of the Summer Office	1818–1824
He Yuanhuai 何元淮	Recorder	1824–1827
He Liangkui 何良奎	Supervisor of the Winter Office	1833–1838
He Shuben 何樹本	Senior Vice-Director	1835–1842

Source: Qu Chunhai 屈春海, "Qingdai Qintianjian ji Shixianke zhiguan nianbiao" 清代欽天監暨時憲科職官年表, *Zhongkuo keji shiliao* 中國科技史料 18, no. 3 (1997): 49–64.

Origins of Mathematical Harmonics and Astronomy, part of which became the textbook for the College of Mathematics and the guidebook for the Astronomical Bureau. It was not surprising to see that the two earliest Principal Instructors of the College of Mathematics were from the He family: He Guoqing 何國卿 and He Guodong 何國棟.[11] With special insight into the intellectual foundation of the Qing Astronomical Bureau, the best career strategy for the He family surely was to send its descendants to the most mathematically demanding section, the Calendar Section, and then to the Section of Heavenly Signs.

The He family was typical of many astronomer families in that the majority of its members clustered in the same section. For instance, among all the officials found in archival documents that had the surname Huang 黃, a surprisingly high proportion belonged to the Section of Heavenly Signs.[12] The surname Huang is too popular to assume that all of them were from the same family. Nevertheless, some assessments based on the name patterns and their service periods are possible. First, the similarity of the given names suggests that Huang Daohua 黃道化 and Huang Daolong 黃道隆 were brothers or cousins. Other records show that they had worked for the Section of Heavenly Signs since the Ming period and that they were Observatory Managers in the Shunzhi reign.[13] When Huang Daolong died on an official trip to Fujian in 1658, his son, Huang Chang 黃昌, had already started working at the Bureau as a Student Astronomer.[14] The name Huang Gong 黃鞏 appeared on archival documents around the same period as Huang Chang. It is highly likely that Huang Gong and Huang Chang were cousins. Both of them became Observatory Managers by 1677.[15] From the mid-Kangxi reign to the end of the Yongzheng reign, no other Huang official is named in the archival documents. Therefore, it is hard to assert that the group of Huang officials mentioned in state papers of the Qianlong and Jiaqing periods were related to the earlier Huang members who served in the Shunzhi and Kangxi reigns. Nevertheless, four of the five Huang officials named in later documents served in the Section of Heavenly Signs. Moreover, the similarity between the names of Huang Dequan 黃德泉 and Huang Deyuan 黃德源, two Observatory Managers during the late Daoguang period, suggests that they were brothers.[16]

A family had to avoid competition among its own members. Sending its members into the same section helped to preserve a family's expertise, but the number of manager-level positions in each section was very limited. Overclustering within a section in which the family was already established would not help a family to gain more control. A reasonable arrangement in such a situation was to send some descendants to an alternative section. It is noteworthy that He Guo'an 何國安, He Tingxu 何廷緒, and He Tingchen 何廷琛 belonged to the Water Clock Section, not the Calendar Section or the Section of Heavenly Signs.[17] Among them, Guo'an might have obtained the post of Water Clock Manager if the Yongzheng emperor had not suspected that the He family had over-expanded.[18] Tingxu and Tingchen were Water Clock Managers, and afterward both became Recorders.

On the other hand, it is also possible that a family might change its specialty over the course of serving the Astronomical Bureau. The example of the Si 司 family, whose members began their careers at the Astronomical Bureau before the Ming-Qing transition, can be used to illustrate such a point. The names of the Si family members are among the earliest to appear on the records related to the Water Clock Section. Si Ergui 司爾珪, Si Ermao 司爾瑁, and Si Ercheng 司爾珵 were Yin-Yang Students when Johann Adam Schall took over the Astronomical Bureau. Si Ergui seemed to maintain a good relationship with the Jesuits. He endorsed Schall's *Response to Concerns over the Notes on Civil Calendar* and lost his job during the Kangxi Calendar Dispute (see Table 4.1). In 1689, Si Ermao became the first Si family member to become a Vice-Director.[19] Throughout the Qing dynasty, more than 20 people from the Si family worked for the Astronomical Bureau.[20] The Si family produced at least five Water Clock Managers; among them, three advanced to Vice-Directors or even Directors. However, by the late Qianlong reign, the Si family diverted some of its members from the Water Clock Section to the Calendar Section. In the late Qianlong and Jiaqing reigns, Si Tinggan 司廷幹 worked as an Observatory Manager while Si Tingdong 司廷棟 was the Supervisor of the Winter Office. Some Si family members continued to work at the Water Clock Section, but Si became one of the frequently seen surnames in records related to the Calendar Section.[21] In 1867, Si Yitian 司以田, an Erudite of the Calendar Section, won special recommendation for his excellent performance in the triennial examination.[22] During the Daoguang reign, Si Yipei 司以培 was the Supervisor of Summer Office and Si Yisun 司以塤 was a Calendar Manager.[23]

Mastering the specialty needed for at least one section was key to an astronomer family's ability to survive in the Astronomical Bureau. However, to maintain steady career progression, a family needed more than knowledge and skills alone. The next section will discuss one of the most important tactics that an astronomer family as a whole employed to prolong its status within the Bureau.

8.2 Remaining in the Astronomical Bureau

One of the biggest differences between the Ming and Qing Astronomical Bureaus was that Han officials of the Qing Astronomical Bureau could transfer out of the Bureau to work for other government departments. Originally, only banner officials who had reached the top of their career ladders at the Bureau were rewarded with higher-ranking positions in other departments. When a Han official reached the upper echelon of the Bureau, his civil service rank and salary continued to rise, but he had to remain in the Astronomical Bureau for his entire life. This restriction was designed to help the Astronomical Bureau to retain proficient astronomers. However, it became a concern to some potential candidates who did not want to spend their whole lives working for the Astronomical Bureau. After the compilation of *Origins of Mathematical Harmonics and Astronomy* had gone on for several years, the Kangxi emperor felt that more mathematicians were required. In 1719, the emperor decreed that Han Bureau officials should be granted similar rights to transfer as banner officials. Following that, a Vice-Director was allowed to leave the Bureau to become a Vice Department Director (*Yuanwailang* 員外郎) of the Six Ministries, and a Calendar Section Supervisor could obtain a post that was equivalent to Department Secretary (*Zhushi* 主事).[24]

However, historical records reveal that not all officials of the Astronomical Bureau appreciated the option to transfer to other government departments. Two decades after the transfer regulations were introduced, Luo'erzhan 羅爾瞻, a newly appointed Manchu Vice-Director, reported a worrisome phenomenon to the Qianlong emperor. In November 1739, Luo'erzhan wrote:

> When an official was at the juncture of being promoted by transferring [to other institutions], he often wrote on the résumé that he prefers having the title elevated but remaining in the current position (*shengxian liuren* 陞銜留任). Currently, within the two Vice-Directors and five Supervisors of Five Offices of my bureau, five have already applied to elevate the titles while remaining in current positions. If in the future any other official who ought to be promoted applies to stay, senior officials are bound to occupy the yaman [Bureau] and attempt to make it their retirement home (*panju yamen xitu yanglao* 盤踞衙門 希圖養老) for the sake of their descendants. In that case, junior officials' career progression will be slowed down, and they will not have a chance to test their talent.[25]

Based on the date the memorial was written, the five officials named by Luo'erzhan must have been Vice-Director Li Tingyao 李廷耀 and the Calendar Section Supervisors: Qin Ning 秦寧, He Guochen 何國宸, Fang Gu 方觳, and Bao Qinhui 鮑欽輝.[26] Moreover, other historical records help us to further examine the phenomenon of elevating the title while remaining in the current position.

The résumés used for the imperial audiences of four of the five officials mentioned earlier are still available. A brief recounting of the contents of these résumés is necessary to understand the career development of the individuals involved. After fulfilling the role as Supervisor of the Middle Office for five years and ten months, He Guochen, a younger brother of He Guozong, received the order to transfer to the Ministry of Punishments as a Department Secretary in October 1729.[27] Guochen did not specifically state on his résumé that he would like to remain in the Astronomical Bureau; however, he did disclose that he was dull and without experience, thus he found the prospect of the potential transfer to be as terrifying as being thrown into deep ice.[28] Li Tingyao originally worked as a Water Clock Manager before becoming a Vice-Director in 1732.[29] Less than a year and a month later, Li received the order to transfer to the Ministry of Punishments to be the Vice-Director of the Left Interrogation Office (*Zuo xianshen si* 左現審司).[30] On his audience résumé, Li begged to remain in the profession of geomancy, stating that he was not familiar with the law and administrative affairs.[31] Qin Ning was a District Graduate before joining the personnel serving in mathematics. After the *Origins of Mathematical Harmonics and Astronomy* was completed, Qin entered the Astronomical Bureau as a Calendar Section Supervisor. The Yongzheng emperor granted his request to continue to stay in the Bureau in March 1734.[32] Eight months after Qin's request was approved, another Supervisor, Bao Qinhui, received the transfer order. Bao was from a Christian family that Jesuit missionaries had brought into the Astronomical Bureau.[33] Qinhui's grandfather was a younger brother of Vice-Director Bao Yingqi, who was Johann Adam Schall's disciple. On his résumé to the Yongzheng emperor, Qinhui wrote, "I worry about my stupidity. Except the knowledge of calendar making, there really is not anything that I can contribute."[34]

The diverse background of the above four officials suggests that applying for an elevated title but remaining in one's current position was a career strategy broadly adopted by the imperial astronomers. These four officials were Han Chinese. However, the Mongolian astronomer Minggantu also applied for permission to remain in the Astronomical Bureau. Minggantu did not leave the Bureau until illness forced him into retirement around 1764.[35] Why did the high officials at the Astronomical Bureau not want to transfer to other institutions? Almost all Bureau officials appealed to stay on the premise that they were unfamiliar with administrative affairs (*buxiao lizhi* 不曉吏治). Is this indeed the reason that led them to think that it would be safer to "occupy the yamen [Bureau] and attempt to make it their retirement home," as Luo'erzhan put it? A reconstruction of the career path of Liu Yuxi 劉裕錫 provides a starting point from which a number of questions can be explored.

Liu Yuxi was one of the five Astronomical Bureau officials recorded in the *Gangzhi* 岡誌, a local history of the Beijing Muslim community that was published in the Qianlong period.[36] The *Gangzhi* described Liu as "calm, elegant, and fond of studying; well learned in astronomy and medicine; and particularly good at making instruments and fanciful things."[37] According to his audience résumé, Liu's joined the Astronomical Bureau to learn calendar making in 1691.[38] By then, the Muslim Section had long ceased to exist in the Astronomical Bureau.[39] The Qing court did not prohibit learning and practicing the Muslim astronomical system in private. But to have a career at the Astronomical Bureau, a Muslim astronomer like Liu would have to study the New Western Method and pass the same examination as his Han colleagues did. One could only wonder if that is the reason why Liu's career at the Astronomical Bureau got off to a slow start. Liu did not obtain the position of Student Astronomer until 1709. At that time, he was well over 30 years old.[40] In contrast, the careers of He Guochen and Bao Qinhui (mentioned earlier) progressed much faster. He and Bao were from Han astronomer families, and they worked for the Astronomical Bureau around the same period as Liu did. Both He and Bao were more than ten years younger than Liu. However, He became a Student Astronomer in 1704 and then an Erudite in 1709.[41] Bao did not progress as fast as He did, but he too became an Erudite earlier than Liu did.[42]

Nevertheless, Liu attracted special attention from the Kangxi emperor and then the Yongzheng emperor. Liu claimed on his résumé that he was able to "pay a tribute to the profound depth of imperial learning" of the Kangxi emperor because he was ordered to work at an inner-court study room of the imperial garden Changchun Yuan, where the emperor had personally taught him mathematics.[43] Liu also worked at the Studio for Cultivating the Youth for some years, presumably for the compilation of the *Origins of Mathematical Harmonics and Astronomy*. Following this, Liu was given the responsibility to translate the calendar into Mongolian and Tibetan. Liu continued to serve in the inner court after the Yongzheng emperor ascended the throne. The Yongzheng emperor allocated him to a range of geographical projects such as drawing up maps of river courses and imperial graves. In March 1725, the Yongzheng emperor bypassed another candidate and elevated Liu to the position of Supervisor of the Winter Office.[44]

Liu Yuxi's career took an unfortunate turn between 1731 and 1732. In January 1731, Liu received an order to transfer to the Ministry of Revenue to be the Secretary of the *Guizhou* 貴州 Department.[45] Liu begged the Yongzheng emperor to allow him to remain in the Astronomical Bureau. He explained:

> Although I am capable of accounting monetary affairs and grain supply, I am not able to understand the law or regulations in detail. Since my heart does not have self-confidence, how dare I try it out rashly? I humbly beg Your Majesty to save me kindly by considering my ability and to allow me to stay at the Astronomical Bureau.[46]

The Yongzheng emperor did not accept Liu's appeal.[47] In just six months, Liu lost his new job at the Ministry of Revenue for reasons unknown. The Yongzheng emperor kindly allowed him to return to the Astronomical Bureau as an Erudite, but Liu seemed too depressed to concentrate on his work. He was dismissed from the Astronomical Bureau after the triennial Metropolitan Inspection in 1732.[48]

Liu Yuxi was not able to regain a government position until the compilation of the *Thorough Investigation of Instruments and Phenomena* (*Yixiang kaocheng* 儀象考成) began. In August 1745, He Guozong and the other directorate asked the Qianlong emperor if Liu Yuxi could be re-employed by the Astronomical Bureau. They told the emperor that Liu had voluntarily worked at the Office of Instrument Production (*Yiqi zaobanchu* 儀器造辦處) and had been "industrious and careful."[49] More importantly, Liu's calculation ability and special talent for instruments would be particularly suitable for teaching the Bureau officials and students. The Qianlong emperor did not approve their petition immediately, but this is not too surprising if one recalls that He Guozong and Guodong had to work at the Office of Compiling Mathematical Treatises and the College of Mathematics for years before regaining civil service ranks and posts.[50] When the treatise *Thorough Investigation of Instruments and Phenomena* was completed in 1754, Liu Yuxi's name appeared at the end of the list of contributors with the title "Erudite of the Astronomical Bureau."[51] At that time, Liu was already 77 years old. There is no evidence to suggest that Liu had ever advanced to any position higher than Erudite. The second half of Liu's life probably would have been more stable and comfortable if the transfer regulations had not forced him to leave the Astronomical Bureau.

Surviving historical records are not sufficient to provide a complete analysis of the career developments after officials were transferred out of the Astronomical Bureau; however, at least two aspects deserve attention. First, Liu Yuxi was not the only individual whose career suffered an unfortunate turn after he was transferred out of the Astronomical Bureau. In the Jiaqing period, former Supervisor of the Winter Office Si Tingdong lost his new job at the Ministry of Revenue within a year because a fire destroyed the granary under his supervision. Following a petition from the Astronomical Bureau superintendent, the emperor allowed 58-year-old Si to return to the Astronomical Bureau as a Student Astronomer.[52] Si was luckier than Liu Yuxi because the promotion system of the Astronomical Bureau

Maintaining a Familial Career 171

had been revised in the early Daoguang reign, so his career was able to advance at a more rapid pace.[53] Still, it took almost a decade before Si regained his original position as a Calendar Section Supervisor.[54]

Second, it was highly likely that the remaining career life span was not sufficient for an official to build a brilliant new career after he transferred out of the Astronomical Bureau. Among the 45 Calendar Section Supervisors and Vice-Directors whose transfer records have been found in the *Complete Collection of the Qing Officials' Résumés* (*Qingdai guanyuan lüli dang'an quanbian* 清代官員履歷檔案全編), 37 were over 50 years old when they received the transfer order (see Figure 8.3). Some of them lived long enough to receive promotions twice or three times after the transfer, but none of their records indicates that any of them had advanced beyond the level of Department Director (*langzhong* 郎中). The Kangxi emperor probably initiated the transfer regulation because he believed that mathematics could be useful to various government tasks, but the astronomers were sent out of the Bureau too late. No wonder some officials would rather turn inward to cultivate family interests within the Astronomical Bureau as opposed to taking the risk of starting a new career outside the Bureau.

Finally, it should be stressed that the Qianlong emperor and his predecessors were also responsible for this retirement home phenomenon. Despite Luo'erzhan's warning, the Qianlong emperor continued to approve Bureau officials' requests to receive elevated titles yet remain in their current positions. For instance, the roster of a routine memorial of February 1766 indicates that Wang Deming 王德明, the Supervisor of the Summer Office, should have transferred to become a Department Secretary at the Ministry of Revenue, but the emperor permitted him to remain in the Bureau.[55] No further evidence is available to provide insight

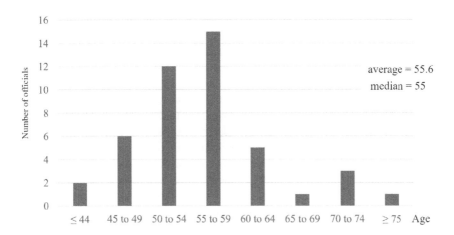

Figure 8.3 Age distribution of high Astronomical Bureau officials when receiving transfer orders.

Source: Qin Guojing 秦國經, ed., *Qingdai guanyuan lüli quanbian* 清代官員履歷檔案全編, 30 vols. (Shanghai: Huadong shifan daxue chubanshe, 1997). Created by the author.

into why Wang's request was granted, but the Qianlong emperor's comments on the case of Senior Vice-Director Sun Shiying 孫士英 revealed his concerns. Sun Shiying received the transfer order in September 1742 after serving the Astronomical Bureau for 54 years. It is likely that Sun was already over 70 years old.[56] The Bureau directorate together petitioned the emperor for Sun's retention, not on the grounds of his irreplaceable knowledge or skills but on the basis of his long and diligent service at the Bureau. The Qianlong emperor replied, "It seems Sun Shiying is not up to the job of Vice Department Director at the Ministry of Punishments. His request to receive an elevated title yet remain as the Vice-Director is granted."[57] Probably the emperor thought that approving the petition submitted collectively by the Bureau directorate was a way to demonstrate his benevolence. Instead of forcing a senior member of the Astronomical Bureau to leave for a new institution, the emperor would rather win the astronomer families' loyalty by allowing him to remain in the Bureau.

Throughout the history of the Qing Astronomical Bureau, it is common to see examples of a Vice-Director or a Supervisor of the Calendar Section remaining in the same position for more than a decade. It seems that as long as the Bureau as a whole could fulfill its duties, the emperor did not pay close attention to the aging problem within the Astronomical Bureau. Nonetheless, Luo'erzhan's warning that younger officials did not have enough opportunities to test out their talent gradually came into fruition during the Qianlong and Jiaqing reigns. A reformation in the administrative system was necessary to stop the Bureau's deterioration.

8.3 The Social Status of Mathematics Students

In March 1831, Zhili Governor Nayan 那彥 delivered two suspects, Han Fangyu 韓方瑜 and Tian Yangzhong 田養中, to the Ministry of Punishments for further investigation. Nayan caught Han and Tian attempting to gain tax benefits by using fake Mathematics Student licenses. According to Nayan's report, Tian admitted that he had purchased a fake license from an acquaintance the previous year. Han, however, insisted that he had taken the entrance examination to the College of Mathematics at the Imperial College in October 1827 and successfully passed the examination. Han claimed that because no vacancy had been available at that time, he was given the license and was permitted to return to his hometown. Both Tian and Han's faked licenses declared that they had earned the privilege of "wearing and using the uniforms of Imperial College Students (*Jiansheng* 監生)," meaning that they were no longer ordinary civilians but, in effect, held the same status as Imperial College Students. Unsure about the official status of Mathematics Students, Nayan did not immediately throw Han and Tian in jail. He requested an explanation from the College of Mathematics first before sending the suspects to the Ministry of Punishments.[58]

On the one hand, the above case shows that the title of Mathematics Student was a socially recognized identity in the Qing period. The College of Mathematics was not a new invention. The earliest state-level College of Mathematics was set up in the Sui 隋 dynasty (581–618) with two Mathematics Erudites (*Suanxue boshi* 算學博士), two Mathematics Instructors (*Suan zhujiao* 算助教), and 80 students. The Tang 唐 (618–907) and Song 宋 (960–1279) dynasties followed suit; they maintained the College of Mathematics whenever they could afford it.[59] It is the historical existence of Mathematics Students that prompted some commoners, such as Tian Yangzheng in 1831 (see earlier), to obtain fake Mathematics Student licenses, though their original intention was to obtain the licenses of Imperial College Students.

On the other hand, Nayan's caution in handling this case indicates that even high officials, who should have been more familiar with the civil service examination system, did not fully understand the statuses of the College of Mathematics and its students. In fact, the producers of the fake licenses did not know them either. Within the civil service examination system, the status of a Mathematics Student was lower than that of an Imperial College Student and roughly equivalent to that of banner Official Students. The entrance examination of the College of Mathematics was indeed held at the Imperial College, but that was only because the College of Mathematics was a subordinate school of the Imperial College. As with banner Official Students, Mathematics Students had to pass a further examination on classical studies to become Imperial College Students.[60] Except for an officially recognized social status, a license of Mathematics Student did not give its holder any tax deduction or financial benefit.

Records in the *Collection of the Qing Vermillion Ink Examination Papers* (*Qingdai zhujuan jicheng* 清代硃卷集成) further testify to Mathematics Students' ambivalent social status. During the Qing era, civil service degree holders often printed the essays composed during the examination as pamphlets. These pamphlets were called *Zhujuan* 硃卷 because of the vermillion ink examination paper used in the examination grading process. Customarily, a *Zhujuan* always began with a simplified genealogy that showcased the family's previous achievements in the civil service. A survey of the surviving *Zhujuan* reveals that official positions at the Astronomical Bureau and College of Mathematics were included in these genealogies, even when the individuals involved were merely Mathematics Students or Astronomy Apprentices at those two institutions. For instance, a Metropolitan Graduate of the Daoguang reign found having an Astronomy Apprentice among his cousins was worth mentioning in the *Zhujuan* genealogy.[61] Another person from the same period counted two Student Astronomers of the Song dynasty among his ancestors.[62] A Provincial Graduate of the Jiaqing reign did not find it too insignificant to report that his wife's great-great-grandfather had been a Student Astronomer.[63] However, only a small number of *Zhujuan* genealogies contain records related to Astronomical Bureau astronomers. While a *Zhujuan* genealogy might easily contain hundreds of entries, it rarely has more than two entries that are relevant to the profession of official astronomer. Not to mention the fact that the majority of the entries are lower-level positions such as Mathematics Student or Student Astronomer.

These characteristics suggest that while families with brilliant records in civil service might divert some of their members to attend the College of Mathematics, it does not necessarily mean that they intended to enter the career of imperial astronomers. Similar to Han and Tian, these families perhaps just wanted to differentiate their members, particularly those who had little hope of succeeding in the civil service examinations, from ordinary civilians by ensuring that they obtained some type of officially recognized status. The reason why few families were seriously interested in their members pursuing a career at the Astronomical Bureau is not hard to understand. A career at the Astronomical Bureau might be stable and secure, but it could hardly bring political power or splendid incomes to the family. Take He Junxi as an example. He had been the Supervisor of the Calendar Section for four decades. Yet, upon his death, the Kangxi emperor gave extra provision to his son, Guozhu, because the emperor knew the He family was on a tight budget.[64] For a civil service degree holder, transferring to the profession of imperial astronomers almost entailed that his previous effort in classical studies was in vain. Ostensibly, civil service degree holders enjoyed several special benefits. After graduating from the College of Mathematics, a Provincial Graduate could skip the level of Student Astronomer and advance to Erudite directly.[65] Similarly, an Instructor at the College of Mathematics could obtain the post of Water Clock Manager after finishing a teaching term if he were a District Graduate and Observatory Manager if he were a Provincial Graduate.[66] However, these benefits were hardly attractive. Gaining a Provincial Graduate degree was the watershed for those who competed in the civil service examinations in the pursuit of governmental jobs. A District Graduate was merely an officially licensed scholar. Many District Graduates sustained their lives by tutoring, and it is not unusual to see a District Graduate living in poverty. In contrast, a Provincial Degree came with the right to request an official post; honor and financial income fell almost instantly to the degree holder. Therefore, it is impractical to expect that a Provincial Graduate, who was already a successful civil service examination candidate, would have much interest in transferring to a less popular profession—not to mention the fact that a transfer would force him to accept the degraded status of a mathematic student. A late-Qing author gave an explicit analysis of the educational reformation:

> The Imperial College includes the program for study astronomy and mathematics . . . but even from the point of view of encouragement, the reward for a Provincial Graduate who passed the examination [for graduating from that program] is merely the post of Astronomical Bureau Erudite. An Erudite is just a petty official with the lowest civil service rank. How can it be possible that a Provincial Graduate will give up his qualification of a District Magistrate and turn to spend many years on [manipulating] counting rods just for obtaining that desolate position?[67]

Those civil service examination candidates who had not obtained the Provincial Graduate degree were more likely to consider a transfer to the career of imperial astronomer. But, ironically, no special treatment was given to a District Graduate or an Imperial College Student.

The career of Wang Lai 汪萊 (1768–1813), a mathematician famous for his interest in Western methods during the Qianlong-Jiaqing period, highlights another problem in the recruitment rules that governed the Astronomical Bureau.[68]

Wang became a District Graduate when he was merely 14 years old. His excellent scholarship in classical study and mathematics had been well known among his contemporaries, but he never obtained the Provincial Graduate degree and lived in poverty. In 1807, Wang won the degree of Tribute Student (*Gongsheng* 貢生) that entitled him to fulfill some minor civil service positions. Thus, Wang came to Beijing to look for a job. Wang's knowledge in mathematics and astronomy would easily qualify him for a role as a high official at the Astronomical Bureau, but there simply was no way for him to secure a position there. He went on to become an Instructor at the Eight Banners Official Schools.[69] Through other courtiers' recommendations, Wang also participated in the amendment of the state *Monograph of Heavenly Signs* (*Tianwen zhi* 天文志) and *Monograph of Astronomical System* (*Shihxian zhi* 時憲志).[70] When the monograph was complete, Wang was rewarded with a job as a District Assistant Instructor (*Xundao* 訓導). In 1813, Wang Lai tried the provincial examination again but soon died of illness and exhaustion.[71] Wang Lai's case demonstrates that the mathematical knowledge acquired before entering the Astronomical Bureau bureaucratic system was little help to one's career advancement. With the exception of the last decade of the Kangxi reign, the Qing state rarely held special examinations to recruit mathematicians. During the majority of the Qing period, civil degree holders received some special rewards for joining the Astronomical Bureau, but self-trained mathematicians did not. This was certainly discouraging to anyone who was considering serving the imperial state with his mathematical knowledge.

By design, the recruitment rules favored descendants of astronomer families. The candidates for selection as Student Astronomers were divided into four groups. Two groups were newcomers to the Astronomical Bureau: Astronomy Apprentices and Mathematics Students. The other two groups were hereditary students who were divided according to the generations their families had served the Bureau. Together, these four groups took turns filling the vacancies of Student Astronomers.[72] A hereditary student supposedly should have learned the craft as part of the education provided by his family; he did not have to go through any formal training at the College of Mathematics. Conversely, the biggest challenge preventing an Astronomy Apprentice or a Mathematics Student from becoming a Student Astronomer was not the graduate examinations but the long wait until a position became available.

In sum, the founding of the College of Mathematics was beneficial to astronomer families. Newcomers began as Mathematics Students; their status was equivalent to that of the Eight Banners Official Students. In contrast, hereditary students could begin with the higher-level position of Student Astronomers without much difficulty. The status of hereditary students was thus raised, although this had little impact on their employment prospects.

8.4 Families in Decline and Criminal Charges

A number of events were symptomatic of the decline of an astronomer family. The first and most obvious sign of decline was the loss of the ability to obtain higher-level positions in the Bureau. At this stage, younger generations still could obtain entrance-level positions at the Bureau because of the quota reserved for hereditary students. In fact, it is common to find that a certain surname lingered on lower-level positions such as Yin-Yang Students and Student Astronomers several decades after it had disappeared from the roster of higher officials. However, the career of these members progressed at a slow pace. They could no longer distinguish themselves through periodical examinations and no longer won extra promotions. Eventually, some would fail the examinations and have their jobs suspended. The worst ones were even involved in petty crimes.

The Zang 臧 family was one of the oldest astronomer families at the Qing Astronomical Bureau. Like He Qiyi 何其義, Zang Wenxian 臧文顯 was already an Erudite before the Ming dynasty ended.[73] After Schall took over the Astronomical Bureau, the Zang family coped with the new leadership and gradually converted to the New Method. Zang Wenxian's name was seen among the endorsers for Schall's *Response to Concerns over the Notes on Civil Calendar*, published in 1662.[74] In November 1653, Zang Yuqing 臧餘慶 became an Astronomical Observer of the Section of Heavenly Signs. Around the same time, Zang Fangxiu 臧樊修 obtained the post of Erudite.[75] The Zang family appeared to have sided with the Jesuits in the Kangxi Calendar Dispute. Zang Yuqing eventually lost his job after refusing Yang Guangxian's request to endorse the Great Concordance system.[76] After the Calendar Dispute ended, the Zang family gradually returned to their former prominence. For some years in the late Kangxi period, both Han Vice-Directors were from the Zang family. Zang Jide 臧積德 was elevated to Junior Vice-Directorship after serving as an Observatory Manager for 30 years.[77] He stayed in the position of Vice-Director from 1707 to 1717.[78] Zang Bichang 臧必昌, perhaps from the Water Clock Section, was the Senior Vice-Director from 1711 to 1724.[79]

Afterward, however, the Zang family never reached the Vice-Directorship again. The Yongzheng period saw only one Zang Yuzhong 臧裕仲, who briefly held the post of Observatory Manager.[80] In the mid-Qianlong period, Zang Dening 臧德寧 from the Water Clock Section became Recorder, but he made no further advancement.[81] By this time, the Zang family was already in decline. In the triennial examination of January 1765, Erudite Zang Cunren 臧存仁 performed so badly that his future career advancement was suspended.[82] The last Zang related to the Astronomical Bureau to be featured in archival documents is a Yin-Yang Student called Zang Xianming 臧顯名. In December 1802, the Astronomical Bureau sent Zang Xianming to the Ministry of Punishments for stealing a bronze tank from the water clocks.[83]

Cases that involved criminal charges, like Zang Xianming's, were rare among the declining astronomer families. Few families were reduced to such a miserable status. After all, the routine tasks of the Astronomical Bureau provided little opportunity for illegal profit and thus the possibility that crimes would be committed was low. Continuous failures in the periodical examinations were alarming enough to make a family consider refraining from sending new members to the Astronomical Bureau.[84] For example, as we will see in the next chapter, the famous He family withdrew from the Bureau during the Daoguang reign after younger family members continued to fail badly in the periodical examinations. It is noteworthy that petty crimes committed by an individual official did not necessarily affect other family members' career advancement. Liu Zhimao 柳芝茂, an Astronomical Observer from 1758 to 1768, failed in the same triennial examination of January 1765 as Zang Cunren. The Bureau punished Liu for his poor grade by banning him from advancement.[85] In August 1768, the Bureau directorate suspected that Liu Zhimao might have tried to forge a sick leave permission. During the investigation, Liu Zhifang 柳芝芳, Zhimao's elder brother and an Observatory Manager, was called in and questioned. Being in the same family and working at the same section, nobody could have known Zhimao better than Zhifang. Zhifang testified against his brother during the investigation of the case that "Liu Zhifang is always discontented with his lot" (*su bu an fen* 素不安分) and that Zhifang, in fact, had been engaging in a civil dispute.[86] Zhifang's testimony caused Zhimao to be dismissed from the Bureau but certainly help to save his own job. This incident did not have a negative impact on Zhifang's career. He went on to become the Vice-Director the next year.[87] Nevertheless, the Liu family did not prosper at the Astronomical Bureau. No further record related to the Liu family dated after the years of Zhifang and Zhimao has been found.

After the Kangxi Calendar Dispute, no criminal charge against an Astronomical Bureau official was fatal enough to bring down an astronomer family in a short time. There were some occasions when the emperor rebuked the Astronomical Bureau for failing to interpret celestial anomalies on time, but these incidents did not result in serious punishments of the Bureau directorate. Because such events tended to occur in the early years of a reign, it was highly likely that such threats were designed to demonstrate imperial authority. For instance, the Revolt of the Three Feudatories (*Sanfan zhi luan* 三藩之亂) lasting from December 1673 to December 1681 was a severe rebellion that not only challenged the young Kangxi emperor's rule but also put the survival of the Qing dynasty in question.[88] In the midst of the rebellion, the Kangxi emperor once addressed the Ministry of Rites on the importance of respecting heavenly signs and ordered the Astronomical Bureau officials ro be investigated for neglecting the duties of interpreting heavenly signs.[89] After Ferdinand Verbiest and others were charged with neglecting their duties, however, the emperor pardoned them all.[90] It is noteworthy that the Kangxi emperor initiated this case. By then he would have known that the Jesuits disliked Chinese traditional divination and astrology. Rather than showing Verbiest personal favor by pardoning them, the emperor instigated the whole case to warn Verbiest that while he had accepted the Western Method of calendar making, Verbiest, in return, had to make sure the Bureau fulfilled all their duties, whether the Jesuits liked it or not.

From the mid-Qianlong reign to the early Daoguang reign, the Qing imperial state left the management of the Astronomical Bureau in the hands of the astronomer families. The Astronomical Bureau was no longer the institution that had caused political turbulence in the early Qing era. Although it had its own specialty and administrative system, the Bureau appeared to be very similar to other government institutions. High officials, such as He Tingxuan 何廷瑄, He Tingzan 何廷

瓚, and He Yuanzi 何元滋, obtained the first grade in the Metropolitan Inspection, but they were not known for distinguished mathematical achievements. Except for Si Tingdong, no other Bureau official made any achievements that were significant enough for his name to be recorded in the *Monograph on Calendar of the Qing Official History*.[91] The Astronomical Bureau was in need of rejuvenation.

Notes

1 IHP 023912.
2 *Qing guoshi*, 6: 484; QHDSL GX 799: 320.
3 IHP 197213.
4 *Qing guoshi*, 6: 484.
5 Ibid.
6 Ibid., 55–6.
7 QGLL 19: 275; Qu, "Qingdai Qintianjian," 57.
8 Qu, "Qingdai Qintianjian," 57–8. Note that He Tingxuan 何廷瑢 is recorded as He Tingxuan 何廷璇. See also QGLL 21: 336 and IHP 053505.
9 See Appendix C.
10 Ibid., 57–61.
11 Wenqing et al., *Guozijian zhi*, 752: 204.
12 See Appendix E.
13 For Huang Daohua, see Xu, "Zhili yuanqi," 1687, and Shi, "Tianwenke," 36–7. For Huang Daolong, see "Shunzhi yuping," 28: 15, and Shi, "Tianwenke," 36–7.
14 Schall, *Xiyang xinfa lishu*, 1338.
15 Shi, "Tianwenke," 37.
16 Ibid., 44. Huang Dequan was an Observatory Manager from 1839 to 1845, while Huang Deyuan served in the same capacity between 1846 and 1857.
17 GYQX 1994.
18 See Chapter 5, Section 5.4.
19 Qu, "Qingdai Qintianjian," 51.
20 See Appendix F.
21 See Chapter 9, Section 9.3 for more on Si Tingdong and the Si family in late Qing period.
22 IHP 182598.
23 QGLL 27: 686; Qu, "Qingdai Qintianjian," 67–8.
24 QHD YZ 534–6.
25 IHP 194605.
26 See the roster in IHP 048439 submitted in March 1737.
27 QGLL 11: 448.
28 Ibid., 453.
29 GYQX 10799; Qu, "Qingdai Qintianjian," 54–5.
30 QGLL 12: 667.
31 Ibid., 672.
32 Ibid., 64–5.
33 See Chapter 1, Section 1.1 and Chapter 3, Section 3.3.
34 QGLL 13: 189–90.
35 Qu, "Qingdai Qintianjian," 57; *Qing guoshi*, 12: 891.
36 *Gangzhi* 岡誌, in *Huizu diancang quanshu* 回族典藏全書, ed. Wu Haiying 吳海鷹 (Lanzhou: Gansu wenhua chubanshe, 2008), 102: 191–6. Besides Liu Yuxi 劉裕錫, the other four were Liu Yuduo 劉裕鐸, Wu Mingxuan 吳明炫, Xue Zongjun 薛宗雋, and Xue Zongwei 薛宗偉. Liu Yuduo was Liu Yuxi's brother. Xue Zongjun was

a Supervisor of the Summer Office in the mid-Kangxi period. Xue Zongjun was his younger brother.
37 Ibid., 194.
38 QGLL 2: 191.
39 The Muslim Section was officially abolished in 1657. See Chapter 2, Section 2.2.4, Chapter 3, Section 3.2 and Section 3.3, and Chapter 4, Section 4.1.
40 QGLL 2: 191.
41 He Guochen was born in 1688. He became a Student Astronomer in 1704 and then an Erudite in 1709. QGLL 11: 453.
42 Bao Qinhui was born in 1689, and he became an Erudite in 1713. Bao did not mention when he became a Student Astronomer in his résumé. QGLL 13: 189. Liu advanced to Erudite in 1714. QGLL 2: 191.
43 Ibid.
44 GYQX 7: 3737–8.
45 Ibid., 25: 14839; QGLL 2: 191.
46 QGLL 2: 192.
47 Ibid.
48 IHP 022183.
49 Ibid.
50 See Chapter 7, Section 7.3.
51 Yunlu, *yixiang kaocheng*, 18.
52 IHP 065595.
53 See Chapter 9.
54 Qu, "Qingdai Qintianjian," 63.
55 IHP 079206.
56 IHP 127466.
57 Ibid.
58 IHP 225728.
59 Li, *Zhongguo Suanxueshi*, 43–7, 100–3; Lee, 515–25.
60 QHDZL QL 625: 131.
61 ZJJC 6: 395.
62 Ibid., 7: 87.
63 Ibid., 93: 206.
64 QJZ KX (BJ), B013820. See Chapter 5, Section 5.2.
65 QHDZL QL 625: 131.
66 Ibid., 625: 130.
67 Zhong Qi 鐘琦, *Huangchao suoxuelu* 皇朝瑣屑錄, CKZB 532: 748–9.
68 On Wang Lai, see Ruan, *Chouren zhuan*, 669–75.
69 Instructors at the Eight Banners Official School were paid the same as those at the College of Mathematics. QHDZL QL 625: 130.
70 Ruan, *Chouren zhuan*, 674.
71 Ibid., 669. QGLL 13: 189.
72 NPM 185064.
73 "Shunzhi yuping," 28: 14.
74 Schall, *Minli puzhu*, 3.
75 "Shunzhi yuping," 28: 15.
76 Huang, *Zhengjiao fengbao*, 524.
77 Shi, "Tianwenke," 37–8.
78 Qu, "Qingdai Qintianjian," 51.
79 Ibid.
80 Shi, "Tianwenke," 39.
81 Qu, "Qingdai Qintianjian," 57.
82 IHP 025061.

83 IHP 195479.
84 See Chapter 9, Section 9.2 for more details on the periodical examinations.
85 IHP 025061.
86 Ibid.
87 IHP 082724.
88 For the Revolt of the Three Feudatories, see Tsao Kai-fu, "The Rebellion of the Three Feudatories against the Manchu Throne in China, 1673–1681: Its Setting and Significance" (Ph.D. diss., Columbia University, 1965).
89 This incidence happened in April 1677. The author thanks Professor Catherine Jami's suggestion on the possible connection between this incident and the Revolt of the Three Feudatories.
90 SL 4: 846.
91 Zhao et al., *Qingshi gao*, 1671–3. See Chapter 9, Section 9.4.

Bibliography

Abbreviations for Archival and Published Sources

CKSB: *Jindai Zhongguo shiliao congkan sanbian* 近代中國史料叢刊三編, edited by Shen Yunlong 沈雲龍. 850 vols. Taipei: Wenhai chubanshe, 1982.
CKZB: *Jindai Zhongguo shiliao congkan sanbian* 近代中國史料叢刊正編, edited by Shen Yunlong 沈雲龍. 1000 vols. Taipei: Wenhai chubanshe, 1966.
GYQX: *Guanyuan quanxuan shiliao* 官員銓選史料 of *Qingdai lizhi shiliao* 清代吏治史料, edited by Ren Mengqiang 任夢強. 34 vols. Beijing: Xianzhuang shuju, 2004.
IHP: Neige daku dang'an 內閣大庫檔案. Institute of History and Philology of Academia Sinica, Taipei. http://archive.ihp.sinica.edu.tw/mctkm2/index.html
NPM: Qingdai gongzhongdang zouzhe ji junjichudang zhejian quanwen yingxiang ziliaoku 清代宮中檔奏摺及軍機處檔摺件全文影像資料庫. National Palace Museum, Taipei. http://npmhost.npm.gov.tw/tts/npmmeta/GC/indexcg.html
QGLL: *Qingdai guanyuan lüli dang'an quanbian* 清代官員履歷檔案全編. Edited by Qin Guojing 秦國經. 30 vols. Shanghai: Huadong shifan daxue chubanshe, 1997.
QHD YZ: *Da Qing huidian (Yongzheng chao)* 大清會典 (雍正朝) [1732]. CKSB 761–90.
QHDSL GX: *Qinding Da Qing huidian shili* 欽定大清會典事例 [1899]. XXSK 798–814.
QHDZL QL: *Qinding Da Qing huidian zeli* 欽定大清會典則例 [1764]. SKQS 620–5.
QJZ KX (BJ): *Qingdai qijuzhuce, Kangxi chao* 清代起居注冊, 康熙朝. Edited by Zou Ailian 鄒愛蓮. 32 vols. Beijing: Zhonghua shuju, 2009.
SKQS: *Yingyin wenyuange sikuquanshu* 景印文淵閣四庫全書. 1500 vols. Taipei: Taipei shangwu yinshuguan, 1986.
SL: *Qing shilu* 清實錄. 60 vols. Beijing: Zhonghua shuju, 1985.
XXSK: *Xuxiu sikuquanshu* 續修四庫全書. 1800 vols. Shanghai: Shanghai guji chubanshe, 2002.
ZJJC: *Qingdai zhujuan jicheng* 清代硃卷集成. Edited by Gu Tingling 顧廷龍. 420 vols. Taipei: Chengwen chubanshe, 1992.

Other Sources

Gangzhi 岡誌. In *Huizu diancang quanshu* 回族典藏全書, edited by Wu Haiying 吳海鷹, 102: 183–429. Lanzhou: Gansu wenhua chubanshe, 2008.
Huang Bolu 黃伯祿. *Zhengjiao fengbao* 正教奉褒 [1884]. In *Zhongguo Tianzhujiao shiji huibian* 中國天主教史籍彙編, edited by Chen Fangzhong 陳方中, 445–575. Taipei: Furen daxue chubanshe, 2003.

Qing guoshi, Jiayetang chaoben 清國史嘉業堂鈔本. 14 vols. Beijing: Zhonghua shuju, 1993.
Ruan Yuan 阮元 et al. *Chouren zhuan huibian* 疇人傳彙編. 2 vols. Taipei: Shijie shuju, 1982.
Schall, Johann Adam. *Minli puzhu jiehuo* 民曆鋪註解惑 [1662]. XXSK 1040: 1–16.
Schall, Johann Adam et al. "Xiyang xinfa lishu, Zoushu" 西洋新法曆書奏疏. In *Mingmo Qingchu Tianzhujiao shi wenxian xinbian* 明末清初天主教史文獻新編, edited by Zhou Yan 周岩, 1235–363. Beijing: Guojia tushuguan chubanshe, 2013.
Shunzhi yuping jingguan zhimingce 順治御屏京官職名冊. In *Wenxian congbian* 文獻叢編, nos. 27, 28. Beijing: National Palace Museum, 1935.
Wenqing 文慶 et al. *Guozijian zhi* 國子監志 [1834]. 2 vols. XXSK 751: 425–769, 752.
Xu Guangqi 徐光啟 et al. "Zhili yuanqi" 治曆緣起. In *Chongzhen lishu fu Xiyang xinfa lishu zengkan shizhong* 崇禎曆書 附西洋新法曆書增刊十種, edited by Pan Naihui 潘鼐匯, 1545–752. Shanghai: Shanghai guji chubanshe, 2009.
Yunlu 允祿 et al. *Qinding yixiang kaocheng* 欽定儀象考成 [1754]. SKQS 793: 1–450.
Zhong Qi 鐘琦. *Huangchao suoxuelu* 皇朝瑣屑錄 [1897]. CKZB 532.

Secondary Sources

Lee, Thomas H.C. *Education in Traditional China, a History*. Leiden: Brill, 2000.
Li Yan 李儼. *Zhongguo Suanxueshi* 中國算學史. Beijing: Shangwu yinshuguan, 1998.
Qu Chunhai 屈春海. "Qingdai Qintianjian ji Shixianke zhiguan nianbiao." 清代欽天監暨時憲科職官年表. *Zhongkuo keji shiliao* 中國科技史料 18, no. 3 (1997): 45–71.
Shi Yumin 史玉民. "Qing Qintianjian Tianwenke zhiguan nianbiao" 清欽天監天文科職官年表. *Zhongkuo keji shiliao* 中國科技史料 21, no. 1 (2000): 34–47.
Tsao Kai-fu. "The Rebellion of the Three Feudatories Against the Manchu Throne in China, 1673–1681: Its Setting and Significance." Ph.D. diss., Columbia University, 1965.

9 The Decline of Missionary Influence and the Nineteenth-Century Reforms of the Astronomical Bureau

9.1 The Declining Influence of European Missionaries

In July 1773, Pope Clement XIV signed a decree to dissolve the Society of Jesus. This decree struck a severe blow to the Catholic mission in Qing China. The nineteenth-century Jesuit biographer of Augustin von Hallerstein (1703–1774), a Jesuit missionary and European Director of the Qing Astronomical Bureau, suggests that his death at the age of 71 shortly after the papal decree reached Beijing may have been caused by his distress at this news.[1] Furthermore, quarrels and anxiety spread among the different missionary groups present in China. In the following decades, the missionaries residing in the Beijing area spent more energy on resolving conflicts among themselves than they did on attempting to improve, or even maintain, their status in the Qing court by introducing new scientific knowledge to China. By mid-1777, the chaos had become so overwhelming that some missionaries repeatedly sought assistance from the Qing court to settle their disagreements over the division of properties.[2]

The Qing court, however, appeared uninterested in becoming involved in the conflict between Catholic missionaries. In fact, the Qing ministers in charge of managing Western missionaries made little attempt to learn or understand the complex factors underlying the conflict. As late as January 1781, European missionaries still had to explain to the ministers the meaning of the papal decree, the different nationalities and religious orders to which the missionaries belonged, the sources of income for purchasing the properties, and the previous processes by which those properties had been managed.[3] Even though the missionaries' explanations seemed consistent and credible, the ministers of the Qing court found handling such quarrels annoying. "If the Westerners serving in Beijing can obey the rules," the ministers wrote in an investigation report to the emperor, "then there is no need for us to handle their household affairs for them."[4] Moreover, the ministers argued, "The Western documents held by missionaries can hardly be trusted. Even if they are authentic, it is irrational to expect documents from hundreds of thousands of miles away to convince everyone."[5] The officials set aside the Western documents, regardless of whether they were decrees from the Pope or European kings, and directly proposed a new property management method to the missionaries.

DOI: 10.4324/9781003008255-9

The ministers' impatience and lack of interest was a reflection of the Catholic missionaries' declining status. This was not the first time that conflicts had arisen among the missionaries. A century earlier, the Kangxi emperor had summoned the missionaries and had personally tried to resolve their conflicts.[6] He wrote to the Pope and even sent some Jesuit missionaries back to Europe as his ambassadors.[7] As a sovereign of China, the Kangxi emperor would not take orders from the Pope, but he was willing to communicate with the papal court. However, such incidents only occurred when the Qing emperor had a use for Jesuit scientific knowledge and skills. The Jesuits earned their status at the Qing court because they made special contributions to the dynasty, not because they had converted the emperors or Manchu high noblemen to their religion. After the death of the Kangxi emperor, succeeding Qing emperors were more interested in Western missionaries' contributions in painting and architecture than in mathematical astronomy. The missionaries no longer appeared more capable than the Chinese court specialists did. No wonder the Qing ministers felt no need to pay special respect to people who could not even maintain order within their own household.

Nonetheless, the Qing court continued to follow the Chinese traditional policy of "cherishing men from afar" (*huairou yuanren* 懷柔遠人) by of reserving some posts at the Astronomical Bureau for European missionaries.[8] By then, assistance from the European missionaries was no longer crucial to ensuring that the Astronomical Bureau could successfully fulfill its duties. Nevertheless, retaining their presence at the Astronomical Bureau would by no means bring any harm to the court. Moreover, the court considered such an act to represent an imperial benevolence to foreigners, in the same way that it allowed the astronomers specializing in the outdated Great Concordance calendar or the Muslim calendar to remain in the Bureau. Whether the Society of Jesus had been dissolved was not a concern to the Qing emperors. Soon after Hallerstein died, the Qianlong emperor filled the post with former Jesuit Félix da Rocha (1731–1781), who had been the Vice-Director of the Astronomical Bureau since 1753.[9] It was not until José Bernardo de Almeida (1728–1805), the last Jesuit Director of the Astronomical Bureau, died in November 1805 and there was no former Jesuit missionary remaining in Beijing that the directorship finally passed to a Franciscan, Alexandre de Gouveia (1751–1808).[10] By that time, the Catholic Church had ruled that Lazarites should take over the Jesuits' work in China. Thenceforward, all succeeding European Directors and Vice-Directors were Lazarites. Unlike the Jesuits, the Lazarites focused on training Chinese missionaries rather than on introducing new European techniques to Qing China.[11] As such, the relationship between European missionaries and the Qing court did not improve after the Lazarites took over.

During the Jiaqing reign, the Qing court became increasingly alarmed by, if not hostile to, Catholic missionary activities. The Yongzheng emperor's ban on Christianity had not been seriously implemented in the capital area. However, the situation changed dramatically in late 1804, after a provincial governor caught a Chinese Christian attempting to deliver letters and maps to Macao on behalf of Pietro Adeodato di Sant'Agostino (1760–1821), a missionary serving as a painter at the Qing court.[12] Adeodato claimed that he sent the maps to seek the papal court's input on how the missionaries' quarrels over the division of properties and parishes should be settled. However, the Qing court considered his behavior to constitute both a crime and a threat to national security.[13] Furthermore, the emperor and the prosecutors were shocked by the number of court officials and bannermen involved in this case. The Jiaqing emperor issued an angry decree expressing his irritation at individuals whose behavior indicated that they would rather be banished to the remote borderland than relinquish their belief in Christianity. In June 1805, the court outlined a new set of regulations that strictly confined and monitored the missionaries' activities.[14]

The Jiaqing emperor's attitude toward Christianity greatly reduced the European missionaries' status at the Qing court. It is noteworthy that in his decree, the emperor described the missionaries as people who had "come to the capital for the purposes of learning the craft [of astronomy]."[15] Apparently, European missionaries were no longer indispensable astronomers to the court and had been relegated to the status of mere craftsmen whose lives and career prosperities were bestowed by the imperial grace. Another case testified to the missionaries' loss of imperial favor during the Jiaqing reign. In 1811, the Astronomical Bureau Director Domingos Joaquim Ferreira (1758–1824) and Vice-Director Verissimo Monteiro da Serra (d. 1852) accused some petty district officers of stealing from their country retreat mansion and kidnapping their tenants.[16] The court immediately investigated this case but with a distinct focus on ascertaining whether the tenants were Christian and identifying whether any recovered item was related to missionary work. At the end of the investigation, no one from the county yamen was punished, while all recovered religious items were destroyed and the Christian tenants were forced to abandon their religion. Usually, the emperors would exempt Western Directors and Vice-Directors from punishments as a show of benevolence to foreigners; but this time, the Jiaqing emperor ordered that their civil service ranks be reduced by four grades.

Although European missionaries were able to keep their positions in the Astronomical Bureau directorate, their importance had been decreasing. While the description of the missionaries as foreigners in Beijing who wished to learn the craft of astronomy was an exaggeration, even Louis Pfister, a Jesuit historian, admitted that the later missionaries "did not compile astronomical records or compute anything. . . . [They] only checked and corrected the computations done by Chinese officials."[17] In contrast, Han and banner officials seemed able to fulfill the essential duties of the Astronomical Bureau. They either had learned to perform the astronomical computations for calendar making and had sufficiently mastered the predictions on solar and lunar eclipses or had somehow managed to cover their faults. The need to cooperate and learn from the European directorate seemed greatly reduced.

Accompanying European missionaries' loss of importance was the Han officials' attempt to oust European missionaries from the Bureau directorate. We may recall the regulation set up at the beginning of the dynasty that European Directors were counted as part of the quota originally set aside for Han Directors. Even though the posts of Directors and Vice-Directors had been adjusted several times up until the Jiaqing reign, the Astronomical Bureau still had no Han Director. Therefore, when José Bernardo died in November 1805, the Han Bureau officials attempted to acquire the post he left behind. In the memorial that nominated the new Director, he was given the title of Han Director, as opposed to Western Director, Moreover, a Han Vice-Director was nominated alongside two Western missionaries.[18] Although Han officials failed to seize the directorship this time, European missionaries would voluntarily give up their posts in the Qing Astronomical Bureau two decades later.

After the mid-Qianlong period, the number of European missionaries in Beijing gradually decreased. In late 1780, there were 16 missionaries living in Beijing.[19] Following the case of Domingos Joaquim Ferreira and Verissimo Monteiro da Serra in 1811, the emperor ordered that all missionaries, with the exception of those who held government positions or who were too old to travel, should be sent to Guangdong and then to Europe.[20] After this deportation, only seven missionaries remained in Beijing.[21] When European Director Joseph Ribeiro (1767–1826) died, the last two European Vice-Directors requested the Daoguang emperor let them retire and return to Europe. The emperor promptly approved their requests and ordered that they be sent to Guangdong under heavy guard so that they would not have to stop on the road or make contact with the local people.[22] Although afterward one of them decided to stay in Beijing to protect the properties of the church, where he remained until his death in 1838, the European missionaries' service at the Qing Astronomical Bureau had finally come to an end.[23]

9.2 Stagnation of Imperial Mathematical Institutions

In July 1826, Jingzheng 敬徵, who had been appointed superintendent of the College of Mathematics and the Astronomical Bureau two years earlier, submitted a memorial to the Daoguang emperor. Jingzheng stated in his memorial that he had been closely supervising the graduation and entrance examinations of the College after a new set of administrative rules had been established in the preceding year. He repeatedly told the Principal Instructor and Instructors at the College of Mathematics to take their teaching responsibilities seriously. However, after a recent inspection to the College, Jingzheng found the lethargic status of the College was not much improved and had to charge its Principal Instructor, Zhang Deyuan 張德源, with "neglectful trifling with official business."[24] Jingzheng wrote in the memorial:

> When questioned [about why none of the teachers and students were at the College of Mathematics], Principal Instructor Zhang Deyuan answered that due to the summer heat, he had told students to meet for class only once during this month and had cancelled the rest of the eight class meetings.... Zhang has the duty to direct and lead [the College of Mathematics], but he does not think about diligently disciplining students.... He reduced the required class schedule and curriculum at will. His neglectful trifling with official business means that he is not suitable for the position of Principal Instructor.[25]

Jingzheng's memorial no doubt reveals the astonishing condition of the College of Mathematics, which was the training ground for future Astronomical Bureau officials, at the time when he was appointed superintendent. But it also suggests that Jingzheng had been striving to rejuvenate these two institutions. What difficulties Jingzheng had encountered, how successful his efforts were, and what impacts Jingzheng's reform brought to the astronomer families will be discussed in the rest of this chapter.

In the Qing dynasty, examinations and seniority were the two factors used to determine an official's career advancement in the Astronomical Bureau. As the balance between these two factors went through several adjustments, it deserves a brief review here. In the Shunzhi reign, seniority had very little influence on a Bureau official's career advancement. Schall, the head of the Astronomical Bureau, used examinations to ensure that new Student Astronomers learned the New Western Method and to deny promotion to staff members who would not learn. As described in Chapter 3, such a system fueled the explosion of the Kangxi Calendar Dispute and the reorganization of the Astronomical Bureau. In 1676, the Kangxi emperor gave his decisive endorsement to the New Method by decreeing that promotions would only be given to Bureau officials who had studied. Moreover, banner Bureau officials were not allowed to transfer to other institutions if they had not studied.[26] In 1681, new regulations specified that vacancies should be filled by holding examination for those who had well studied.[27] However, it is not clear how the Bureau chose the examination candidates and what the contents of the examinations were.

The triennial examination system was not established until 1745. Before that, examinations were held when vacant positions arose. The purpose of the triennial examinations was different; it provided a means to measure the progress of lower-level officials and trainees. Therefore, the Bureau directorate, Recorders, and those who already reached the highest positions of each section—Calendar Section Supervisors, Observatory Managers, and Water Clock Managers—were not included in the triennial examinations. In contrast, officials from the Calendar Managers down to the Student Astronomers and Yin-Yang Students all had to take and pass the triennial examinations. After the examinations, the best performers were rewarded with special promotions. Conversely, those who failed the examinations had their rights of promotion suspended and repeated failures resulted in the loss of their jobs.[28] From the Qing state documents preserved in the Archive of the Grand Secretariat at the Institute of History and Philology of the Academia Sinica in Taiwan, eight memorials that reported the triennial examination results to the emperor have been found. Their dates ranged from 1765 in the Qianlong reign to 1867 in the Tongzhi 同治 reign. As the following discussion will show, these memorials provide critical information for evaluating the efficiency of the Astronomical Bureau's triennial examination system.

The first handful of the triennial examination examinations seemed to have been implemented rather dutifully. For instance, the report of the examination held in January 1765 informed the emperor in detail that one examinee should be given a special promotion, four examinees should be suspended, and one examinee who

Table 9.1 Triennial examinations, Qianlong and Jiaqing reigns

Year	Qianlong		Jiaqing
	1765	1792	1804
Pass	?	114	120
Pass with Excellence	1	4	0
Pass and Reinstall	1	0	0
Fail and Suspend	4	0	0
Fail and Demote	0	0	1
Fail and Discharge	0	0	0
Examinees	?	118	121

Sources: IHP 025061, 092494, 157745.

had made sufficient progress since the previous examination should have his suspension removed.[29] It is noteworthy that the person who received special promotion was Chen Jixin 陳際新, who indeed would prove his mathematical talent in the future by completing Minggantu's *Quick Methods for the Circle's Division and Precise Ratio* (*Geyuan milü jiefa* 割圜密率捷法).[30]

However, by the end of the Qianlong reign, the examination system seemed to have deteriorated into being simply formulaic and its effectiveness became questionable. None of the examinees failed the examination of 1792, for example; yet four officials were given recommendations. The examination of 1804 failed only one examinee and made no recommendation (see Table 9.1).[31] In sum, with the exception of only one person, everyone who attended these two examinations passed. Interestingly, the person who failed the examination of 1804 was an Erudite.[32] One can only wonder how he had passed previous examinations and had advanced from the position of Student Astronomer to his current role. The potential power of the examination system for managing Bureau officials was clearly not in use. Similarly, the examination system had lost its rewarding power. The four officials who won recommendations in 1792 included one official of the Erudite level from each section and one Student Astronomer. That Student Astronomer, in fact, had already won the recommendation in a previous examination; however, because no position had become available over the previous three years, he had not been able to receive any promotion.[33] The fact that no suitable position had become available in three years indeed confirmed what Luo'erzhan had described and warned the emperor about in 1739: "Junior officials' career progression will be slowed down and they will not have a chance to test their talent."[34]

A lethargic Astronomical Bureau could not retain potential astronomers and mathematicians effectively. The case of Luo Shilin 羅士琳 (1789–1853) demonstrates this.[35] Luo was the author of the *Sequel to the Biographies of Mathematicians and Astronomers* (*Xu chouren zhuan* 續疇人傳 or *Chouren zhuan xubian* 疇人傳續編), to which he added several specialists of the Astronomical Bureau, including Minggantu and Chen Jixin. It is highly likely that Luo was familiar with their achievements because he had been a Student Astronomer in the late Jiaqing period. In the early years, Luo's interests were in Western learning (*xixue* 西學) rather than in traditional Chinese mathematics. However, according to the *History of the Qing Empire* (*Qing guoshi* 清國史), Luo was not able to advance his career at the Bureau because his colleagues were too jealous of his excellent ability in mathematical astronomy.[36] Luo left Beijing discouraged and eventually lost his passion for Western mathematics. He turned his efforts to studying the newly rediscovered *Jade Mirror of the Four Unknowns* (*Siyuan yujian* 四元玉鑑), the highest-level treatise on Chinese algebra that had been written by Zhu Shijie 朱世傑 in 1303. For the rest of his life, Luo advocated the power of traditional Chinese mathematics.[37]

From the late Qianlong era to the end of Jiaqing reign, the Astronomical Bureau and the College of Mathematics were on a downward spiral. These two institutions were not yet dysfunctional when the Daoguang emperor ascended the throne in 1820. Nevertheless, if the lethargy continued, the astronomer families and the two institutions where they earned a living were unlikely to escape a miserable end.

9.3 Attending to Details and Efficiency

Similar to his predecessors, Jingzheng (1784–1851) was a trusted minister handpicked by the emperor to be the superintendent of the Astronomical Bureau and the College of Mathematics. Jingzheng's father, Yongxi 永錫 (d. 1821), was the sixth-generation Prince Su 肅親王.[38] Yongxi was also the superintendent of these two institutions during the last two years of his life.[39] When Yongxi died in the first year of the Daoguang reign (1821), Jingzheng's elder brother inherited the title of Prince Su. Nonetheless, Jingzheng's administrative ability soon made him an indispensable assistant to the new emperor. By the end of 1823, besides being the Vice Minister of Works, Jingzheng was also managing the Imperial Household Department (*Neiwufu* 內務府) and the Yuanming Garden (*Yuanming Yuan* 圓明園) for the Daoguang emperor. In May 1824, the Daoguang emperor gave Jingzheng the responsibility of managing Western missionaries and superintending the Astronomical Bureau and the College of Mathematics.[40] Throughout his career, Jingzheng often concurrently managed several accounting offices and engineering projects that the emperor had assigned to him.

Jingzheng reformed the Astronomical Bureau steadily but not hastily. Three months after becoming superintendent, Jingzheng sent the first warning signal to the Astronomical Bureau officials. He discharged the Manchu Director E'erdengbu 額爾登布, who had been too sick to come into the office. Since E'erdengbu was almost 70 years old, Jingzheng suggested the emperor should not wait for the old man's recovery but instead pressure him to retire.[41] The fact that E'erdengbu had been the Director for 14 years without transferring to another institution was not unique but was highly suspicious.[42] We have seen the memorial submitted by the directorate in September 1742 that begged the emperor to let the aged Senior Vice-Director Sun Shiying 孫士英 remain in the Bureau.[43] Perhaps, E'erdengbu, like Sun Shiying, had felt too old to learn the required skills for alternative positions.

The discharge of E'erdengbu did not necessarily mean that Jingzheng wanted to strictly implement the transfer requirements as Luo'erzhan had suggested. Nonetheless, he used it to warn the staff that the Astronomical Bureau had no position for those who could not contribute.

In January 1826, Jingzheng reported to the emperor that the administrative system of the College of Mathematics was in terrible disarray and had to be rebuilt.[44] First of all, a new official seal of the Principal Instructor had to be made because the current one was nowhere to be found and the Principal Instructor, Zhang Deyuan, did not even know if it ever existed. Second, Jingzheng found that the College of Mathematics had stopped updating its accounting records before 1755 and there was no way to know if supplies of stationery that should have been given to students and teachers had indeed been distributed or who had taken them instead. Jingzheng proposed that beginning that year, the College of Mathematics should be obliged to submit its accounting records together with those of the Imperial College for verification. Third, the College of Mathematics needed a new clerk because the current one was not knowledgeable enough to help resolve the above issues. In fact, he was not even hired according to the normal recruitment process. Finally, Jingzheng found that a Teaching Assistant had not been paid any salary between the time he graduated from the College of Mathematics and assumed the post of Student Astronomer. During such a period, Jingzheng suggested, a Teaching Assistant should be granted the monthly stipend of a Mathematics Student so that his studies would not be interrupted.

After attempting to rebuild its administrative system, Jingzheng turned his attention to the teachings of the College of Mathematics. In July 1826, Jingzheng had Zhang Deyuan demoted from Principal Instructor to Instructor after finding out that the classes of the College of Mathematics did not meet on schedule.[45] Eight years later, Zhang's name appeared again in a job review that had been written by the Manchu Director of the Astronomical Bureau on behalf of Jingzheng, who had been sent by the emperor to survey some provincial construction projects. "Zhang worked diligently," the Director wrote, "but his teaching of the students assigned to him did not always bring satisfactory achievements."[46] The Director did not recommend a promotion for Zhang, as would normally be awarded to those who had successfully completed their teaching terms. Instead, he suggested that Zhang should remain in his current post for one more term. The emperor approved the suggestion without further ado. Since there is no further mention of Zhang in the archival documents dated after 1834, we can only guess that Zhang probably ended his career as a disgraced Instructor at the College of Mathematics.

In addition to removing incompetent officials such as E'erdengbu and Zhang Deyuan, Jingzheng attempted to speed up potential astronomers' career advancements. In July 1821, Chen Jie 陳杰 passed the entrance examination of Astronomer Apprentice and immediately voluntarily himself to work for the Calendar Section. Jingzheng noticed Chen's talent after he became the Superintendent in May 1824, and he began to look for opportunities to promote Chen. A year later, Jingzheng felt he had enough evidence to make a special recommendation for

Chen. After holding the 1825 triennial examination, he wrote to the Daoguang emperor:

> Because my bureau was calculating the coming solar and lunar eclipses from 1826 to 1835, I ordered this trainee [Chen Jie] to submit a copy of his own calculation. Surprisingly, his calculation was accurate to the second. Moreover, the periodic examination has just been held on the Bureau officials and trainees. When the answer sheets were graded the next day, they were interviewed and questioned. This trainee's calculation was very detailed. It proved that he was indeed good at mathematics.[47]

The emperor agreed that Chen should immediately become a staff member of the Astronomical Bureau and awarded him the post of Student Astronomer. Henceforth, Chen worked concurrently at the Calendar Section and the Section of Heavenly Signs, specializing in astronomical observation, and "higher officials relied heavily on him."[48] In May 1836, Chen Jie, by then an Erudite, obtained the Principal Instructorship of the College of Mathematics.[49] Sources differ on what happened to Chen afterward. The *Veritable Records* states that Chen was dismissed from the College of Mathematics in November 1838 because of malfeasance in administering the examination.[50] *The Third Addition to the Biographies of Mathematicians and Astronomers* written by Zhu Kebao 諸可寶, avoids mentioning malfeasance, and tells us instead that Chen retired from the Astronomical Bureau in 1839 due to "leg problems."[51] Either way, Chen returned to his hometown and continued to teach mathematics. He wrote *The Great Achievements of Computational Methods* (*Suanfa dacheng* 算法大成), and his faith in the Western mathematics used in the Astronomical Bureau never wavered.[52]

Jingzheng's most important contribution to the administrative system of the Astronomical Bureau was his attention to the triennial examination system. During his superintendency of the Astronomical Bureau, Jingzheng administered the triennial examinations seven times. Fortunately, the results of four of the seven examinations are preserved in the Archive of the Grand Secretariat at the Institute of History and Philology (IHP) of the Academia Sinica, Taiwan. Table 9.2 summarizes the results of those four examinations together with an additional examination that was held during a later period. Jingzheng held his first triennial examination in May 1825, just one year after being appointed superintendent. However, in comparison to the previous examinations listed in Table 9.1, the results of the 1825 examination contained a higher number of examinees who passed with excellence or failed. The triennial examination was designed to monitor and maintain the level of mathematical knowledge that was deemed essential to the success of the Astronomical Bureau. As Table 9.1 shows, by the end of the eighteenth century, the triennial examinations had become formulaic and thus had little effect on a person's career progression in the Astronomical Bureau. The 1825 examination, nonetheless, began to resume the practice of adjusting the Bureau staff members' positions according to their mathematical knowledge. It rewarded

Table 9.2 Triennial examinations, Daoguang and Tongzhi reigns

Year	Daoguang				Tongzhi
	1825	1828	1837	1843	1867
Pass	116	88	113	102	84
Pass with Excellence	4	8	6	5	11
Pass and Reinstall	0	1	1	0	0
Fail and Suspend	4	11	5	11	0
Fail and Demote	1	4	2	0	0
Fail and Discharge	1	9	0	3	0
Total Examinees	126	121	127	121	95
Total Absence	?	5	21	18	32

Sources: IHP 170696, 205793, 197248, 216304, 182598.

the best four examinees with special promotions and punished the worst six with suspension, demotion, and even discharge.

The outcomes of later triennial examinations administered by Jingzheng were even more severe than the one held in 1825. It seems possible that Jingzheng may have felt that the Bureau officials and students had already been given enough time to polish their knowledge, and so a more demanding standard of examination was appropriate, The 1828 examination failed 24 examinees; 11 of them were banned from future promotion, and nine were discharged directly.[53] We may recall that the report of the 1792 examination mentioned a candidate who had not yet received the promotion due to him from the previous examination because no suitable position had become available. This was clearly no longer acceptable, and it was only through discharging incompetent members that the Astronomical Bureau could ensure vacant positions were available to capable officials and trainees. Similarly, banning incompetent officials or students from promotion prevented them from advancing to higher positions of seniority alone and thus made those positions available to other officials.

To make the triennial examination system more powerful, Jingzheng submitted a proposal to the Daoguang emperor soon after the 1828 examination. Originally, the examination results had no impact on the Student Astronomers who passed but did not win special promotion, because their career advancement depended on their seniority of service alone. Jingzheng claimed that these Student Astronomers needed further stimulation so that they would not neglect their studies. Therefore, Jingzheng stated that he had discussed the issue with the Bureau directorate and had identified a fairer way of utilizing the triennial examination system. Together they proposed that Student Astronomers should be divided into two groups according to their examination grades. Within each group, members were still ordered according to seniority. However, only after all the members of the first group had advanced to Erudites or higher-level positions could the members of the second group begin to receive promotion.[54] The Daoguang emperor approved this new rule, and it was put into effect immediately.

Jingzheng was an administrator who paid great attention to detail. Rather than adopting large-scale reformation at once, he focused on ensuring that every stage of the administrative processes was precisely and effectively implemented. Such a focus did not require the Superintendent to have distinct mathematical knowledge, but it certainly consumed a great deal of time and energy. Nevertheless, that was exactly what a trusted and capable Superintendent like Jingzheng could do for the emperor. Jingzheng introduced very few rules to the administrative system of the Astronomical Bureau and the College of Mathematics. In particular, he did not change the system of employing the hereditary astronomer families. Nonetheless, his attention to detail and efficiency would not allow an individual or a family that did not contribute to remain in the Astronomical Bureau. The next section will describe how Jingzheng's administration led to the downfall of the He family and the rise of new astronomer families and how it led to new achievements within the Astronomical Bureau.

9.4 The Downfall of the He Family and the Rejuvenation of the Astronomical Bureau

The case of He Yuanpu 何元溥 illustrates the decay of the He family and the lethargic condition of the Astronomical Bureau in the late Qianlong and Jiaqing reigns. He Yuanpu was the only person to fail the 1804 examination. At that time, he was already an Erudite but he failed the examination so miserably that, instead of being suspended from future advancement, he was demoted to Fed-by-salary Student Astronomer.[55] But afterward, He Yuanpu was able to remain in the position of Fed-by-salary Student Astronomer for more than two decades. One could only wonder whether He Yuanpu might have remained at the Astronomical Bureau for the rest of his life if Jingzheng had not become the superintendent of the Astronomical Bureau.

The triennial examinations held during Jingzheng's superintendency struck the He family severely. In the first examination administered by Jingzheng in 1825, two out of the six people who failed the examination were from the He family. One of them was He Yuanpu, and he was further demoted to Fed-by-grain Student Astronomer as a result of "making too many mistakes during the examination."[56] In the 1828 examination, the performance of the He family did not improve but deteriorated. Out of the 24 failed examinees, 4 were bannermen and 20 were Han Chinese astronomers, who belonged to 12 surnames. Among these 12 surnames, only Chen 陳, Li 李 and He had more than one person who failed the examination; each of the surnames Chen and Li had 2 persons (one Erudite and one Student Astronomer), but the surname He had 7 (see Table 9.3).[57] According to Jingzheng's report, He Yuangan 何元淦, though already an Erudite, "was not versed in the principles of mathematics" and should be demoted to the entry-level position of Fed-by-grain Student Astronomer.[58] He Yuanpu and He Yuanrun 何元潤 had made so many mistakes on the examination sheets that they "should be discharged to set a warning to others."[59] Erudite He Yuanqi 何元淇, who also failed the 1825 examination and was in suspension, could not demonstrate enough improvement

Table 9.3 He officials who failed the 1828 examination

Title	Name	Punishment
Erudite, Calendar Section	He Yuangan 何元淦	Demotion
Erudite, Calendar Section	He Yuanqi 何元淇	Suspension
Fed-by-salary Student Astronomer	He Liangcheng 何良成	Demotion
Astronomical Observer	He Yuandu 何元渡	Suspension
Fed-by-grain Student Astronomer	He Yuanpu 何元溥	Discharge
Fed-by-grain Student Astronomer	He Yuanrun 何元潤	Discharge
Fed-by-grain Student Astronomer	He Yuanhui 何元洄	Suspension

Source: IHP 205793.

to be reinstated. In fact, He Yuanqi's examination performance never seemed to improve. His name was not seen among those who failed the 1837 examination, but he did fail the 1843 examination.[60] Moreover, by 1843, He Yuanqi had already been demoted to the position of Fed-by-salary Student Astronomer and the examination outcome resulted in his suspension once again.[61] Worst, He Yuanqi was not the only member of the He family to fail the 1837 and 1843 examinations. In 1837, Yin-Yang Student He Liangkai 何良楷, probably a brother or cousin of He Liangcheng, failed the triennial examination.[62] In 1843, He Jun 何均, a Fed-by-grain Student Astronomer of the Section of Heavenly Signs, failed the examination and was suspended.[63]

To be sure, some early nineteenth-century He family members still took the study of mathematical astronomy seriously. For example, Erudite He Yuanying 何元瀛 won special promotion by passing the 1816 examination with excellence. He Liangtang 何良棠 and He Shuben 何樹本 passed the 1825 and 1828 examinations with excellence, respectively. Around the same period, He Liangkui 何良奎, originally a Calendar Section Erudite, was the Principal Instructor at the College of Mathematics between 1826 and 1831.[64] It is noteworthy that besides He Guoqing 何國卿 and He Guodong, He Liangkui was the only Principal Instructor at the College of Mathematics from the He family from 1751 onward.[65] In 1835, He Shuben was the Senior Vice-Director of the Bureau, He Liangkui held the post of Supervisor of the Winter Office, and He Liangkai served as Observatory Manager. In the past, their high positions would have offered those family members who were not competent enough to hold their positions great protection. However, the strictly administered examinations that had become the norm in recent years reduced this level of protection. None of the He family members was able to pass the 1837 or 1843 examination with excellence. By this time, the He family must have been aware that the end of its career at the Astronomical Bureau was approaching.

Nevertheless, Jingzheng's reform of the Astronomical Bureau could not have succeeded if he simply expelled the decaying He family and other incompetent Bureau staff. What Jingzheng needed was to find some capable officials to ensure that the Astronomical Bureau could fulfill its duties for the imperial state without any disruption and, hopefully, to raise the Bureau's knowledge level and technical skills. This is why soon after becoming the superintendent, Jingzheng made a special recommendation for Chen Jie, a talented newcomer to the Astronomical Bureau. Within the hereditary astronomer families, Jingzheng also found officials who were eager to contribute their expertise, for instance, former Supervisor of the Winter Office Si Tingdong and former Calendar Manager Fang Luheng 方履亨.

Si Tingdong, whose dramatic ups and downs of career have been briefly mentioned in Chapter 8, Section 8.2, was in fact a talented astronomer. Soon after advancing to Erudite in 1795, Si Tingdong found new methods to improve the accuracy of calculating the moon and five planets' positions. Tingdong urged the Astronomical Bureau to adopt his new calculation methods. However, according to the preface written by Fang Luheng in 1822 for Si Tingdong's treatise, *New Methods for Calculating Encroachments and Parallax* (*Lingfan shicha xinfa* 凌犯視差新法), "At that time the Supervisors could not harmoniously come to an agreement. Therefore for more than 20 years, nobody discussed it again."[66] The decades after 1795 was a period when the He family still enjoyed great influence over the administration of the Astronomical Bureau. He Tingying 何廷瑛 was the Bureau Vice-Director between 1794 and 1802, while He Tingzan 何廷瓚 the Supervisor of the Summer Office between 1781 and 1805 and He Yuanhao 何元浩 the Supervisor of the Middle Office between 1791 and 1798. Perhaps they rejected Si Tingdong's proposal for fear that it would threaten the He family's dominate position in the Bureau. Si Tingdong eventually became the Supervisor of the Winter Office in 1813, but by that time he was probably too disheartened to advocate his new methods. Five years later, he transferred to the Ministry of Revenue to oversee a large granary. Within ten months, an accidental fire destroyed the granary and cost Tingdong his job. It was only by the Astronomical Bureau superintendent's petition based on his expertise on mathematics that Tingdong was allowed to return to the Bureau as a Fed-by-grain Student Astronomer.[67]

Fang Luheng was a lifetime colleague of Si Tingdong and his career at the Astronomical Bureau also suffered dramatic setbacks. Tingdong and Luheng were probably of a similar age, for they both passed the entrance examination required for hereditary students to become astronomer students in 1780. Afterward, Luheng studied with Tingdong under the supervision of Tingdong's elder brother, Observatory Manager Si Tinggan.[68] Fang Luheng was promoted to Erudite in 1795, the same year as Tingdong.[69] But when a calendar piracy case occurred in 1816, the angry Jiaqing emperor demanded that all officials in charge of calendar publication, Fang Luheng included, be severely penalized.[70] As a result, Fang Luheng's position was reduced from Calendar Manager to Fed-by-grain Student Astronomer.[71]

When Jingzheng became the superintendent of the Astronomical Bureau, Si Tingdong and Fang Luheng had been trying to re-climb the career ladder. They surely were willing to contribute their expertise in exchange for a rejuvenation of their personal careers and family prosperity. By the end of 1822, Si Tingdong had secured support from Fang Luheng, the Calendar Section Supervisors, and some senior Erudites. In the years to come, Si Tingdong's methods were gradually adopted by the Astronomical Bureau to calculate the Seven Governors calendar, which gave detailed information on the movements of the sun, moon, and five visible planets.[72] In the meantime, Si Tingdong and his students, mainly Du Xiling 杜熙齡, worked on preparing a treatise that would explain the new calculation methods and included all necessary calculation tables. Thanks for the triennial examinations administered by Jingzheng, Si Tingdong and Fang Luheng won special recommendations for passing with excellence each time. By the time the treatise, *New Methods for Calculating Encroachments and Parallax,* was published in 1833, Si Tingdong had once again become a Calendar Section Supervisor and Fang Luheng even advanced to Vice-Director.[73] By the time Jingzheng retired from public service in 1845, the Astronomical Bureau had managed to repair the instruments of the observatory, update astronomical constants, and publish them with new stellar tables in the *Addition to the Thorough Investigation of Instruments and Phenomena* (*Yixiang kaocheng xubian* 儀象考成續編).

The *Addition to the Thorough Investigation of Instruments and Phenomena* was the last mathematical treatise published by the Qing Astronomical Bureau, and its roster of contributors was populated by the members of newly empowered hereditary astronomer families.[74] The Si and Du 杜 families, for instance, each had four members listed in the roster. Before the 1820s, only one Supervisor of the Spring Office had the surname Du.[75] With the exception of only one year, the roster of every annual calendar between 1842 and the end of the dynasty included at least one member of the family.[76] From the Daoguang reign onwards, the Du family produced eight Calendar Section Supervisors.

In contrast, the roster of the *Addition to the Thorough Investigation of Instruments and Phenomena* did not contain anyone surnamed He. This absence of He officials is striking, because the imperially commissioned mathematical treatises published in earlier times had always included a significant number of contributors from the He family. In April 1846, the Astronomical Bureau nominated two Erudites—He Weimin 何維敏 and He Liangtong 何良桐—to fill the vacant position of Water Clock Manager. By then, He Shuben, He Liangkai, and He Liangtang either had died or had left the Astronomical Bureau.[77] The Daoguang emperor appointed He Weimin Water Clock Manager, but neither Weimin nor Liangtong ever reached any higher position. No record related to the He family dated after this nomination has been found.

Notes

1 For the life of Augustin von Hallerstein, see Pfister, *Notices biographiques*, 753–7. Note that Pfister does not provide any evidence for the claim on the cause of Hallerstein's death. Ibid., 757.
2 Zhongguo diyi lishi dang'anguan, *Qing zhongqianqi*, 312–23.
3 Yan Zonglin 閻宗臨, *Chuanjiaoshi yu zaoqi hanxue* 傳教士與早期漢學 (Zhengzhou: Daxiang chubanshe, 2003), 218–27.
4 Ibid., 223.
5 Ibid.
6 Zhongguo diyi lishi dang'anguan, *Kangxichao Manwen*, 448–9.

7 Zhongguo diyi lishi dang'anguan, *Qing zhongqianqi*, 14.
8 See James Hevia, *Cherishing Men from Afar: Qing Guest Ritual and the Macartney Embassy of 1793* (Durham: Duke University Press, 1994) for an extensive discussion on this traditional diplomatic policy.
9 Pfister, *Notices biographiques*, 774. When the news of the suppression of the Society reached Beijing, Félix da Rocah promptly declared himself ex-Jesuit. See Davor Antonucci, "In the Service of the Emperor: Félix da Rocha S.J. (1731–1781) and Qianlong's 'Ten Great Campaigns'," *Orientis Aura: Macau Perspectives in Religious Studies* no. 3 (2018): 64.
10 For the biographical information of José Bernardo de Almeida, see Pfister, *Notices biographiques*, 886–8. For Alexandre de Gouveia, see Lin et al., *Lishi yihen*, 142. For the nomination and election of the new Bureau Director after the death of Almeida, see IHP 060732.
11 Geng Sheng 耿昇, "Qianshihuei Chuanjiaoshi Zaihua Huodong Kaoshu" 遣使會傳教士在華活動考述, *Journal of Sino-Western Cultural Studies* 中西文化研究 1 (2008): 2–8.
12 Zhongguo diyi lishi dang'anguan, *Qing zhongqianqi*, 829–30.
13 Ibid., 832–4.
14 Ibid., 852–5.
15 Ibid., 846.
16 IHP 119761.
17 Pfister, *Notices biographiques*, 886n3.
18 IHP 060732.
19 Yan, 225.
20 Zhongguo diyi lishi dang'anguan, *Qing zhongqianqi*, 923–4.
21 Ibid., 925. See also SL 31: 325–6.
22 IHP 292204–004, SL 34: 740, 749.
23 Lin et al., *Lishi yihen*, 145–6.
24 IHP 129844.
25 Ibid.
26 IHP 091507. See Chapter 4, Section 4.3. At the time Han officials were not allowed to transfer to other institutions. QHD KX 291.
27 Ibid.
28 QHDZL QL 625: 149–50; IHP 216304.
29 IHP 025061.
30 Minggantu and Chen, *Geyuan milü jiefa*, 1–2.
31 IHP 157745.
32 Ibid.
33 IHP 092494.
34 IHP 194605. See Chapter 8, Section 8.2.
35 For Luo Shilin's life, see Guo Qingzhang 郭慶章, "Luo Shilin ji qi shuxue yanjiu" 羅士琳及其數學研究 (master's thesis, National Taiwan Normal University, 2005), 29–68.
36 *Qing guoshi*, 12: 702.
37 Written by Zhu Shijie 朱世傑 in 1303, *Siyuanyujian* brough Chinese algebra to its highest level.
38 For a biography of Jingzheng, see *Qing guoshi*, 9: 627–32. The first-generation Prince Su Hoogu 豪格 (1609–1648) was the Shunzhi emperor's uncle and Regent Prince Dorgon's eldest brother. In the Qing period, a title of prince was diminished by one rank when it was passed to the next generation. For his extraordinary service to the founding of the dynasty, Hoogu won for his descendants the privilege that the title of Prince Su was allowed to be passed to the next generation without rank dropping. The title of Prince Su and other titles which enjoyed the same privilege were often called Princes of the Iron Cap (*Tie maozi wang* 鐵帽子王). Elliott, *The Manchu Way*, 80.

39 Qu, "Qingdai Qintianjian," 62.
40 *Qing guoshi*, 9: 627.
41 IHP 162826.
42 Qu, "Qingdai Qintianjian," 61–2.
43 IHP 127466. See Chapter 8, Section 8.2.
44 IHP 119130.
45 IHP 129844.
46 IHP 131038, 129844.
47 IHP 129743.
48 Ruan, *Chouren zhuan*, 765.
49 IHP 224166.
50 SL 37: 918.
51 Ruan, *Chouren zhuan*, 765.
52 Ibid., 766.
53 IHP 205793.
54 NPM 060148.
55 IHP 157745.
56 IHP 170696.
57 IHP 205793.
58 Ibid.
59 Ibid.
60 IHP 197248; IHP 216304.
61 IHP 216304.
62 IHP 197248.
63 IHP 216304.
64 Wenqing et al., *Guozijian zhi*, 752: 205.
65 Ibid., 752: 204–5.
66 Fang Luheng 方履亨, preface to *Lingfan shicha xinfa* 凌犯視差新法 (Beijing, 1833. Tohoku University Library, Wasan shiryo Fujiwara bunko 3283), 3. Si Tingdong wrote similar statements in his own preface.
67 IHP 065595.
68 Si Tingdong 司廷棟, preface to *Lingfan shicha xinfa*, 5.
69 IHP 125793.
70 IHP056490; NPM 49325; SL 32: 265.
71 IHP 236998.
72 Fang, preface to *Lingfan shicha xinfa*, 4.
73 Qu, "Qingdai Qintianjian," 63.
74 *Qinding yixiang kaocheng xubian* 欽定儀象考成續編 [1842], XXSK 1035: 271–2.
75 Qu, "Qingdai Qintianjian," 58. Du Zhaoxiong 杜兆熊 held the position of Supervisor of the Spring Office from September 1771 to October 1777. See also IHP 043162 and QGLL 20: 641.
76 Qu, "Qingdai Qintianjian," 58–69.
77 Ibid., 63–4; Shi, "Tianwenke," 44.

Bibliography

Abbreviations for Archival and Published Sources

CKSB: *Jindai Zhongguo shiliao congkan sanbian* 近代中國史料叢刊三編, edited by Shen Yunlong 沈雲龍. 850 vols. Taipei: Wenhai chubanshe, 1982.
IHP: Neige daku dang'an 內閣大庫檔案. Institute of History and Philology of Academia Sinica, Taipei. http://archive.ihp.sinica.edu.tw/mctkm2/index.html

NPM: Qingdai gongzhongdang zouzhe ji junjichudang zhejian quanwen yingxiang ziliaoku 清代宮中檔奏摺及軍機處檔摺件全文影像資料庫. National Palace Museum, Taipei. http://npmhost.npm.gov.tw/tts/npmmeta/GC/indexcg.html

QGLL: *Qingdai guanyuan lüli dang'an quanbian* 清代官員履歷檔案全編. Edited by Qin Guojing 秦國經. 30 vols. Shanghai: Huadong shifan daxue chubanshe, 1997.

QHD KX: *Da Qing huidian (Kangxi chao)* 大清會典 (康熙朝) [1690]. CKSB 711–30.

QHDZL QL: *Qinding Da Qing huidian zeli* 欽定大清會典則例 [1764]. SKQS 620–5.

SKQS: *Yingyin wenyuange sikuquanshu* 景印文淵閣四庫全書. 1500 vols. Taipei: Taipei shangwu yinshuguan, 1986.

SL: *Qing shilu* 清實錄. 60 vols. Beijing: Zhonghua shuju, 1985.

XXSK: *Xuxiu sikuquanshu* 續修四庫全書. 1800 vols. Shanghai: Shanghai guji chubanshe, 2002.

Other Sources

Minggantu 明安圖 and Chen Jixin 陳際新. *Geyuan milü jiefa* 割圜密率捷法. XXSK 1045.

*Qinding yixiang kaocheng xubi*an 欽定儀象考成續編 [1842]. XXSK 1035.

Qing guoshi, Jiayetang chaoben 清國史嘉業堂鈔本. 14 vols. Beijing: Zhonghua shuju, 1993.

Ruan Yuan 阮元 et al. *Chouren zhuan huibian* 疇人傳彙編. 2 vols. Taipei: Shijie shuju, 1982.

Si Tingdong 司廷棟 and Du Xiling 杜熙齡. *Lingfan shicha xinfa* 凌犯視差新法. Beijing, 1833. Tohoku University Library, Wasan shiryo Fujiwara bunko 3283.

Wenqing 文慶 et al. *Guozijian zhi* 國子監志 [1834]. 2 vols. XXSK 751: 425–769, 752.

Zhongguo diyi lishi dang'anguan 中國第一歷史檔案館, ed. *Kangxichao Manwen zhupi zouzhe quanyi* 康熙朝滿文朱批奏摺全譯. Beijing: Zhongguo shehui kexue chubanshe, 1996.

———. *Qing zhongqianqi xiuang Tianzhujiao zihua huodong dang'an shiliao* 清中前期西洋天主教在華活動檔案史料. 4 vols. Beijing: Zhonghua shuju, 2003.

Secondary Sources

Antonucci, Davor. "In the Service of the Emperor: Félix da Rocha S.J. (1731–1781) and Qianlong's 'Ten Great Campaigns'." *Orientis Aura: Macau Perspectives in Religious Studies* 3 (2018): 61–80.

Elliott, Mark C. *The Manchu Way: The Eight Banners and Ethnic Identity in Late Imperial China*. Stanford: Stanford University Press, 2001.

Geng Sheng 耿昇. "Qianshihui chuanjiaoshi zaihua huodong kaoshu" 遣使會傳教士在華活動考述. *Journal of Sino-Western Cultural Studies* 中西文化研究 1 (2008): 1–18.

Guo Qingzhang 郭慶章. "Luo Shilin ji qi shuxue yanjiu" 羅士琳及其數學研究. Master's thesis, National Taiwan Normal University, 2005.

Hevia, James. *Cherishing Men from Afar: Qing Guest Ritual and the Macartney Embassy of 1793*. Durham: Duke University Press, 1994.

Lin Hua 林華 et al. *Lishi yihen: Li Madou ji Ming Qing xifang chuanjiaoshi mudi* 歷史遺痕：利瑪竇及明清西方傳教士墓地. Beijing: Zhongguo renmin daxue chubanshe, 1994.

Pfister, Louis. *Notices biographiques et bibliographiques sur les Jésuites de l'ancienne mission de Chine. 1552–1773*. 2 vols. Shanghai: Imprimerie de la Mission catholique, 1932–34.

Qu Chunhai 屈春海. "Qingdai Qintianjian ji Shixianke zhiguan nianbiao" 清代欽天監暨時憲科職官年表. *China Historical Materials of Science and Technology* 中國科技史料 18, no. 3 (1997): 45–71.

Shi Yumin 史玉民. "Qing Qintianjian Tianwenke zhiguan nianbiao" 清欽天監天文科職官年表. *China Historical Materials of Science and Technology* 中國科技史料 21, no. 1 (2000): 34–47.

Yan Zonglin 閻宗臨. *Chuanjiaoshi yu zaoqi hanxue* 傳教士與早期漢學. Zhengzhou: Daxiang chubanshe, 2003.

10 Conclusion

Research on a hereditary astronomer family working for the Qing Astronomical Bureau might begin by locating the family's genealogy, then searching the archives to collect data related to family members so that the story emerging from the genealogy could be enriched, challenged, or even reconstructed. However, the research for this book proceeded in the reverse order. It did not construct genealogies before beginning the main investigation, nor did it allow existing genealogies to determine the research framework or to define the storylines of the families studied here. Instead, it began by examining the archives that contain records of the Qing Astronomical Bureau, abstracting the data on Bureau astronomers, and then rebuilding the possible familial relations among them. Only then, having located possible astronomer families of the Qing Astronomical Bureau, and identified their common patterns or distinct characteristics, was it possible to construct some of these family histories in parallel with one another, and thereby contribute to the social history of the Qing Astronomical Bureau.

This book develops its narrative mainly by following the history of the He family, but its research results open up the possibilities for investigating many more astronomer families who worked at the Astronomical Bureau through successive generations. Whether these were the Christian Bao family, the Huang family of the Section of Heavenly Signs, or the Si family whose members were employed by the Bureau from the first to the last day of the Qing dynasty, each family had its distinct traits that this book could only touch on briefly. These families and many others who have not been mentioned all deserve detailed research in their own right.

This book intends to establish hereditary astronomer families as among the important actors in the history of mathematical sciences in the Qing dynasty. In contrast with the emperor's interest in maintaining his rule, or European missionaries' goal of spreading Christianity, imperial astronomers of the Qing Astronomical Bureau sought family prosperity, and they achieved that goal by mastering the knowledge and skills needed to fulfill their professional duties. The hereditary astronomers of the Astronomical Bureau obtained state patronage because they embodied the sovereign's vision of imperial mathematics, which was not static but changed in the course of time. By tracing the rise and fall of different astronomer families from the late Ming period to the early Kangxi reign, one sees how

DOI: 10.4324/9781003008255-10

astronomer families strove to balance protecting their own interests with adjusting to the state's changing demands for their specialties. Moreover, hereditary astronomer families did not just passively react to the state's demands; they can be shown to have been critical factors in a full reconstruction of the stories of the Kangxi Calendar Dispute and the amendment of the Timely Modeling calendar in the early Qianlong reign.

However, since their profession was under the patronage of the state, Bureau astronomers had to perform functions that were not (in modern terms) "science oriented." This is perhaps best revealed by closely examining how the Qing court handled solar eclipse incidents. Observing an eclipse was a highly politicized event involving the monarch, court ministers, local governors, petty officials, and "all people under heaven"—that is, the mass of imperial subjects. Before an eclipse occurred, the Bureau officials' duties were indeed scientific; they marshaled all their mathematical knowledge to provide the emperor with a prediction as accurate as they could produce. However, during and after the eclipse, their tasks became politically sensitive. Publicizing the discrepancy between prediction and observation might disturb social and political stability, a situation that the emperor would definitely not want to happen. Therefore, historians should recognize that Bureau officials were not only technical specialists but also government bureaucrats responsible for assisting the monarch in maintaining social and political stability, no matter if it was accomplished by scientific knowledge or by political performance. Instead of considering the concealment of the discrepancy as malfeasance, historians should be aware that Bureau astronomers were compelled to do so to a certain extent. Such compromise was the price that a technical specialist who chose a state-patronized profession had to make, a fact which was no doubt well known within astronomer families.

This research also reevaluates the Yongzheng emperor's role in the history of astronomy in the Qing dynasty. The lack of Qing state records of the 1730 solar eclipse is significant, for it reveals the incident's political sensitivity rather than the Yongzheng emperor's indifference to astronomy. The inaccurate prediction of the 1730 solar eclipse exposed the Yongzheng emperor to a crisis of mathematical astronomy that his father, the Kangxi emperor, had already pointed to as a risk, given the lack of expertise at the Qing court. However, neither the Kangxi emperor's *Thorough Investigation of Astronomical Phenomena* nor the group of young mathematicians he trained was able to resolve the crisis. The Yongzheng emperor had to seek help from Jesuit specialists whose loyalty had been in doubt since the Kangxi era and whose missionary work he himself had banned. The Yongzheng emperor was in a difficult situation because he had to maintain his father's and his own authority by not arousing any suspicion of the validation of the *Thorough Investigation*. The Yongzheng emperor resolved the crisis by concealing the fact that he knew the prediction would fail and by accepting his officials' interpretation that the unexpected eclipse was a heavenly approval of his rule. Furthermore, to improve the accuracy of future predictions, he accepted the Jesuits' suggestion to correct the Tychonic system of astronomy that the dynasty had been using by substituting solar and lunar tables based on the new Newtonian system. However, the replacement was not publicized and even the Bureau astronomers were not taught the theoretical basis of the new tables.

On the other hand, by the end of his reign, the Yongzheng emperor seemed to have come to a similar realization as his father did of the imperial state's need for a new generation of trustworthy mathematicians. Mathematics courses were added to the curriculum of the Eight Banners Official Schools. In contrast to the College of Mathematics founded in the early Qianlong period that aimed at training mathematics specialists to work at the Astronomical Bureau, the Yongzheng mathematics program aimed to produce a group of Manchu officials who could serve in different government departments. Unfortunately, the Yongzheng emperor died in 1735 and his mathematics program was closed in 1738. The succeeding emperors never again had the vision of cultivating officials who were both scholars in Confucian classics and mathematicians, such as He Guozong and Mei Juecheng.

In the succeeding Qianlong reign, the Qing dynasty reached its heyday; so did the astronomer families' control of the Astronomical Bureau. Soon after the Qianlong emperor ascended the throne, Jesuit missionaries were ordered to explain the Newtonian astronomy underlying the new solar and lunar tables to their Chinese colleagues at the Bureau. Afterward, the Jesuits stopped introducing new European techniques to China, and their status at the Qing court declined. By the end of the eighteenth century, the Astronomical Bureau had become stagnant. Although it continued to produce the calendar for the state, its astronomical theories and instruments were not updated. At that point, it seemed that the Qing Astronomical Bureau would follow the same fate as its predecessor in the Ming Dynasty by becoming the property of the hereditary astronomer families and gradually losing the ability to provide the state with satisfactory predictions of eclipses.

However, the story of the Qing Astronomical Bureau ended with a different twist when Jingzheng, a capable minister, was appointed superintendent in 1824. Instead of initiating a large-scale reformation, the method Jingzheng adopted to rejuvenate the Bureau was merely to reinforce the periodical examination system that had existed since 1745. New and more proficient families replaced the old and incompetent ones, such as the He family. By the time Jingzheng retired from public service in 1845, the Astronomical Bureau had managed to repair the instruments of the observatory and had published the *Addition to the Thorough Investigation of Instruments and Phenomena* (*Yixiang kaocheng xubian* 儀象考成續編) with updated astronomical constants. The achievements of Jingzheng's superintendency remind historians of Chinese astronomy to carefully evaluate the relationship between the Bureau's administration and the hereditary astronomer families. The Astronomical Bureau relied heavily on its members' familial relations to recruit and train new employees, but it was prone to corruption precisely because of such relations. Thus, a powerful administrative system was essential as a corrective. It turned out that the examination system was able to effectively stimulate learning and competition, if not among individual staff members, then at least between the different astronomer families of the Bureau.

On February 3, 1912, nine days before the last Qing emperor abdicated, the Astronomical Bureau dutifully submitted the next year's calendar for imperial approval.[1] Among the names of officials listed on that calendar was Vice-Director Si Bingjun 司秉鈞. The Si family had served the Qing court since the day it was established in Beijing. However, in the last decade of the Qing dynasty, only Bingjun's name could be found on the Bureau's rosters.[2] Perhaps the changing social and political conditions had made the Si family consider the profession of being an Astronomical Bureau astronomer much less attractive than before. The first Opium War (1839–1842) ended before Jingzheng left the Astronomical Bureau. In the following decades, the political, social, and intellectual crises that Qing China encountered were far more severe than could be resolved by compiling a new treatise or training new mathematicians. In fact, the Qing court never included the Astronomical Bureau and its imperial astronomers in its reformation efforts. Although the hereditary astronomer families served the Qing court until its last day, their story had become part of the past and ceased before the dynasty ended.

Notes

1 NPM 184913.
2 Rongbaozhai 榮寶齋, ed., *Guangxu wushen chunqiu liangji juezhi quanlan* 光緒戊申春秋兩季爵秩全覽 [1908], CKZB 380: 298–302, 1148–51; Neige Yinzhuju 內閣印鑄局, ed., *Xuantong sannian dongji zhiguanlu* 宣統三年冬季職官錄 [1914], CKZB 290: 523–37.

Bibliography

Abbreviations for Archival and Published Sources

CKZB: *Jindai Zhongguo shiliao congkan sanbian* 近代中國史料叢刊正編, edited by Shen Yunlong 沈雲龍. 1000 vols. Taipei: Wenhai chubanshe, 1966.
NPM: Qingdai gongzhongdang zouzhe ji junjichudang zhejian quanwen yingxiang ziliaoku 清代宮中檔奏摺及軍機處檔摺件全文影像資料庫. National Palace Museum, Taipei. http://npmhost.npm.gov.tw/tts/npmmeta/GC/indexcg.html

Other Sources

Neige Yinzhuju 內閣印鑄局, ed. *Xuantong sannian dongji zhiguanlu* 宣統三年冬季職官錄 [1914]. CKZB 290.
Rongbaozhai 榮寶齋, ed. *Guangxu wushen chunqiu liangji juezhi quanlan* 光緒戊申春秋兩季爵秩全覽 [1908]. CKZB 380.

Appendix A
Reconstructed Family Tree of the Baos

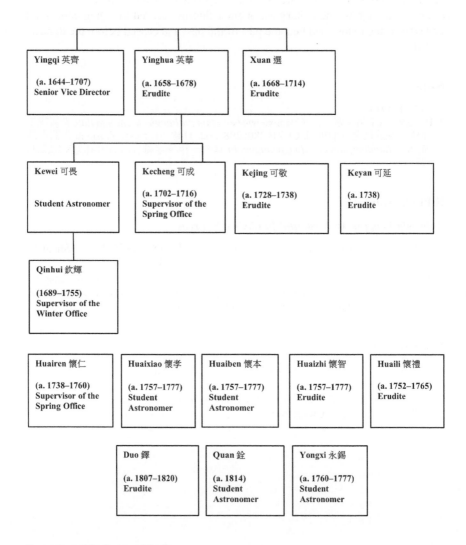

Reconstructed family tree of the Baos
Created by the author

Appendix B
The Ge Family

B.1 Biographical Information Extracted From the Genealogy of the Ge Family

The Fifth Generation

    Jiugong 九功, Erudite
    Jiushao 九韶, Erudite

The Sixth Generation

    Kunheng 坤亨, Erudite
    Jinheng 近亨, Director
    Qianheng 乾亨, Erudite
    Qianheng 謙亨, Supervisor of the Spring Office
    Dazhong 大中, Erudite

The Seventh Generation

    Yunhu 允祜, Senior Vice-Director
    Yunqing 允清, Recorder
    Yunjing 允靖, Supervisor of the Five Offices
    Yuncheng 允澄, Official Astrologer
    Shougong 守躬, Director
    Zhigong 治躬, Erudite
    Yunling 允齡, Supervisor of the Summer Office
    Fengnian 豐年, Supervisor of the Summer Office

The Eighth Generation

    Shixian 士賢, Erudite, Calendar Section
    Shiying 士英, Erudite, Water Clock Section
    Chengyin 承胤, Erudite

Chengxu 承緒, Calendar Manager
Weixiang 維相, Calendar Section
Chengzhi 承祉, Calendar Section

The Ninth Generation

Zhangzhen 掌鎮, Erudite
Zhangrong 掌戎, Erudite
Jiwen 繼文, Supervisor of the Spring Office
Jie 杰, Calendar Section
Chunzhi 淳治, Calendar Section
Jizong 繼宗, Section of Heavenly Signs

The Tenth Generation

Guoqi 國琦, Erudite
Yusheng 于陞, Erudite

Source: Ge Dingyi 戈定一, *Luoyang Geshi zongpu shiliujuan* 洛陽戈氏宗譜十六卷 (Jiangsu: Wenxintang, 1949), 15: 128–41. Shanghai Library, 923668–83. https://jiapu.library.sh.cn/#/jiapu:STJP003477

B.2 Biographical Information Extracted From the Great Concordance Calendars

Name	Title	Period*
Ge Qianheng 戈乾亨	Supervisor of the Winter Office	1585–1594
Ge Kunheng 戈坤亨	Calendar Manager	1586–1588
Ge Qianheng 戈謙亨	Calendar Manager	1594
	Official Astrologer	1597–1610
	Supervisor of the Spring Office	1612–1619
Ge Jinheng 戈近亨	Calendar Manager	1605–1614
	Official Astrologer	1616
	Supervisor of the Winter Office	1617–1625
Ge Fengnian 戈豐年	Calendar Manager	1617–1619
	Official Astrologer	1620–1623
	Supervisor of the Summer Office	1624–1632
Ge Shunnian 戈舜年	Official Astrologer	1637–1643
Ge Chengke 戈承科	Calendar Manager	1617
	Official Astrologer	1619
	Supervisor of the Spring Office	1620–1632
Ge Yongling 戈永齡	Official Astrologer	1617–1619
	Supervisor of the Summer Office	1620–1621

Name	Title	Period*
Ge Yonghu 戈永祜	Calendar Manager	1624
Ge Yongjing 戈永靖	Calendar Manager	1634–1643

Sources: Ming Qintianjian, *Da Ming Datong li* (Taipei: National Central Library), Microfilms, 305.3 06315–06338; Beijing tushuguan chubanshe guji yingyinshi, *Guojia tushuguancang Mingdai Datongliri huibian*, 6 vols.

*Periods are approximations because some years of the Great Concordance calendars are missing in the collections.

Appendix C
The He Family

Name	Title	Active period
Qiren 其仁		
Qiyi 其義	Erudite	1644–1666
	Calendar Manager	1666–1676
Luoshu 雒書	Erudite	1644–1666
	Supervisor of the Summer Office	1666–1684
Luotu 雒圖	Erudite	1655–1678
Junxi 君錫	Supervisor of the Winter Office	1666–1710
	Supervisor of the Spring Office	1710–1713
Junchong 君寵	Student Astronomer	1678
Junfan 君藩	Erudite	1719–1727
Junhui 君惠	Erudite	1727–1736
	Calendar Manager	1736–1738
	Supervisor of the Spring Office	1739–1743
Guoning 國寧	Erudite	1701–1708
Guozhu 國柱	Calendar Manager	1711–1712
	Vice-Director	1723–1724
Guozong 國宗	Superintendent	1745–1757
Guoan 國安	Erudite	1724
Guochen 國宸	Student Astronomer	1704–1709
	Erudite	1709–1723
	Supervisor of the Middle Office	1724–1744
Guodong 國棟	Supervisor of the Middle Office	1751–1767
Guoxiu 國秀	Student Astronomer	1716–1719
	Erudite	1719–1741
	Calendar Manager	1741–1744
	Recorder	1744–1745
	Supervisor of the Summer Office	1745–1758
Guoqing 國卿	Supervisor of the Spring Office	1745–1755
Guozheng 國政	Student Astronomer	1738–1742
Guoxun 國勳	Student Astronomer	1733–1748
Guoxiang 國相	Erudite	1755
Guoqing 國慶	Student Astronomer	1757–1777
Tingxu 廷緒	Erudite	1748–1757
	Water Clock Manager	1760–1766
	Recorder	1766–1768
	Astronomical observer	1768–1773

Appendix C The He Family 209

Name	Title	Active period
Tinglu 廷祿	Student Astronomer	1741–1757
	Erudite	1760
	Supervisor of the Middle Office	1767–1772
	Vice-Director	1773–1774
Tingxuan 廷璿	Student Astronomer	1746–1760
	Calendar Manager	1768–1772
	Supervisor of the Middle Office	1773–1774
	Vice-Director	1775–1781
Tingji 廷基	Student Astronomer	1757–1760
	Erudite	1765
Tinglin 廷琳	Student Astronomer	1757–1777
Tingyan 廷琰	Student Astronomer	1757–1777
Tingying 廷瑛	Student Astronomer	1757–1770
	Erudite	1777
	Supervisor of the Spring Office	1778–1794
	Vice-Director	1794–1802
Tingxuan 廷瑄	Student Astronomer	1760
	Erudite	1770
	Supervisor of the Winter Office	1771–1780
Tingchen 廷琛	Student Astronomer	1757–1760
	Water Clock Manager	1770–1777
	Recorder	1782–1786
Tingjie 廷玠	Student Astronomer	1757–1777
Tingwan 廷琬	Student Astronomer	1757–1765
Tingxian 廷憲	Student Astronomer	1757–1777
Tinghuang 廷璜	Student Astronomer	1760–1777
Tingxun 廷珣	Student Astronomer	1768–1770
Tingjue 廷珏	Student Astronomer	1770
Tingzan 廷瓚	Student Astronomer	1770
	Erudite	1777
	Supervisor of the Summer Office	1782–1804
Tingmei 廷玫	Student Astronomer	1768–1777
Tingli 廷理	Erudite	1787–1788
Bangjun 邦俊	Student Astronomer	1748–1765
	Erudite	1770
	Supervisor of the Summer Office	1774–1777
Tianfu 天福	Student Astronomer	1748–1760
	Observatory Manager	1769–1781
Tiangui 天貴	Erudite	1757–1765
Tianshou 天壽	Student Astronomer	1757–1765
	Erudite	1770
Longwu 隆武	Student Astronomer	1793–1794
	Erudite	1794–1812
Yuanhao 元浩	Student Astronomer	1760–1765
	Erudite	1768–1786
	Supervisor of the Middle Office	1795–1797
Yuanhong 元泓	Student Astronomer	1757–1777
Yuanfu 元富	Student Astronomer	1777
	Erudite	1788
	Water Clock Manager	1798–1800

(*Continued*)

(Continued)

Name	Title	Active period
	Recorder	1803–1805
	Supervisor of the Middle Office	1805–1808
	Observatory Manager	1812–1818
Yuanzi 元滋	Student Astronomer	1777–1807
	Erudite	1807–1816
	Calendar Manager	1816–1821
Yuanze 元澤	Student Astronomer	1781
	Erudite	1781–1788
Yuanpai 元派	Erudite	1787–1801
Yuanhai 元海	Erudite	1788–1809
	Supervisor of the Winter Office	1809–1811
Yuanji 元濟	Student Astronomer	1793
	Erudite	1793–1806
Yuantai 元泰	Erudite	1794–1808
	Recorder	1808–1809
	Supervisor of the Summer Office	1809–1813
Yuanpu 元溥	Erudite	1796–1804
	Student Astronomer	1804–1828
Yuanyong 元湧	Student Astronomer	1802–1803
	Erudite	1803–1820
Yuanhuai 元淮	Erudite	1804–1812
	Observatory Manager	1812–1821
	Recorder	1823–1826
Yuanying 元瀛	Student Astronomer	1810
	Erudite	1810–1816
	Supervisor of the Summer Office	1816–1823
Yuangan 元淦	Student Astronomer	1814–1815
	Erudite	1815–1828
	Student Astronomer	1828
Yuandu 元渡	Student Astronomer	1816
	Astronomical observer	1827–1831
Yuanqi 元淇	Erudite	1824–1828
	Student Astronomer	1843
Yuanrun 元潤	Student Astronomer	1828
Yuanhui 元泂	Student Astronomer	1828
Chaolian 朝璉	Erudite	1797–1801
Shuben 樹本	Student Astronomer	1816–1828
	Erudite	1830–1833
	Observatory Manager	1834
	Senior Vice-Director	1834–1841
Liangkui 良奎	Erudite	1821
	Supervisor of the Winter Office	1832–1837
Liangtang 良棠	Student Astronomer	1825
	Observatory Manager	1830–1837
Liangcheng 良成	Student Astronomer	1828
Liangqi 良棨	Erudite	1830–1834
Liangkai 良楷	Yin-yang student	1837
Liangtong 良桐	Student Astronomer	1843
	Erudite	1843–1857
Liangshan 良善	Erudite	1847–1856
Weimin 維敏	Erudite	1840–1846
	Water Clock Manager	1846–1848
Jun 均	Student Astronomer	1843

Appendix D
The Zhou Family

Name	Title	Active period
Ziyu 子愚	Calendar Manager	1589–91
	Official Astrologer	1592–93
	Supervisor of the Winter Office	1594–1613
	Vice-Director	1614
	Director	1623
Yin 胤	Calendar Manager	1620
	Official Astrologer	1622
	Supervisor of the Autumn Office	1624–1633
	Junior Vice-Director	1634–1664
	Senior Vice-Director	1664
Xiao 曉	Erudite	1638
	Official Astrologer	1644–1645
Tong 統	Erudite	1644–1664
	Calendar Manager	1666–1685
Shichang 士昌	Student Astronomer	1631–1638
	Erudite	1644–1662
Shitai 士泰	Student Astronomer	1638
	Erudite	1644–1665
	Supervisor of the Autumn Office	1666–1672
Shicui 士萃	Student Astronomer	1638
	Erudite	1644–1665
Daye 大液	Student Astronomer	1678
Shiqi 世琦	Recorder	1686–1687
	Supervisor of the Middle Office	1688–1692
Shitai 世泰	Erudite	1694–1699
	Observatory Manager	1699–1723

Appendix E
The Huang Family

Name	Title	Active period
Hongxian 宏憲	Calendar Department Official	1633–1645
Zixian 子賢	Erudite	1635–1646
Daohua 道化	Official	1637
	Observatory Manager	1645–1646
Daolong 道隆	Observatory Manager	1645–1658
Gong 鞏	Student Astronomer	1644–1658
	Observatory Manager	1662–1666
	Observatory Manager	1669–1690
Chang 昌	Student Astronomer	1658
	Erudite	1666
	Erudite	1668–1673
	Observatory Manager	1677–1681
Tingji 廷極	Erudite	1737–1739
Fengru 奉儒	Astronomical Observer	1737–1741
	Observatory Manager	1742–1747
Zhenkui 振奎	Student Astronomer	1757
Xian 銑	Erudite	1796–1808
	Calendar Manager	1808–1809
Depu 德溥	Student Astronomer	1814
Dequan 德泉	Student Astronomer	1814
	Erudite	1832
	Observatory Manager	1839–1845
Deyuan 德源	Observatory Manager	1846–1857

Appendix F
The Si Family

Name	Title	Active period
Ergui 爾珪	Ying-Yang Person	1647
	Erudite	1647–1684
Ermao 爾瑁	Ying-Yang Person	1649
	Erudite	1649
	Water Clock Manager	1684
	Junior Vice-Director	1689–1701
Ercheng 爾珵	Ying-Yang Person	1674
	Erudite	1674–1684
Jing 敬	Erudite	1715–1725
Mu 牧	Erudite	1738
Wenyu 文郁	Erudite	1738
Wenjing 文靖	Student Astronomer	1757–1760
	Erudite	1761–1786
	Water Clock Manager	1787
	Recorder	1787–1792
Chengju 宸榘	Ying-Yang Student	1757–1765
Hongze 鴻澤	Student Astronomer	1751
Hongpu 鴻溥	Student Astronomer	1757
	Erudite	1760–1768
	Vice-Director	1787–1793
Hongying 鴻英	Erudite	1788–1807
	Water Clock Manager	1807
	Recorder	1814–1815
	Supervisor of the Summer Office	1815–1816
	Vice-Director	1817–1827
	Director	1827–1834
Tinggan 廷幹	Erudite	1777
	Observatory Manager	1782–1807
Tingdong 廷棟	Student Astronomer	1781–1787
	Erudite	1796–1808
	Recorder	1810–1812
	Supervisor of the Winter Office	1812–1818
	Student Astronomer	1820–1825
	Erudite	1826–1828
	Supervisor of the Autumn Office	1829–1834
Tingben 廷本	Student Astronomer	1839–1840

(*Continued*)

(Continued)

Name	Title	Active period
	Erudite	1845–1851
Zhaonian 兆年	Student Astronomer	1814
Yan 晏	Erudite	1834–1841
Zhi 智	Erudite	1834–1837
	Water Clock Manager	1845–1851
	Junior Vice-Director	1858–1861
Jin 晉	Erudite	1837–1839
	Supervisor of the Middle Office	1839–1858
Chang 昶	Erudite	1845–1854
Yitian 以田	Student Astronomer	1845–1852
Yipei 以培	Supervisor of the Summer Office	1878–1888
Yixun 以塤	Calendar Manager	1884–1898
Bingjun 秉鈞	Student Astronomer	1890
	Recorder	1902–1907
	Junior Vice-Director	1908–1911

Appendix G
Register of Metropolitan Officials According to the Shunzhi Imperial Screen

Current title	Name	Registration	Initial position or degree	Date[1]
Director	Tang Ruowang 湯若望[2]			
Senior Vice-Director	Liu Youqing 劉有慶	Shuntian 順天	Student Astronomer	SZ3/6
Junior Vice-Director	Zhou Yin 周胤	Zhejiang 浙江	Student Astronomer	SZ2/3
Recorder	Zhang Sheng 掌乘	Shuntian	Confucian scholar 儒士	SZ3/6
Supervisor of the Middle Office	Jia Liangqi 賈良琦	Shuntian	Student Astronomer	SZ2/3
Supervisor of the Spring Office	Song Kecheng 宋可成	Shuntian	District Graduate 生員	SZ10/10
Supervisor of the Summer Office	Li Zubai 李祖白	Shuntian	Imperial College Student 監生[3]	SZ10/6
Supervisor of the Autumn Office	Song Fa 宋發	Shuntian	Confucian scholar	SZ3/6
Supervisor of the Winter Office	Zhu Guangxian 朱光顯	Shuntian	Student Astronomer	SZ3/6
Official Astrologer	Zhang Wenming 張問明	Shuntian	Student Astronomer	SZ15/9
Official Astrologer	Chen Zhengjian 陳正諫	Shuntian	Student Astronomer	SZ10/10
Calendar Manager	Ge Jiwen 戈繼文	Jiangnan 江南	Student Astronomer	SZ3/6
Calendar Manager	Yin Kai 殷鎧	Shuntian	Confucian scholar	SZ15/9
Erudite	Zuo Yuhe 左允和	Shuntian	Student Astronomer	SZ2/3
Erudite	Bao Yinghua 鮑英華	Jiangnan	Confucian scholar	SZ15/9
Erudite	Sun Youben 孫有本	Shuntian	Confucian scholar	SZ3/6
Erudite	Jiao Yingxu 焦應旭	Shuntian	Confucian scholar	SZ1/12
Erudite	Ge Guoqi 戈國琦	Jiangnan	Student Astronomer	SZ13/11

(Continued)

(Continued)

Current title	Name	Registration	Initial position or degree	Date[1]
Erudite	Bao Yingqi 鮑應齊	Shuntian	Confucian scholar	SZ3/6
Erudite	Song Keli 宋可立	Shuntian	Confucian scholar	SZ3/6
Erudite	Zhang Guangxiang 張光祥	Shuntian	Student Astronomer	SZ2/3
Erudite	Zang Wenxian 臧文顯	Jiangnan	Student Astronomer	SZ2/3
Erudite	Zuo Yudeng 左允登	Shuntian	Student Astronomer	SZ2/3
Erudite	Zhou Shichang 周士昌	Zhejiang	Student Astronomer	SZ2/3
Erudite	Zhou Shitai 周士泰	Zhejiang	Student Astronomer	SZ2/3
Erudite	Zhou Shicui 周士萃	Zhejiang	Student Astronomer	SZ2/3
Erudite	Zhou Tong 周統	Zhejiang	Student Astronomer	SZ2/3
Erudite	He Qiyi 何其義	Zhejiang	Student Astronomer	SZ2/3
Erudite	He Luoshu 何雒書	Zhejiang	Student Astronomer	SZ2/3
Erudite	Xue Wenbing 薛文炳	Jiangnan	Student Astronomer	SZ2/3
Erudite	Xue Wenhuan 薛文煥	Jiangnan	Student Astronomer	SZ2/3
Erudite	Dong Yiming 董一鳴	Shanxi 山西	Student Astronomer	SZ3/6
Erudite	Liu Yingchang 劉應昌	Shuntian	Student Astronomer	SZ13/11
Erudite	Jia Liangqing 賈良慶	Shuntian	Student Astronomer	SZ2/3
Erudite	Li Guanghong 李光宏	Shuntian	Student Astronomer	SZ15/9
Erudite	Jia Wenying 賈文英	Shuntian	Student Astronomer	SZ6/2
Erudite	Fangxiu 臧樊修	Jiangnan	Confucian scholar	SZ10/10
Erudite	Xu Hu 徐瑚	Shuntian	Confucian scholar	SZ10/10
Erudite	Huang Gong 黃鞏	Shuntian	Student Astronomer	SZ15/9
Erudite	Zuo Youqing 左有慶	Shuntian	Student Astronomer	SZ10/10
Erudite	Liu Biyuan 劉必遠	Shuntian	Student Astronomer	SZ12/1
Erudite	He Luotu 何雒圖	Zhejiang	Student Astronomer	SZ12/10

Current title	Name	Registration	Initial position or degree	Date[1]
Observatory Manager	Li Zhigui 李之貴	Shuntian	Student Astronomer	SZ2/3
Observatory Manager	Li Guangxian 李光顯	Shuntian	Erudite	SZ15/9
Observatory Manager	Huang Daolong 黃道隆	Shuntian	Student Astronomer	SZ2/3
Observatory Manager	Zhang Qichun 張其淳	Fujian 福建	Student Astronomer	SZ10/3
Astronomical Observer	Zang Yuqing 臧餘慶	Jiangnan	Student Astronomer	SZ10/10
Erudite	Wang Ye 王燁	Shuntian	Student Astronomer	SZ2/3
Erudite	Li Guangda 李光大	Shuntian	Student Astronomer	SZ2/3
Water Clock Manager	Du Ruyu 杜如預	Shuntian		SZ5/7
Water Clock Manager	Yang Hongliang 楊弘量	Huguang 湖廣	Yin-Yang Person	SZ11/10
Timekeeper	Zhao Yingrui 趙應瑞	Shuntian	Yin-Yang Person	SZ4/9
Erudite	Sheng Ming 盛銘	Shuntian	Yin-Yang Person	SZ2/3
Erudite	Jin Yanshou 金延壽		Erudite	SZ16/1
Erudite	Ge Shiying 戈士英	Shuntian	Yin-Yang Person	SZ17/6
Erudite	Ou Jiwu 歐繼武	Shuntian	Yin-Yang Person	SZ4/1
Erudite	Si Ergui 司爾珪	Shuntian	Yin-Yang Person	SZ4/9
Erudite	Si Ermao 司爾瑁	Shuntian	Yin-Yang Person	SZ6/2
Erudite	Zhang Huafeng 張化鳳	Shuntian	Yin-Yang Person	SZ11/10
Erudite	Si Ercheng 司爾珵	Shuntian	Yin-Yang Person	SZ13/11
Muslim Supervisor of the Autumn Office				
Erudite	Ma Weilong 馬惟龍	Shuntian	Student Astronomer	SZ2/3
Erudite	Ma Ziyi 馬子義	Shuntian	Student Astronomer	SZ2/3
Erudite	Ji Dengzhou 繼登洲	Shuntian	Student Astronomer	SZ2/3
Erudite	Ma Yicai 馬以才	Shuntian	Student Astronomer	SZ10/10

Source: *Shunzhi yuping jinggua zhimingce* 順治御屏京官職名冊, *Wenxian congbian* 文獻叢編 (Beijing: National Palace Museum, 1935) 28: 14–16.

Notes

1 In the format of the year and the month of the Shunzhi reign.
2 Tang Ruowang 湯若望 was Schall's Chinese name. His full title listed here was Director Wearing Rank Two Button, Honorific (Commissioner of) Office of Transmission in Charge of the Affairs of the Astronomical Bureau, One Additional Level (*Jianzheng jia erpin dingdai tongzheng shisi guan qintianjian shi jia yiji* 監正加二品頂帶通政使司管欽天監事加一級).
3 Li Zubai's full degree was Imperial College Student in the category of supplementary list (to the passers of the Provincial Examination) (*Fubang Jiansheng* 副榜監生).

Appendix H
Units Used in the Qing Era

H.1 Time

ri 日 = day
shi 時 = double hours; 1 *ri* = 12 *shi*

Double hours	Modern time
zi 子	11 p.m.—1 a.m.
chou 丑	1 a.m.—3 a.m.
yin 寅	3 a.m.—5 a.m.
mao 卯	5 a.m.—7 a.m.
chen 辰	7 a.m.—9 a.m.
si 巳	9 a.m.—11 a.m.
wu 午	11 a.m.—1 p.m.
wei 未	1 p.m.—3 p.m.
shen 申	3 p.m.—5 p.m.
you 酉	5 p.m.—7 p.m.
xu 戌	7 p.m.—9 p.m.
hai 亥	9 p.m.—11 p.m.

ke 刻 = quarter; 1 *shi* = 8 *ke*

Ke	Time in a double hour
chu chuke 初初刻	first quarter
chu yike 初一刻	second quarter
chu erke 初二刻	third quarter
chu sanke 初三刻	fourth quarter
zheng chuke 正初刻	fifth quarter
zheng yiki 正一刻	sixth quarter
zheng erke 正二刻	seventh quarter
zheng sanke 正三刻	eighth quarter

fen 分 = minute; 1 *ke* = 15 *fen*
miao 秒 = second; 1 *fen* = 60 *miao*

H.2 Eclipse Magnitude

In Qing state documents, the solar eclipse's magnitude is defined as the fraction of the Sun's diameter covered by the Moon. Similarly, the Moon eclipse's magnitude is the fraction of the Moon's diameter covered by the Earth's shadow.

1 *fen* 分 = 1/10 diameter
1 *miao* 秒 = 1/100 *fen* 分
1 *wei* 微 = 1/100 *miao* 秒

Index

Note: Page numbers in *italics* indicate a figure and page numbers in **bold** indicate a table on the corresponding page.

Adeodato di Sant'Agostino, Pietro 183–184
Almeida, José Bernardo de 183, 185
Antai 安泰 89
Asali 阿薩禮 79
astrologer *see* Official Astrologer
astrology 20, 50, 177; *see also* divination
Astronomical Bureau (*Qintianjian* 欽天監): age distribution when receiving transfer orders *171*; career ladder for Han official *83*; career ladder for Manchu official *80*; career ladder for military Han official *82*; career ladder for Mongol official *81*; civil service ranks of **27**; conversion to New Method 57; disciples of Verbiest in 152; factionalism of 58; gnomon 43; map showing physical location in Beijing *17*; Ming 37, 39, 44, **51**, 59; New Method in 37–60; nineteenth-century reforms and rejuvenation of 182–195; officials in 1645 **38**; officials in 1658 **53**; personnel quotas in 1690 **75**; personnel quotas in 1732 **76**; personnel quotas in 1764 **76**; personnel quotas in 1818 **77**; Qing Astronomical Bureau 1645 proposed re-organization **51**, 52; officials purged during Kangxi calendar dispute 70; organization of (Qing) 16–31; researching the history of 1–7; Schall's vision for 37, 52–54; Sections of 19–30; solar eclipse prediction produced by 40, *129*; Superintendents and Directorate 29–30; Yongzheng emperor's administrative policy 116–119; *see also* Schall

Astronomical Observer (*Jianhou* 監候) 24–25
astronomy: calendrical 144; compilation publications on 104, 106, 108, 110, 167, 168; He family 84–85, 106, 193; hereditary astronomer families, Ming Dynasty 35–44; Jesuit system of 44–45, 47, 148; Kangxi emperor's decree regarding 78; Korean 131; Luo's excellent abilities in 188; Minggantu and 3; New and Old Astronomer families during Shunzhi reign 54–60; Newtonian system 202; official character of Chinese astronomy 60n1; Qing period 126; Western system of 45, 47, 139n20, 146, 201; Yang Guangxian's ignorance of 86; *see also* mathematical astronomy
Astronomy Apprentices (*Yiye tianwensheng* 肄業天文生) 24, 153, 173, 175; *see also* Student Astronomers

Bao 鮑 family 3, 200; Duo 鮑鐸 12n14; Kecheng 2; Qinhui 鮑欽輝 1, 2, 4, 6, 148, 150, 157, 168, 169; Quan 鮑銓 12n14; Yinghua 鮑英華 **54**, 70, 74, **215**; Yingqi 鮑英齊 2, 32n53, **51**, **54**, 57, 59, 69, 74, 85, 91; Xuan 鮑選 74; family tree *204*
Baozhangshi 保章氏 (official responsible for astronomical prognostication) 11
Baozhangzheng 保章正 (official astrologer) 11–12, 58; *see also* Official Astrologer
Beijing: Korean embassies in 131–133; Manchu march into 83; Qing 2, 17–18,

222 Index

44–45; Qing (map) *17*; water clock 21; Westerners in 182–184
Bernardo, José *see* Almeida, José Bernardo de
Bi Lianqi 畢璉器 **70**
Biographies of Mathematicians and Astronomers (*Chouren zhuan*) (Ruan Yuan) 2, 5, 11n8, 84; *Sequel* (Luo Shilin) 187; *Third Addition* (Zhu Kebao) 190
Book on Calendrical Astronomy in Reverent Accord (*Qinruo lishu* 欽若曆書) 104
Books on Calendrical Astronomy According to the New Method (*Xinfa lishu* 新法曆書) 144

calendar: calculations 17; civil 19; new (Jesuit) 8; official 6, 7, 16; 'people's calendar' 19; *see also* Great Concordance system; Kangxi Calendar Dispute; Latitude-Longitude Degrees of Seven Governors (*Qizheng jingwei chandu shix- ian li* 七政經緯躔度時憲曆)
calendar making 2; Astronomical Bureau's responsibility to produce 17; *Book on Calendrical Astronomy in Reverent Accord* (*Qinruo lishu* 欽若曆書) 104; *Books on Calendrical Astronomy According to the New Method* (*Xinfa lishu* 新法曆書) 144; career of 3; constants used in 10; Newtonian system 126, 137, 201, 202; Tychonic system 137
Calendar Manager (*Sili* 司曆, or *Sishu* 司書) 24–25
Calendar Section (*li ke* 曆科) 1, 5, 19–21
Changchun 暢春Garden 103, 169
Chang'e 常額 80, 81
Chengde 承德, city of 100; Summer Palace 102–103, 107, 110
Chengde (Manchu high official) 成德 150–151
Chen Houyao 陳厚耀 101, 102
Chen Jie 陳杰 190, 192, 194
Chen Jixin 陳際新 3, 187, 189
Chen Zhengjian 陳正諫 **215**
Chosŏn Kingdom 7, 107, 131; *see also* Korea; *Veritable Records of the Chosŏn Dynasty*
Collected Statutes of the Great Ming (*Da Ming huidian* 大明會典, or *Ming Statutes*) 36

Collected Statutes of the Great Qing (*Da Qing huidian* 大清會典) 5, 18, 24, 29, 75–79, 151
Collection of the Qing Vermillion Ink Examination Papers (*Qingdai zhujuan jicheng* 清代硃卷集成) 5, 173
College of Mathematics (*Suanxue* 算學) 3, 36, 151–156; He Guozong and 161; location of 159n73; origin of 172–173; *see also* Mathematics Student, Principal Instructor
Complete Collection of the Qing Officials' Résumés (*Qingdai guanyuan lüli dang'an quanbian* 清代官員履歷檔案全編) 6, 171

Dai Jinxian 戴進賢 [Ignaz Kögler] 137, *see also* Kögler, Ignaz
Daoguang 道光 emperor: ascent to throne 188; *see also* Jingzheng 敬徵
Daoguang 道光 reign 8, 19; Du family 195; He family 163, 176–178, 195; Huang family 166; Si family 166–167, 171; triennial examinations **191**
divination 18, 20, 29; Chinese theories of 55; Chinese traditional 177; earthquake detector 72; of eclipse 129–130; interpretation of 21, 28
Du杜 family 195; Ruyu 杜如預 **54**, 56, 69, **70**, **217**; Xiling 杜熙齡 195

Eclipse Measurement (*Ce shi* 測食) (Schall) 43
eclipses: calculating 20, 52, 57, 71; causes of 20; competitions for predicting 44–45; divination of 129–130; Great Concordance system used to predict 86; magnitude (Qing era) 220; politicization of the observation of 201; predictions of 6, 20–21; Rescue Ritual used for 95n106; *see also* lunar eclipse; solar eclipse
E'erdengbu 額爾登布 188–189
Eight Banners Official Schools (*Baqi guanxue* 八旗官學) 2, 10; mathematics program at 149, 156, 202; He Guodong as teacher at 154, 155; quota of Student Astronomers divided among 81; Sun Jiagan's plan to improve 151; Wang Lai as Instructor at 175; Yongzheng emperor's support of 150
Encroachments 20
Encroachments calendar 20, 22; Muslim system used to calculate 22, 59, 72; New

Methods for Calculating Encroachments and Parallax (Si Tingdong) 194, 195; Qing courts abolishing of 32n40; Wu Mingxuan's involvement with 72
Erudite (*Boshi* 博士) 24, **27**; in Astronomical Bureau **53**, 56, 58, 72, **75–77**; Calendar Section 60, 79, 88, 107, 155, 167; Clepsydra (*Louke boshi* 漏刻博士) 36; Mathematics (*Suanxue boshi* 算學博士) 172; Muslim 37; Old Method 85; in Section of Heavenly Signs 52, 69, 87; wait period for Student Astronomer to become 84; Water Clock Section 117, 118; see also Ge family; He family; Huang family; Si family; Zhou family
Essence of Numbers and Their Principles (*Shuli jingyun* 數理精蘊) 104; *Imperially Composed Essence of Numbers and Their Principles* 155
Exact Meaning of the Pitch-pipes (*Lülü zhengyi* 律呂正義) 104

Fang Gu 方榖 168
Fang Luheng 方履亨 194–195
Ferreira, Joaquim 184
First Collection of the Imperial Birthday Ceremony 103
Fulin 福臨 (emperor) 45, 62n48

Gao Qizhuo 高其倬 134–135
Gate of Declaring Military Power (*Xuanwu men* 宣武門) 44
Gate of Heavenly Peace (*Tianan men* 天安門) 17
Gate of the Great Qing (*Da Qing men* 大清門) 17
Ge family 戈 40, **205–206**; Chengke 戈承科 43, 52, 71, **206**; Fengnian 40; Guoqi 戈國琦 **54**, 57, 71, 74; Jiugong 戈九功 40; Jiwen 戈繼文 **54**, 57, 71; Ning 40; Shiying 戈士英 **57**, **217**; Zhili branch 40
Gemei 戈枚 79, 94n74
Grand Canal 105, 115
Grand Empress Dowager 69
Grand Minister Concurrently Managing Bureau Affairs (*Jianguan jianshi dachen* 兼管監事大臣) 29
Grand Minister Managing Bureau Affairs (*Guanli jianshi dachen* 管理監事大臣) 29, 30
Grand Secretariat 45–46, 52, 149
Great Achievements of Computational Methods (*Suanfa dacheng* 算法大成) (Chen Jie) 190

Great Concordance (*Datong* 大統) system 8, 11n3, 22, 60, 70, 176; co-existence with Muslim astronomers' system 59; Dorgon's discarding of 53; eclipse prediction using 86–87; He family and 83, 89, 91, 163; Kangxi emperor and 89–90; limitations of 39; Ming-era *48*; non-dismissal of scholars specializing in 74, 183; persistence of 44, 58; return to/re-establishing of 68–69, 71, 88; rosters of 40; Schall's New Method compared to 46; solar year system of 31n22; Watching for the Ethers (*Houqi* 候氣) as means to improve 72; Zang Yuqing's refusal to endorse 176
Great Reckoning (*daji* 大計) 19
Great Wall 45
Grimaldi, Philippus Maria 101
Guangxu 光緒 reign xiv
Gucong 顧琮 144–148, 151

Hallerstein, Augustin von *162*, 182–183
Han Chinese 10, 46; career ladder for officials at Astronomical Bureau *82–83*; military Han Supervisor 25; Manchu Chinese compared to 26; personnel quotas for Student Astronomers at Astronomical Bureau 23, **23**
Hao Benchun 郝本純 **70**
He 何 brothers/family **193**, **208–210**; downfall of 192–195; imperial empowerment of 99–104; Kangxi emperor and 99–111; Kangxi Calendar Dispute and 82–91; Korean Astronomical Bureau and 130–134; in Timely Modeling calendar **165**; Yongzheng emperor and 111–119
He Guochen 何國宸 107, 140, 147, 168, 169
He Guodong 何國棟 99; dishonorable discharge of 154; downfall of 117; as rising star in officialdom 116; as teacher at Eight Banners Official Schools 154–155
He Guozhu 何國柱 8, 84, 99, 102, 104, 106–114, 174; downfall of 117; Hong Jung Ha versus 131; Kangxi emperor and 132, 149; embassy to Korea 107–108; as rising star in officialdom 116
He Guozong 何國宗 2, 8, 10, 29, 30, 85, 99, 102, 104–106; admittance to Hanlin Academy 106; amendment of Timely Modeling System and 148, 154; downfall of 117; Gucong and 144–148;

Later Part and 151; memorials written by 105; new astronomical theory learned by 146; *Origins of Mathematical Harmonics and Astronomy* 135; Qianlong emperor and 170; retirement of 163; as rising star in officialdom 116; Tian Wenjing and 115–116; Yongzheng emperor and 115–116, 138

He Junxi 何君錫 8, 84–85, 88–91, 102, 104–109; as disciple of Yang Guangxian 95n3; Great Concordance system and 99, 132, 163; Hŏ Wŏn 許遠 and 132; plans for his children 116, 163; recommendation of Old Method 89–91; stagnant career of 99

He Liangcheng 何良成 193, **193**
He Liangkai 何良楷 193, 195
He Liangkui 何良奎 **165**, 193
He Liangtong 何良桐 195
He Luoshu 何雒書 8, 84–91, 95n101
He 何 officials who failed 1828 examination **193**
He Qiyi 何其義 **54**, 84–86, 88, 90, 176
He Shuben 何樹本 **165**, 195
He Weimin 何維敏 195
He Yuanpu 何元溥 192
He Yuanqi 何元淇 192–193
He Yuanrun 何元潤 192
Hong Jeong-Ha 洪正夏 131, 132
Hongli 弘曆 19
Hongwu 洪武 emperor 35, 39
Hoogu 豪格 196n38
Horng, Wann-Shang 130–131
Hŏ Wŏn 許遠 108, 132
Huang 黃 family **212**; Chang 黃昌 69, **70**, 166; Daohua 黃道化 166; Daolong 黃道隆 166, **217**; Dequan 黃德泉 166; Deyuan 黃德源 166; Gong 黃鞏 **54**, 56, 69, **70**, 166; Hongxian 黃宏憲 51
Huang Guochai 黃國材 112, 115

Imperial City Beijing 45
Imperial College (*Guozi jian* 國子監) 151, 156, 172–174
Imperial College of Physicians (*Taiyiyuan* 太醫院) 18
Imperial Diarist 112
Imperial Diary (*Qiju zhu* 起居注) 5, 91
imperial mathematical institutions, stagnation of 185–188
imperial mathematics 111–112, 116

Jartoux, Pierre 3
Jesuits 44–54, 182–184; Bao family's reliance on 2–3; Bao Qinhui and 168; Bao Yingqui and 91; control of Astronomical Bureau 83, 86; decline of power at Astronomical Bureau 149; dislike of divination and astrology 177; Gucong and 146–147; He Guozong and 148; Kangxi emperor and 100–101, 111, 116, 148; in Ming China 44, 57, 100; Mingtu and 4; Newtonian systems introduced by 138n2, 202; New Western Method introduced by 31n22, 53; Qianlong emperor and 202; Qing astronomers and 146; Qing court and 8, 149; shift in power at Astronomical Bureau 104, 149; Si Ergui and 166; tables of solar and lunar orbits made by 137; Western theories transmitted to China by 146; Yongzheng emperor and 119, 201; Zang family and 176; *see also* Ricci; Schall von Bell; Verbiest

Jia Liangqi 賈良琦 51, 52, **54**; New Method learned by 63n83; possible death of 59; punishment extended to family members of 69
Jiao Yingxu 焦應旭 **51**, **54**, 85
Jiaqing 嘉慶 emperor: attitude toward Christianity 183–184; Song Shu and 130, 137n5
Jiaqing 嘉慶 reign 3, 161, 163, 166; career of Wang Lai during 174; Catholic missionary activities during 183–184; Si Tinggan during 167, 170; triennial examinations **187**
Jingzheng 敬徵 (Daoguang emperor) 9–10; departure from Astronomical Bureau 203; as superintendent of Astronomical Bureau 30, 185–186, 188–195, 202

Kangxi Calendar Dispute (*Kangxi lizheng* 康熙曆爭) 8, 68–91, 126, 152, 177; emergence of He family 82–91; officials purged from Astronomical Bureau during **70**; reorganization of Astronomical Bureau due to 75–82; Si Ergui and 167; Zang family 176
Kangxi 康熙 reign **2**, 23; civil service ranks of Astromical Bureau officials during **27**; Muslim officials during 37; Rescue Rituals during 127; solar eclipse during 136

Kangxi 康熙 emperor 3, 9, 18, 26, 72; on the Calendar Dispute 78; death of 174; declining favoritism towards Jesuits 100, 101; He brothers and 83, 91, 99–111, 112, 116, 118, 132, 149, 154, 163; Liu and 169; New Western Method and 88–90; trips to South China 115; Verbiest and 73, 89–90; Yinzhi 胤祉 third son of 103

Kangxi Thorough Investigation of Astronomical Phenomena (Kangxi lixiang kaocheng 康熙曆象考成) 133, 135, 144, 147

knowledge reproduction 144–156; College of Mathematics 152–156; Timely Modeling System 144–149; Yongzhen Mathematics Program 149–152

Kögler, Ignaz 135, 137, 144–147

Korea: Chinese calendars distributed in 16; Chosŏn Kingdom 7, 107, 131; He Guozhu's special embassy to 99, 107–108; Korean Astronomical Bureau and He family 130–134, 138, 140n59; Yi Seonggye 李成桂 (King)131; see also Veritable Records of the Chosŏn Dynasty

Later Part of Thorough Investigation of Astronomical Phenomena (Lixiang kaocheng houbian 曆象考成後編) 145–146, 148, 151, 156

Latitude-Longitude Degrees of Seven Governors (Qizheng jingwei chandu shix- ian li 七政經緯躔度時憲曆) calendar (Seven Governors calendar) 20, 72–73, 137, 155–156, 195

Lazarites 183

Le'ersen 勒爾森 29, 30, 148, *162*

Li Guangda 李光大 **54, 217**

Li Guanghong 李光宏 69, **70**, 87, 91

Li Hua 李華 **51**

Liu Biyuan 劉必遠 57, **70, 216**

Liu Youqing 劉有慶 **51**, 52, **54**, 56, 57, 59, 69

Liu Youtai 劉有泰 **54**, 57, 58, 59, 69, **70**

Liu Yunde 劉蘊德 **51**, 58, 59

Liu Yuxi 劉裕錫 169–170, 176

Li Wei 李衛 134

Li Zubai 李祖白 **51, 54**, 56, 69, **70, 215**

Li Zicheng 李自成 45

Longobardo, Nicolò 40, 43

Longkodo 隆科多 117, 123n110

lunar eclipse 6, 40; divination of 139n15; Muslim astronomical system to predict 22; predictions of 6, 20–21, 44, 184; see also solar eclipse

lunar motions 145, 147

lunar orbits 137, 138, 144, 145

lunar tables 137, 148; Newtonian 201–202

Luo Shilin 羅士琳 11n8, 187–188

Luo'erzhan 羅爾瞻 167–169, 171–172, 187, 189

Ma Weilong 馬惟龍 88, **217**

Mamboo 滿保 112–115, 123n91

Manchu Chinese 72; career ladder at Astronomical Bureau *80–81*; Director of the Astronomical Bureau 73; as new rulers of China 83, 85; personnel quotas at Astronomical Bureau **75–77**, 78; regulations for selection of 79

Manchu emperor 47

Manchuria 45

mathematical astronomy: College of Mathematics 152–156; as hereditary profession 2–4, 35–44; He family and 108, 131, 147–149, 193; Jesuits' teaching of Kangxi emperor 89; meeting to improve accuracy of 73; Luo's excellent abilities in 188; Ming Astronomical Bureau's study of 85; Origins of Mathematical Harmonics and Astronomy (Lüli yuanyuan 律曆淵源) 2, 3, 110, 115, 135, 165, 167–170; Qing court 68; Tychonic 8, 45; Western 45, 47; Yang's incompetence in 70, 86

mathematical institutions: stagnation of 185–188

mathematical knowledge: essential 190; He family and 111; importance of 78, 80; Wang Lai and 175

mathematical treatises 27, 102, 195; compilation of 147; Office of Compiling Mathematical Treatises (Xiu suanshu chu 修算書處) 103–104, 150; publication of 105; Western 144

mathematics see imperial mathematics

Mathematics Student (Suanxuesheng 算學生) 78, 152–156; social status of 172–175

Mei Juecheng 梅瑴成 2, 105, 106, 117, 145–148, 151, 202; as Director General of Later Part 146, 151

Mei Wending 梅文鼎 101

Mei Yi 梅鈫 105

226 *Index*

memorials *see* palace memorials
Mercury (planet) 60
Ming Dynasty 28, 62, 68; *Collected Statutes of the Great Ming* 36, 38; hereditary astronomer families 35–44
Minggantu 明安圖 2–4, 102, 110, 117, 144–147, 169; *Quick Methods for the Circle's Division and Precise Ratio* (*Geyuan milü jiefa* 割圓密率捷法) 187
Mingtu 明圖 137, 140n52
Mingxin 明新 3, 4
Ministry of Personnel 19, 27, 56, 58; coordination with Ministry of Rites 18; nomination of two candidates to position of Manchu Vice-Director 80; *see also* palace memorials
Ministry of Punishments 73; Li Tingyao's transfer to 168; Sun Shiying at 172; thief Zang Xianming sent to 176; two suspects delivered to 172
Ministry of Revenue 108–109; He Guazhu assigned to 149; Liu Yuxi's transfer to 170; Si Tingdong's transfer to 193
Ministry of Rites 26; adoption of New Method and 59; calendars distributed by 16; Dorgon and 46–47, 49–50; examination of staff members of Astronomical Bureau by 36; Kangxi emperors address on the importance of respecting heavenly signs 177; Office of Scrutiny for Rites 47, 49–50; quota of Student Astronomers 55; recruitment of court mathematicians 101; recruitment of experts on calendars 40; Rescue Ritual on day of eclipse ordered by 127–128, 134, 136; Schall's trial and 52; selection of Astronomical Bureau officials for promotion 18; Timely Modeling system and 46
Ministry of War 110, 111, 112, 113; He Guozhu's directorship at 118
Ministry of Works 1; Zhaohai made Vice Department Director 154
Mongol Chinese 94n72
Monteiro da Serra, Verissimo 184
moon *see* lunar eclipse
Muslim calendar 183
Muslim Erudites 37, 56, **217**
Muslims in Beijing: *Gangzhi* 岡誌 169
Muslim Section (*Huihui ke* 回回科) 22, **38**, **53**; adoption of New Method and 59–60; abolition of 19, 52, 169, 179n39; Student Astronomers 39, 49; Supervisor of the Autumn Office 25, 56–57, **217**; *see also* Liu Yuxi; Wu Mingxuan

Muslim system: calculating eclipses 31n37, 46, 86–87; Encroachments calendar 72

New Methods for Calculating Encroachments and Parallax (Si Tingdong) 194, 195
New Treatise on the Instruments at the Observatory (*Xinzhi lingtai yixiang zhi* 新製靈臺儀象志) 147
New Western Method (*Xiyang xinfa* 西洋新法) 8; adoption of 19; calendar dispute and 86, 90–91; Ge Jiwen and 71; He Junxi's mastery of 131–132; He Luoshu's hostility to 86; Kangzhi emperor's reinstatement of 88, 89, 132; Luotu's learning of 84; Muslim Section and 19, 22; shift from Old Method to 35–60; removal of phrase, "According to the New Western Method" (*yi Xiyang xinfa* 依西洋新法) from the calendar cover 69; Qing court's abandoning of 68; Qing court's adoption of 85, 152; Yang's attack on 70–71
North Pole, measuring of 110, 154

Observatory Manager (*Lingtailang* 靈臺郎) 25–26
Office of Amending the Timely Modeling System 148; *see also* Timely Modeling system
Office of Instrument Production (*Yiqi zaobanchu* 儀器造辦處) 170
Office of Compiling Mathematical Treatises (*Xiu suanshu chu* 修算書處) 2, 103–104, 110, 150, 170; *see also* mathematical treatises
Official Astrologer 28–29, 36, **37**, **38**, **51**, **53**, **54**; Ge family 205, **206**; Li Youtai 57, 58; Yin Kai **70**; Zhang Wenming **70**, **215**; Zhou family **211**
Origins of Mathematical Harmonics and Astronomy (*Lüli yuanyuan* 律曆淵源) 2, 3, 110, 115, 135, 165, 167–170
Ou Jiwu 歐繼武 **70**, **217**

palace memorials (*zouzhe* 奏摺) 5–7, 19; Gao Qizhou 134–135; Grimaldi 100–101; Gucong 144–148; He Guozong 105, 121n34; Jingzheng 185–186; Li Tianjing 84; Li Wei 134; Luo'erzhan 168; Mei Juecheng 151; Mingtu 137; Minister of Personnel 117; Ministry of Personnel 58, 91, 113, 118; recorders and scribes of 26–28; Schall

39, 46, 49–50, 52–53, 55; Tian Wenjing 115; Verbiest 74, 89–90, 147; Wu Mingxuan 59, 72; Xu Guangqi 83; Yang Guangxian 69; Zhou Ziyu 43
Pereira, Andreas 137, 140, 144–146
Pereira, Tomás 100, 146
Pfister, Louis 184
Principal Instructor (*Zhujiao* 助教) 154–156; Chen Jie 190; He Guodong 154–155, 165; He Guoqing 165, 193; He Liangkui 193; Zhang Deyuan 185, 189

Qianlong 乾隆 emperor 19, 26, 29, 128; College of Mathematics and 151–152, 156; Fang Luheng's demotion by 194; Gucong and 144–145, 147; rehabilitation of He Guozong 148; retirement home phenomenon under 171–172; Sun Shiying, case of 172
Qianlong 乾隆 reign 6; Astronomical Bureau during 177, 188; *Collected Statutes* 25; compilation project of astronomical treatises during 9; European missionaries in Beijing during 185; He family during 138, 148, 163–166, 192; He Guozong's career during 105, 138; hereditary astronomer families' prestige and power during 161–177; Huang family during 166; Si family during 167; triennial examinations **187**
Qing Era: archival sources related to 7; army 46; astronomers 2, 4, 10, 146; Beijing *17*, 44, 131; biographies 5; *Collection of the Qing Vermillion Ink Examination Papers* (*Qingdai zhujuan jicheng* 清代硃卷集成) 173; *Complete Collection of the Qing Officials' Résumés* (*Qingdai guanyuan lüli dang'an quanbian* 清代官員履歷檔案全編) 6, 171; history of mathematical astronomy during 126; Korea and 108, 131, 133; mathematicians 2; Ming-Qing transition 85; Muslim astronomical system during 169; official compilation projects of mathematical works 105; spying on astronomers 78; state documents 6, 8; Timely Modeling calendar *162*; units used in 219; *see also Astronomical Bureau*; *Collected Statutes of the Great Qing* (*Da Qing huidian* 大清會典); He brothers/family; Jesuit missionaries
Qing Emperors 119; reign titles of xiv
Qing Empire: founding of 45

Qin Ning 秦寧 168
Qu Chunhai 屈春海 5
Quick Methods for the Circle's Division and Precise Ratio (*Geyuan milü jiefa* 割圓密率捷法) (Minggantu) 187

Rescue Ritual (*jiuhu* 救護) 20, 22, 31n37, 89–90, 127–128
Response to Concerns over the Notes on Civil Calendar (Schall) **54**, 56, 58, 60, 85, 167, 176
Ribeiro, Joseph 185
Ricci, Matteo 44–45; Rules of 100
Rites Controversy (*Liyi zhi zheng* 禮儀之爭) 3, 12n13
Rites of Zhou (*Zhou li* 周禮) 28, 157n25
Rocha, Félix da 183

Sanbao 三保 80
Schall von Bell, Johann Adam ("Schall") 8, 55; administrative power of 26, 29; Bao Yingqi and 57, 59; calendar reform by 45–47; civil service rank of 55; disciples of **51**, 86, 168; Dorgon and 56–57, 127; *Eclipse Measurement* written by 43; Emperor's friendship with 55, 60; endorsers of *Response to Concerns over the Notes on Civil Calendar* **54**; execution (interrupted) of 69, 72; false accusations against 52–53; Ge Guoqi and 71; as head of Astronomical Bureau 58, 68–69; Kangxi calendar dispute and 68–69, 152; Korean Astronomical Bureau and 131–132; life of 13n36; numbers of Astronomical Bureau officials reported by **38**, 39; Ministry of Rites' threats to 49–50, 63n68; Muslim staff dismissed by 52; New Method of 8, 31, 37–60, 72, 127; reorganization of Astronomical Bureau proposed by **51**, 52; reorganization plan of 1645 37–38, 84; rehabilitation of reputation of 74; *Response to Concerns* **54**, 56, 58, 60, 85, 167, 176; as Ricci's successor 45; Shunzhi emperor and 68; solar eclipse prediction of 31n28, *87*, *88*; state calendar of 1644 produced by 56; trial of 68; Wu and 60; Xiaozhuang (Empress Dowager) and 64n93; Yang Guangxian's persecution of 69, 75, 86; Yin Kai and 59; Zang family and 176; Zhou Ziyu and 43
Section of Heavenly Signs (*Tianwen ke* 天文科) 6, 20, 22, 24, **27**, 55; Astronomical Bureau officials in 1645

38; Astronomical Bureau officials in 1658 38; Astronomical Observer of 176; College of Mathematics and 153; Huang family in 166; Instruction Erudite 37; New Method scandal and 69; personnel quotas of Astronomic Bureau in 1690 75; Qing Astronomical Bureau 1645 proposed re-organization 51, 52; Student Astronomer numbers/quotas 39, 55, 81
Seven Governors *see* Latitude-Longitude Degrees of Seven Governors calendar (*Qizheng jingwei chandu shix- ian li* 七政經緯躔度時憲曆)
Shi Yumin 史玉民 5, 6
Shunzhi 順治 emperor: Schall and 68
Shunzhi Imperial Screen: Register of Metropolitan Officials **215**
Shunzhi 順治 reign: Astronomical Bureau 83; death of Chongzhen emperor in relationship to 45; He family during 84, 85, 88, 147; Huang family during 166; New and Old Astronomer families 54–60; Rescue Ritual during 127; revision of policies of 68; Schall's difficulty finding staff during 152; seniority influence on career advancement during 186; Water Clock Section 23; Zuo family, absence of records during 74
Sichen 司辰 (Timekeeper) 24, 38
Sichen 司晨 (Timekeeper) 24, 38
Si 司 family **213–214**; Ercheng 司爾珵 166–167, **217**; Ergui 司爾珪 **54**, **70**, 166, **217**; Ermao 司爾瑁 166–167, **217**; Tinggan 司廷幹 167, 194; Tingdong 司廷棟 167, 170, 178, 194–195; Yipei 司以培 167; Yisun 司以塤 167; Yitian 司以田 167
solar eclipse: of 1664 59; of 1665 86, *87*, *88*; of 1676 89, 91; of 1730 126–138; Astronomical Bureau's inaccurate prediction in 1610 40; Astronomical Bureau's failure to predict in 1629 39; Astronomical Bureau's prediction in 1849 *129*; challenges to Astronomical Bureau's ability to predict 44; Dorgon's sending of ministers to observe 46–47; eclipse magnitude 220; Muslim Section's methods to predict 22, 59; theory of 55; Yang's inability to evaluate different illustrations of 69; *see also* Rescue Ritual
solar orbits 144–145
solar tables 148, 202
solar terms 20, 31n22
Song Fa 宋發 **51**, **54**, **70**

Song Kecheng 宋可成 **51**, **54**, **70**
Song Keli 宋可立 **51**, **70**
Sources Related to China in the Veritable Records of the Chosŏn Dynasty (*Chaoxian Lichao shilu zhong de Zhongguo shiliao* 朝鮮李朝實錄中的中國史料) 7
Sources Related to the Personnel Administration in the Qing Dynasty (*Qingdai lizhi shiliao* 清代吏治史料) 7
Student Astronomer (*Tianwensheng* 天文生) 23–24; Fed-by-grain (*Shiliang* 食糧) 23; Fed-by-salary (*Shifeng* 食俸) 23; personnel quotas at the Astronomical Bureau 23, **23**
Studio for Cultivating the Youth (*Mengyang zhai* 蒙養齋) 103; Chengde at 151; discontinuation of mathematical activities at 149; He Guodong as personnel at 110, 144, 150; Gucong at 144, 147; Mathematics Office at 111, 152; Mei Juecheng at 151; "Praises Written by Courtiers of the Studio for Cultivating the Youth" (He Guozong) 99, 102; temporary status of 108
Stumpf, Bernard-Kilian 101
sun *see* solar eclipse
Sun Jiagan 孫嘉淦 151
Su 肅親王 (Prince) 188, 196n38
Sun Shiying 孫士英 172, 188
Sun Youben 孫有本 **51**, **54**, 56, **215**
Supervisor of the Five Offices (*Wuguanzheng* 五官正) 25

Tan Tai 談泰 3
Thomas, Antoine 95n3, 100
Thorough Investigation of Astronomical Phenomena (*Lixiang kaocheng* 曆象考成) 144–145, 154–156; Astronomical Bureau and 104, 148; corrections to 145; crisis of mathematical astronomy and 201; inaccuracy of 138; *Imperially Composed Thorough Investigation of Astronomical Phenomena* 138; Mingtu's observations regarding 137; nine years required to finish 147; predictive inaccuracy of Timely Modeling system exposed by 130, 133; Yunlu's and He Guozong's claims regarding 135
Thorough Investigation of Instruments and Phenomena (*Yixiang kaocheng* 儀象考成) 170, 195; *Addition to the Thorough Investigation of Instruments and Phenomena* (*Yixiang kaocheng xubian* 儀象考成續編) 202

Tian Wenjing 田文鏡 115–116
Timely Modeling calendar (*shixian li* 時憲曆, *shixian shu* 時憲書) 19, *162*, 163, *164*; Dorgon's naming 46; He officials appearing in **165**
Timely Modeling (*shixian* 時憲) system: amending 144–149, 154, 201; predictive inaccuracy of 130, 133
Tongzhi 同治 reign xiv, 186; triennial examinations **191**

Ursis, Sabatino de 40, 43

Verbiest, Ferdinand 73–74, 89–91, 100, 147, 152
Veritable Records of the Chosŏn Dynasty 7, 90, 107, 131, 190

Wang Lai 汪萊 174–175
Water Clock Manager (*Qiehuzheng* 挈壺正) 25–26; Si family 167
Water Clock Section (*Louke ke* 漏刻科) 21, 23; He family 166; Si family 166; Zang family 176
Wu Mingxuan 吳明炫 57, 59, 60
Wu Zhiyan 武之彥 **51**

Xianfeng 咸豐 reign xiv
Xiaozhuang (Empress Dowager) 64n93
Xuantong 宣統 reign xiv
Xue Wenbing 薛文炳 **54**, **216**
Xu Guangqi 徐光啟 43–44, 83, 144, 156n2; *see also* New Western Method
Xu Huan 徐瑛 **51**
Xu Maode 徐懋德 [Andreas Pereira] 137; *see also* Pereira, Andreas

Yang Guangxian 楊光先 21, 68–73; dismissal of 73–74, 88; charges raised against Schall 75; *I Have No Alternative* (*Budeyi* 不得已) 70–71; observation of 1665 solar eclipse 88; Zang Yuqing and 176
Yang Hongliang 楊弘量 **54**, 56, 69, **70**
Yin Kai 殷鎧 **51**, **54**, 56, 58, 59, **70**, **215**
Yin-Yang Person (*Yinyangren* 陰陽人) 23, 38–39, **75**
Yin-Yang Student (*Yinyangsheng* 陰陽生) 22–24, **76**, **77**; triennial examination of 186
Yinlu 胤祿 *see* Yunlu
Yinti 胤禵 *see* Yunti
Yinzhen 胤禛 *see* Yongzheng emperor
Yinzhi 胤祉 103, 106, 110–113, 123n83

Yi Seonggye 李成桂 (King of Korea) 131
Yongzheng 雍正 emperor 5, 111; assumption of throne 123n83; ban on Christianity 183; calendar-making improved by 144; death of 150, 202; He family and 105–106, 111–119, 147, 163, 166; Jesuits and 148; Liu Yuxi and 169–170; Qin Ning and 168; solar eclipse of 1730 and 126–129, 133–138, 201; understanding of the imperial state's need for mathematics 202
Yongzheng 雍正 reign: Bao Qinhui during 1–2, 4; deterioration of Qing official calendar during 7; Korean astronomers and 132; Mathematics Program 149–152, 153, 156, 202; Zang family during 176
Yunli 允禮 149–150, 157n27
Yunlu 允祿 112, 123n83, 135, 138, 145
Yunti 允禵 113, 123n83
Yunzhi 允祉 *see* Yinzhi

Zang 臧 family 176; Bichang 臧必昌 176; Cunren 臧存仁 176, 177; Jide 臧積德 176; Fangxiu 臧樊修 176; Wenxian 臧文顯 **54**, 176, **216**; Xianming 臧顯名 176; Yuqing 臧餘慶 **70**, 176, **217**; Yuzhong 臧裕仲 176
Zhang Deyuan 張德源 159n70, 185, 189
Zhang Gong 張肱 3
Zhang Guangxiang 張光祥 **54**, **216**
Zhang Huafeng 張化鳳 **70**, **217**
Zhang Qichun 張其淳 **54**, 56, 69, **217**
Zhang Sheng 掌乘 **51**, **54**, 56, 58, **215**
Zhang Shoudeng 張守登 **43**
Zhang Wenming 張問明 **54**, **70**, **215**
Zhang Yingtian 張應田 105
Zhang Youzhuan 掌有篆 **51**
Zhang Zhao 張照 105, 121n40
Zhaohai 照海 155–156
Zhou family **211**: Shichang 周士昌 **54**, **216**; Yin 周胤 43, 52, **54**, 57, **70**, **211**; Ziyu 周子愚 40, 43 61n30, **211**
Zhu Guangda 朱光大 **51**
Zhu Guangxian 朱光顯 **51**, **54**, **70**
Zhu Guangyin 朱光蔭 **51**
Zhu Xingshu 朱廷樞 **51**
Zu Chongzhi 祖沖之 3
Zu Gengzhi 祖暅 3
Zuo family 74: Chengsi 左承嗣; 57–58; Chengye 左承業 57–58; Youqing 左有慶 58, 60, **215**; Yuhe 左允和 **215**

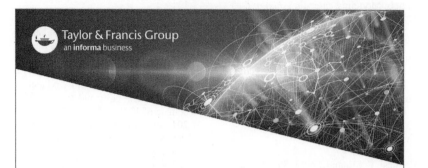